T0203537

Faecal Sludge
and Septage Treatment

Praise for this book

'In the developing world's rapidly growing cities, safe management of sanitation is of ever growing importance. As universal sewerage still remains a (pipe) dream for many, it is widely recognized that we must improve the effectiveness of non-networked sewerage options for the many, to complement sewerage access for the few. To address this neglected but crucial part of the urban sanitation system, Kevin Tayler's *Faecal Sludge and Septage Treatment* is a timely resource that provides practitioners with much-needed technical support to diagnose, plan and manage FSM services.'

Dr Darren Saywell, Director, Water Services, AECOM International Development, USA

'The urgency in providing safe acceptable sanitation to millions of people in the global South requires a different mind-set to traditional approaches. The rapid urbanization, lack of dependable water and electricity supply add to the challenges. This publication is a valuable contribution to the body of technical guidance for sanitation professional and students in developing countries. I see it as becoming the standard text for all sanitation courses in the global South.'

Professor Chris Buckley, Pollution Research Group, University of KwaZulu-Natal, Durban, South Africa

'One of the key essences in safely managed sanitation is to properly treat the collected faecal sludge or septage. Information and step-by-step guidance in planning and designing the treatment facilities in this book are necessary for professionals and design engineers.'

Dr Thammarat Koottatep, Associate Professor, School of Environment, Resources and Development, Asian Institute of Technology, Pathumthani, Thailand

Faecal Sludge and Septage Treatment

A guide for low- and middle-income countries

Kevin Tayler

PRACTICAL ACTION
Publishing

Practical Action Publishing Ltd
Rugby, Warwickshire, UK
www.practicalactionpublishing.org

A catalogue record for this book is available from the British Library.
A catalogue record for this book has been requested from the Library of Congress.

ISBN 978-1-85339-987-9 paperback
ISBN 978-1-85339-986-2 hardback
ISBN 978-1-78044-986-9 library pdf
ISBN 978-1-78044-987-6 epub

Citation: Tayler, K. (2018) *Faecal Sludge and Septage Treatment: A guide for low- and middle-income countries*, Rugby, UK, Practical Action Publishing, <http://dx.doi.org/10.3362/ 9781780449869>

Since 1974, Practical Action Publishing has published and disseminated books and information in support of international development work throughout the world. Practical Action Publishing is a trading name of Practical Action Publishing Ltd (Company Reg. No. 1159018), the wholly owned publishing company of Practical Action. Practical Action Publishing trades only in support of its parent charity objectives and any profits are covenanted back to Practical Action (Charity Reg. No. 247257, Group VAT Registration No. 880 9924 76).

This work was reviewed for contents and technical accuracy by staff from The World Bank and staff from the Bill & Melinda Gates Foundation. The findings, interpretations and conclusions expressed in this work are those of the author and do not necessarily reflect the views of Bill & Melinda Gates Foundation, or the views of The World Bank, its Board of Executive Directors, or the governments they represent. Neither the Bill & Melinda Gates foundation, nor The World Bank, guarantee the accuracy of the data included in this work.

Cover design by Mercer Design
Printed in the United Kingdom
Typeset by vPrompt eServices, India

Contents

List of figures, photos, tables, and boxes

Figures

Photos

Tables

Boxes

About the author

Kevin Tayler is a chartered civil engineer with experience of planning and design for wastewater treatment in the UK, as well as over 35 years' experience in countries of the global South. During those 35 years, he has been involved with many aspects of urban development, including urban infrastructure, and in particular the provision of water and sanitation services. In recent years, his work has included a strong focus on septage management, including septage treatment.

Acknowledgements

The seed of the idea for a book such as this was planted by the Bill & Melinda Gates Foundation (BMGF) in 2010, when it asked the author to carry out a scoping study for a text book on decentralized faecal sludge management. Alyse Schrecongost managed the work on behalf of the BMGF. BMGF decided not to go ahead with the project at that stage, but it led indirectly to several years' engagement with faecal sludge management issues in Indonesia, working with the Water and Sanitation Program (WSP) team in Jakarta. This book draws on that experience, which was facilitated by many members of the WSP team, in particular Isabel Blackett, Reini Siregar, Budi Darmawan, Maraita Listyasari, and Inni Arsyini. The book also draws on the insights and experience of Foort Bustraan and his colleagues in the USAID Indonesia Urban Water, Sanitation and Hygiene (IUWASH) team, who collaborated closely with the WSP team on investigations into aspects of faecal sludge management. Working with WSP, Freya Mills carried out work on sludge accumulation rates in pits and septic tanks, which informs Chapter 3 of the book.

Andy Peal, Isabel Blackett, Peter Hawkins, Andy Cotton, and Rebecca Scott provided useful comments on an early draft of the book. Following further review of this draft by the World Bank and the BMGF, the consulting firm Stantec was engaged to contribute additional material to the book. The Stantec team contributed its knowledge of conventional and innovative treatment technologies and information on initiatives from several countries. It is largely responsible for the mathematical formulae and worked examples that guide readers through the design process. Michael McWhirter provided overall direction to the Stantec team, Chengyan Zhang led the team and was a major contributor to its input. Jeannette Laramee, Jeovanni Ayala-Lugo, Tyler Hadacek, and Mengli Shi made important contributions and Oliver Tsai, Chris Machado, and Charlie Alix also provided contributions and/or senior review. The Stantec team also contacted specialists with knowledge of specific technologies and initiatives. These included Nick Alcock and Santiago Septien for information on the black soldier fly and LaDePa system initiatives, respectively, both in eThekwini, South Africa, Andreas Schmidt for information on biodigester use and performance, Aubrey Simbambi for information on the Kanyama faecal sludge treatment plant in Lusaka, Zambia, Rohini Pradeep for information on the Devanahalli faecal sludge treatment plant performance in Bangalore, India, and Stephen Sugden for information on the Water for People biochar/pyrolysis initiative in Kenya. Particular mention must be made of Linda Strande and others at Eawag/Sandec, who provided detailed review comments on all chapters, particularly the first three chapters and the chapters on drying beds.

Georges Mikhael provided information on the domed biodigester in Lusaka and the Sistema Biobolsa biodigesters in Antananarivo and Kumasi. Biodigester treatment initiatives in other locations came from various sources. Anthony Kilbride and Max Affre provided information and feedback on the SOIL bin-composting initiative in Haiti and the Sistema Biobolsa anaerobic digestion system, respectively. Information on the treatment plant in Sittwe, Myanmar, which serves camps housing internally displaced Rohingya people, was gathered in the course of a consultancy for the Paris-based NGO, Solidarités International. Thanks are due to Elio de Bonis, who was the lead consultant and Emmett Kearney, who was the main point of contact with Solidarités International in Myanmar during the consultancy and to Alberto Acquistapace, who provided information on the performance of the hopper-bottomed gravity thickener that was constructed in response to the consultancy recommendations. Teddy Gouden provided information on the latest situation with regard to the LaDePa and black soldier fly initiatives in South Africa. Ashley Muspratt checked and corrected the box on the Pivot Works initiative in Kigali.

The World Bank and the BMGF provided detailed review and suggestions for improvement at all stages of the project. The review process was led and coordinated by Jan Willem Rosenboom at the BMGF and Ruth Kennedy-Walker and Rebecca Gilsdorf at the World Bank. Special mention should be made of Duncan Mara, Emeritus Professor at the University of Leeds in the UK, who provided a detailed review of the final draft of the book. Comments and suggestions on earlier drafts were received from both World Bank and the BMGF staff members and consultants and external specialists. World Bank reviewers included Martin Gambrill, Jean-Martin Brault, Ravikumar Joseph, Srinivasa Podipireddy, Edkarl Galing, Shafick Hoossein, Bill Kingdom, and Mutsa Prudence Mambo. BMGF reviewers included Roshan Shrestha, Dennis Mwanza, John Duffy, and Doulaye Kone. Dorai Narayana and Dave Robbins both contributed extensive comments and suggestions in their capacity as BMGF consultants. External reviewers included Linda Strande and the Eawag/Sandec team, Professor Chris Buckley from the University of KwaZulu-Natal in South Africa, and Dave Wilson of eThekwini Water and Sanitation, Durban, South Africa.

For Practical Action Publishing, Clare Tawney was a supportive content development manager at all stages of the development of the book while Chloe Callan-Foster managed the copy-editing and production process.

While thanks are due to all the individuals and organizations identified above, the final responsibility for the contents of the book, the views expressed in it, and any errors in the text lies with the author.

Acronyms and abbreviations

AASHTO	American Association of State Highway and Transportation Officials
ABR	anaerobic baffled reactor
AF	anaerobic filter
AOR	actual oxygen requirement
AS	activated sludge
ASR	activated sludge reactor
BMGF	Bill & Melinda Gates Foundation
BOD	biochemical oxygen demand
BOD_5	five-day biochemical oxygen demand
BORDA	Bremen Overseas Research and Development Association
BSF	black soldier fly
C	carbon
CBS	container-based sanitation
CFR	US Code of Federal Regulations
COD	chemical oxygen demand
DS	dry solids
E. coli	*Escherichia coli* (bacterium)
Eawag	Swiss Federal Institute of Aquatic Science and Technology
ET	evapotranspiration
EFD	Excreta Flow Diagram
FAO	Food and Agriculture Organization
FC	faecal coliform
FIDIC	International Federation of Consulting Engineers
FOG	fats, oil, and grease
FSTP	faecal sludge treatment plant
g	gram
GLS	gas–liquid–solids
HRT	hydraulic retention time
IDP	internally displaced person
IWA	International Water Association
kg	kilogram
kW	kilowatt
LaDePa	latrine dehydration and pasteurization
m	metre
MBBR	moving bed biofilm reactor
MJ	megajoule
MLSS	mixed liquor suspended solids
mm	millimetre

MPN	most probable number
N	nitrogen
NGO	non-government organization
NH_3-N	ammonia nitrogen
NH_4-N	ammonium nitrogen
NO_3	nitrate
O&G	oil and grease
OA	oxygenation efficiency
P	phosphorus
PF	peak factor
PFU	plaque forming unit
QMRA	quantitative microbial risk assessment
RBC	rotating biological contactor
Sandec	Department of Sanitation, Water and Solid Waste for Development
SBR	sequencing batch reactor
SDG	Sustainable Development Goals
SLR	solids loading rate
SOP	standard operating procedure
SOR	surface overflow rate
SRT	solids retention time
SSC	solids separation chamber
SSWM	Sustainable Sanitation and Water Management toolbox
STT	settling-thickening tank
TAN	total ammoniacal nitrogen
TDS	total dissolved solids
TKN	total Kjeldahl nitrogen
TS	total solids
TSS	total suspended solids
UASB	up-flow anaerobic sludge blanket
UPTD	Unit Pelasana Teknis Daerah (local technical implementation unit)
USAID	United States Agency for International Development
US EPA	United States Environmental Protection Agency
VDS	volatile dissolved solids
VS	volatile solids
VSS	volatile suspended solids
WB	World Bank
WC	water closet
WEF	Water Environment Federation
WHO	World Health Organization
WSP	Water and Sanitation Program (World Bank)
WSUP	Water and Sanitation for the Urban Poor

CHAPTER 1

Introduction to faecal sludge and septage treatment

This chapter sets the scene for the rest of the book. It explains the importance of faecal sludge management in urban areas in which many people rely on on-site and decentralized sanitation facilities and emphasizes the place of treatment in the overall sanitation service chain. It defines terms used throughout the book, explains why faecal sludge and septage treatment is important, and identifies broad treatment objectives. After a brief explanation of this book's place in relation to other similar publications and faecal sludge planning tools, it lists subsequent chapters, briefly summarizing their contents.

Keywords: urban sanitation, faecal sludge, septage, definitions, treatment objectives, indicators

The challenge of urban sanitation

The world is urbanizing rapidly. The number of people living in cities is projected to increase by 50 per cent from 4 to 6 billion between 2016 and 2045. Much of this growth is occurring in low-income and lower middle-income countries (United Nations, 2015; World Bank, 2016). Formal service providers often struggle to meet the demand for housing, infrastructure, and services created by rapid urbanization. This is especially true for sanitation provision. Many towns and cities are without sewerage and, even where it exists, formal sewerage provision is often confined to central business districts and high-income areas. Developers and individual households respond to this situation by providing their own sanitation facilities. These typically consist of a dry direct-drop toilet or a pour-flush water closet (WC), from which excreta are flushed to a pit, tank, or the nearest drain. Connections to drains may incorporate an interceptor tank, which holds some solids while allowing digested solids and liquid to discharge to the drain. Facilities with on-site storage remove excreta from living spaces, reducing people's exposure to pathogens and improving the local environment. However, sludge accumulates in pits and tanks, eventually exposing people to insanitary conditions unless the pits and tanks are either replaced or emptied. Construction of a replacement pit is possible in low-density rural and peri-urban areas but lack of space often precludes this option in higher-density urban areas. The only option for households living in these areas is to arrange to have pits and tanks emptied when they are full. Protection of public health and the environment requires that the material removed is then transported away from residential areas and treated

http://dx.doi.org/10.3362/9781780449869.001

or otherwise dealt with in a way that allows for its subsequent safe reuse or disposal. Failure to arrange for safe faecal sludge removal, transport, and treatment will result in sanitation conditions that fail to meet the Sustainable Development Goal (SDG) requirement for safely managed sanitation services: that excreta are safely disposed of in situ or transported and treated off-site.

The purpose and intended readership of this book

This book deals with the treatment of faecal material and supernatant water removed from on-site and decentralized sanitation facilities and systems. Its main focus is on treatment facility design but this can never be viewed in isolation. Rather, it must reflect local conditions, start from a realistic assessment of the load on the plant, and take account of the final destination of the liquid and solid products of treatment. With this in mind, the first part of the book provides general guidance on the ways in which the context will influence treatment plant choices and designs, and sets out the steps to be followed when planning for a new or improved treatment facility. Later chapters focus on the selection and design of systems for the treatment of faecal material removed from on-site and decentralized sanitation facilities. The early chapters should be of interest to municipal planners and engineers with treatment plant design responsibilities. The later, more technical, chapters will be of interest mainly to design engineers. Those with more general interests should also benefit from reading the short review sections that conclude each chapter other than this introductory chapter.

Definitions and meanings

Before going further, it is useful to define the key sanitation-related terms and concepts used in this book.

Excreta is the collective term used for human wastes. They consist of *faeces*- wet solids with a high organic content, and liquid *urine*. The term *sanitation* refers to systems for the collection and safe disposal of excreta and wastewater generated in households, businesses, and communal buildings, rather than the wider definition that also includes stormwater management and solid-waste management.

Dry sanitation systems do not use water to flush excreta away from the toilet. Users defecate directly through a hole into a pit or vault lying directly under the toilet cubicle. Such toilets are sometimes referred to as *direct-drop* toilets. The material held in the pit or vault is thus a combination of faeces, urine, and any water used for anal cleansing and to clean the toilet floor. In some cases, toilet cubicles are also used for bathing, and all or part of the used bathing water is discharged to the pit or vault.

In the past, some dry systems involved defecation into a bucket located below the latrine floor, which would be replaced by a cleaned and sanitized bucket at intervals of a few days, with full buckets taken to a central location for disposal, preferably but not always involving treatment. From the mid-20th century onwards, these *bucket* systems were officially discouraged because they were correctly perceived as being unhygienic. Recent years have seen increased interest in container-based sanitation (CBS) approaches that have emerged as an alternative service approach for those not served by sewers or on-site sanitation systems. CBS consists of an end-to-end service – i.e., covering the whole sanitation service chain – that collects excreta hygienically from toilets designed with sealable, removable containers (also called cartridges) that are regularly replaced by the service provider, who also strives to ensure that the excreta is safely treated and then disposed of or reused.

Water-borne or *wet* sanitation systems rely on water to flush faeces away from toilets, usually but not always through a *water seal*, formed by inserting an inverted 'U' in the discharge pipe. The term for the resulting mixture of faeces, urine, flush water, and any anal cleansing water is *black water*. *Grey water* or *sullage* is wastewater generated by other domestic activities, including laundry, bathing, cleaning, and cooking. Households using water-borne sanitation generate both black and grey water. Those using dry sanitation only generate grey water. *Domestic wastewater* is created when black and grey water are combined.

On-site systems retain most of the solid material close to the toilet in a pit or tank while, in most cases, allowing liquid to percolate into the *ground*. This book uses the term *leach pit* for a pit serving a flush or pour-flush toilet from which water percolates directly. Many installations that are described in reports as septic tanks are, in fact, leach pits. *Septic tank systems* consist of a watertight *septic tank*, usually followed by a soakaway or drainfield from which water percolates into the ground. A *soakaway* is a pit which receives the septic tank effluent and allows it to soak into the ground. Soakaways may be filled with stones or be open pits lined with open-jointed brickwork or blockwork. The stone-filled option has less capacity but is easier to construct and less prone to collapse. *Drainfields* consist of horizontal stone-filled trenches and usually incorporate an open-jointed pipe running close to the top of the trench. In areas with a high water table, the drainfield may be raised in an artificial *mound* if the height of the toilet can also be raised. Prefabricated, open-bottomed domed or half-barrel *leaching chambers* provide an alternative form of drainfield. *Cess pits* retain both faecal solids and liquid in a watertight tank and require more frequent emptying than other types of on-site system.

Off-site systems remove solids and liquid from the vicinity of the toilet. *Sewered* systems remove wastewater from residential areas through a system of pipes or sewers, referred to collectively as *sewerage*. CBS systems require frequent removal of containers and so they also fall into the off-site category. This book uses the term *hybrid* for systems such as solids-free sewers that retain solids on-site in a tank or pit while conveying liquid off-site in sewers or drains. Tilley et al. (2014) include more detailed information on the various sanitation systems.

Views on the meaning of the terms septage and faecal sludge vary: some authors refer to all the materials collected from pits, vaults, and septic tanks as faecal sludge, while others refer to them collectively as septage. Neither of these conventions is entirely satisfactory. The water content of material taken from poorly draining leach pits and septic tanks will normally be higher than 95 per cent, causing it to act as a liquid so that it cannot accurately be described as sludge. The solids content of material removed from dry pit latrines will normally be higher, except where the water table is high and/or water from a bathroom is discharged to the pit. In this book the term *faecal sludge* refers to the material, largely consisting of faecal solids and urine, which accumulates at the bottom of a pit, tank, or vault. The material that accumulates in pits that either receive or retain little or no wastewater consists almost entirely of faecal sludge. Material removed from dry pits, containerized systems and those wet systems in which percolation from the sides and base of the pit removes all excess water, will consist almost entirely of faecal sludge. The term *septage* is used to refer to the solids and liquids which are removed from a pit, tank, or vault in a wet sanitation system. Septage comprises faecal sludge, the supernatant *water* that accumulates above it, and material that is lighter than water that forms a *scum* layer on the liquid surface. Faecal sludge may behave as a *non-Newtonian fluid*, flowing poorly if at all until it is stirred (Chhabra, 2009). This will have implications for the treatment options.

A distinction is often made between *high-strength* faecal sludge and *lower-strength* septage, with the strength defined in terms of oxygen demand and suspended solids concentration. This distinction is qualitative, rather than quantitative, and should not obscure the fact that both faecal sludge and septage exert a high oxygen demand, have a high solids content, and contain large numbers of pathogens. Without effective management, including treatment, both will harm the environment, public health, or both. Chapter 3 gives further information on typical strengths of faecal sludge and septage.

More definitions for specific processes and technologies are given at appropriate points in this and later chapters.

The need for treatment

Engineers and urban managers sometimes assume that sewerage followed by wastewater treatment is the only viable urban sanitation option. There are circumstances in which sewerage is the best option, particularly where sewers are built to appropriate standards such as those of the Brazilian condominial sewerage system (Melo, 2005). Indeed, people in many cities have taken matters into their own hands and have built informal sewers to remove wastewater from their neighbourhoods. However, there are few cities with 100 per cent sewer coverage and this situation is unlikely to change in the near future. Poor construction and maintenance, inadequate falls, and the absence of treatment facilities mean that the sewer systems that do exist are often inadequate. This leaves most people dependent on on-site systems. A recent study of 12 cities in Latin America, Africa, and Asia concluded that around 64 per cent of all households in the 12 cities relied on on-site sanitation (WSP, 2014). Figures from individual cities varied from 51 per cent for Santa Cruz, Bolivia, through 72 per cent for Phnom

Penh, Cambodia, 88 per cent for Manila, the Philippines, and 89 per cent for Maputo, Mozambique, to 90 per cent for Kampala, Uganda. Comparison with figures quoted by the World Health Organization (WHO) in the mid-2000s suggests that on-site sanitation coverage is changing slowly (Eawag/Sandec, 2006) and that a high proportion of urban dwellers will continue to rely on on-site sanitation for many years to come. While technologies to contain and treat excreta on-site exist, they have not yet been widely implemented. The reality is that almost all towns and cities will continue to need systems for emptying pits and tanks, removing and either reusing or disposing of the contents in a way that harms neither public health nor the environment. Safe reuse and disposal both require effective provision for treatment. Sludge transport and treatment systems are also required where decentralized sewer systems convey wastewater to local treatment plants that lack sludge treatment facilities.

The sanitation service chain

Removal, storage, and treatment of the contents of on-site tanks, pits, and vaults are links in the sanitation service chain. Different organizations use different versions of the chain. The World Bank (WB) identifies five links in the chain: user interface/containment, emptying/collection, conveyance, treatment, and end-use/disposal. The Bill & Melinda Gates Foundation (BMGF) chain includes a different five links: capture, storage, transport, treatment, and reuse. The BMGF's use of the term 'sanitation value chain' highlights its belief that excreta are a potential resource and should not be viewed solely as a problem. Neither chain is completely disaggregated. The WB chain bundles together capture and storage in the term containment, while the BMGF chain omits removal. The BMGF chain works well for the on-site sanitation facilities that generate faecal sludge and septage and so this book uses that chain, while recognizing that removal and transport of pit and tank contents can be undertaken independently of one another. With these points in mind, the chain becomes:

> Capture – Storage – Removal and transport – Treatment – End use/safe disposal

Options for capturing excreta range from a simple hole in a slab, through pour-flush and cistern-flushed toilets, to urine-diversion toilets that are designed to separate faeces from urine. Storage is only required for on-site and hybrid systems. The arrangements for excreta capture and storage will have a strong influence on subsequent links in the chain, as will be explained in more detail in Chapter 2. Both on-site and sewered systems can include provision for reuse of treated material. While not essential, this preserves resources, and can generate income to partly offset the cost of treatment. This book provides detailed guidance on the treatment stage of the non-networked service chain, referring to other stages in the chain where necessary to explain their influence on treatment choices and outcomes.

The objectives of faecal sludge and septage treatment

The overall objective of faecal sludge management is to ensure that the faecal material removed from on-site and decentralized sanitation facilities is dealt with in a way that protects both public health and the environment and does not create a local nuisance. The objective of treatment is to convert unpleasant and potentially harmful faecal sludge and septage into inoffensive products that harm neither public health nor the environment and are easy to handle. In sensitive environments, it may also be necessary to reduce the nutrient content (for example, nitrogen and phosphorus) of any liquid effluent discharged directly or indirectly to watercourses.

Excreta and public health

Faeces contain many microorganisms. If the person who excreted the faeces is infected with a faecal–oral disease, these microorganisms include the pathogen (disease-causing organism) that causes disease. It is difficult and expensive to identify and measure pathogens directly and so indicator organisms are used to assess whether they are likely to be present, as explained below.

Urine is mainly water but also contains urea and trace elements, including sodium, potassium, and phosphate. If uncontaminated with faeces or blood, it is free of almost all pathogens, although cross-contamination of urine by pathogens from faeces is difficult to prevent. Schistosomiasis (bilharzia), when caused by *Schistosoma haematobium*, is one important disease that is transmitted in urine.

Seepage water from pits and septic tank soakaways/drainfields may contaminate groundwater, particularly where the water table is high or the subsoil is fractured or highly permeable, posing a health risk to those who use untreated water from a nearby well or borehole for drinking and other household purposes. The level of risk depends on various factors, including the nature of the subsoil, the presence of fissures in the underlying rock, the construction details of wells, and the depth from which the water is drawn. For further information on assessment of the risk of groundwater contamination from on-site sanitation see Lawrence et al. (2001). The key point to note here is that regular desludging of pits and septic tanks is unlikely to fully eliminate potential risks because removing the sludge will still leave highly contaminated liquid to escape into the ground.

Excreta and the environment

Faeces consist largely of water and organic compounds. In the presence of bacteria, the latter break down into simpler components, using oxygen available in the environment in the first instance. For faecal material discharged to a watercourse, this oxygen is available in the receiving water but the high oxygen demand of the excreta will quickly reduce the oxygen content of the water. Where the oxygen demand from the faecal material exceeds the oxygen availability in the receiving water, anaerobic conditions will result, generating odours, killing aquatic organisms including fish, and generally making the environment less pleasant. On-site sanitation systems protect the environment by containing much of the faecal material in a pit, vault, or tank, but this material eventually requires removal. The material removed during desludging will have high organic, suspended solids, and ammonia concentrations and will adversely affect the quality of any watercourse to which it is discharged. Treatment is needed to reduce its extremely high oxygen demand and suspended solids concentration to levels that do not affect fish and other aquatic life in the receiving water.

Based on the above, specific objectives of faecal sludge and septage treatment are to:

- *Reduce the water content of sludge*, thus making it easier to work with and transport. The aim will normally be to reduce the water content to the point at which the sludge acts as a solid and can be handled with spades.
- *Reduce the oxygen demand and suspended solids content of the liquid fraction that is discharged to the environment* to the point at which discharging it to watercourses will not deplete oxygen levels or cause a build-up of solids to levels that may harm aquatic life.
- *Reduce pathogens from the liquid effluent*, to allow its safe disposal or end use. Pathogen reduction will be required when the effluent is to be used for irrigation or aquaculture. It should also be considered when liquid effluent is discharged to a watercourse upstream of a point at which people bathe or extract water. However, in this case, it will usually be better to explore alternative disposal/discharge arrangements: for instance, moving the discharge point downstream.
- *Reduce pathogen concentrations in sludge* sufficiently to allow its safe end use or disposal as part of the solid waste stream. Reducing sludge pathogen concentrations will be particularly important if the intended end use involves spreading treated sludge on agricultural land.

Faecal sludge and septage contain high concentrations of ammonia, other nitrogenous compounds, and nutrients. It may be necessary to reduce the concentration of these compounds, particularly where the addition of nutrients to a watercourse may lead to eutrophication. Chapter 8 provides a brief introduction to these issues.

It will not be possible to achieve these objectives unless the financial and organizational requirements for effective plant operation are in place. Plans for improved septage and sludge treatment should therefore consider the actions needed to ensure that these requirements can be met.

Key indicators and measures

The pathogens present in excreta are of four main types: viruses, bacteria, protozoa, and helminths. Tests are available to identify individual pathogens, but testing for all possible pathogens requires specialized laboratory procedures and a high level of effort and expenditure. The more common procedure when assessing risk from bacterial pathogens is to use indicator bacteria as a proxy for the presence of pathogens. The most commonly used indicator bacteria are faecal coliforms and *Escherichia coli* (*E. coli*). *E. coli* are a specific type of faecal coliform and predominate in the human gut and the vast majority of *E. coli* are non-pathogenic. Studies on polluted freshwater bodies in Brazil found that *E. coli* concentrations consistently comprised about 80 per cent of total faecal coliform concentrations (Hachich et al., 2012). From studies in Ohio in the USA, the US Geological Survey derived the equation log EC = 0.932 (log FC) + 0.101, where EC is the *E. coli* concentration and FC is the faecal coliform concentration. This equation gives EC to FC ratios in the range 0.4–0.5 at the faecal coliform concentrations to be expected for strong wastewater and septage. Another equation, derived by the Ohio River Valley Water Sanitation Commission predicts slightly lower EC to FC ratios (Francy et al., 1993). One person may excrete more than 10^{11} faecal coliforms in one day. The black water flushed from WCs may contain up to 10^9 faecal coliforms per 100 ml. These figures compare with typical national standard requirements that there be no *E. coli* or faecal coliforms in a 100 ml sample of drinking water and that the faecal coliform concentration in wastewater used to irrigate crops eaten raw should not exceed 1,000 MPN/100 ml. MPN means most probable number and is another way of measuring concentration of certain microorganisms when assessing concentrations in faecal sludge, septage, and wastewater. Because the standard faecal coliform test identifies some non-faecal bacteria that grow at the 44°C temperature used for the test, *E. coli* are now the preferred indicator (Edberg et al., 2000).

Numerous protozoa inhabit the human intestinal tract. Many are non-pathogenic, some can cause mild disease, but a few, for instance *Giardia intestinalis*, *Cryptosporidium parvum,* and *Cryptosporidium hominis*, can cause acute diarrhoea. It is possible to detect protozoan cysts and oocysts in wastewater and faecal sludge, but the approach normally adopted is to focus on the detection of helminth (worm) eggs as an indicator of protozoa survival through different stages of treatment. These can persist for months or even years in sludge and therefore present a greater health risk than protozoan (oo)cysts. Viable *Ascaris lumbricoides*, a common helminthic pathogen, eggs are the most commonly used indicator for helminth infections. Tests may also be carried out to establish the presence of *Trichuris trichiura*, another helminthic pathogen. Ayres and Mara (1996) provide further information on analytical methods for the enumeration of helminth eggs and faecal coliform bacteria in wastewater samples. Unless the organization with septage management responsibilities has its own specialist laboratory staff, it will be necessary to engage an organization with specialist knowledge to plan and conduct monitoring programmes for indicator bacteria and pathogens such as *Ascaris* and *Trichuris*.

The measures for oxygen demand are:

- *Chemical oxygen demand (COD)*: a measure of the oxygen equivalent of the organic material contained in wastewater that can be oxidized chemically using dichromate in an acid solution. In effect, it is a measure of all the organic material contained in the wastewater.

- *Biochemical oxygen demand (BOD)*: a measure of the oxygen demand exerted by the readily bio-oxidizable organic material contained in a wastewater sample over a given time period. BOD is normally determined over a five-day period at 20°C and is referred to as BOD_5. Another justification for using the five-day figure is that the onset of nitrification, which would distort carbonaceous oxygen demand results, normally does not occur until after five days.

Both COD and BOD are expressed as concentrations in milligrams per litre (mg/l), which is equivalent to grams per cubic metre.

The indicator for solids content, *total suspended solids* (TSS), is also expressed as a concentration in mg/l. Wastewater also contains dissolved solids, and suspended and dissolved solids together comprise the *total solids* (TS) content of the wastewater. *Volatile suspended solids* (VSS) and *volatile solids* (VS), normally expressed as percentages, are indicators of the readily biodegradable fractions of TSS and TS, respectively.

Information on the solids content of faecal sludge and septage may be presented in terms of either TSS or TS. TS figures can be misleading because they may include high levels of total dissolved solids (TDS) that were already present in the uncontaminated water as salinity, hardness, or both. Given the fact that these solids are both dissolved and inorganic, neither physical settlement nor biological processes will remove them. In view of this, the main focus of wastewater and septage sampling should be on TSS rather than TS.

How this book relates to other publications

Wastewater treatment textbooks include chapters on septage treatment but focus mainly on the fairly sophisticated approaches adopted in industrialized countries (see for instance Burton et al., 2013). The US Environmental Protection Agency's *Handbook on Septage Treatment and Disposal* (US EPA, 1984) and its *Fact Sheet on Septage Treatment/Disposal* (US EPA, 1999) cover much the same ground as this book, but they are now some decades old and focus on the needs of the USA rather than low- and lower-middle-income countries (for brevity, this book refers to both low- and lower-middle-income countries as lower income countries). *Faecal Sludge Management: Systems Approach for Implementation and Operation* (Strande et al., 2014) covers all aspects of faecal sludge management and includes theoretical and practical material, including examples, on options for faecal sludge treatment. It draws on the reports and research findings of the Department Water, Sanitation and Solid Waste for Development (Sandec) of the Swiss Federal Institute of Aquatic Science and Technology (Eawag) and the organizations with which it collaborates. Sandec/Eawag has also produced a detailed guide on economic aspects of low-cost faecal sludge management (Steiner et al., 2002). However, there is no textbook or guide with a primary focus on the technical aspects of faecal sludge and septage treatment in low-income countries. This book is concerned primarily with treatment process selection and design, covering both process design and the design details that experience has shown are key to successful plant operation in these countries. It also provides a critical assessment of technologies described in other publications and identifies some other technologies that might be options for faecal sludge and septage treatment. References to relevant publications and research findings are included throughout the book.

Structure of book and brief description of contents

The rest of this book is structured as follows:

Chapter 2 explores the context for treatment. It deals first with treatment as a component of the complete faecal sludge/septage management cycle and then with the options for safe disposal. It introduces the three main options: land treatment, co-treatment with wastewater, and provision of specialized faecal sludge/septage treatment plants, explaining that the remainder of the book focuses on the last of these options. Explanations of need and demand, and the importance of distinguishing between them, follow. The influence of legislation, institutions, and finance on treatment technology choices is then explored, with the need to ensure that available funds can cover operational costs emphasized. Finally, the chapter addresses the need to recognize and allow for the fact that the context for treatment is not constant and may change over time.

Chapter 3 deals with planning for faecal sludge and septage treatment. It sets out the steps in the planning process, starting from assessment of need and demand for septage treatment, and moving on to determination of the planning area, decentralization options and their impact on treatment plant service areas and locations, assessment of hydraulic, organic, and suspended solids loads, and technology choice. The chapter includes references to documents that provide guidance on the wider aspects of sanitation and faecal sludge management planning.

Chapter 4 introduces treatment processes and technologies. It develops the material on treatment objectives contained in this introduction and identifies the options for treating high-strength faecal sludge and septage. Process options for providing complete treatment packages for septage and faecal sludge are then described and the technology options at each stage in these treatment packages are introduced. The advantages, disadvantages, and limitations of co-treatment of faecal sludge and septage with municipal wastewater are briefly discussed.

Chapter 5 covers the important subject of planning and design for effective operation. It emphasizes the need to ensure that the processes and technologies selected are compatible with available management systems and resources, and the importance of designing with operators in mind. Tasks that are difficult to do are likely to be neglected, with consequences for the medium- to long-term performance of treatment units.

Chapter 6 examines arrangements for receiving and screening sludge and, where necessary, removing grit. It also refers to arrangements for mixing additives to sludge in order to stabilize it and/or improve its settling characteristics.

Chapter 7 deals with options for solids–liquid separation. These include technologies that rely on sedimentation, percolation and evaporation, and mechanical sludge presses.

Chapter 8 explores the range of options that are available for treating the liquid portion of separated septage. For small flows and where land is available, the technologies described might be used to treat the whole of the septage flow. Information is provided on both anaerobic and aerobic technologies and options for linking them to achieve satisfactory effluent standards are explained.

Chapter 9 is concerned with the options for dewatering sludge. These options should normally be deployed after solids–liquid separation, but for small flows, particularly those with high solids contents, they may be deployed immediately after preliminary screening and grit removal as an alternative to other solids–liquid separation options. Technologies covered include planted and unplanted drying beds, and various forms of sludge presses.

Chapter 10 examines the options for additional treatment required to render liquid effluent and dried sludge suitable for disposal to the environment or end use. The chapter is concerned mainly with options for dried sludge, which will normally have a higher reuse value than the small volume of liquid effluent produced in septage treatment plants.

References

Ayres, R.M. and Mara, D.D. (1996) *Analysis of Wastewater for Use in Agriculture – A Laboratory Manual of Parasitological and Bacteriological Techniques*, Geneva: WHO <www.who.int/water_sanitation_health/publications/labmanual/en> [accessed 14 January 2018].

Burton, F.L., Tchobanoglous, T., Tsuchihashi, R. and Stensel, H.D. (2013) *Metcalf & Eddy, Inc.: Wastewater Engineering: Treatment and Resource Recovery*, 5th edn, New York: McGraw-Hill Education.

Chhabra, R.P. (2009) *Non-Newtonian Fluids: An Introduction*, Kanpur: Indian Institute of Technology <www.physics.iitm.ac.in/~compflu/Lect-notes/chhabra.pdf> [accessed 8 March 2017].

Eawag/Sandec (2006) 'Urban excreta management: situation, challenges, and promising solutions', presented by Eawag at the *1st International Faecal Sludge Management Policy Symposium and Workshop, Dakar, Senegal* <http://siteresources.worldbank.org/INTWSS/Resources/eawag.pdf> [accessed 13 March 2017].

Eawag/Sandec (2017) Management of excreta, wastewater and sludge [online] <www.eawag.ch/en/department/sandec/main-focus/management-of-excreta-wastewater-and-sludge> [accessed 17 November 2017].

Edberg, S.C., Rice, E.W., Karlin, R.J. and Allen, M.J (2000) '*Escherichia coli*: the best biological drinking water indicator for public health protection', *Journal of Applied Microbiology Symposium Supplement* 88: 106S–16S <www.ncbi.nlm.nih.gov/pubmed/10880185> [accessed 13 March 2017].

Francy, D., Myers, D. and Metzker, K. (1993) *Escherichia coli and Fecal Coliform Bacteria as Indicators of Recreational Water Quality*, Denver, CO: US Geological Survey <https://pubs.usgs.gov/wri/1993/4083/report.pdf> [accessed 21 February 2017].

Hachich, E., Di Bari, M., Christ, A., Lamparelli, C., Ramos, S. and Sato, M. (2012) 'Comparison of thermotolerant coliforms and *Escherichia coli* densities in freshwater bodies', *Brazilian Journal of Microbiology* 43(2): 675–81 <http://dx.doi.org/10.1590/S1517-83822012000200032> [accessed 22 February 2017].

Lawrence, A.R., Macdonald, D.M.J., Howard, A.G., Barrett, M.H., Pedley, S., Ahmed, K.M. and Nalubega, M. (2001) *Guidelines for Assessing the Risk to Groundwater from On-Site Sanitation*, Nottingham: British Geological Survey <http://nora.nerc.ac.uk/id/eprint/20757/1/ARGOSS%20Manual.PDF> [accessed 14 January 2018].

Melo, J.C. (2005) *The Experience of Condominial Water and Sewerage Systems in Brazil: Case Studies from Brasília, Salvador and Parauapebas*, Lima: Water and Sanitation Program Latin America <www.wsp.org/sites/wsp.org/files/publications/BrasilFinal2.pdf> [accessed 24 January 2018].

Steiner, M., Montangero, A., Koné, D. and Strauss, M. (2002) *Economic Aspects of Low-cost Faecal Sludge Management: Estimation of Collection, Haulage, Treatment and Disposal/Reuse Costs*, Dübendorf: Department of Water and Sanitation in Developing Countries, Swiss Federal Institute for Environmental Science & Technology <www.eawag.ch/fileadmin/Domain1/Abteilungen/sandec/publikationen/EWM/Project_reports/FSM_LCO_economic.pdf> [accessed 14 January 2018].

Strande, L., Ronteltap, M. and Brdjanovic, D. (2014) *Faecal Sludge Management: Systems Approach for Implementation and Operation*, London: IWA <www.sandec.ch/fsm_book> [accessed 17 November 2017].

Tilley, E., Ulrich, L., Lüthi, C., Reymond, Ph. and Zurbrügg, C. (2014) *Compendium of Sanitation Systems and Technologies*, 2nd revised edn, Dübendorf: Swiss Federal Institute of Aquatic Science and Technology (Eawag) <www.iwa-network.org/wp-content/uploads/2016/06/Compendium-Sanitation-Systems-and-Technologies.pdf> [accessed 27 February 2017].

United Nations, Department of Economic and Social Affairs, Population Division (2015) *World Urbanization Prospects: The 2014 Revision* (Report No. ST/ESA/SER.A/366) [online] <https://esa.un.org/unpd/wup/> [accessed 13 March 2017].

US EPA (1984) *Handbook: Septage Treatment and Disposal*, Washington, DC: EPA <https://nepis.epa.gov/Exe/ZyPDF.cgi/30004ARR.PDF?Dockey=30004ARR.PDF> [accessed 19 June 2018].

US EPA (1999) *Decentralized Systems Technology Fact Sheet: Septage Treatment/Disposal* (Report No. EPA 932-F-99-068), Washington, DC: EPA <https://www3.epa.gov/npdes/pubs/septage.pdf> [accessed 15 January 2018].

World Bank (2016) Urban development [online] <www.worldbank.org/en/topic/urbandevelopment/overview> [accessed 20 February 2017].

WSP (2014) *The Missing Link in Sanitation Service Delivery: A Review of Fecal Sludge Management in 12 Cities*, Washington, DC: World Bank <www.wsp.org/sites/wsp.org/files/publications/WSP-Fecal-Sludge-12-City-Review-Research-Brief.pdf> [accessed 13 March 2017].

CHAPTER 2

Faecal sludge and septage treatment in context

Planning and design decisions should take account of the context within which treatment facilities are to operate. This chapter examines the ways in which contextual factors can affect these decisions. It first examines the ways in which treatment requirements are influenced by arrangements earlier in the sanitation service chain and the intended arrangements for disposal/end use of the products of treatment. The need for realistic assessment of demand for services is emphasized and the roles of legislation and effective institutions in creating and responding to demand are explored. The chapter stresses the need to match technologies to available financial, management, and operational resources. Recognizing that contextual factors are not fixed, the final section of the chapter is concerned with possible measures to create an improved context for treatment.

Keywords: sanitation service chain, demand, legislation, institutions, resources

Introduction – the sanitation service chain

Assessment of faecal sludge and septage treatment requirements must start from an understanding of the main sanitation options and the ways in which they influence subsequent links in the sanitation chain. Figure 2.1 presents the various options, showing the ways in which the choices between various wet and dry toilet systems and on-site and off-site disposal options affect the type of treatment required. Inevitably a diagram such as this simplifies reality. In particular, the material removed from leach pits may have the characteristics of either septage or of faecal sludge, depending on the amount of water retained in the pit. The diagram can be used as an aid to initial assessment of sanitation systems and treatment needs, to be followed by more detailed investigation of the situation in the field. Tilley et al. (2014) provide further information on the various toilet options.

Figure 2.1 shows three basic options for the removal, transport, and treatment of excreta and wastewater from water-flushed systems: sewerage followed by wastewater treatment; hybrid systems; and on-site septic tanks and leach pits.

Sewerage followed by wastewater treatment

Sludge produced during wastewater treatment is normally treated at the wastewater treatment plant. However, local plants serving decentralized sewerage will often have no provision for sludge treatment, in which case it

http://dx.doi.org/10.3362/9781780449869.002

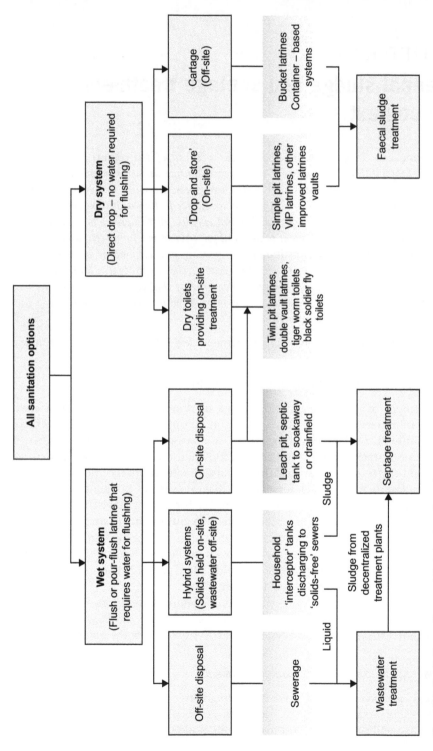

Figure 2.1 Sanitation options and their treatment needs

may be appropriate to treat sludge separated during the treatment process in a septage treatment plant.

Hybrid systems

Hybrid systems retain solids on-site in an interceptor tank, while discharging liquid through a sewer for off-site treatment or safe disposal. Regular desludging of septic tanks will be required if sewers are to remain solids-free. The solids content of the material removed during regular desludging will vary, depending on factors such as the emptying frequency, but removed material will normally be treatable as septage rather than faecal sludge.

On-site septic tanks and leach pits

Septic tanks retain solids, supernatant liquid, and scum, and must be regularly desludged. Best practice design and operation of a septic tank typically involves desludging at intervals of 2–4 years but in practice desludging can take place at intervals ranging from months to decades. The solids content of material removed from septic tanks will normally be less than 5 per cent and, in this book, such material is referred to as septage. Leach pits, which may exist in large numbers, may go for many years without desludging. When they are desludged, the nature of the material removed will depend on conditions in the pit. In areas with some combination of high water table, poorly draining pits, and discharge of sullage water to the pit, the material removed from pits is likely to include supernatant water and it can be described as septage. The solids content of material removed from well-drained pits serving pour-flush toilets is likely to be much higher and this material may be better described as faecal sludge. Cesspits, tanks that hold both solids and liquid in a sealed pit or tank, will require frequent emptying, as will those leach pits and septic tanks that retain water because either the water table is high or the drainage paths below the pit, soakaway, or drainfield have become clogged with solids. In both cases, the material removed will be septage rather than sludge.

Almost all dry systems retain solids in a pit or vault located directly underneath the toilet, allowing any excess moisture to percolate into the soil. They fall into three broad categories, conventional 'drop and store' systems, container-based and other cartage systems, and self-contained on-site systems, the first two of which require provision for removal and treatment of faecal sludge.

Conventional drop and store systems

These systems include various types of pit latrine and vault toilet. Pit latrines retain faecal material for several years, during which time both its volume and the concentration of pathogens decrease. These systems require removal of partly digested faecal sludge at infrequent intervals. The solids content of the sludge will vary, depending on local conditions. Investigations in Durban, South Africa, where people deposit solid waste in pits, revealed typical solids contents of over 20 per cent (Nwaneri, 2009). This is at the upper limit of the solid content of material removed from pit latrines, but suggests that material from dry single drop and store latrines will usually be classifiable as faecal sludge. Exceptions to this general rule are possible where some combination of a high water table, poorly draining soils, and discharge of bathroom wastewater to the pit occurs. In these circumstances, the pit may contain supernatant water so that material removed has the characteristics of septage rather than faecal sludge.

Container-based systems and other cartage systems

These systems require faecal sludge removal at intervals of a week or less. The short retention period in the container leaves little time for digestion, so the volume and strength of the faecal sludge produced by these systems are likely to be higher than those of faecal sludge removed from pit latrines and septic tanks. Additionally, it is common for these systems to separate urine from the excreta and wiping materials, which results in even stronger faecal sludge.

Self-contained on-site systems

Self-contained systems are designed to allow on-site transformation of faecal solids into safe and inoffensive soil-like material, which can be manually removed. These include dry twin-pit and twin-vault systems, and toilet systems that use worm composting to treat faecal material. In theory, these sanitation technologies remove the need for off-site transport and treatment. In practice, while showing promise, none of these solutions are likely to remove the need for more 'traditional' approaches to faecal sludge and septage management , especially in urban and peri-urban contexts, in the foreseeable future.

This brief overview of the various sanitation options and their treatment needs leads to the following conclusions:

- Many people in the towns and cities of lower-income countries rely on on-site sanitation.
- While options for dealing with wastes on-site exist, they are either subject to operational difficulties or are yet to be implemented at anything approaching a city-wide scale.
- Most towns and cities in lower-income countries will therefore need faecal sludge/septage removal, transport, and treatment/disposal systems for the foreseeable future.
- The characteristics of the material to be removed will depend on the type of toilet, the drainage characteristics of the soil and the design of the pit. Dry systems will normally produce faecal sludge, although pit latrines that penetrate the water table and/or receive wastewater

from washrooms may contain supernatant water. Pits that penetrate the water table are not desirable but the possibility that they may exist cannot be ignored. Water-flushed systems are more likely to produce septage, and the quantities of sludge and supernatant water will depend on the level of the water table and the efficacy of the drainage mechanism from the pit.

Options for faecal sludge and septage disposal

Material removed from on-site facilities, decentralized treatment facilities, and interceptor tanks is unpleasant, has a strong smell, may contain a large number of pathogens, and will certainly exert a high oxygen demand. If dumped indiscriminately, it will cause environmental degradation and pose a threat to public health. If spread on agricultural land without adequate controls, it will pose a threat to the health of agricultural workers and consumers of the agricultural produce grown on the land on which it is spread. Faecal sludge or septage discharged to agricultural and forest land may contaminate watercourses, adversely affecting their condition. Treatment and disposal systems for this material must therefore be designed to protect both public health and the environment. The US EPA identifies the following broad options for septage disposal (US EPA, 1984):

- independent septage treatment;
- co-treatment with sewage;
- land disposal of untreated septage.

In lower-income countries the general lack of sewer networks and sewage treatment means that independent faecal sludge and septage treatment will usually be the preferred option for new faecal sludge management initiatives. In areas where there is an existing or planned sewer network, co-treatment of septage with sewage (municipal wastewater) may be possible, although septage pre-treatment to separate solids from liquid will always be desirable. It may be possible to co-treat faecal sludge with separated wastewater solids, although some form of digestion prior to co-treatment may be desirable to reduce odours. When considering co-treatment, it is critical that the load generated by faecal sludge and septage is assessed in relation to the capacity of wastewater treatment facilities to accept that load. The assessment should cover both the organic and suspended solids load carried in the liquid fraction of separated sludge/septage and the volume of separated solids. The co-treatment of liquid from septage and faecal sludge in a wastewater treatment plant is discussed in Chapter 9.

Land disposal of untreated faecal sludge or septage adds nutrients and carbon to the soil but poses risks to the health of agricultural users and consumers of farm produce. Because of its benefits, it was once the norm in the USA and Europe, a point that is illustrated by the description in the 1984 US EPA Septage Treatment and Disposal handbook of land disposal as 'the most frequently used technique for septage disposal in the United States'. Since then, increased concern about the risks has led all developed countries to either ban or severely restrict the use of untreated and partially treated faecal matter on land. Land disposal is still practised in many low- and lower-middle-income countries, usually informally with minimal regulation, and the challenge for sanitation planners is to identify appropriate responses to this situation.

When assessing possible responses, lessons can be learned from experience in the USA and Europe. The 1984 US EPA handbook identified three broad options for land disposal: land spreading, sub-surface incorporation, and burial. Land spreading was the simplest option but usually led to problems with pathogens, flies, and other vectors. The handbook suggested that sub-surface incorporation, with sludge ploughed into the land immediately after discharge, provided a better option. When assessing options, it will also be useful to assess the risks associated with current land disposal practices. Box 2.1 provides an example from northern Ghana of what this might entail.

The pit-composting method described in Box 2.1 is similar to the trenching methods used in Malaysia (Narayana, 2017). It has also been trialled in

---

Box 2.1 Unregulated land disposal in Tamale, Ghana

Farmers around the city of Tamale in northern Ghana purchase untreated septage from suction tanker operators and use it as a soil conditioner/fertilizer (RUAF, 2003). The crops grown on the land fertilized with septage are mainly cereals, including maize, sorghum, and millet. Farmers purchase septage from suction truck drivers during the dry season. The most common practice is for the septage to be delivered to points that the suction trucks can reach and left in the open for the remainder of the dry season. During this period, the high temperature, high solar radiation, and low humidity create the conditions for effective drying. At the end of the dry season, the farmers spread the dried sludge evenly over their land. The long drying time allows deactivation of pathogens and so is likely to reduce the health risk to workers, but helminths can remain in the dried septage for long periods, leading to a risk of infection. Workers report problems with itching and swollen feet when incorporating the dried sludge into the soil. These symptoms could be an early indication of hookworm infection and might also be associated with mycetoma, a chronic, progressively destructive disease caused by fungus and some types of bacteria which is known to affect agricultural workers in tropical climates.

Some farmers compost sludge in pits. They dig pits, place rice or maize straw in the bottom of the pit, and pour sludge onto the straw. They then cover the sludge with another layer of straw, repeating the process until the pit is full. The pit contents are then left to compost throughout the dry season, from November to the end of March. Farmers then empty the pits and apply the dry mixture of sludge and straw evenly across their fields. This method is less widely used than the first method because it requires more crop residue than is available to some farmers, and is relatively labour intensive. Its advantages are that the digested sludge produced is easy to apply and results in good soil characteristics, in particular soil bulk density.

These methods are only viable during the dry season and so do not provide a year-round response to septage disposal needs. In this respect, and in their potential to transmit pathogens, they are far from ideal. Nevertheless, they provide benefits to farmers, who may resist efforts to discontinue them.

South Africa, where Partners in Development and the University of KwaZulu-Natal investigated deep trench burial of faecal sludge from pit latrines for forestry and land reclamation purposes (Still et al., 2012). They found that trees grown on entrenched sludge had about 60 per cent more biomass than control trees after 25 months. Monitoring boreholes were installed downstream of the deep trench burial site, and nitrate, phosphorus, and pH fluctuations in these boreholes remained within acceptable ranges throughout the study, even though the volumes of sludge buried were significantly in excess of normally accepted rates for agricultural application. Tests revealed significant numbers of helminth ova in freshly exhumed pit-latrine sludge. However, after almost three years of burial, less than 0.1 per cent of these ova were viable (i.e., potentially infective). The study concluded that, provided contamination of surface soil is prevented, deep trench burial in a suitable location can be a viable option for faecal sludge disposal.

The work in South Africa shows that there are potentially safe options for land disposal. However, the safety of land disposal practices depends on strong regulation, which may be difficult to guarantee in countries without strong regulatory systems. Low permissible application rates mean that a large land area will be required, with disposal to agricultural land usually requiring the cooperation of many landowners. If the farms accepting fresh or treated sludge are widely scattered, the logistics and cost of transport are likely to become problematic. Forest land holdings will often be larger, with many owned by the state, but access may be a problem. In established forest areas, sub-surface incorporation may be impossible because the close spacing of trees prevents the use of ploughs. A better option may be to focus on areas that are being prepared for tree planting, the approach followed in the KwaZulu-Natal example.

Private and public needs and the importance of demand

As explained in the introduction to this chapter, a need for septage or faecal sludge management is likely to exist wherever sanitation facilities retain faecal solids at the household or community level. Need is a rather imprecise term and it is legitimate to ask: what is the nature of the need, and who experiences it? Households with overflowing leach pits that flood the area around their houses will feel an urgent need to have the leach pit emptied. If the tanker crew that empties their pit then discharges the resulting septage to a watercourse, it will contribute to the pollution of the wider environment, creating a need for action to both prevent indiscriminate dumping and clean up any pollution that has resulted from previous dumping. There is an important distinction between these two needs. The first is a private need that affects household members and their immediate neighbours. The second is a public need that affects all those whose quality of life will be adversely affected by the environmental pollution resulting from indiscriminate dumping.

The concept of demand helps to clarify the options for meeting private and public needs. Economists define demand as willingness and ability to pay for a good or service. People's willingness to pay for their overflowing pit or tank to be emptied but not for the subsequent safe treatment and disposal of the pit/tank contents illustrates the fact that demand is normally greater for private than for public goods and services. Without demand, effective provision of a good or service will be very difficult. The experience in many towns and cities is that households discharge faecal wastes to open drains, depressions, and water bodies, sometimes, but not always, via small septic tanks. These practices reduce the demand for pit and tank emptying services. In the case of direct discharge there is no stored sludge to be removed. Where discharge is via a tank, solids will be washed out with the water discharged from the tank. This will prolong the time for which the tank will continue to function without desludging, often indefinitely. Even where faecal material is removed from household facilities, it may be dumped or sold to farmers for use as a soil conditioner/fertilizer rather than delivered to a treatment plant. These practices can lead to greatly reduced loading on treatment facilities while posing threats to both public health and the environment. These examples show that lack of demand does not necessarily indicate absence of need. Underloading of treatment plants designed to address needs but without consideration of demand will occur where demand for treatment is limited. This may result in operational difficulties and reduced income for the organization operating the treatment plant, which may make the operational difficulties worse. In such situations, the following action may be required:

- Introduce or strengthen and enforce regulations that prevent harm to health and/or the environment.
- Inform demand, ensuring that people, and in particular decision-makers, are aware of the need to consider the whole sanitation service chain and why it is important to them.
- Develop systems for charging for services that provide mainly public goods. An example from the Philippines is the introduction of small monthly charges, added to water bills, which were intended to cover the cost of scheduled emptying but also cover the cost of treatment.

The regulatory approach might involve new building regulations prohibiting toilet connections to the drainage system and specifying a minimum vertical distance between leach pits, soakaways, and drain fields and the water table. Improved and more relevant regulations will normally require legislation, as discussed in more detail under the legislation sub-heading below. The key to successful regulation is enforcement, and planners should recognize that effective enforcement will require effective systems for vetting designs and inspecting construction. Such systems require resources, which will often only be available once appropriate institutional strengthening measures have been taken. They are unlikely to be effective in 'informal' areas; i.e., those that have developed outside formal planning and regulatory systems.

Informal development accounts for a high proportion of housing in many countries and, by its very nature, is difficult to regulate.

Education is required to inform demand. This might involve promotion campaigns, based on key messages about the public and private benefits of improved septage management and the consequences of failing to follow good practice. Like effective enforcement of regulations, education requires institutional and financial resources, suggesting that functioning septage management and treatment systems are reliant on the existence of effective institutional and financial systems. One important focus of education should be on the need to ensure that tanker operators can gain access to pits and tanks without breaking cover slabs. This action will be most effective if it is undertaken in parallel with the introduction of national regulations and laws and municipal by-laws that specify appropriate construction and access arrangements for on-site tanks and pits.

The main point to take from this discussion of need and demand is the importance of taking account of demand when assessing treatment requirements. In some cases, this will result in a staged approach to treatment provision, linked to efforts to increase demand over time. This point is considered in more detail in Chapter 3.

Legislation

Legislation provides the framework within which septage management takes place. It may exist in the form of national laws, directives, regulations, and standards or more locally as municipal directives and by-laws. The areas of legislation that are likely to affect efforts to improve septage management in general and septage treatment in particular include:

- *Environmental legislation* relating to air and water quality standards and limits on the discharge of wastes to the environment.
- *Legislation on institutional powers and responsibilities* covering the distribution of powers and responsibilities between different utility or public service organizations, the scope for creating specialist organizations to take on tasks such as faecal sludge management, and possible roles for the private sector.
- *Sanitation codes, standards, and guidelines*, which specify the types of sanitation that are allowable and the form that sanitation facilities should take.
- *Licensing requirements for operators.*
- *Codes, standards, and guidelines* that refer specifically to faecal sludge disposal.
- Any existing legislation on tariffs, tipping fees and other financial matters.

Legislation will be strongest if national laws and standards provide a framework within which local government bodies can develop their own by-laws and standards. For instance, Section 503 of the US Code of Federal Regulations (CFR) Title 40 provides the national framework for the use or disposal of treatment-plant biosolids. Individual states and city administrations refer to this when developing their own guidelines and legislation. The Government of Brazil sets out similar standards in its Resolution 375 (Conselho Nacional do Meio, 2006). Where national codes and standards make no specific reference to faecal sludge and septage disposal, it may be possible to base by-laws and standards on the guidance provided for sludge produced at sewage treatment plants. If no such guidance exists, the development of national guidelines should be a priority. These should include guidelines on procedures to be followed and standards to be achieved for the various end-use possibilities.

Legislation will only be effective if it is enforced. Enforcement depends on systems to monitor the activities of households and sanitation service providers and impose sanctions on those who fail to comply with relevant rules and regulations. Sanctions require clear statements of the penalties for non-compliance and effective legal arrangements for ensuring that those penalties are enforced. Effective monitoring requires access to clear guidance on standards, together with effective institutional arrangements for carrying out monitoring activities. While these conditions are often difficult to realize in practice, action to realize them must form part of any effort to improve faecal sludge management.

Institutional structures, systems, and capacities

The term institution can be used to describe an organization or, more widely, a 'significant practice, relationship, or organization in a society or culture' (Merriam-Webster on-line dictionary definition). Another definition is Douglass North's: 'humanly devised constraints that structure political, economic and social interactions' (North, 1990). Institutions, in the sense given by North and the wider Merriam-Webster definition, provide the framework within which septage and faecal sludge management activities take place. Effective institutions increase the likelihood that a particular septage management initiative will work, while poor and inappropriate institutions can undermine even the best technical approaches to septage/faecal sludge management and treatment. It is therefore important to assess septage management options, including treatment technology options, in relation to existing and possible future institutions. Figure 2.2 is a diagrammatic representation of the factors that influence how institutions work.

Mental models

Figure 2.2 illustrates the point that institutions cannot be seen in isolation from the attitudes, assumptions, and perceptions, collectively referred to as 'mental models', that are prevalent in society. The concept dates from the 1940s but its use in relation to municipal governance owes much to the work of Douglass North and Elinor Ostrom (World Bank, 2015: Chapter 3).

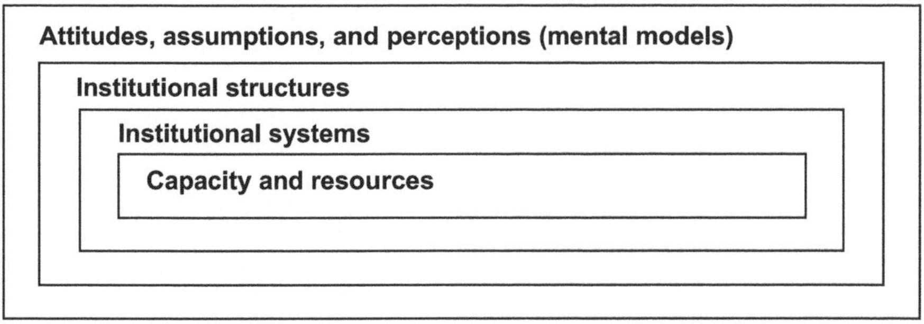

```
┌─────────────────────────────────────────────────────────────────────┐
│  Attitudes, assumptions, and perceptions (mental models)              │
│  ┌──────────────────────────────────────────────────────────────┐    │
│  │  Institutional structures                                     │    │
│  │  ┌─────────────────────────────────────────────────────┐      │    │
│  │  │  Institutional systems                               │      │    │
│  │  │  ┌──────────────────────────────────────────┐        │      │    │
│  │  │  │  Capacity and resources                   │        │      │    │
│  │  │  └──────────────────────────────────────────┘        │      │    │
│  │  └─────────────────────────────────────────────────────┘      │    │
│  └──────────────────────────────────────────────────────────────┘    │
└─────────────────────────────────────────────────────────────────────┘
```

Figure 2.2 Factors that influence the performance of institutions

Mental models shape personal and group priorities, which influence the objectives and working methods of the organizations to which they belong. Effective septage/faecal sludge management will only be possible if key decision-makers and potential service users believe that safe management of faecal sludge and septage is important. Demand for treatment will depend on attitudes to the environmental consequences of indiscriminate dumping. Where sanitation and environmental degradation have low priority for both decision-makers and the general public, action to raise awareness among members of both groups must be a high priority.

Institutional structures

Institutional structures influence the way in which responsibilities for sanitation services, including septage treatment, are distributed. The distribution of responsibilities may be either *spatial*, with different organizations taking responsibility in different areas, or *functional*, with different organizations and groups taking responsibility for different types of activity, including different links in the sanitation service chain. In practice, institutional structures may involve both spatial and functional distribution of responsibilities. In most countries:

- Higher levels of government set objectives, allocate the capital funding required to facilitate action to meet those objectives, and develop the overarching legislation and regulations that govern the actions of other stakeholders. National and regional organizations are also responsible for setting standards and monitoring effluents.
- Faecal sludge and septage removal and transport services are provided by municipalities, the private sector, or some combination of the two. The services provided by the private sector should be regulated by the municipality, but there are many situations in which this regulation is absent or ineffective. In some cities, for instance, Dakar, private-sector operators have set up associations of emptiers that provide some degree of self-regulation.

- Responsibility for treatment normally rests with local government or a water and sanitation utility, although operation is sometimes outsourced to the private sector.
- Households are responsible for providing and maintaining their own on-plot sanitation facilities.

Where existing service providers do not provide good faecal sludge management, the possibility of creating a body to provide these services, including faecal sludge and septage treatment, across several local government or utility service areas should be considered. This body might be a public company, a specialist department within a sewerage utility or solid waste management agency, or a private-sector organization, working with several municipalities through some form of management contract. It might be responsible for services across a whole region or province, or a defined area within that region or province, and would probably be empowered to subcontract some tasks to other organizations.

Where municipalities have limited powers to employ and pay suitably qualified workers and/or septage management has low priority for municipal decision-makers, it will be worthwhile to explore alternatives to municipal management of septage/faecal sludge removal, transport, and treatment services. Possible options include:

- Assigning responsibility for septage and faecal sludge management to a higher-level government body.
- Management by a public or private-sector operator, in accordance with contracts or agreements with individual local government bodies.
- Management by a public or private-sector operator in accordance with a contract or agreement with a group of local government bodies.
- Vesting powers to provide these services in an existing specialist organization such as a water and sewerage utility.

The public-sector operator might be a specialist public-sector organization set up with the remit of managing septage- and faecal-sludge-related services on behalf of local government. When considering alternative institutional structures, it will be important to assess the extent to which they provide scope for development of the basic management and operational skills required for septage/faecal sludge management.

Institutional systems

The quality of service provision will be influenced by:

- the systems that govern relationships between different groups and organizations; and
- the internal systems that govern the way in which each group or organization functions.

An important external relationship is that between pit and tank emptiers and the organization with responsibility for operating the treatment plant. The strength of this relationship will depend on systems being in place to define roles, ensure effective communication between the parties to the relationship, and resolve any disagreements that may arise. The effectiveness of these systems will, in turn, influence the volume of faecal sludge/septage that reaches the treatment plant. The relationship between the organization with responsibility for planning and designing treatment facilities and that with responsibility for operating those facilities is also important. The organization with operational responsibilities should be involved in the planning and design process from the beginning so that the design reflects its views, concerns, and operational experience.

Internal systems determine where responsibilities for decision-making lie within organizations. If those with formal responsibility for operational matters neglect that responsibility, routine operational decisions will be left to untrained, and perhaps unmotivated, staff. The result may be that the operational procedures followed in practice are significantly different from those required by official guidelines and standard operational procedures. Possible consequences include:

- failure of operational staff to keep accurate records of tanker deliveries to the treatment plant;
- delayed or neglected desludging of treatment units, including tanks, ponds, and anaerobic reactors, leading to sludge accumulation and poor plant performance; and
- haphazard loading of drying beds, resulting in poor drying and increased pathogen concentrations in partly dried sludge.

Such problems will be exacerbated if there is a high turnover of operational staff because many are employed on temporary contracts.

Capacity and resources

The poor record-keeping and haphazard loading of drying beds cited in the previous sub-section could be blamed, at least partly, on poorly trained staff. This shows that an operational system can fail if the staff employed to implement that system lack appropriate technical and/or managerial knowledge and skills. Financial resources are similarly important. The reason for delayed desludging of anaerobic ponds might be a lack of funds, the non-availability of equipment, or some combination of the two. These examples illustrate the need to go beyond a concern with systems to consider the human, financial, and other resources needed to implement them. Training can help to address capacity issues but will only do so when combined with action to address any structural and systemic constraints on capacity building. One common problem stems from the often low rank of staff holding septage management responsibilities within local government and water and sewerage utility hierarchies. This applies to both managers and workers and has two consequences:

- Workers may lack the basic educational background that would enable them to benefit from training. This is particularly important when treatment systems include mechanized units requiring skilled and knowledgeable operational staff.
- Once trained, both managers and workers may seek better, more highly paid jobs so that any benefits that have accrued from their training are lost.

These examples illustrate the key point that capacity building should never be just about training. It must also encompass action to develop systems to ensure that managers and workers:

- once trained, have scope to apply that training; and
- are incentivized to stay, perhaps by raising awareness that faecal sludge management will offer them opportunities to enhance their status and gain promotion to higher and more responsible positions.

Where government systems are rigid, the only way to offer these opportunities may be through setting up an alternative structure, as suggested in the sub-section on institutional structures.

The next sub-section, which deals with financing options, emphasizes the point that it will be best to integrate all aspects of septage/faecal sludge management in a single operation, using funds generated from charges for septage and faecal sludge to cover the cost of treatment. This requires an effective organization to manage the integrated process, a condition that applies even when this organization outsources some tasks to private-sector organizations.

In many towns and cities, the informal sector makes a major contribution to housing and services provision. It includes households and builders who construct sanitation facilities without reference to formal planning and building standards and codes, unlicensed pit and tank emptiers, and septage tanker operators. By definition, informal activity is unregulated and this means that it is largely unaffected by legislation. When considering institutional options, it is important to be aware that any attempt to introduce scheduled pit and tank emptying will require integration of informal sector pit and tank emptying services into the formal system.

Financial considerations

Responsibilities for financing the capital and recurrent costs of publicly provided services are often divided:

- Central government and international donors provide funds for treatment plant construction and purchase of tankers and other types of delivery vehicle.
- Local service providers cover operational costs, including maintenance and perhaps repair and replacement costs.

- Households are responsible for capital and maintenance costs of household facilities, and potentially some part of the costs for collection and transport.

Continued operation of faecal sludge and septage management services depends on the availability of funds to cover operational costs. As already stated in the discussion on demand, removal and local transport services provide private benefits and it is therefore relatively easy to persuade on-site sanitation users to pay for them. Even so, both public- and private-sector sludge tanker operators may struggle to cover costs where pits are large and/ or fill slowly so that demand for pit and tank emptying services is limited (Tayler et al., 2013). Financing septage and faecal sludge treatment services is more difficult. Because treatment is a public good that safeguards the environment and thus provides benefits to society as a whole, it is difficult to get customers to pay for it directly. Possible sources of funds to finance treatment are outlined below.

Charging sludge tanker operators for each load delivered to the treatment facility

This mechanism can be a good source of revenue where there is a high demand for tank and pit emptying and there are incentives to ensure that all material removed from pits and tanks is delivered to the treatment plant. Its use will be most appropriate where households pay a fee for each emptying/sludge removal event, either to a private or public sector provider. It requires effective systems for estimating and recording loads and levying charges. Investigations in several Indonesian cities in 2012 revealed that income from delivery charges covered only a small fraction of treatment plant operating costs, partly because of poor collection performance. (Tayler et al., 2013). It is possible that the imposition of delivery charges will deter private-sector operators from delivering to the plant, resulting in a reduction in the volume of faecal sludge delivered to the plant and a corresponding increase in the incidence of uncontrolled dumping directly to the environment. However, investigations in Sri Lanka found that, tanker drivers did deliver to conveniently located discharge points, resulting in an increase in the volume of septage delivered for treatment (Ravikumar Joseph – personal communication). The main point to take from this discussion is that income from delivery charges will depend on the local situation and should be investigated accordingly.

Income from sale of treated sludge

Treated sludge can be sold as a soil conditioner, fuel, source of protein, or building material. The first of these has historically been the most common form of resource recovery, but options that produce energy have the potential to produce more income (Diener et al., 2014). Where sludge is to be sold for agricultural use, it will be important to ensure that treated sludge is free of pathogens. Whatever the intended use of treated sludge, it must be socially acceptable and systems must be in place to market it and deliver it to customers. Chapter 10 provides further information on efforts to develop uses for dried sludge.

Transfer of funds from the municipal budget

This is the normal option for funding treatment costs in most countries. The amount transferred is often insufficient to cover all operating costs because faecal sludge treatment has a relatively low priority for municipal decision-makers.

Imposition of a surcharge on the charge made for another service

Surcharges have been imposed on water bills in some towns in the Philippines to cover the cost of scheduled pit and tank emptying and the associated transport and treatment services. This option has the merit of simplicity but is only possible where most people have a water connection. It might also be possible to add the surcharge to electricity bills or property taxes. Some states in India have explored the second option (see, for instance, Swachh Maharashtra Mission, 2016). Both pose some administrative challenges: in the case of electricity because it is rarely a municipal responsibility, and in the case of property tax because some properties are exempt from tax. The Maharashtra Government document quoted above suggests the alternative of introducing a new sanitation tax, noting that this would be possible under existing legislation.

Cross-subsidy

Cross-subsidy from profits on public-sector septage removal and transport services has potential, but will require an integrated approach to ensure that the organization with financial responsibility for treatment benefits from the income generated by pit and tank emptying services. Cross-subsidies from water supply or sewerage tariffs could also be used.

It will rarely be possible to cover all costs by charging for service delivery and selling treated products. Some subsidy from municipal funds will be necessary. These in turn may be subsidized by transfers from higher levels of government. Even where such subsidies cannot be avoided, the aim should always be to develop other funding sources in order to minimize reliance on subsidy.

An integrated approach does not require that one organization has to carry out all septage management tasks. The responsible organization may well wish to contract out pit and tank emptying services, and indeed the operation of septage treatment plants. However, it is essential that private-sector service providers work within a framework set by the main service provider organization, which must ensure sufficient funds are available – through a mix of the above-described options – to cover the capital and operation and maintenance costs associated with treatment.

Other external factors that influence treatment choices

The feasibility of faecal sludge and septage treatment technologies will depend on the availability and cost of the external inputs required for their successful operation. These inputs include spare parts, land, water and power, and the specialist operational knowledge and skills required for treatment process operation. Knowledge of the local situation in relation to each of these inputs is necessary when assessing the feasibility of different approaches and technologies. Key factors that are common to most treatment technologies are examined in more detail in Chapter 6. Factors that influence process choices are discussed in Chapter 4.

Potential changes in faecal sludge and septage management

The context within which faecal sludge management takes place will change over time. Demographic growth will result in both increased population and, potentially, a change in population distribution. Increased sewerage coverage may reduce the need for specialized faecal sludge and septage treatment facilities. Changes in faecal sludge and septage management practices can also affect the need for treatment. Those with responsibility for treatment services will have limited ability to affect such changes and should allow for them when planning for the future. There are other areas in which they can initiate and support change. Indeed, change may be essential if the legal, institutional, and financial constraints identified earlier in this chapter are to be overcome. When planning faecal sludge or septage treatment and understanding the context that it will operate in, it is important to consider how that context could change. Questions to be asked when assessing the likelihood of and need for change include:

- What changes are possible now, and what will be their consequences?
- What constraints stand in their way?
- What realistic options exist to address those constraints?
- How are the attitudes of service users and providers likely to change over time?

An example of a change that will influence treatment requirements is the change in load that will result from the introduction of scheduled pit and tank emptying services. This change is likely to encompass an increase in the volume of faecal sludge and/or septage requiring treatment and a reduction in its strength. Constraints on city-wide introduction of scheduled emptying include shortage of funds to finance the service, lack of information about existing on-site sanitation facilities to plan the scheduled desludging, lack of vacuum tankers, and lack of institutional capacity to manage a greatly expanded septage removal and transport operation. A solution to the shortage of funds associated with this could be to add a surcharge to water bills to pay for the service. As already noted, such a surcharge was used in some towns in the Philippines to cover the cost of scheduled emptying.

Another change that could impact treatment is the introduction of a public-private partnership in which the private-sector operator is contracted to conduct certain parts of the sanitation service chain, such as collection and/or treatment. This option will often be constrained by the ability of the organization with overall septage management responsibility to manage the greatly enlarged and more complex operation required to implement it. In this respect, it is worth noting that the working practices required of private-sector operators under a scheduled emptying regime managed by a public-sector organization will be different from those of unregulated providers operating in a competitive market. One response to these constraints might be to focus on scheduled emptying in selected areas in the first instance. This will provide time for gradual development of the capacity to manage scheduled services.

Changes in end-use practices, perhaps stemming from efforts to overcome resistance to the use of safely treated products, may result in increased revenue but may also require changes in treatment to ensure the safety of treated products.

Key points from this chapter

This chapter has explored the ways in which decisions about treatment process options need to take account of the context in which they operate. Key points emerging from this chapter include the following:

- The characteristics of the material to be treated will be influenced by the arrangements for capturing and storing excreta at the household level. Pit latrines and well-drained leach pits produce relatively dry faecal sludge, while septic tanks, leach pits with poor drainage, and pit latrines that penetrate the water table will usually produce more watery septage.
- Independent treatment facilities will usually be the best option for dealing with faecal sludge and septage.
- Where wastewater treatment facilities with spare capacity exist, co-treatment with wastewater is a possible septage treatment option. When considering this option, the effects of septage strength and characteristics on treatment processes must be taken into account. Solids–liquid separation of septage will always be advisable prior to co-treatment, with the separated liquid and solid fractions treated with wastewater and separated sewage sludge, respectively.
- Co-treatment of faecal sludge with the wastewater treatment plant sludge is possible but prior biodigestion of the faecal sludge may be advisable to reduce odour problems.

- Various options exist for land disposal of faecal sludge and septage, but these pose risks to both public health and the environment. Land disposal should only be considered if disposal sites with suitable hydro-geological conditions and topography are available, and the institutional systems to regulate it effectively are in place.
- Plans for faecal sludge and septage treatment must take account of both need and demand, both at the time of planning and at the planning horizon. Demand for treatment may be inhibited by the fact that sanitation users are reluctant to pay for a service that is a public rather than private good. Where this is the case, a combination of education and enforced regulations will usually be required to increase demand.
- Efforts to provide improved faecal sludge management services will only be successful if they are backed by relevant legislation. It will be particularly important to define roles and responsibilities in relation to various aspects of faecal sludge management.
- Plans for improving faecal sludge management, including treatment, should take account of resource availability and institutional capacity. Particular attention should be paid to any opportunities and constraints presented by existing systems. Where institutional strengthening is required, the short-term focus will normally have to be on options for improving existing institutional systems. In the longer term, it may be necessary to consider structural changes. These might involve the creation of a body with specific responsibility for faecal sludge management in one or more local government areas, depending on local circumstances.
- Responsibilities for faecal sludge and septage treatment are often split, with capital funding provided by higher levels of government while operational costs are borne by local government. Failure to cover operational costs will result in poor plant performance and may lead fairly quickly to plant failure. Some income can be generated by charging sludge tanker operators to deliver to the treatment plant and by the sale of treated products. However, neither is likely to cover the full cost of treatment.

References

Conselho Nacional do Meio Ambiente (2006) Resolução No. 375 de 29 de Agosto de 2006: Define critérios e procedimentos, para o uso agrícola de lodos de esgoto gerados em estações de tratamento de esgoto sanitário e seus produtos derivados, e dá outras providências. Diário da União, 28 August 2006, Part 1, 141–146 <http://www.mma.gov.br/port/conama/res/res06/res37506.pdf> [accessed 3 February 2018].

Diener, S., Semiyaga, S., Niwagaba, C., Muspratt, A., Gning, J., Mbéguéré, M., Ennin, J., Zurbrugg, C. and Strande, L. (2014) 'A value proposition: resource recovery from faecal sludge – Can it be the driver for improved sanitation?' Resources Conservation and Recycling 88: 32–8 <https://doi.org/10.1016/j.resconrec.2014.04.005> [accessed 11 May 2018].

Narayana, D. (2017) *Sanitation and Sewerage Management: The Malaysian Experience*, FSM Innovation Case Study, Seattle, WA: Bill & Melinda Gates Foundation <www.susana.org/_resources/documents/default/3-2760-7-1503648469.pdf> [accessed 26 October 2017].

North, D.C. (1990) *Institutions, Institutional Change, and Economic Performance*, New York, NY: Cambridge University Press.

Nwaneri, C.F. (2009) *Physico-Chemical Characteristics and Biodegradability of Contents of Ventilated Pit Latrines (VIPs) in eThekwini Municipality*, MSc thesis, University of KwaZulu-Natal <http://citeseerx.ist.psu.edu/viewdoc/download?doi=10.1.1.719.9526&rep=rep1&type=pdf> [accessed 25 February 2017].

RUAF (2003) *Faecal Sludge Application for Agriculture in Tamale, Ghana* <www.ruaf.org/sites/default/files/Faecal%20Sludge%20Application_1.pdf> [accessed 13 March 2017].

Still, D., Louton, B., Bakare, B., Taylor, C., Foxon, K. and Lorentz, S. (2012) *Investigating the Potential of Deep Row Entrenchment of Pit Latrine and Wastewater Sludges for Forestry and Land Rehabilitation Purposes*, Gezina, South Africa: Water Research Commission <www.susana.org/en/resources/library/details/1679> [accessed 13 March 2017].

Swachh Maharashtra Mission (Urban) (2016) *Guidelines for Septage Management in Maharashtra*, Urban Development Department, Government of Maharashtra <https://swachh.maharashtra.gov.in/Site/Upload/GR/Septage_Management_Guidelines_UDD_020216.pdf> [accessed 26 October 2017].

Tayler, K., Siregar, R., Darmawan, B., Blackett, I. and Giltner, S. (2013) 'Development of urban septage management models in Indonesia', *Waterlines* 32(3): 221–36 <http://dx.doi.org/10.3362/1756-3488.2013.023> [accessed 11 May 2018].

Tilley, E., Ulrich, L., Lüthi, C., Reymond, Ph. and Zurbrügg, C. (2014) Compendium of Sanitation Systems and Technologies, 2nd revised edition, Dübendorf, Switzerland: Swiss Federal Institute of Aquatic Science and Technology (Eawag) <www.iwa-network.org/wp-content/uploads/2016/06/Compendium-Sanitation-Systems-and-Technologies.pdf> [accessed 27 February 2017].

US EPA (1984) *Handbook: Septage Treatment and Disposal*, Cincinnati, OH: Municipal Environmental Research Laboratory <https://nepis.epa.gov/Exe/ZyPDF.cgi/30004ARR.PDF?Dockey=30004ARR.PDF> (accessed 19 June 2018).

World Bank (2015) *World Development Report 2015: Mind, Society, and Behavior*, Washington, DC: World Bank <http://dx.doi.org/10.1596/978-1-4648-0342-0> [accessed 11 May 2018].

CHAPTER 3
Planning for improved treatment

This chapter deals with the decisions and actions required before detailed design of treatment facilities can begin. It focuses on planning for faecal sludge and septage treatment but notes the desirability of integrating plans for treatment into overall sanitation plans. It emphasizes the importance of identifying actual rather than assumed problems, based on informed assessment of existing conditions. Methods and procedures for preliminary assessment are identified and described and those for detailed assessment are introduced, with references to resources that should be useful in conducting detailed assessments. Procedures for determining planning and service areas and assessing the merits of a decentralized approach to treatment are described. The chapter next identifies the factors that will influence treatment plant location. A description of procedures for estimating hydraulic, organic, and suspended solids loads follows. The final section of the chapter explores the factors that will affect technology choice.

Keywords: preliminary assessment, planning area, plant location, load assessment, technology options

Introduction

This chapter deals with the planning decisions required when developing proposals for new and improved faecal sludge and septage treatment facilities. It does not attempt to provide guidance on wider faecal sludge and sanitation planning activities. Where possible, development of plans for improved treatment should take place within the context provided by an overall sanitation plan. However, this will not always be possible because either no such plan exists or the resources to produce a plan are not available. Where this is the case, the aim should be to collect enough information on other links in the sanitation service chain to facilitate informed choices on treatment options. The approach set out in this chapter draws on the concepts set out in *Sanitation Planning: A Guide to Strategic Planning* (Tayler et al., 2003). The Sustainable Sanitation and Waste Management (SSWM) toolbox includes an introduction to strategic sanitation planning (SSWM, n.d.). Much of this is based on the Tayler et al. book which emphasizes the importance of understanding the existing situation, identifying clear objectives, and charting a stepwise course from the existing situation towards those objectives, taking account of institutional and financial constraints and opportunities. Other planning approaches provide suggestions on what the stepwise approach might entail and how it might be implemented (see, for instance, Parkinson et al., 2014 and Lüthi et al., 2011).

http://dx.doi.org/10.3362/9781780449869.003

Chapters 14–17 of Strande et al. (2014) provide detailed guidance on planning for faecal sludge management, covering assessment of the existing situation (Chapter 14), stakeholder analysis and engagement (Chapters 15 and 16), and planning for integrated faecal sludge management systems (Chapter 17). This chapter does not attempt to replicate this guidance but rather focuses on the points that are of specific importance to planning for new and improved treatment facilities. Faecal sludge and septage treatment is a public good, with benefits that extend beyond individual geographically or socially based communities. For this reason, the chapter stresses the need to engage with stakeholders while recognizing that planning for improved treatment is unlikely to be community led.

In order to assess the existing situation, it will be necessary to collect information relating to the following:

- *The nature and extent of existing sanitation services*, taking account of all the links in the sanitation chain and including information on typical characteristics of material removed from pits and tanks.
- *The way in which those services are likely to change* in the future.
- *Any problems and deficiencies with these services*, including those that relate to the institutional structures and systems that determine the ways in which services are delivered.
- *The availability of resources*, including both physical resources, such as land and power supply, and institutional resources in the form of organizations with the technical and management skills to operate treatment processes of varying degrees of complexity.
- *Existing and potential future markets* for the products of treatment.

Information on existing sanitation facilities and faecal sludge/septage collection and transport, and the ways in which these are likely to change in the future, is required to assess the likely short- and longer-term loading on proposed treatment plants. Changes over the planning period will include those, such as population growth, that will be largely independent of planned interventions and those achieved through interventions that aim to amend and improve services and the institutional and financial systems that support them. An example of the latter would be an increase in the volume of material to be treated following the introduction of scheduled pit and tank emptying. Information on problems and deficiencies with existing services will help planners and designers to avoid repeating the mistakes of the past. Operational problems must be considered in relation to institutional and financial arrangements, with particular emphasis on identifying any shortfall in the funds required to cover operational maintenance, repair, and replacement costs.

Broad objectives were identified in Chapter 1 and are explored in more detail in Chapter 4. In order to chart a route from the existing situation to achievement of overall objectives, plans must explore choices, identify actions to be undertaken, and combine those actions into an overall programme. The programme should identify intermediate objectives, achievement of which will facilitate implementation of later programme activities. Intermediate objectives might include ensuring the availability of the following:

- *A database of existing sanitation facilities and their pit and tank emptying needs.* This will be required where there are plans to move from 'on-call' to scheduled emptying.
- *Information on characteristics of material to be treated.* Because of the variable nature of faecal sludge and septage, this will require a comprehensive sampling and testing programme, based on composite samples taken from representative faecal sludge/septage transport vehicles. This will give information on the current situation. When designing for future conditions, allowance should be made for possible changes in characteristics caused by changes in the sanitation chain, for instance expansion of access to household water supply or the introduction of scheduled emptying. This may require a degree of judgement but it may be possible to inform this judgement by obtaining information on material removed from regularly emptied pits and tanks.
- *Effective management systems and supply chains for proposed treatment processes.* This is an important intermediate objective in all cases and is a prerequisite for the implementation of mechanized treatment technologies.

As far as is possible, decisions should be information-based rather than reliant on untested assumptions. Judgement will be required where there are gaps or inconsistencies in the available information. To improve the quality of decision-making, the options for collecting and analysing additional information with the aim of filling gaps and resolving inconsistencies should always be explored.

Overview of treatment plant planning and design process

Planning works best when it follows a logical process in which each step builds on the outputs and outcomes of previous steps. Figure 3.1 is a diagrammatic representation of the process described in this book. It shows the activities required at each stage, together with information needs and the factors that may influence planning choices. The feedback arrows point to the fact that the process is not linear. Information collected and choices made at some stages in the planning process may result in a need to revisit earlier decisions. The key point to take from this is that planning will often be an iterative rather than a linear process.

The steps set out in Figure 3.1, from initial assessment to technology assessment and choice, are now examined in more detail. Chapter 4 provides further information on technology options and choices.

Other relevant factors   **Task**   **Information requirements**

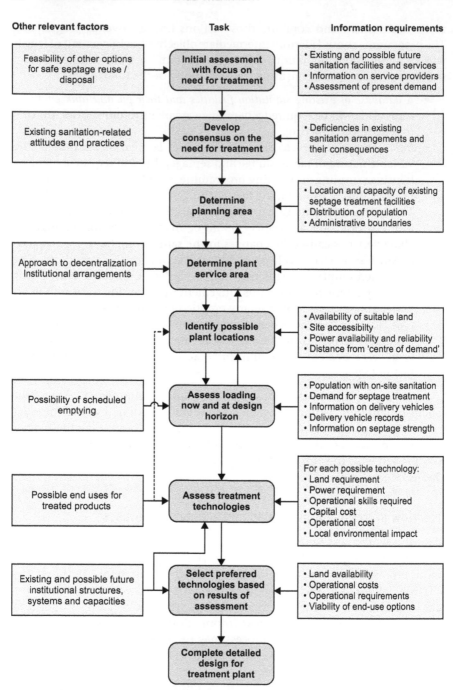

Figure 3.1 Steps in the planning process

Preliminary assessment

Overview and initial meetings

The first step in planning for improved faecal sludge and septage treatment is to make a preliminary assessment of the existing situation in order to:

• determine what information exists or can be gathered; and
• identify gaps and deficiencies in that information.

The starting point for assessment should be to meet the people with official responsibility for managing faecal sludge management and faecal sludge/septage treatment services. This meeting will provide opportunities to obtain an initial idea of existing services, request access to existing information, identify the main stakeholders in faecal sludge management provision, and arrange to meet those stakeholders. Use it to determine whether the public sector is involved in pit and tank emptying services, whether there are records relating to those services, and, where treatment facilities already exist, whether those records cover faecal sludge/septage deliveries to the facilities.

Meetings with government officials also provide an opportunity to explore institutional arrangements and the extent to which existing legislation supports those arrangements. Points to be explored during these meetings include responsibilities for different aspects of faecal sludge management and the extent to which these responsibilities are defined in national and local legislation. Meetings with government officials will also provide information on any formal arrangements for the reuse of dried sludge. Government officials may know something about informal end-use arrangements but investigation of these arrangements will normally require follow-up discussions with tanker operators and the farmers and others to whom they deliver.

Obtaining reliable information on the activities of private-sector tanker operators and pit emptiers will often be more difficult, particularly where their activities are unregulated. The first task will be to identify private and community sector operators. Government officials may be able to provide leads, particularly where the private-sector operators are already delivering loads to treatment plants.

Secondary information

Sources of information that may be already available include existing plans and records, reports prepared by government and international agencies, any previously implemented behaviour change and sanitation marketing studies, consultants' reports, and census data. Additional information can be gathered through review of satellite images, field observation, and talking to key stakeholders, including both the users and providers of services.

When considering existing plans, it is important to ask the questions:

- How realistic is this plan, and what is the likelihood that it will be implemented?
- In the event that it is implemented, what, if any, impact will it have on faecal sludge management services?

The first question is important. If a plan is unrealistic, proposals based on the assumptions and time-scales set out in the plan will be equally unrealistic.

Official surveys may provide information on existing sanitation facilities. For instance, in Indonesia, health departments carry out regular surveys that provide information on the number of households with access to on-site sanitation facilities, although they provide little detailed information on those facilities. Census records often include information on sanitation but this information may lack detail making it impossible to separate out information on different types of sanitation.

Using satellite images to plan for field visits

Satellite images are a good source of information on the extent and nature of development. Comparison of satellite images and other sources of spatial information from different years provides an indication of the scale and direction of new development. Information from satellite images can also be used to identify the location and extent of different types of development and this information can then be used to plan a programme of field visits to areas representing different types of development. Figure 3.2 is a Google Earth image of part of central Dhaka in Bangladesh. The larger buildings

Figure 3.2 Satellite image of part of Dhaka, Bangladesh

on the right-hand side of the image are in the high-income Gulshan area, while the area of small, tightly packed buildings in the top left-hand corner of the image are in the Korai informal settlement. Sanitation provision is very different in the two areas, with consequences to be assessed when developing plans for septage and faecal sludge treatment.

Field visits

Field visits provide opportunities to gain a broad understanding of existing sanitation facilities and services, their strengths and their weaknesses, and the opportunities and problems that they present. Initial information collection should encompass observation and conversations with sanitation users and service providers, both of which should focus on existing sanitation facilities and services. Some aspects of existing facilities and services will be obvious at the street level while others will require visits to houses, picked at random but, as far as is possible, representative of houses in the surrounding area. Box 3.1 summarizes the findings from field visits to the areas shown in Figure 3.2.

Initial appraisal can lead to erroneous conclusions if the information obtained is interpreted incorrectly. Most reports on Dhaka say that people living outside formally sewered areas rely on on-site sanitation systems. In fact, as illustrated by the examples given in Box 3.1, most people in Dhaka rely on hybrid systems that retain some solids but are connected to drains and informally provided sewers. Because solids escape with the tank effluent, demand for pit and tank emptying services is much lower than would be the case with fully on-site systems.

Box 3.1 Findings of field visits in Gulshan and Korai, Dhaka, Bangladesh

Most buildings in Gulshan are multi-storey apartments. Visits to areas where similar buildings were under construction revealed the existence of large septic tanks located under the buildings, with effluent connections to the drainage system. In Gulshan, the drainage system consists of covered drains and piped sewers, which discharge locally and are not connected to the formal sewer system.

Buildings in Korai are typically single or double storey and many people live in rented rooms grouped together in multi-occupancy 'holdings'. Most sanitation facilities are pour-flush toilets, most of which are connected to crude covered drains and sewers which, like those in Gulshan, discharge locally. In some cases, the 'P' trap on the toilet is omitted so that excreta drop directly into a pit.

Sanitation facilities with septic tanks connected to drains and sewers will continue to function after a fashion, even when septic tanks are full of solids. This means that the widespread practice of connecting household sanitation facilities directly or indirectly to the drainage system reduces demand for pit and tank emptying services. This, in turn, reduces the volume of material available for delivery to treatment plants. In Dhaka, this led to a situation in which there were no tanker-based pit emptying services prior to 2015, other than two small 'vacutug' machines, which have a very low capacity (WSUP, 2017). Manual emptying services do exist, mainly in low-income areas, but the informal nature of these services means that little information is available on them.

This example illustrates the need to base conclusions on accurate assessment of local conditions, rather than preconceived assumptions about those local conditions. Two further examples will help to illustrate this point. In Indonesia, most households discharge toilet wastes to crude leach pits, which require emptying at infrequent intervals. It would seem reasonable to assume that this is because people connect the leach pits to drains, as in Dhaka. In practice, field visits in several towns revealed that this was rarely the case, so that there must be another reason for the lack of demand for emptying services. In Mekelle, Ethiopia, many higher income households discharge all their wastewater to large leach pits with dry stone walls. At first sight, this approach is similar to that adopted in Indonesia, but the discharge of sullage water to the pits increases the hydraulic loading, with the result that some require emptying at intervals of a year or less. This results in a relatively high volume of watery septage. In contrast, lower-income houses mostly rely on dry pit latrines, sometimes building a new latrine when the old one is full. The important point to take from these examples is that sanitation practices vary between countries, between towns and cities, and within towns and cities.

Preliminary field visits should provide opportunities to determine the accessibility of existing tanks and pits. Questions to ask when looking at accessibility include 'where are tanks and pits located?', 'how close are they to roads that are wide enough to permit vehicle access?' and 'what, if any, provision is made for inserting a suction hose?' Answers to these questions will provide guidance on action required to facilitate removal of pit and tank contents, which in turn will influence the amount of faecal sludge/septage delivered to the treatment plant.

Talking to sanitation users and service providers

Interviews and observation can reveal much about the concerns, priorities, and activities of different stakeholders. In particular:

- Household members can provide information on the frequency with which their pits/tanks are emptied, what they pay for emptying services, and any problems that they face in accessing those services. Initial discussions can also help planners to understand people's priorities and identify possible drivers for change.
- Builders can provide information on how they construct sanitation facilities. Their information will provide an indication of the extent to which common construction norms and practices differ from those required by any formal regulations.
- Tanker operators, both public and private sector, and manual emptiers can provide information on the demand for their services, their working practices, and any obstacles that they face when attempting to empty tanks and pits.

- Plant operators can provide useful information on how they operate existing treatment plants, any operational problems that they experience, and any action that they have taken to overcome those problems.
- Those who use dried sludge for agricultural and other purposes will provide an indication of demand for end uses. In the event that present end-use practices are unsafe, these discussions will indicate a need to consider how treatment for end use can be included in the treatment process.

Information on the attitudes and practices of households, builders, and tanker operators should be related to the various types of development identified during the initial assessment of the planning area.

Informal discussions and formal interviews will help to identify key issues, thus providing a starting point for more detailed investigation of those issues. When trying to find out about existing activities and procedures it is important to ensure that interviewees discuss what they actually do rather than what they think you expect them to do. This requires that subjects are approached in a neutral way, avoiding leading questions as far as is possible. Where possible, approach a subject in more than one way and compare the findings. For instance, it will be useful to compare what people say they do with observation of what they do. When assessing the operational practices followed by tanker operators, builders, or plant operators, it will always be useful to ask an operator to demonstrate how they approach a task, noting any challenges and issues that they face in carrying out the task.

Group discussions with tanker operators and/or manual emptiers should be used to build on the initial impressions gained through observation and informal discussions with individual service providers. Box 3.2 provides an example of how a discussion with a group of tanker operators revealed limited utilization of available tanker capacity, suggesting a lack of demand for septage

---

Box 3.2 Lessons learned from group discussion with tanker operators in Tegal, Indonesia

Investigations led by the author in Tegal, Central Java, Indonesia revealed that public-sector pit emptying services had been non-operational for several months but that several private-sector entrepreneurs were providing pit emptying services. All of these entrepreneurs used small tankers, maximum capacity 3 m³, consisting of a pump and locally fabricated tank mounted on a pick-up truck body. A meeting with all the active tanker operators in the city revealed that their number had increased from three to seven over a period of three to four years. At the beginning of this period, the three active operators did good business but by the time of the group meeting no operator was emptying more than about three pits per week. Given the lack of effective public service provision, this meant that not more than 1,000 pits were being emptied each year in a town with a population of about 250,000 and almost no sewerage. This implied limited demand for pit emptying services. It seemed that the relatively low cost of purchasing a second-hand pick-up truck and converting it to carry a pump and septage tank had enticed operators into the market with the result that capacity now exceeded demand.

removal services. Assessment of the implications of such findings will be essential when assessing the short-term loading on the treatment plant.

Analysis based on preliminary investigations

Analysis of existing records can provide useful information on the current demand for pit and tank emptying services and hence on the likely load on an existing or proposed septage treatment plant. The author's experience in Palu, the capital of Central Sulawesi Province in Indonesia, provides an example. The estimated 2013 population of the city was about 360,000. All sanitation in the town was on-site, with sullage discharged separately to soakaways or the public drainage system. The only pit emptying service for the 70,000 on-site toilet systems and 45 shared sanitation units in the town was that provided by Palu municipality. The complete absence of private-sector operators was an indicator that this service was meeting all existing demand. The municipality kept good records, showing that, on average, about 1,400 pits and tanks were emptied each year. This equates to an average emptying rate per pit or tank of once in 50 years. This high figure is an indication of low demand for emptying services. Extensive site visits revealed very few connections from pits and tanks to drains and watercourses and so ruled out the possibility that low demand resulted from the escape of solids into the drainage system. Further investigation suggested that the low demand for emptying stemmed partly from the relatively large size of the pits and partly from the low solids accumulation rate.

Detailed investigation and analysis

Preliminary investigation of the type outlined above can lead to broad conclusions, but more detailed investigations will normally be required to obtain the reliable and accurate information required for treatment plant design. These investigations should cover the attitudes and behaviours of potential users of faecal sludge management services, any barriers to changes in their sanitation-related practices, and possible drivers for those changes. The first step in carrying out these investigations will be to separate potential users into groups living in different types of settlement. Within those groups, further segmentation will be required, based on factors such as housing conditions, tenure status, social status, and income. Income security, level of education, gender of the household head, and tenure status are all likely to influence ability and willingness to pay for feacal sludge management services. Explore willingness to pay for services in relation to possible financial mechanisms, recognizing that different approaches may be required for different segments of the potential 'customer' base.

The planning tools identified at the beginning of this chapter provide guidance on carrying out these investigations. For information on these and other planning tools, including an assessment of their scope, strengths, and weaknesses, see WaterAid (2016).

Household surveys provide a more rigorous approach to the assessment of people's sanitation-related practices, views, and priorities. They can provide useful information on existing sanitation provision, current septage management practices, awareness of the health risks associated with poor sanitation, and willingness to pay for improved services. A general introduction to social survey methods is Oxfam's field guide, which draws on work on water and sanitation services in Juba, South Sudan (Nichols, 1991). For an introduction to participatory methods, see Dayal et al. (2000). Chapter 14 of Strande et al. (2014) provides a guide to assessing the existing faecal sludge management situation.

The Excreta Flow Diagram (EFD) is a tool for presenting information on the flow of excreta through each link in the sanitation service chain and may be used to present information on excreta flows and whether or not these are effectively dealt with. The EFD Promotion Initiative has developed a toolbox to provide guidance on producing an EFD, which is available at SFD (2017). This includes a tool for generating an EFD once information on sanitation conditions in the city is available. The accuracy and relevance of the EFD will depend on the quality of available information on sanitation facilities and excreta flows and the assumptions made when interpreting that information. In the likely event that there are gaps and inconsistencies in the available information, the EFD should help to identify them so that steps can be taken to fill gaps and clarify inconsistencies. Figure 3.3 shows a typical EFD. For further information on the EFD and associated tools see Peal et al. (2014)

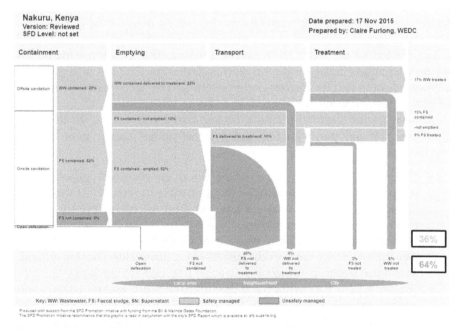

Figure 3.3 Example EFD showing excreta flows in Nakuru, Kenya

Participatory workshops and consultation exercises are useful in assessing attitudes to proposals. They tend to be better for confirming consensus than for negotiating differences but are useful in identifying areas of concern and, hence, of potential opposition to proposals. Only when areas of concern and opposition are identified and understood will it be possible to respond to them.

The main point to take from this brief overview of social survey methods and participatory approaches is that decisions should take account of both specialist knowledge and local knowledge. Specialist knowledge provides understanding of the factors that affect decisions relating to sanitation and faecal sludge management while local knowledge will help professionals to understand the ways in which local factors might constrain or facilitate possible courses of action.

Develop consensus on the need for faecal sludge and septage treatment

Where most households and businesses rely on on-site sanitation, the need to manage faecal sludge will normally be clear. Unfortunately, need does not always lead to action. The explanation for this lies, at least partly, in the distinction between public and private goods identified in Chapter 2. Demand for goods, that provide private benefits, including removal of septage from overflowing tanks, will normally be much greater than that for public goods, such as the environmental protection provided by treatment. This leads to situations in which unregistered operators remove faecal sludge from pits and tanks, often using insanitary methods, and then dump it on the nearest convenient open ground or into the nearest manhole or watercourse. The challenge in such situations will be to convince both the public and policy-makers of the need for action to improve the situation with regard to the later stages in the sanitation service chain. The EFD can be a powerful advocacy tool in that it illustrates issues relating to the treatment and disposal of excreta using a simple diagram that is easy to understand.

Arguments for treatment should be fact-based and tailored to the local situation. Key arguments for improving faecal sludge management include the following:

- Sludge that remains in pits and tanks for many years will consolidate to the point at which it is difficult or impossible to remove. At this stage, households will have to pay a large amount to either have the sludge removed or build a new facility.
- Without regular desludging, typically at intervals of 3–5 years, solids will pass through septic tanks, eventually blocking drainfield/soakaway systems, which will lead to ponding of wastewater near people's dwellings.
- Similarly, failure to periodically desludge leach pits and pit latrines will eventually lead to blocking of the drainage paths below the pit so that the pit no longer drains effectively and requires frequent emptying.

- The long-term viability of decentralized wastewater treatment plants serving local sewer systems is dependent on provision of effective systems to remove, transport, and treat sludge. Neglect of desludging needs will lead to their eventual failure and the discharge of untreated effluent to local water bodies.
- Removing faecal sludge from the local environment and ensuring that it is properly treated or otherwise safely managed will have health benefits for both the local and wider communities.

Most of these arguments focus on either private or local benefits of improved faecal sludge management. They will not lead directly to more demand for treatment but will increase demand for pit and tank emptying and transfer of faecal sludge and septage out of communities. Their impact will be limited where the majority of the population uses pits and tanks with connections to the drainage system. As noted earlier, such systems will continue to operate for years without desludging, albeit with little or no impact on effluent quality, to the detriment of the wider environment. Where such systems are the norm, the challenge will be to develop political awareness and will to initiate action to change existing insanitary practices. Arguments for change might focus on the possible consequences if tanks are not regularly desludged: for instance, blocking of solids-free sewers and sludge accumulation in open drains.

While efforts to promote improved septage management should emphasize private benefits whenever possible, they cannot ignore public benefits. There will always be a need to raise awareness of the health and environmental benefits of good septage management systems that incorporate effective treatment. Experience worldwide is that action to improve public health and environmental conditions is impossible without strong governmental commitment. For instance, municipalities rather than the private sector led the way in providing sewage treatment in European cities during the 19th and 20th centuries. Unlike water supply, which has clear private good characteristics, sewage treatment is primarily a public good. This example suggests a need to ensure that political leaders and senior administrators are convinced of the value of septage/faecal sludge treatment. This will be much easier if national legislation to support the implementation of effective septage/faecal sludge management systems is in place.

Determining the planning area, the plant service area, and location

Planning area

Ideally, faecal sludge/septage treatment plants should be compatible with any regional or country-wide plans and strategies. Whether or not such plans and strategies exist, the first planning task at the local level will be to establish the service area of the proposed faecal sludge management initiative. Factors that will influence the extent of the planning area include:

- any existing and already planned provision for septage treatment;
- the settlement pattern;
- the distribution of on-site and sewered sanitation facilities; and
- administrative responsibilities and boundaries.

Planning must start from consideration of the existing situation but should also aim to take account of possible changes over the proposed planning period. The most obvious of these will be changes in settlement pattern as towns and cities grow.

Each planning area might be served by one centralized treatment plant, two or more smaller decentralized plants, or a combination of a larger centralized plant and one or more smaller plants. Table 3.1 lists possible settlement patterns and identifies likely administrative scenarios and planning and service areas for each settlement pattern.

Where responsibility for faecal sludge management is devolved to the local level, the default assumption is often that each local authority or water and sanitation utility should be responsible for treating septage and faecal sludge from within its own area. In practice, private-sector tanker operators may deliver septage to a plant from areas outside the formally defined service area. Indeed, informal surveys in Indonesia revealed that some private operators delivered septage loads to treatment plants over distances exceeding 50 km. In most cases, the contribution of such loads will be small enough to ignore at the planning stage. For instance, the author's analysis of records on septage loads delivered to the Palu treatment plant in Central

Table 3.1 Influence of possible geographical and administrative scenarios on planning area

Settlement pattern	Administrative arrangements	Planning and service areas
Predominantly rural area with several small towns	One or more district administrations	One or more administrative districts, depending on distances and population density
Predominantly rural area dominated by one medium-sized town	District administration including the town	Administrative district, centred on town
Area dominated by one large town	Town administered separately from surrounding areas	Town plus parts of surrounding rural districts
Area dominated by two medium-to-large towns	Separate municipal administrations and perhaps rural district administration/s for surrounding areas	If possible, develop integrated plan to serve both towns, even if administrative factors require that each town has its own treatment facility
Large city or conurbation	May be unitary administrative authority or divided between two or more administrative districts	Planning should cover the whole city although treatment facilities may be located to serve smaller service areas based on administrative boundaries

Sulawesi, Indonesia showed that less than 3 per cent of the loads delivered to the plant originated in the two rural districts that adjoin the Palu urban administrative area.

There are situations in which urban development has expanded beyond formal municipal boundaries into surrounding administrative areas that are still officially classed as rural. Where this is the case, it will be necessary to consider the whole of the built-up area when assessing the likely demand for septage and faecal sludge management services, including treatment.

Chapter 2 referred to possible institutional arrangements that might involve a single organization taking responsibility for treatment facilities in several service areas. Where such arrangements exist or are proposed, it may be necessary to extend the planning area beyond the limits of a single municipality or district. The points outlined above suggest the following approach to determining the planning area:

- Obtain the best possible plan showing the area of interest and surrounding areas.
- Identify built-up areas and mark them on a copy of the plan. If possible, link to a database giving details of the population of each built-up area.
- Identify administrative boundaries and plot them on a copy of the plan.
- Identify any existing wastewater treatment and septage/faecal sludge treatment plants and plot their approximate service areas – based on available plans and conversations with treatment plant managers and pit and tank emptying operators.
- Identify any sewered areas, checking the situation with regard to connections to the sewers (bearing in mind that the presence of a sewer does not mean that households have connected to it).
- Based on the information obtained from the steps listed above, determine areas that are currently without access to faecal sludge/septage treatment services.
- Assess the size of the market for pit and tank emptying services in each area identified.
- Discuss the findings with local stakeholders, focusing particularly on the ways in which the areas with access to services relate to the settlement pattern and administrative boundaries and agree the extent of the planning area.

With the planning area agreed, at least in outline, attention can turn to demarcation of treatment plant service areas within the overall planning area.

Determining the plant service area

Most existing septage treatment plants are centralized, in the sense that one plant serves one town, city, or district. This does not have to be the case, and recent years have seen considerable interest in the possibility of decentralized treatment provision, with several smaller treatment facilities spread around the area. Conversely, there will be situations in which several towns or districts can cooperate to provide a shared treatment plant. Table 3.2 sets out the potential advantages and disadvantages of centralized and decentralized approaches.

There may be situations in which a combination of centralized and decentralized provision will be desirable and the meaning of centralized and decentralized will be different for large cities and smaller towns. Use Table 3.2 as a starting point for assessing the merits and demerits of more

Table 3.2 Advantages and disadvantages of centralized and decentralized approaches

Centralized approach	Decentralized approach
Advantages:	Advantages:
Economies of scale associated with larger centralized plant, resulting in reduced capital and perhaps operational costs. (But note that this advantage will reduce if simpler and cheaper treatment technologies can be used for smaller decentralized facilities.)	Reduced haul distances, resulting in reduced transport costs, reduced haulage time, and hence an increase in the number of pits and tanks that can be emptied using a given number of vehicles. (But note that a similar effect can be achieved with the use of transfer stations.)
Small number of centralized plants may be easier to manage than a large number of smaller decentralized plants.	Dispersed availability of treated products, resulting in reduced travel distances and/ or an increase in the number of potential users where the intention is to sell treated liquid and/or solids as agricultural inputs.
Land may already be available, for instance on part of an existing solid waste landfill site.	
A single site, some distance from existing development, is less likely to attract opposition than multiple sites close to existing houses.	Smaller loading on individual plants will mean that less land is required at each plant for any given technology, allowing the use of simpler and cheaper technologies
Disadvantages:	Disadvantages:
Longer haul distances, leading to higher vehicle requirements and increased transport costs	Potential difficulties in finding suitable land at several decentralized locations.
The high loading on a single plant will require either a large site or adoption of sophisticated mechanical/ electromechanical treatment technologies.	Potential opposition from people living near proposed treatment plant sites.
Large sites may only be available at some distance from centres of population. Such sophisticated treatment technologies require skilled operators and may incur high maintenance costs.	Potential difficulty of monitoring performance, ensuring compliance with discharge standards, and managing operation and maintenance at several dispersed treatment sites.
	Inability to reach minimum loading required for some technologies to cover their costs. (This may be particularly important for approaches that rely on income from sale of treated products – see Chapter 10.)

and less centralized approaches. Detailed assessments can follow, taking into account geographic, technical, and institutional factors.

One variation on the approaches outlined in Table 3.2 will be to combine a centralized treatment plant with local transfer stations. This approach will, in theory, facilitate efficient use of both small emptying and transport vehicles, designed to operate where access is restricted, and larger tankers, which will provide an efficient option for transporting sludge and septage over longer distances.

Reduction in the average haul distance will be particularly important:

- in large towns and cities, where average haulage distances to a centralized plant are long and traffic congestion may lead to significantly increased haulage times; and
- where workers remove faecal sludge from pit latrines manually and transport it to the treatment site in handcarts, as is the case for some systems in Africa.

Mukheibir (2015) provides information on transfer station options, including simple transfer stations that hold both solid and liquid waste; options that provide some degree of solids–liquid separation before discharge of separated liquid to a sewer, soakaway, or constructed wetland; and mobile transfer stations. Transfer station proposals should take account of the design principles set out in this book. Where the aim is to achieve solids–liquid separation, a steep floor slope will ensure that sludge accumulates in one place and will make it easier to withdraw sludge without removing supernatant water. Chapter 7 includes further discussion of this point.

Mukheibir notes the need for easy access to transfer station sites and sufficient space to park both small septage collection vehicles and the larger tankers that transfer stored septage to the treatment facility. In practice, as for decentralized treatment plants, the challenge will often be to find land that is both central to the area that the transfer station is to serve and acceptable to local residents. Experience with solid waste shows that people often oppose proposals to site transfer stations near their homes because they fear, often correctly, that poor facility management will lead to deterioration of the local environment. Mobile transfer stations, each consisting of a large tank mounted on a trailer, are one option for overcoming this problem. Each tank should be large enough to hold material removed from several pits or tanks. It will be advisable to make each tank as large as is compatible with haulage vehicle capacity and the size and condition of local roads. These transfer tanks would remain in one location for a limited period and should therefore be more acceptable to people living locally. During this period, the aim would be to empty several local pits and/or tanks and deliver the contents to the transfer tank. Once full, a tractor or tractor unit would tow the tank away and deliver its contents to the treatment facility.

Methods for assessing the most economical approach to plant location are available but the practical reality is that plant location choices are often determined by the availability of land. This will influence the approach to decentralization. While each decentralized plant may require less land than a single centralized plant, land acquisition for public purposes is rarely straightforward. Local residents are likely to object and the high cost of land and complicated land acquisition processes may limit the choice of treatment plant location to sites already owned by government.

A decentralized approach might involve the addition of new facilities over time. This scenario would involve initial provision of a single treatment plant in a reasonably central location, followed by construction of additional plants in strategic locations, phased to match an increase in demand for septage management services. One advantage of this approach is its potential for supporting the incremental development of management capacity through a 'learning by doing' approach.

Plant location

Ideally, the treatment plant should be located centrally within its service area. In practice, other factors will influence the choice of location. The most important of these is the need for separation from residential development. Some national guidelines give stringent directions on this: for instance, the minimum separation recommended in Indonesian guidelines is 2 km. This guidance is similar to the recommended separation of at least 500 m and preferably 1 km given in guideline documents for the location of anaerobic waste stabilization ponds (Arthur, 1983). In practice, many treatments plants are located within less than 500 m of houses, as illustrated by the examples given in Box 3.3.

The overall conclusion from these and other examples is that, while issues such as odour mean that it is desirable to keep treatment plants as far from

---

Box 3.3 Examples of distance between treatment plants and housing

The plant serving Palu in Central Sulawesi, Indonesia is located on elevated ground some distance from the town but the distance to the nearest houses is less than 200 m.

Development, some of it residential, surrounds the two treatment plants in Indonesia's capital, Jakarta and the Keputih treatment plant in its second city, Surabaya.

The Kingtom faecal sludge reception facility in Freetown, Sierra Leone is located in the centre of the city and is surrounded by residential development. and even includes some houses within its perimeter. Like many septage treatment plants, the Kingtom facility is located on the same site as a solid waste landfill.

Decentralized plants in Lusaka, Zambia, which provide partial treatment, are located in the informal housing areas that they serve. Workers deliver faecal sludge to the Lusaka plants in handcarts, which limits the distance that the plants can be from the areas that they serve and so makes it almost inevitable that they will be close to residential development.

housing development as is possible, there is little point in setting separation standards that are impossible to implement in practice.

Even if separation standards are completely relaxed, local communities may resist efforts to site a treatment plant in their neighbourhood. This opposition may reduce if the proposal to build the plant is accompanied by promises of benefits to the community if it accepts the proposal. This approach was successful in Dumaguete in the Philippines, where the local community was offered incentives to host the treatment plant in the form of improved roads, promises of jobs for local residents, a health centre, and a scholarship programme (David Robbins, personal communication). The cost of the incentives was funded from the tariff charged for scheduled emptying and constituted only a small proportion of the overall cost of the programme.

High land prices around built-up areas will also influence site selection. When assessing possible sites, the possibility that land that is currently beyond the urban fringe will be developed during the lifetime of the proposed treatment plant should be taken into account.

A common response to these challenges is to accept that treatment plants must be located some distance from built-up areas, often on land adjacent to that already occupied by a solid waste landfill. In some countries, it may be necessary to take account of customary ownership arrangements when assessing possible sites. Another option is to locate treatment plants more centrally but to reduce space requirements and odour problems by adopting a more mechanized approach and choosing unit processes that can be enclosed so that they do not emit odours. This approach will be more appropriate for larger cities, where the systems required to support mechanized technologies are more likely to be available.

Tanker travel time will be a key determinant when assessing the viability of possible sites. Travel times and speeds are obviously very dependent on local conditions. When allowance is made for the time to pick up septage from a client and discharge it at the treatment plant, an average one-way travel time of 45 minutes should allow around three round trips per day. This is a subjective figure but is about the level of activity achieved in places where there is demand and traffic conditions are not a major constraint. Assuming an average travel speed of 20 km per hour, this suggests that the average trip length should not exceed 15 km, less if traffic or road conditions result in a slower average travel speed. A shorter average round trip time is desirable, as this will increase the volume of septage transported by a single tanker. These figures can be used for preliminary assessment. However, every situation will be different and detailed assessment will require information on travel speeds and loading and discharge times obtained from field monitoring of tanker operations (see Box 3.4). Analysis should allow for the possibility that large tankers may service more than one pit or tank per trip.

Box 3.4 Two examples of preliminary analysis of existing systems

Tanker delivery records in Palu, Indonesia showed that a 4 m³ capacity tanker could serve three to four pits or tanks per day, requiring an average round trip time, including pit/tank emptying and septage discharge, of around two hours. Approximate analysis, using satellite images, suggests that the average haul distance was of the order of 8 km, which would give an average travel speed of 16 km/h if it is assumed that travel time accounted for about 50 per cent of the time required for a round trip. Records of tractor-trailer unit operation for a system serving communal toilets in internally displaced person (IDP) camps in Sittwe, Myanmar also revealed an average of three to four round trips per day. In this case, analysis of satellite image mapping suggests that average distance travelled was of the order of 5 km. The use of tractor-trailer units rather than vacuum tankers and the poor state of the roads serving the IDP camps suggest that the average speed was less than that in Palu. Workers pumped latrine contents into barrels and transported them to pick-up points within the various IDP camps using handcarts. The barrels were then loaded onto the tractor-trailer units. In both cases, the analysis given here is crude but could be refined with further information on actual septage loading, haul distances, and round trip times.

Other points to consider when assessing possible treatment plant sites include:

- *Access.* The access road from the public highway to the treatment plant site should be paved, without steep gradients. It should preferably have sufficient width to allow two tankers to pass. Where this is not possible, frequent passing places should be provided. Ideally, the site should be located in an area where congestion on the public highway will not cause problems for tankers seeking access. Access through residential areas should be avoided as far as is possible. Any bridges along planned access routes should provide sufficient height to allow tankers to pass.
- *Land prices.* Land prices will increase the capital cost of 'extensive' systems such as sludge drying beds, waste stabilization ponds, and constructed wetlands, unless government land is already available. However, land prices in city-fringe areas tend to rise over time. If land is acquired to allow provision of drying beds, ponds, and constructed wetlands, none of which require heavy civil engineering works, the land becomes an asset that can be sold at a later date when the treatment plant site is relocated or extensive facilities are replaced by less extensive, enclosed, mechanized facilities.
- *The availability of utility services, in particular electricity and water.* In the case of water, it may be possible to supply a remote site from a local groundwater source.
- *Topography.* Ideally, the site should provide sufficient slope to allow the liquid treatment part of the plant to work largely by gravity. A gentle slope will be best for siting of treatment processes such as waste stabilization ponds while a flat site will suit many solids handling processes. With careful design, units with a smaller footprint can be located on land

that slopes more steeply. However, it will be best to avoid sites with steep slopes, which might be susceptible to land slips and are likely to require costly civil engineering works and steeply graded access roads.

- *Geology and hydrogeology.* Avoid areas with rock close to the surface and/or a high water table, both of which are likely to involve high construction costs. A high water table will also affect liquid disposal options because disposal via soakaways and drainfields will be difficult and will adversely affect groundwater quality. Consult relevant organizations to ensure that a proposed site does not fall within an environmentally sensitive area.
- *Susceptibility to flooding.* Treatment plants should not be located on land that is susceptible to flooding. A typical design criterion used in developed countries is that a site should not be at risk of flooding more often than once every 50 or 100 years. Where it is impossible to avoid using an area that is subject to occasional flooding, the design should ensure that treatment units are raised sufficiently to keep them clear of the highest predicted flooding level.
- *Proximity to a water body.* The treated liquid fraction of the septage will normally be discharged to a water body. For small plants, discharge of treated liquid to a drainfield or soakaway may be possible if the water table is some distance beneath the surface and the ground has good percolation characteristics.
- *Tree cover.* To avoid obstruction of solar radiation, trees should not be located close to ponds and drying beds. They may be located near site boundaries, at an appropriate distance from ponds and drying beds, to screen the site from public view.

The aim should be to identify sites with sufficient land to provide for treatment needs for at least 30 years and preferably longer. Where planning systems are strong and planning decisions lead to action, it should be possible to select preferred sites within the context provided by an overall land-use planning framework. The more likely scenario in many countries will be that these conditions do not apply and it will not be possible to link site selection to an overall planning framework. Where planning systems are weak and informal development is widespread, it will be unwise to assume that a site earmarked for a particular purpose will remain undeveloped indefinitely.

Box 3.5 provides information on the steps to be taken to identify a suitable treatment plant site.

The lack of suitable land and/or opposition from local residents may mean that it is difficult to identify a reasonably central site that provides both sufficient area to accommodate non-mechanized treatment technologies and sufficient separation from residential development to avoid opposition from local residents. The options in such circumstances are to either:

- select a less central site and accept greater septage transport distances; or
- select a mechanized and enclosed technology.

Box 3.5 Steps in identifying and assessing a suitable treatment plant site

1. Obtain the best available map showing the whole planning area, preferably in electronic form so that additional copies can be made.
2. On this map, plot major roads, built-up areas, and the locations of any existing solid waste dump/landfill sites, wastewater and septage treatment facilities. Provide information on topography, preferably using contours, but, if these are not available, by demarcating the approximate limits of steeply sloping areas. Also show the approximate limits of areas that are susceptible to flooding.
3. Identify areas that might provide suitable treatment sites, focusing particularly on travel distance from population centres, separation from existing and planned development, and proximity to a main road.
4. Obtain information on land prices in these areas and identify any currently unused government-owned land.
5. At this stage, the aim will be to have identified areas suitable for siting a treatment plant or plants. The next step will be to identify and further investigate possible treatment plant locations within these areas. This will require discussions with landowners to ascertain their willingness to sell or, in the case of government departments, transfer land.
6. Based on discussions and assessed land prices, identify sites for further, more detailed investigation.

The second option will only be viable if it is possible to provide the technical and managerial systems required for operation of the mechanized technology. Planners also need to recognize that the operating costs of mechanized systems will tend to be much higher than those of non-mechanized systems and make a realistic assessment of the possibility and consequences of power cuts.

Regardless of the various points discussed above, the availability of land will often influence the choice of site for a new faecal sludge or septage treatment plant. Purchase of even the relatively small area of land required for mechanized treatment options may be difficult, particularly where there is strong local opposition to siting a treatment plant on it. In such circumstances, it may be necessary to fall back on the use of government-owned land, even when this land is not optimally located.

Once a suitable site has been chosen, a survey of the site will be required. This should show all existing structures, spot levels with contour lines interpolated, and the location of the site boundaries.

Load assessment

Realistic load assessment is critical for successful treatment plant operation. The plant will fail if the actual loading is significantly higher than the design loading. Conversely, a low loading may lead to hydraulic and biological problems, which make it difficult for operational staff to operate the plant effectively. Load assessment must take account of:

- the hydraulic load on the plant – expressed as the volume of faecal sludge and/or septage delivered to the treatment plant in a given time;

- the organic load on the plant, expressed as either the COD or BOD_5 of the material delivered to the plant in a given time;
- the solids loading: the mass of TSS delivered to the plant in a given time.

Planners often base load estimates on assessed need. However, as was explained in Chapter 2, where the objective need for septage/faecal sludge removal and treatment exceeds user demand for these services, design based on assessed need will overestimate the loading on a treatment plant, at least in the short term. There will be situations in which much of the sludge that accumulates in pits and tanks remains in-situ and others in which material is removed but does not reach the treatment facility. The proportions will vary from place to place, depending on the type of on-site sanitation, the ways in which households manage those facilities, and the effectiveness of removal and transport services. However, failure to remove all the sludge that accumulates in pits and tanks and transport it for treatment is the rule rather than the exception. Reasons for this situation vary, depending on local circumstances, but the most common scenarios are as follows:

- Householders connect pour-flush toilets to large pits that go for many years without emptying, with some apparently never emptied, perhaps due to loss of digested solids into the surrounding groundwater.
- Some pits and tanks have overflows to drains and water bodies that allow digested sludge to escape and thus reduce the demand for septage removal services.
- Pits and tanks are inaccessible, which makes it difficult or even impossible to desludge them. Inaccessibility may be due to location – for instance a householder may have built an extension over the tank and be very reluctant to break a nicely tiled floor to gain access to a tank located under a kitchen – or the lack of an access pipe or cover. The second situation is easier to deal with but it will still deter people from having their tank or pit emptied until the last possible moment.
- The equipment available cannot handle thick sludge, leading to a situation in which most of the material removed is supernatant water. This problem will be particularly acute where sludge is allowed to consolidate to the point at which it is only removable by hand, a practice that is extremely unpleasant and hazardous for workers. Not surprisingly, workers leave this material, removing only the supernatant liquid. Eventually, consolidated sludge accumulates to the point at which the only option is to abandon the pit and build another.
- Tanker crews sell sludge directly to farmers or dump it illegally, again reducing the amount of sludge taken to the sludge treatment plant.

These situations and practices are, to varying degrees, undesirable but they are widespread and not confined to low-income countries. For instance, official records from Florida, USA show around 100,000 septic tanks emptied each year. This number is less than 4 per cent of the 2.6 million septic tanks in the state, representing an average emptying rate of once every 25 years for each tank (Florida Department of Health, Bureau of On-site Sewage Programs, 2011).

Planners should identify and, as far as is possible, quantify existing practices, determine how these practices will affect demand in the short term, and assess the likely impact of future changes on the quantity and quality of material delivered for treatment. Interviews with sludge tanker operators and records of septage loads delivered to existing treatment facilities will provide information on existing practices. Assessment of any gap between the quantity of septage removed from pits and tanks and the quantity delivered for treatment will provide an indication of the immediate need for treatment. Future demand will depend on the ways in which plans respond to undesirable practices: do they accept the existing situation and reduce treatment plant load estimates accordingly, or do they include realistic proposals to reduce and eventually eliminate undesirable practices such as indiscriminate septage dumping? It will always be better to plan to eliminate undesirable practices but plans should, as far as possible, be flexible to accommodate uncertainty about the extent and pace of future change. They need to allow for:

- the short-term situation in which demand for services may be limited.
- a future scenario in which positive action creates awareness and introduces incentives to encourage regular septage removal and delivery. This positive action leads to an increase in the loading on the plant.

As with all aspects of planning, efforts to create demand for good septage/ faecal sludge management practices will be more effective if they start from analysis of available information. Box 3.6 illustrates what this might mean in practice.

The analysis in Box 3.6 suggests that any efforts to promote increased emptying frequency, perhaps encompassing scheduled emptying, should focus on the sub-districts with the highest demand. This staged approach to increasing emptying frequency would have to be taken into account when assessing the rate at which loading on the treatment plant would increase over time.

Assessment of hydraulic loading

This section describes three methods of assessing the hydraulic loading on a treatment plant. The first uses information on current pit and tank emptying activity and is best suited to assessing short-term loading. The second uses information on the total number of on-site sanitation facilities, while the third relies on information on the design population and the rate of

---

Box 3.6 Investigation of demand patterns in Palu, Indonesia

As described earlier in this chapter, assessment of pit emptying activities in Palu, Indonesia, showed that pits were being emptied on average only about once in 50 years. The low level of demand seemed to preclude the possibility of introducing scheduled emptying across the city as a whole. However, the once in 50 years figure was clearly an average that masked variations in demand for pit and tank emptying services. In order to understand this better, the municipal records were analysed in more detail in order to ascertain where demand for emptying services was highest. This exercise revealed that almost 30 per cent of the pits emptied were in just 4 sub-districts out of a total of 44 sub-districts (9 per cent), and that over 58 per cent were in 11 sub-districts, about 25 per cent of all sub-districts. The sub-districts with higher demand were in older areas with relatively high population densities In these sub-districts, all households had water piped into their house either from the municipal system or from their own groundwater sources. In contrast, the records showed almost no demand for emptying services from peripheral sub-districts with lower population density and a lower frequency of water piped into the house.

One possible explanation for the variation in demand is that *cubluks* (septic tanks) in peripheral areas were newer and had not yet filled. Another explanation, which was supported by subsequent investigation, was that, in the areas with higher demand, higher water use, combined with the tendency for drainage paths beneath *cubluks* to become blocked over time, eventually leading to hydraulic overloading of the *cubluks* and hence a need for more frequent emptying. The blocked drainage paths mechanism is similar to the mechanism observed when septic tank desludging is neglected, resulting in failure of subsequent soakaways and drainfields.

---

sludge accumulation. All methods present some difficulties. Where sufficient information is available, it will be advisable to calculate future demand using more than one method and review the validity of the assumptions underlying each method if the results differ widely.

Assessment of existing tank and pit emptying activity

The simplest option for assessing the current hydraulic load on an existing or proposed treatment plant is to gather information on current pit and tank emptying activity.

The volume (V) to be treated in a year is given by the equation:

$$V = nt_c$$

where V is in m³ per year, n is the number of tanker loads delivered during a year, and t_c is the mean tanker capacity in m³.

This is a simple method and will be easy to implement where there are good records of existing pit/tank emptying and transport services. Where investigation suggests that the average tanker capacity is greater than the average tank/pit volume, an added factor should be included to allow for the fact that tankers do not run full. Information on the number of pits and tanks emptied each year may be available from existing records. But these records may be deficient and it will always be advisable to check their accuracy and reliability by surveying the activities of pit and tank emptying operators. Where records do not exist, it will be necessary to obtain information on existing services. Suggested steps for obtaining this information are as follows:

- Identify all tanker operators working in the planning area.
- Prepare a simple record sheet.
- Meet with all tanker operators, if possible in a group meeting.
- Ask operators to complete the record sheet over a period of at least two weeks and preferably longer.
- Collect record sheets and analyse to obtain information on average number of pits/tanks emptied per week and average volume of faecal sludge/septage removed.

If possible, this exercise should be repeated during two distinctly different seasons in order to obtain an understanding of the way in which loading varies over the course of a year. It will be worthwhile to encourage tanker operators to continue to record their activities, stressing the potential benefits to the efficiency and effectiveness of their operations.

Points to be considered when assessing the results of this exercise:

- There is a chance that lack of capacity is suppressing demand. To check whether this is the case, the extent to which existing emptying and transport services are operating at full capacity should be ascertained. Conversely, it may be that demand is being suppressed by the inaccessibility of pits and tanks. The example of Malaysia (Box 3.8) highlights the importance of keeping records of both successful and unsuccessful attempts to empty pits and tanks.
- Tankers may not always carry a full load so that estimates based on the number of tanker trips will be too high. This will be more likely where tanker capacity tends to be higher than average pit and tank capacity.
- Prediction of future hydraulic loading requires an estimation of the growth in carrying capacity.

Where there is supressed demand and/or plans are in place to increase demand, this method will underestimate loading at the design horizon and one of the methods described below will be a more appropriate option for assessing hydraulic loading.

Future hydraulic loading based on mean pit/tank sizes and assumed emptying frequency

The hydraulic load on a treatment plant can be assessed using information on the number of tanks and pits to be emptied within its service area, an estimate of the average tank/pit size, and an assumed emptying interval. When using this approach, the equation for the hydraulic loading is:

$$V = \frac{Nv_t c_r}{T}$$

Where: V is the volume delivered to the treatment plant in m³ per year;

N is the number of pits and tanks in the service area;

v_t is the average pit/tank capacity in m³;

c_r is the proportion of on-site facilities that are regularly desludged; and

T is the average interval between pit/tank desludging events in years.

This equation assumes complete emptying of tanks each time they are desludged. Where typical tank sizes are larger than the average tanker/ sludge removal vehicle capacity, it is likely that the volume removed will be determined by the tanker volume rather than the tank volume. Where this is the case, t_c should replace v_t in the equation. Where an area contains more than one type of sanitation facility, for instance both dry pit latrines and larger septic tanks, the loads from each type of facility should be assessed separately.

This method will work well for areas with scheduled emptying services. The main challenge in such areas will be to identify all the existing on-site facilities and to estimate average pit and tank volumes. Builders and others who construct pits and tanks should be able to provide information on the range of pit sizes that they construct, but it will always be best to check their information by observing the construction of new pits and tanks in the field. Areas without scheduled emptying services present the additional problem of determining average pit/tank emptying intervals. In many places, as shown by the case of Palu, the average pit and tank emptying interval may be much greater than the 3–5 years that is typically taken as the optimum. The challenge for planners and designers is to assign a realistic value to the emptying interval and assess how it is likely to change over time. This will be particularly difficult where nominally on-site pits and tanks are connected to drains and sewers so that solids can escape through the connections, thus reducing the demand to have tanks emptied. The activities of unregistered pit and tank emptying operators, who may be discharging at locations other than officially designated treatment/disposal sites, will also affect the hydraulic load.

Future loading based on per-capita sludge accumulation rate

Another option for assessing future volumetric loading is to base calculations on the per-capita sludge accumulation rate. The equation for the volume (V, m³) for this option is:

$$V = \frac{Pq c_o c_r}{1000}$$

where: P is the estimated population of the service area, including allowance for population growth and, where appropriate, any transient population, for instance tourists and migrant workers;

q is the average volume removed per person each year (litres per capita per year), comprising the faecal sludge accumulation rate and an allowance for any supernatant water removed with the sludge;

c_o is the proportion of the population served by on-site and decentralized sanitation facilities requiring septage removal, transport, and treatment services, expressed as a fraction; and

c_r is the proportion of on-site facilities that are regularly desludged.

The population of the service area may be estimated using census data. Another method is to multiply the number of households by the average household size. Information on the number of households may be available from social surveys. Alternatively, where households occupy single buildings, it may be possible to estimate the number of buildings from satellite images. This option should not be used where either several households occupy one building or one household occupies more than one dwelling. In most cases, the best option will be to start from census data, using other methods to check and confirm estimates where necessary. Future population estimates must include an allowance for future population growth.

The sludge accumulation rate depends on a number of factors, including temperature, whether or not it is possible to add extraneous material to pits and tanks, and the retention time before a pit or tank is emptied. Box 3.7 summarizes information on sludge accumulation rates taken from a number of sources and covering various types of on-site sanitation. Note the low ranges observed in most cases.

This approach is best suited to areas in which pit latrines and/or dry leach pits are the most common form of on-site sanitation. It will underestimate the volume of material requiring removal and treatment where that material includes supernatant water from septic tanks and wet leach pits, in some cases significantly so. For instance, the estimated volume of septage removed from pits and tanks in Dakar, Senegal is around 6,000 m³/day (Bäuerl et al., 2014). Calculations based on the population served by regularly emptied pits and tanks suggest that this equates to almost 600 litres per capita per year. This high figure must include a very high supernatant water volume, a conclusion that is supported by the 4.5 g/litre solids content of the septage, which indicates a 99.55 per cent water content. Where calculations show that the volume of septage removed is well above the range suggested at the end of Box 3.7, the long-term aim should arguably be to improve on-site sanitation facilities to reduce infiltration and ensure effective exfiltration.

A key challenge with methods based on the number of on-site facilities and the per-capita sludge accumulation rate is to calculate c_r, the proportion of on-site facilities that will regularly be desludged. This is particularly true where there is currently limited demand for septage removal, transport,

---

Box 3.7 Information on sludge accumulation rates

A study including physical measurements in 107 pits and septic tanks in six cities across Indonesia revealed mean and median annual sludge accumulation rates of 25 litres per capita per year and 13 litres per capita per year, respectively. The difference between the mean and median rates resulted from high accumulation rates in a small number of pits. Only 8 per cent of the facilities investigated were conventional septic tanks; 83 per cent were single-pit *cubluks* and 6 per cent were small fibreglass tanks. Twenty-two per cent of the facilities tested had an outlet to a drain, which would result in some reduction in sludge accumulation rate. Nevertheless, the results show generally low accumulation rates (Mills et al., 2014).

A compilation of data on pit latrine filling rates from sites in Southern Africa showed that accumulation rates typically fell within the range 10–70 litres per capita per year. Further study revealed per-capita latrine filling rates in the range 21–64 l/year and that pits typically filled at a rate of between 200 and 500 l/year, regardless of the number of users. Based on these findings, the report on the investigations recommended that pits should be designed using a figure of 40 litres per capita per year, while pit emptying programmes should be based on a figure of 60 litres per capita per year (Still and Foxon, 2012).

Sludge accumulation rates obtained from studies in North America typically lie in the range 60–125 litres per capita per year for retention times greater than three years, with a reduction in average accumulation rate with increased retention time (see for instance Brandes, 1977 and summary in Chapter 3 of Lossing, 2009). Septic tank accumulation rates in warmer climates are likely to be lower. Studies in South Africa revealed rates in the range 27–54 litres per capita per year (Norris, 2000).

The key point to take from these figures is that sludge accumulation rates are usually of the order of 25–70 litres per person per year. Apparently higher rates are likely to include supernatant water and will not therefore represent the actual sludge accumulation rate.

---

and treatment services. For instance, the experience in Indonesia is that lack of demand for these services has resulted in a situation in which almost all septage treatment plants are underloaded. Comparison of information on current pit emptying activity with that on the total number of on-site sanitation facilities can be used to assess the current situation. However, it is also necessary to consider how this demand might grow over time. Box 3.8 lists some of the factors that will influence future demand. Given the difficulty in assessing the combined effect of these factors, load projections will always be provisional. This suggests the advisability of taking a phased approach to treatment facility provision, with plans amended in the light of operational experience. Chapter 5 provides more information on this point.

Because of the many uncertainties associated with each approach to calculating the hydraulic loading, it will always be worthwhile to cross-check findings obtained using different calculation methods.

Assessment of growth in demand requires judgement and assessments will always be subject to uncertainty. The design report should clearly state the assumptions made when assessing growth in demand. Clear assumptions provide a basis for future modification of operational procedures in response to operational experience. Where densification and increased traffic flows may affect ability to deliver to a particular site, the design report should include

---

Box 3.8 Assessing future demand

Points to consider when assessing future demand include:

- *Past trends.* Do any available records show an increase in demand over time? If so, is sufficient information available to allow more detailed analysis to determine (a) where demand is increasing; and (b) the reasons for that increase?
- *Likely changes in sanitation provision.* Are there plans to extend sewerage into new areas and, if so, how many people are likely to connect?
- *Changes in septage management practices.* Are there plans to introduce scheduled pit emptying? Demand will increase after the introduction of scheduled emptying. Improvements in the equipment used to empty pits, efforts to improve the accessibility of pits and tanks, and enforcement of legislation to ban practices such as connections from domestic septic tanks to the drainage system will also tend to increase the volume of material delivered for treatment.
- *Stronger regulation.* Legislation to discourage illegal dumping of faecal sludge and septage at locations other than official treatment sites will tend to lead to an increase in loading on those sites. The impact of legislation will depend on the systems and resources that are available to enforce it. Without enforcement, its effect will be limited.
- *Efforts to promote more frequent pit emptying.* It is reasonable to assume that initiatives to promote pit and tank emptying will lead to an increase in demand for emptying. The challenge for planners is to estimate the size of this increase.
- *Changes in sanitation practices resulting from increased urban density.* In particular, plot subdivision and the resultant increase in housing density will tend to preclude construction of new pits when old pits are full, leaving emptying as the only viable option.
- *Release of suppressed demand.* Suppressed demand results from a lack of serviceable septage removal and transport vehicles. One indicator of possible suppressed demand is that tankers are fully used, making 3–4 trips per day and perhaps working at weekends. If demand is supressed by lack of transport capacity, action to increase both transport and treatment capacity will be required. Another indicator is a high proportion of failed attempts to empty tanks. Data from Malaysia show that in recent years, only about 40 per cent of attempts to empty tanks on demand have been successful (Narayana, 2017: Figure 7). The main reason for the high proportion of unsuccessful desludging attempts is likely to be that tanks either cannot be found or are inaccessible. The proportion of successful attempts was less than 30 per cent when scheduled emptying was the norm.
- *Decrease in demand on a particular facility because of construction of new facilities in surrounding areas.* It is possible that, even where demand remains high, increased traffic congestion will lead to increased journey times so that the volume of sludge delivered to a particular treatment plant reduces.

---

reference to the possibility of building new treatment plants in the future rather than expanding the existing plant.

This discussion points to the need to base hydraulic loading estimates on the best possible assessment of demand. The following points should be borne in mind when assessing demand:

- Where the water table is high and/or percolation mechanisms from pits and soakaways have become blocked, demand for pit and tank emptying is likely to be high.

- Where a high proportion of pits and tanks discharge excess liquid to the drainage system, initial demand for emptying service is likely to be low. The extent to which this situation might change in the future will depend on the ability of government to enforce regulations and by-laws that ban discharge of partly treated effluent to the drainage system.
- Large pits will take many years to fill and many years may elapse before they contribute to demand. Where liquid retention in pits and soakaways is not causing problems for sanitation users, the demand for tank emptying services is likely to be low.

Assessment of organic and suspended solids loadings

It is possible to calculate the organic loading on a planned wastewater treatment plant by multiplying the contributing population by an appropriate estimate of the per-capita BOD or COD and TSS loadings. This approach is not suitable for calculating the load on faecal sludge and septage treatment plants because digestion and the loss of dissolved material with percolating water result in marked changes in the COD, BOD, and TSS of faecal sludge held in pits and septic tanks over time.

The other method for calculating organic and suspended solids loadings is to multiply the estimated hydraulic loading by an assumed or estimated influent BOD or COD concentration. The BOD loading rate is therefore:

$$\lambda_{BOD} = \frac{QL_i}{1000}$$

where: λ_{BOD} is the BOD loading rate in kg/day;
Q is the daily flow rate in m³/day; and
L_i is the influent BOD concentration (mg/l)

Similar equations will apply for the loading rates for COD and TSS with the BOD concentration replaced by the COD and TSS concentrations, respectively.

The accuracy of the loading estimate depends on the accuracy of information on the hydraulic load and influent concentration. Challenges for designers of faecal sludge and septage treatment plants include:

- the wide variability in faecal sludge/septage strength between locations;
- the wide variability in strength of individual samples taken from faecal sludge/septage at specific locations; and
- the likelihood that the strength of the material to be treated will change as emptying practices change.

Table 3.3 illustrates the first point. The wide range of strengths listed in the table illustrates the desirability of obtaining site-specific information at the design stage.

A useful indicator of the likely biodegradability of faecal sludge and septage is the COD to BOD$_5$ ratio. As a rule, the lower the ratio, the greater will be the biodegradability of the material. The COD to BOD ratios of the materials

Table 3.3 Information on septage strength from various places

Location and type	BOD	COD	TSS	Comments
Accra septage	600–1,500	7,800	4,760	TSS based on 40% non-volatile total solids Koné and Strauss (2004)
Accra public toilet sludge	7,600	49,000	52,500	Koné and Strauss (2004)
Septage from various locations	840–2,600	1,200–7,800	12,000–35,000	Koné and Strauss (2004), summarized in Strande et al. (2014)
Kampala septage	–	24,962	19,140	Author's analysis of mean of 56 samples with very wide range of strengths listed in Schoebitz et al. (2016): median concentrations were significantly lower
Manila septage	3,800	37,000	72,000 (TS figure)	Quoted in Heinss et al. (1999)
Indonesia, samples from septage delivered to eight treatment plants	5,000	12,700	18,000	Mean results from 160 samples from septage delivered to eight septage treatment plants (IUWASH, 2016, unpublished document)
Maximo Paz, Argentina	2,800	Not recorded	11,500	Figures from Fernández et al. (2004) appear to be average obtained from multiple samples, each made up of three sub-samples from a tanker load
Albireh, Palestine	434 (165–1,107)	1,243 (181–9,315)	3,068 (76–13,044)	Taken from Al Sa'ed and Hithnawi (2006) 'Large number of samples' over period of four months
Ouagadougou, Burkina Faso (septic tanks)	1,453	7,607	7,077	Figures for septic tanks and pit latrines taken from paper by Bassan et al. (2013), which also indicated large variations around mean figures quoted here
Ouagadougou, Burkina Faso (pit latrines)	1,480	12,437	10,982	

Note: All values are in mg/l

listed in Table 3.3 range from around 2.5, recorded by the Indonesian study, to almost 10 for Manila. These ratios compare with a typical COD to BOD_5 ratio of around 2 for domestic wastewater. These are mean figures and the ratios recorded from individual samples may vary widely. For example, COD to BOD_5 ratios recorded for individual loads to one treatment plant in the USA ranged from 2.7 to 8.4 (US EPA, 1977). Nevertheless, average COD to BOD_5 ratios obtained from a number of samples provide a good indication of the degree to which the material to be treated includes digested sludge, with higher ratios indicating the presence of digested material.

The best way to deal with the wide variability in sludge characteristics at a particular site will be to obtain information on characteristics from composite samples. Composite samples should:

- be taken from tanker trucks or other vehicles used to transport faecal sludge and septage;
- include samples from as many truck loads as possible;
- include samples taken at intervals through the discharge process, thoroughly mixed together.

Individual composite samples, while better than unmixed samples, will still provide information on a fraction of all the material delivered for treatment. In order to ensure that sampling results are representative of the whole load, it will be necessary to take at least 20 and preferably more composite samples, typically spread over several days. The mean of the results obtained from this exercise should provide an acceptably accurate estimate for the septage/faecal sludge strength at a particular time of the year. It is possible that sludge and septage characteristics will vary over the year. With this in mind, it will be best to take and analyse sets of composite samples at intervals throughout the year.

Where a treatment plant will receive material from different types of on-site sanitation, for instance dry pit latrines and wet leach pits and septic tanks, it will be necessary to assess the hydraulic, organic, and suspended solids loads from each type of sanitation separately. This will require composite sampling and analysis of loads delivered from each type of sanitation, together with information of the volume of material expected from each type of sanitation. The load on the plant is then the sum of the loads from each type of sanitation. The equation for BOD load from a combination of pit latrines and septic tanks would then be:

$$\lambda_{BOD} = \frac{(QL_i)_{\text{Pit latrines}} + (QL_i)_{\text{Septic tanks}}}{1000}$$

The characteristics of incoming material may change over time as either sanitation facilities or pit and tank emptying practices change. In particular:

- The strength of incoming septage will tend to reduce with increased pit and tank emptying frequency as the ratio of accumulated sludge to supernatant water decreases.
- The strength of both septage and faecal sludge will increase if improved sludge removal methods lead to increased removal of concentrated sludge from the bottom of pits and tanks.

The effect of such changes is difficult to predict. Some idea of likely differences in strength might be obtainable by comparing the strengths of material taken from frequently and infrequently emptied facilities. Regardless of this, designers should recognize that operational experience may reveal that actual hydraulic, organic, and suspended solids loadings are different from those assumed in design. This experience should be used to:

- recommend changes in operational practices designed to ensure that they respond to the actual rather than assumed situation; and
- make changes in the design assumptions used when planning new treatment facilities.

Allowance for flow variations

The flow to a septage treatment plant will vary from day to day and from month to month, depending on how many tankers arrive. It will also vary over the course of each day, not least because delivery is only possible during plant opening times. Peak instantaneous flow rates will depend on the maximum discharge rate from individual tankers and the number of tankers that can discharge simultaneously. The normal approach to dealing with variations over a single day, between days, and between months is to estimate the average flow to a plant over a year and apply appropriate peak factors to calculate the peak-month, peak-day, and peak-hour flows. The peak instantaneous flow can be assessed by recording the rate at which tankers discharge their loads.

Table 3.4 lists appropriate flow rates for use in the design of septage treatment facilities.

Table 3.4 Flow rates used in design of various treatment units

Unit	Flow rate to be used for design
Septage reception facilities and screens	Maximum instantaneous flow – for tankers the flow when the tanker is full – modified as necessary to allow for flow attenuation through the reception facility
Units that retain septage for average of less than one day (sedimentation tanks and gravity thickeners)	Peak hourly discharge
Units with retention time between one day and one week (anaerobic baffled reactors, Indonesian style solids–liquid separation chambers)	Peak daily discharge
Units with retention time between one week and two months (ponds, West African style settling-thickening tanks, conventional drying beds)	Peak monthly discharge
Units with retention time greater than two months (planted drying beds)	Average discharge

Analysis of records of deliveries to an existing septage treatment plant can provide information on peak month and day factors. To assess the peak month factor, analyse the complete set of records to calculate the mean rate of septage delivery to the plant, identify the month with the highest septage delivery, and use the records for this month to calculate the mean delivery rate during this month. Dividing the peak monthly figure by the mean figure for the year as a whole gives the peak month factor. The approach to calculating the peak day factor is similar except that the focus will be on identifying the peak recorded daily flow, or perhaps the average of the 10 highest recorded daily flows, and dividing this by the mean daily flow. When using this approach, be aware that limited septage removal and transport capacity may suppress peak demands.

If good records are not available, or there is reason to believe that lack of capacity is suppressing peak demand, it will be necessary to estimate peak month and day factors. Analysis of information obtained from nine treatment plants, five in the US and four in Norway, revealed peak month factors ranging from 1.3 to 2.5, with 10 of the 16 results recorded lying in the range 1.7–2.1 (US EPA, 1984). Analysis of delivery records to the Devanahalli septage treatment plant in Karnataka, India (based on information provided in Pradeep et al., 2017) shows a peak month factor of 1.61. The highest monthly number of loads was in August, which was also the month with the highest rainfall. Based on these figures, a peak month factor of 2.0 should be used in the absence of site-specific information.

Peak day factors for the four Norwegian plants referred to above varied from 2.94 to 4.88 (US EPA, 1984). These are probably typical findings for temperate climates. Information on peak day factors in lower income countries with warm climates and clear seasonal variations in rainfall is limited. It is unlikely that the maximum daily rate of delivery will exceed 1.5 times the average rate of delivery during the peak month. For a peak month factor of 2.0, this would give a peak day factor of 3.0. However, the only reliable way to assess peak day factors will be to collect daily information on the volume of material/number of loads delivered to an existing plant over a period of at least one year.

The simplest way to calculate the peak hourly discharge is to divide the total daily discharge by the number of hours that the plant is open to receive tankers, perhaps increasing the resulting figure slightly to allow for the fact that some periods during the day will be busier than others. For instance, if a plant receives 120 m^3 of septage during an eight-hour delivery period, the average flow during the eight-hour period is 15 m^3/h, three times the 5 m^3/h figure calculated over the whole day. If an added peak factor of 1.33 is applied to allow for variations in the rate at which tankers discharge over the eight-hour period, the design flow becomes 15 × 1.33 m^3/h or 20 m^3/h, which is four times the flow rate averaged over the whole day.

The other option for assessing the peak hour flow is to estimate the maximum possible septage delivery rate, based on the typical tanker capacity and the time taken for a tanker to back up to the septage reception point, discharge its load, and move out of the way ready for the next tanker to back into place. Field observation at an existing septage treatment plant will be required to obtain the information required for this approach. The peak flow calculated using this method will represent the upper bound of the range of possible peak hourly flow values, based as it is on the assumption that septage discharge takes place continuously with no 'down time' when a tanker is not backing into place, discharging its contents, or moving away from the discharge area. Chapter 6 gives further information on the options for assessing peak instantaneous flows.

Technology choices

Technology assessment requires information on the following aspects of each technology:

- its land requirement;
- its power requirement;
- the knowledge and skills required for its operation, maintenance, and repair;
- the adequacy of the supply chain for the materials and spare parts that it requires;
- its overall cost, including capital and discounted recurrent costs;
- its operational cost;
- its likely environmental impact, particularly any local impact on air or water quality.

These aspects are linked in various ways. For instance, there may be links between the cost of replacement parts and the inadequacy of the supply chain. The root causes of deficiencies in operational knowledge and skills may be institutional, in which case efforts to train staff without changing the institutional structures and systems within which they operate will be ineffective.

Two questions are important when assessing a technology or process:

- How well does this technology solve the problem?
- How might it fail?

Asking these questions will help to eliminate technologies and approaches that are inappropriate because either they do not address the problem to be solved or the conditions required for their successful operation cannot be guaranteed.

As noted in Chapter 2, no situation is static and conditions may change in the future. Strategies for improving faecal sludge management should include measures to overcome institutional, financial, and other constraints. In doing so, they may create conditions that allow a wider choice of technology. It is important to ensure that the measures included in the strategy are realistic, starting from the existing situation and clearly identifying the steps required to achieve the necessary conditions for the successful introduction of proposed technologies.

After ruling out inappropriate or impractical technologies, attention can turn to comparative assessment of the technologies that remain. This should include assessment of their capital and recurrent costs. The standard approach to cost comparison is to discount all costs and any income back to a single net present cost. The discount rate applied is critical to the results of net present cost calculations. For instance, if the choice is between two technologies, one with a high capital cost and low operating cost and the other with a low capital cost and high operating cost, a high discount rate will favour the option with the high capital cost while a low discount rate will favour that with a high operating cost. Take advice from economic and financial specialists when choosing the discount rate.

Capital and operating costs of mechanized treatment processes will usually be higher than those of non-mechanized processes, a point illustrated by the findings from the Philippines summarized in Box 3.9.

The comparisons set out in Box 3.9 suggest that a non-mechanized treatment option will be cheaper than a mechanized option except where land prices are very high. The USAID comparisons only considered treatment costs and, as indicated in Chapter 2, a full cost comparison must take account of costs incurred to provide the other links in the sanitation chain.

Box 3.9 Comparison of costs of mechanized and non-mechanized options for the Philippines

A comparison exercise undertaken in the Philippines suggested ratios of capital costs for mechanized and non-mechanized schemes ranging from about 2.5 for a plant capacity of 15 m³/day down to about 1.25 for a plant capacity of 380 m³/day (USAID, 2013). The costs include those of land, plant, and sludge tankers. The fully mechanized system costs assumed automatic sludge/solid waste separation, mechanical press or centrifuge sludge dewatering, and high-rate aeration of filtrate. Those for 'non-mechanized' systems include mechanical screening, waste stabilization ponds, and sludge drying beds. The land cost assumed was US$46 per square metre. For a 70 m³/day plant, the capital cost of a mechanized plant was cheaper than that of a non-mechanized plant once the land cost exceeded about US$350 per square metre.

A similar exercise for operational costs found that the estimated mechanized system costs were marginally higher than those for the non-mechanized system for a 15 m³ per day capacity plant, increasing with increasing plant capacity to reach a ratio of about 2.35:1 for a 380 m³/day capacity plant. The comparison included the costs of personnel, office costs, and water quality tests as well as direct treatment costs. Personnel included plant manager, operators, maintenance technician, chemist, secretary-clerk, utility person, security guard, driver, and labourers. In practice, this level of staffing will not be required for small treatment plants. The assumed costs of water quality testing were the same for both mechanized and non-mechanized systems, as were personnel and office costs for plants with capacities up to 60 m³/day. For larger plants, the comparison assumed higher costs for mechanized than for non-mechanized plants but the difference did not exceed about 10 per cent for any size of plant. Treatment costs included those of power and chemicals (polymers for mechanical sludge treatment and chlorine for effluent disinfection).

It is possible to envisage situations in which choosing a mechanized technology would enable the treatment plant to be moved closer to centres of population, leading to a reduction in septage transport costs that might exceed the additional cost of mechanized treatment. If initial investigations suggest that this scenario is possible, it will be advisable to extend cost comparisons to include septage transport costs.

Another reason for choosing a mechanized option might be that conveniently located and available sites are too small to accommodate a non-mechanized system. This is probably more pertinent to wastewater treatment facilities than to septage treatment facilities. Septage flows are much smaller than wastewater flows, and septage treatment usually requires much less land than wastewater treatment for sewered sanitation serving the same population despite the fact that septage is much stronger than municipal wastewater. The USAID investigation summarized in Box 3.9 estimated the land requirements for a 70 m³/day plant as 1,100 m² and 4,000 m² for mechanized and non-mechanized systems, respectively. It would be possible to provide the 4,000 m² required for the non-mechanized system on a site 100 metres long by 40 metres wide, which is not a particularly onerous requirement. The use of anaerobic technologies to treat the liquid fraction of the septage would reduce the area required for the non-mechanized option. Treatment plants can utilize a combination of mechanized and non-mechanized technologies. For instance, where power and appropriate management systems are available, screw presses to separate solids from liquid can be followed by non-mechanized treatment of supernatant water.

One further point is pertinent to any discussion of capital and operational costs. In many countries, capital costs are borne by higher levels of government, perhaps with support from international agencies, while local organizations meet operational costs. Local government and other local organizations are often financially constrained and this means that they may face difficulty in finding the finance required for effective service provision. This is particularly true for septage treatment, which is essentially a public good, for which people will be reluctant to pay directly and is often a low priority for decision-makers. Where funding to meet recurrent costs is limited, a technology or approach with low operational costs is more likely to succeed than one with high operational costs, despite the fact that the net present cost of the second option is lower than that of the first. With this in mind, costs comparisons should cover both net present costs and operational costs, with the latter assessed against the best possible estimate of the available operational budget.

Key points from this chapter

This chapter has dealt with the steps required before detailed design begins. In particular, it has examined the factors that will affect the choice of treatment plant site and procedures for determining the hydraulic, organic, and suspended solids loads on the plant. Key points to take from the chapter include:

- Planning should always be information-based and should start from an assessment of the existing situation. Rapid assessment, based on existing records, field observation, and conversations with service users and providers, can provide useful information on existing facilities and services. It will help to identify areas requiring more detailed investigation prior to detailed design.
- The first task will be to determine the planning area. This will be influenced by physical realities, in particular, existing settlement patterns and administrative boundaries. It should be determined in consultation with local government and service providers.
- Treatment plant locations will depend on their service areas, which, in turn, will depend on the degree to which treatment provision is to be decentralized.
- A decentralized approach to treatment will result in reduced haul distances for both untreated faecal sludge and septage and the useful end-products of treatment. Conversely, it will increase labour requirements for the operation and maintenance of treatment facilities. Where operational skills are limited, the need to deploy the workforce over several sites will mean that decentralization will work best with fairly simple technologies.
- Regardless of theoretical considerations, factors such as the availability of government land will often govern the choice of treatment plant location.
- Factors to be considered when assessing the loading on the plant include the proportion of the population served by on-site and decentralized sanitation systems, the types of sanitation facility found in the service area, the demand for pit and tank emptying and transport services, and the nature and effectiveness of pit and tank emptying and transport services in the area. The figures from Malaysia quoted in this chapter show that pit and tank accessibility can also have an important bearing on loads.
- In the absence of initiatives to increase the number of sewer connections, demand for tank and pit emptying services will increase as the population increases. If effectively enforced legislation on delivery to treatment plants exists, this will result in a steadily increasing load on septage treatment facilities. Where the current demand for pit and tank emptying services is low, a major increase in treatment plant loading will often be dependent on a change from on-call to scheduled emptying.
- The organic and suspended solids loads on treatment facilities will depend on the strength of the material to be treated. For design purposes, loading calculations should use mean organic and suspended solids loading figures, obtained by averaging the results from as many

samples as possible. To allow for the high variability of faecal sludge and septage, these samples should be composite samples.

- Choices between more and less mechanized treatment technologies should take account of the management requirements of each technology, including the skills required to operate the technology and monitor its performance, the supply chains required to ensure the availability of spare parts, and the dependence of the technology on difficult tasks that are required at infrequent intervals.
- Choices will also be influenced by costs, particularly recurrent costs. Where financial resources are limited, it may be best to select technologies with lower operational costs, even if their discounted cost is more than that of technologies with high operational costs.

References

Al Sa'ed, R.M.Y. and Hithnawi, T.M. (2006) 'Domestic septage characteristics and cotreatment impacts on Albireh Wastewater Treatment Plant efficiency', *Dirasat Engineering Sciences* 33(2): 187–97, Amman: University of Jordan <https://journals.ju.edu.jo/DirasatEng/article/view/1430> [accessed 26 January 2018].

Arthur, J.P. (1983) *Notes on the Design and Operation of Waste Stabilization Ponds in Warm Climates of Developing Countries*, World Bank Technical Paper Number 7, Washington, DC: World Bank <http://documents.worldbank.org/curated/en/941141468764431814/pdf/multi0page.pdf> [accessed 26 January 2018].

Bassan, M., Tchonda, T., Yiougo, L., Zoellig, H., Mahamane, I., Mbéguéré, M. and Strande, L. (2013) 'Characterization of faecal sludge during dry and rainy seasons in Ouagadougou, Burkino Faso', paper presented at the *36th WEDC International Conference, Nakuru, Kenya*, Loughborough: Water, Environment and Development Centre, University of Loughborough <https://wedc-knowledge.lboro.ac.uk/resources/conference/36/Bassan-1814.pdf> [accessed 7 February 2018].

Bäuerl, M., Edthofer, M., Prat, M-A., Trémolet, S. and Watzal, M. (2014) *Report on the Financial Viability of Faecal Sludge End-Use in Dakar, Kampala and Accra*, London: Trémolet Consulting <www.tremolet.com/publications/report-financial-viability-faecal-sludge-end-use-dakar-kampala-and-accra> [accessed 26 January 2018].

Brandes, M. (1977) *Accumulation Rate and Characteristics of Septic Tank Sludge and Septage*, Research Report W63, Toronto, Canada: Applied Science Section, Pollution Control Branch, Ministry of the Environment <https://ia802708.us.archive.org/32/items/accumulationrate00bran/ACCUMULATIONRATE_00_BRAN_07915.pdf> [accessed 26 January 2018].

Dayal, R., Wijk-Sijbesma, C.A. van and Mukherjee, N. (2000) *Methodology for Participatory Assessments With Communities, Institutions and Policy Makers: Linking Sustainability with Demand, Gender and Poverty* [pdf], METGUIDE, Washington, DC: World Bank – Water and Sanitation Program <www.ircwash.org/sites/default/files/Dayal-2000-Metguide.pdf> [accessed 27 February 2017].

Fernández, R.G., Inganllinella, A.M., Sanguinetti, G.S., Ballan, G.E., Bortolotti, V., Montangero, A. and Strauss, M. (2004) *Septage Treatment Using WSP, Proceedings, 9th International IWA Specialist Group Conference on Wetlands Systems for Water Pollution Control* and *6th International IWA Specialist Group Conference on Waste Stabilization Ponds, Avignon, France, 27 September – 1 October 2004.*

Florida Department of Health, Bureau of Onsite Sewage Programs (2011) *Report on Alternative Methods for the Treatment and Disposal of Septage* <www.floridahealth.gov/environmental-health/onsite-sewage/_documents/septage_alternatives.pdf> [accessed 18 November 2017].

Heinss, U., Larmie, S.A. and Strauss, M. (1999) *Characteristics of Faecal Sludges and their Solids–Liquid Separation*, Eawag/Sandec <https://www.sswm.info/sites/default/files/reference_attachments/HEINSS%20et%20al%201994%20Characteristics%20of%20Faecal%20Sludges%20and%20their%20Solids-Liquid%20Seperation.pdf>.

Indonesia Urban Water, Sanitation, and Hygiene (IUWASH) (2016) *IPLT Technology Options Section Guide*, Appendix B, Jakarta, Indonesia: IUWASH (unpublished document).

Koné, D. and Strauss, M. (2004) 'Low-cost options for treating faecal sludges (FS) in developing countries: challenges and performance', paper presented at the *9th International IWA Specialist Group Conference on Wetlands Systems for Water Pollution Control* and the *6th International IWA Specialist Group Conference on Waste Stabilization Ponds, Avignon, France, 27 September – 1 October* <https://www.eawag.ch/fileadmin/Domain1/Abteilungen/sandec/publikationen/EWM/Journals/FS_treatment_LCO.pdf> [accessed July 2018].

Lossing, H.A. (2009) *Sludge Accumulation and Characterization in Decentralized Community Wastewater Treatment Systems with Primary Clarifier Tanks at Each Residence*, MSc thesis, Kingston, Ontario: Department of Civil Engineering, Queen's University <https://qspace.library.queensu.ca/handle/1974/1854> [accessed 26 January 2018].

Lüthi, C., Morel, A., Tilley, E. and Ulrich, L. (2011) *Community-led Urban Environmental Sanitation Planning: CLUES*, Dübendorf: Eawag <www.eawag.ch/en/department/sandec/projects/sesp/clues> [accessed 4 October 2017].

Mills, F., Blackett, I. and Tayler, K. (2014) 'Assessing on-site systems and sludge accumulation rates to understand demand for pit emptying in Indonesia', In *Proceedings of 37th WEDC International Conference, Hanoi, Vietnam*, Loughborough: Water, Engineering and Development Centre, University of Loughborough <https://wedc-knowledge.lboro.ac.uk/resources/conference/37/Mills-1904.pdf> [accessed 26 January 2018].

Mukheibir, P. (2015) *A Guide to Septage Transfer Stations*, report for SNV Netherlands Development Organisation by Institute for Sustainable Futures, University of Technology, Sydney, Australia <www.snv.org/public/cms/sites/default/files/explore/download/a_guide_to_septage_transfer_stations_-_october_2016.pdf> [accessed 11 January 2018].

Narayana, D. (2017) *Sanitation and Sewerage Management: The Malaysian Experience, FSM Innovation Case Study*, Seattle, WA: Bill & Melinda Gates Foundation <www.susana.org/_resources/documents/default/3-2760-7-1503648469.pdf> [accessed 4 February 2018].

Nichols, P. (1991) *Social Survey Methods: A Field Guide for Development Workers*, Oxford: Oxfam GB <https://policy-practice.oxfam.org.uk/publications/social-survey-methods-a-field-guide-for-development-workers-115403> [accessed 15 February 2018].

Norris, G. A. (2000) *Sludge Build-Up in Septic Tanks, Biological Digesters and Pit Latrines in South Africa*, South Africa: Water Research Commission <www.wrc.org.za/Knowledge%20Hub%20Documents/Research%20Reports/544-1-00.pdf> [accessed 26 January 2018].

Parkinson, J., Lüthi, C. and Walther, D. (2014) *Sanitation 21: A Planning Framework for Improving City-wide Sanitation Services*, IWA/Eawag/GIZ <www.iwa-network.org/filemanager-uploads/IWA-Sanitation-21_22_09_14-LR.pdf> [accessed 4 October 2017].

Peal, A., Evans, B., Blackett, I., Hawkins, P. and Heymans, C. (2014) 'Fecal sludge management: analytical tools for assessing FSM in cities', *Journal of Water, Sanitation and Hygiene for Development* 4(3), 371–83 <http://dx.doi.org/10.2166/washdev.2014.139>.

Pradeep, R., Sarani, S. and Susmita, S. (2017) 'Characteristics of faecal sludge generated from onsite systems located in Devanahalli', paper presented at the *4th FSM Conference, Chennai, India* <www.susana.org/_resources/documents/default/3-2741-7-1488813934.%20et%20alpdf> [accessed 3 November 2017].

Schoebitz, L., Bischoff, F.,Ddiba, D., Okello, F., Nakazibwe,R., Niwagaba, C.B., Lohri, C.R. and Strande, L. (2016) *Results of Faecal Sludge Analyses in Kampala, Uganda: Pictures, Characteristics and Qualitative Observations for 76 Samples*, Dübendorf: Swiss Federal Institute of Aquatic Science and Technology (Eawag) <www.eawag.ch/fileadmin/Domain1/Abteilungen/sandec/publikationen/EWM/Laboratory_Methods/results_analyses_kampala.pdf> [accessed 7 February 2018].

SFD (2017) *SFD Toolbox*, Eschborn, Germany: Sustainable Sanitation Alliance (SuSanA), Deutsche Gesellschaft für Internationale Zusammenarbeit (GIZ) GmbH <http://sfd.susana.org/toolbox> [accessed 4 February 2018].

SSWM (no date) 'City sanitation plans' [online] <www.sswm.info/content/city-sanitation-plans-csp> [accessed 18 November 2017].

Still, D. and Foxon, K. (2012) *Tackling the Challenges of Full Pit Latrines Volume 2: How Fast Do Pit Toilets Fill Up? A Scientific Understanding of Sludge Build Up and Accumulation in Pit Latrines*, WRC Report No. 1745/2/12, Gezina, South Africa: Water Research Commission <www.wrc.org.za/Pages/DisplayItem.aspx?ItemID=9759&FromURL=%2fPages%2fKH_DocumentsList.aspx%3fd t%3d%26ms%3d2%3b67%3b%26d%3dTackling+the+challenges+of+full+pit+latrines+Volume+2%3a+How+fast+do+pit+toilets+fill+up%3f+A+scient ific+understanding+of+sludge+build+up+and+accumulation+in+pit+latrin es%26start%3d121> [accessed 26 January 2018].

Strande, L., Ronteltap, M. and Brdjanovic, D. (2014) *Faecal Sludge Management: Systems Approach for Implementation and Operation*, London: IWA <www.sandec.ch/fsm_book> [accessed 17 November 2017].

Tayler, K., Parkinson, J. and Colin, J. (2003) *Urban Sanitation: A Guide to Strategic Planning*, Rugby: Practical Action Publishing <https://doi.org/10.3362/9781780441436> [accessed 7 February 2018].

USAID (2013) *Philippine Water Revolving Fund Follow-up Program: Business Case and Model Contract for a Septage Management Project under a Public Private Partnership Agreement*, Manila, Philippines: USAID <https://smartnet.niua.org/sites/default/files/resources/PA00JMVP.pdf> [accessed 26 January 2018].

US EPA (1977) *Feasibility of Treating Septic Tank Waste by Activated Sludge*, Cincinnati, OH: Municipal Environmental Research Laboratory, EPA <https://nepis.epa.gov/Exe/ZyPDF.cgi/9101BHQM.PDF?Dockey=9101BHQM.PDF> [accessed June 2018].

US EPA (1984) *Handbook: Septage Treatment and Disposal*, Cincinnati, OH: Municipal Environmental Research Laboratory.

WaterAid (2016) *Comparison of Tools & Approaches for Urban Sanitation*, September 2016 <https://nepis.epa.gov/Exe/ZyPDF.cgi/30004ARR.PDF?Dockey=30004ARR.PDF> [accessed 19 June 2018]

WSUP (2017) *From Pilot Project to Emerging Sanitation Service: Scaling up an Innovative Public Private Partnership for Citywide Faecal Waste Collection in Dhaka* <https://www.wsup.com/content/uploads/2017/08/05-2017-From-pilot-project-to-emerging-sanitation-service.pdf> [accessed 5 October 2017].

CHAPTER 4

Introduction to treatment processes and technologies

This chapter introduces faecal sludge and septage technologies and explains the options for combining these technologies to achieve treatment objectives, which are often defined in terms of national and international standards. It emphasizes the point that proposals for treatment of faecal sludge and septage must take account of their high strength and partly digested nature. Treatment units and their functions are introduced and linked to the main stages in treatment: reception and preliminary treatment, solids–liquid separation, liquid treatment, solids dewatering, and treatment to allow safe end use. The benefits of solids–liquid separation prior to separate treatment of the liquid and solid fractions of the influent are emphasized. While the chapter is mainly concerned with separate treatment of septage and faecal sludge, options for co-treatment with wastewater are discussed. The last section of the chapter outlines a process for developing the process design and choosing appropriate technologies.

Keywords: treatment objectives, treatment processes, high strength, partially stabilized influents, co-treatment, treatment units

Treatment objectives

As stated in Chapter 1, the basic objective of treatment is to render the material treated safe for either reuse or disposal to the environment. Septage and faecal sludge treatment processes aim to do this by 'stabilizing' faecal waste, converting it from its untreated condition, in which it is unpleasant, unstable, high in pathogens, and has a high oxygen demand, to products that are stable, low in pathogens, and have a low oxygen demand. All septage treatment processes, and most faecal sludge treatment processes, produce a liquid effluent and a sludge residue. Specific treatment objectives are as follows:

- Reduce the oxygen demand, suspended solids, and nutrient concentrations in the liquid fraction of the effluent as required to comply with national environmental regulations.
- Reduce pathogen concentrations in the liquid fraction to levels that allow safe discharge or reuse.
- Reduce the water content of sludge to the point at which the sludge acts as a solid, is much reduced in volume, and so is easier and cheaper to handle and transport.
- Reduce pathogen numbers in sludge to levels that allow its safe end use or disposal. Treated sludge intended for end use is usually referred to as a biosolid.

http://dx.doi.org/10.3362/9781780449869.004

In order to ensure that objectives relating to effluent disposal and reuse and biosolids reuse are met, both individual countries and international organizations set effluent and biosolids standards.

Effluent discharge standards

Most countries have formulated national standards for discharges to waterbodies. These typically cover oxygen demand, suspended solids, and nutrients. National standards for pathogens are less common, but international organizations such as the World Health Organization (WHO) and Food and Agriculture Organization (FAO) define acceptable pathogen numbers for liquid effluents and biosolids intended for agricultural use.

Effluent discharge standards in many countries are similar to the original 'Royal Commission' standards that were developed in the UK early in the 20th century. These set maximum allowable five-day biochemical oxygen demand (BOD_5) and total suspended solids (TSS) concentrations of 20 mg/l and 30 mg/l, respectively. In areas where the receiving environment is particularly sensitive, higher BOD_5 and TSS standards will be required, together with maximum allowable standards for nutrients, including ammonia, nitrate, total nitrogen, and phosphorus. Some countries specify minimum standards in terms of chemical oxygen demand (COD) rather than BOD_5. Table 4.1 summarizes the Malaysian standards, which cover both BOD and COD, together with ammonia nitrogen (NH_4-N), nitrate (NO_3), phosphorus (P), and oil and grease (O&G).

Standard B is the generally applicable standard, while Standard A applies to specified locations upstream of drinking water supply intakes. In this respect, and in specifying higher NH_4-N, NO_3, P, and O&G standards for effluents discharged to stagnant water, the Malaysian standards illustrate the point that discharge standards should relate to the nature of the receiving water body and potential water uses downstream of the discharge point.

Table 4.1 Malaysian wastewater discharge standards

Parameter	Effluent discharge to river or stream				Effluent discharge to stagnant water (ponds and lakes)			
	Standard A		Standard B		Standard A		Standard B	
	Absolute	Design	Absolute	Design	Absolute	Design	Absolute	Design
BOD_5	20	10	50	20	20	10	50	20
SS	50	20	100	40	50	20	100	40
COD	120	60	200	100	120	60	200	100
NH_4-N	10	5	20	10	5	2	5	2
NO_3	20	10	50	20	10	5	10	5
P	N/A	N/A	N/A	N/A	5	2	10	5
O&G	5	2	10	5	5	2	10	5

Source: SPAN (2009)

The standards also distinguish between an absolute figure, which should never be exceeded, and a lower design figure, set at a level that should ensure that the absolute standard will always be met. The distinction between absolute and design standards recognizes and takes account of the inevitable variation in effluent sampling results. The more common practice is to specify a standard that must not be exceeded in more than a small proportion, typically around 5 per cent, of all the samples taken. As already noted in Chapter 1, the most common approach to assessing the likelihood that pathogens are present is to test for indicator bacteria. National effluent discharge standards do not normally place limits on indicator bacteria numbers in effluents discharged to watercourses. Rather, they focus on ensuring acceptable outcomes, specifying acceptable levels for the presence of indicator bacteria and, in some cases, specific pathogens, in treated potable water and water bodies used for recreation (see, for instance, Government of South Africa, 1996). Table 4.2 reproduces the 1989 WHO-guidelines for using treated wastewater in agriculture. Intestinal nematodes include *Ascaris, Trichuris,* and the hookworms *Ancylostoma* and *Necator.*

Recognizing that these guidelines are unnecessarily strict, the 2006 WHO guidelines recommend a quantitative microbial risk assessment (QMRA) approach to determining acceptable pathogen levels in irrigation water (World Health Organization, 2006). The data required for QMRA-based approaches may not be available at the local level, with the result that planners must often rely on the more conservative 1989 guidelines. Blumenthal et al. (2000) provide further information on the theoretical thinking that underlies the 2006 guidelines.

Per capita production of septage will typically be of the order of 100 litres per person per year, which compares with typical sewage flows of 50–150 litres per person per day, depending on the water supply and household plumbing arrangements. Although these figures will vary greatly, depending

Table 4.2 1989 WHO Guidelines for using treated wastewater in agriculture

Category	Reuse condition	Exposed group(s)	Intestinal nematodes (arithmetic mean, no. of eggs per litre)	Faecal coliforms (geometric mean, no. per 100 ml)
A	Irrigation of crops likely to be eaten uncooked, sports fields, public parks	Workers Consumers Public	≤1	≤1,000
B	Irrigation of cereal crops, industrial crops, fodder crops, pasture, and trees	Workers	≤1	No limit
C	Localized irrigation of crops in Category B if exposure to workers and the public does not occur	None	Not applicable	Not applicable

on local circumstances, they illustrate the fact that the volume of liquid effluent produced by a septage treatment plant will be significantly lower than that produced by a sewered system serving the same population. Given the relatively small volume of liquid effluent produced by septage treatment plants, and the difficulty of producing an effluent that meets the WHO unrestricted irrigation guidelines, a good option for disposal of the liquid effluent will be to use it locally for irrigation of trees and other crops that require minimal worker contact.

Solids disposal and reuse standards and guidelines

National and international guidelines place restrictions on pathogen concentrations in biosolids that are to be used in agriculture and aquaculture. Like the guidelines for use of treated effluent for irrigation, the WHO guidelines cover both pathogens, as represented by either faecal coliforms or *Escherichia coli*, and intestinal nematodes. The US EPA distinguishes between Class A and Class B biosolids, suitable for unrestricted and restricted use, respectively. Few if any guidelines exist for biosolids use for purposes other than agriculture. In the absence of such guidelines, the focus for non-agricultural uses should be on removing any health risk to workers. Chapter 10 provides further information on the WHO guidelines and other relevant international standards. Where it is not possible to achieve the standards required for reuse, the solid products of treatment processes should be disposed of to a controlled landfill.

Dealing with high strength, partly stabilized faecal sludge and septage

Many of the treatment processes described in this book are similar to processes used for the treatment of municipal wastewater. However, faecal sludge and septage differ from municipal wastewater in two important respects. First, they are much stronger than municipal wastewater and, second as already noted, the volume received at treatment plants is much lower than the volume of wastewater generated by an equivalent population. These differences are considered in turn below.

The figures quoted in Table 3.3 show that septage COD and TSS concentrations often exceed 5,000 mg/l and may reach 50,000 mg/l. Dry faecal sludge may be even stronger. Studies in South Africa found that the moisture content of pit latrine contents typically lies in the range 60–80 per cent, giving solids contents in the range 20–40 per cent and TSS concentrations in excess of 200,000 mg/l (Bakare et al., 2012: Figure 4). These figures compare with typical municipal wastewater COD and TSS concentrations in the ranges 500–1,200 mg/l and 200–600 mg/l, respectively (Henze and Comeau, 2008). Nitrogen concentrations in faecal sludge and septage are similarly high, with ammonia nitrogen (NH_4-N) concentrations typically ranging from 300 to 2,000 mg/l. This range compares with typical concentrations of around 40 mg/l for municipal wastewater.

The high strength of faecal sludge and septage results in the following treatment challenges:

- Their high solids content leads to high sludge accumulation rates in tanks and ponds. Designers must allow for the operational implications of this.
- Their high organic strength increases their treatment needs well above those of conventional wastewater. This often creates a need for multiple treatment processes, deployed in series.
- The high ammonia content may inhibit biological processes, reducing the efficacy of treatment and resulting in liquid effluent nitrogen concentrations that exceed discharge standards.
- High nutrient concentrations in treated effluent may make it difficult to meet discharge standards. Most nutrients in faecal sludge and septage are present in dissolved form and remain in the liquid stream after sedimentation (Henze and Comeau, 2008). This means that high nutrient levels in effluent may be an issue, particularly for co-treatment with wastewater. This will be true even after initial solids–liquid separation of septage.

The point concerning volume can be illustrated by comparing total per capita wastewater production with sludge accumulation rates in on-site pits and tanks. The first may exceed 100 litres per person per day while, as shown by the figures in Box 3.7, the latter are unlikely to exceed 100 litres per person per year. Even allowing for the fact that septage includes both accumulated sludge and supernatant water, the volume of septage will be less than 1 per cent of the volume of wastewater generated by a sewered system serving the same population. This has implications for treatment technology selection, and is considered further in Chapters 6–10.

The biodegradability of the material to be treated will also affect treatment choices. Faecal sludge and septage differ from wastewater and from one another in the biodegradability of their liquid and solid fractions. Figure 4.1 illustrates this point. It is based on Table 9.3 in the publication *Faecal Sludge Management: Systems Approach for Implementation and Operation* (Lopez-Vazquez et al., 2014), which draws on information taken from several sources.

The fractions given in Figure 4.1 relate to particular cases and actual fractions will vary, depending on local circumstances. Nevertheless, it is possible to use the figure to draw the following conclusions:

- *Fresh faecal sludge contains a high proportion of biodegradable material.* Figure 4.1 shows an average of 84 per cent biodegradable COD, of which around one-fifth is 'readily biodegradable' and the remainder 'slowly biodegradable'.
- *Digested faecal sludge contains a much higher proportion of non-biodegradable material.* The average shown in Figure 4.1 is 56 per cent, of which almost 85 per cent is particulate and hence potentially settleable.

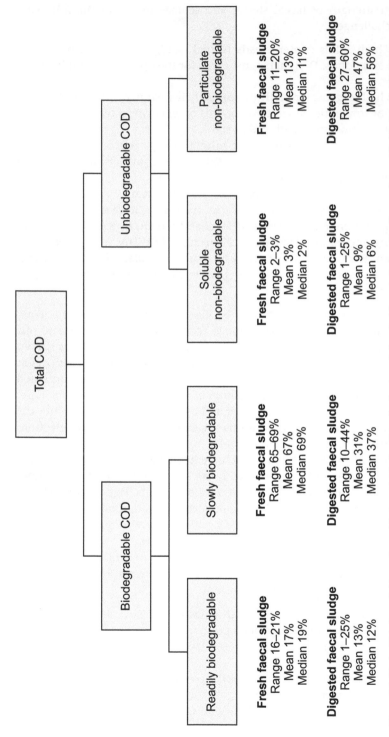

Figure 4.1 Typical biodegradable and non-biodegradable fractions for fresh and digested faecal sludge; the figures for readily biodegradable COD are the sum of figures given for acidogenic bacteria, fermentable organic matter, and volatile fatty acids

Source: Lopez-Vazquez et al. (2014: Table 9.3)

- *The biodegradable proportion of digested faecal sludge, while smaller than that of faecal sludge, is still likely to be significant.* The average shown in Figure 4.1 is 44 per cent, of which around 30 per cent is readily biodegradable.

The reduced biodegradability of digested faecal sludge stems from the fact that it is partly stabilized, having experienced anaerobic conditions in pits and tanks for several years. Investigations in South Africa found that readily biodegradable material exists in a fairly thin layer at the top of dry pit latrines but that the bulk of the contents have low biodegradability (Bakare et al., 2012). As already noted in Chapter 3, the COD to BOD_5 ratio of the sludge is a good indicator of stabilization. For fresh faecal sludge it will normally be around 2, similar to that of municipal wastewater. For fully digested sludge it may rise to 10 or more.

Differences in the biodegradability of septage and faecal sludge affect treatment choices. In particular:

- Faecal sludge removed from frequently emptied public toilets and container-based sanitation (CBS) systems offers considerable scope for further biological treatment. Biodigestion is an option for this type of sludge. It will reduce odour problems while preparing the sludge for further biological treatment.
- Faecal sludge removed from dry pit latrines is likely to provide limited scope for further biological treatment. It will normally be best to view it as a solid requiring further dewatering rather than a liquid to be treated.
- Septage removed from infrequently emptied septic tanks, wet leach pits, and wet pit latrines offers less scope for biological treatment. Most of its non-biodegradable COD is associated with particulate matter, as is a high proportion of its biodegradable COD. Removal of this material from the liquid flow will render the liquid more amenable to treatment and so septage treatment should normally include initial separation of solids from liquid.

A high proportion of the nutrients in faecal sludge and septage are present in dissolved form and remain in the liquid stream after sedimentation (Henze and Comeau, 2008). The presence of these nutrients, particularly total nitrogen and ammonia, must be taken into account when assessing treatment options for the liquid fraction of septage.

These points should be taken into account when assessing the options for linking technologies to achieve the objectives identified at the beginning of this chapter.

Treatment units and their functions

No single-unit process can achieve all the objectives listed earlier in this chapter. Faecal sludge and septage treatment plants must therefore include a number of treatment units, linked in a way that ensures effective achievement of the objectives. These units must provide some or all of the following functions:

- *Faecal sludge/septage reception.* From vacuum tankers, smaller vehicles, and hand carts used for manual emptying.
- *Removal of gross solids, grit, fats, oil, and grease (FOG), and floating objects.* These might otherwise be caught in or clog pipes and/or settle in subsequent treatment units, causing blockages and impairing performance.
- *Stabilization of fresh faecal sludge to reduce odours and render it more amenable to follow-up treatment processes.*
- *Solids–liquid separation.* This allows the size of subsequent treatment units in septage treatment plants to be reduced.
- *Treatment of the liquid removed from septage or faecal sludge.* This reduces the organic loading and ammonia and pathogen contents to levels that are compatible with the intended disposal/reuse arrangements for the liquid effluent.
- *Solids dewatering.*
- *Reduction of the pathogen content of treated liquid and separated sludge.* Pathogen levels must be compatible with proposed disposal/reuse arrangements.

Figure 4.2 shows the options for combining treatment processes to achieve overall treatment objectives.

All the treatment paths shown on Figure 4.2 involve faecal sludge/septage reception and coarse screening to remove gross solids. Grit and FOG removal and stabilization of fresh faecal sludge may be required, depending on the nature of material to be treated and the requirements of later treatment processes. Following preliminary treatment, Figure 4.2 shows three options:

1. *Provide solids–liquid separation* followed by separate treatment for the solid and liquid fractions of the influent.
2. *Treat the influent as a liquid* with a focus on reducing the organic load, as in a conventional wastewater treatment plant. This process produces sludge, which must then be treated as a slurry.
3. *Treat the influent as a slurry*, to be dewatered sufficiently to allow it to be handled as a solid. Excess water removed from the sludge must then be treated as a liquid.

The first and second options are suitable for septage treatment while the third option is more appropriate for the treatment of faecal sludge. Solids–liquid separation will be the preferred option for septage, except for smaller treatment plants in places where management and operational skills are limited.

Separated liquid will require treatment to reduce liquid oxygen demand and suspended solids loading and to dewater sludge. Further treatment to reduce pathogen numbers to safe levels may be necessary, particularly where the treated effluent is to be used for 'unrestricted' irrigation. Similarly, dewatered solids may require further treatment to remove pathogens, reduce water content further, or both.

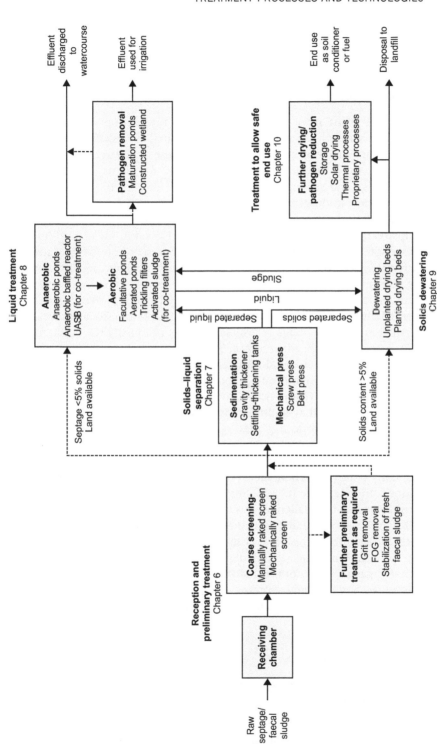

Figure 4.2 Faecal sludge and septage treatment stages and options.
Note: Dashed lines indicate routes followed in some but not all cases

The next sub-section provides further information on the various treatment stages shown in Figure 4.2. Chapters 7–10 give detailed information on the options for each stage.

Reception and preliminary treatment

Every treatment plant must include provision for reception of incoming material. Coarse screening to remove large objects such as trash and textiles is also essential since such objects might otherwise cause downstream blockages and/or damage downstream treatment processes. At plants that receive both faecal sludge and septage, it will be advisable for each to have its own reception facilities, leading to partly or wholly separate treatment streams. Where septage is to be co-treated with wastewater, it is possible to add the septage upstream of the treatment plant screens. However, given the desirability of separating solids from the liquid septage stream prior to co-treatment with wastewater, separate reception and preliminary treatment facilities will normally be required.

Grit removal is often omitted, on the premise that grit contributes only a small proportion of the solids that accumulate in tanks and ponds. The assumption is that a small increase in sludge accumulation does not justify the additional complexity associated with grit removal. This is a reasonable assumption for small facilities that receive material from tanks and pits with lined walls. It may not be justified where a significant proportion of incoming material comes from unlined pit latrines. Grit removal will be essential for plants that rely on mechanical equipment if that equipment is susceptible to damage by grit.

FOG can block pipework and may reduce effectiveness of downstream treatment processes. In particular, FOG accumulates in the scum layer at the surface of anaerobic ponds and reactors, and may affect their performance unless regularly removed. Where faecal sludge or septage is directed to drying beds without prior treatment, FOG may prevent evaporation and so slow the drying process. The challenge, as explained in Chapter 6, is to provide facilities for FOG removal that are both effective and simple.

Options for stabilizing fresh faecal sludge and reducing odour and vector attraction problems include partial digestion and lime stabilization. Both present challenges and will not normally be either appropriate or desirable for well-digested faecal sludge and septage.

Chapter 6 details arrangements for reception and preliminary treatment of septage and faecal sludge.

Solids–liquid separation

Solids–liquid separation prior to separate treatment of the liquid and solid fractions of septage has the following advantages:

- It reduces the organic load exerted by the liquid component, so reducing the land and/or power requirements for treatment of that component.

- It removes settleable material from the liquid stream, so reducing the sludge accumulation rate and hence desludging requirements in subsequent liquid treatment units.
- By removing settleable material, which contains a high proportion of non-biodegradable solids, it increases the biodegradable proportion of the liquid stream.

These advantages mean that the treatment process for septage should include a dedicated solids–liquid separation stage, except where the solids content of the septage is low, the proposed plant is small, management capacity is limited, and land availability is not a constraint. In these circumstances, direct discharge to anaerobic ponds will be an option if the challenge of regular desludging can be met. Solids–liquid separation will always be desirable before co-treatment with wastewater.

The main mechanisms used for solids–liquid separation are sedimentation, filtration, and pressure. Sludge separated using physical sedimentation will typically have a solids content in the range 5–10 per cent and will require further dewatering. The solids content of the cake produced by mechanical presses, which use a combination of pressure and filtration, typically lies in the range 15–30 per cent. This means that follow-up dewatering needs will be either reduced or, in some cases, removed altogether. Chapter 7 provides further information on the various solids–liquid separation options, identifying the pre-conditions for their use and setting out their advantages and disadvantages.

Liquid treatment

As already noted, both faecal sludge and septage are much stronger than municipal wastewater and this will normally remain the case even after solids–liquid separation. One consequence of this is that treatment of the liquid stream will often require several treatment stages. Deployment of anaerobic processes ahead of aerobic processes will reduce power costs and/or land requirements. Because anaerobic processes are temperature dependent, the advantages of this arrangement will be greatest in hot climates. A second consequence will be that the sludge accumulation rate in anaerobic treatment units and sedimentation tanks will be higher for septage, and particularly for faecal sludge, than for wastewater. If ponds and tanks are not desludged regularly, sludge will rapidly accumulate in them, reducing their capacity and blocking flow paths. The results will be poor plant performance and, eventually, complete system failure. A third point to be considered is the possibility that the ammonia content of faecal sludge and septage will inhibit treatment processes. This point is explored further in Chapter 8.

As shown in Figure 4.2, liquid treatment processes produce solids, which will require periodic removal followed by dewatering along with previously separated solids. Conversely, solids dewatering processes will produce liquid filtrate, which will require treatment if no other safe disposal option is available. While the volume of this liquid will normally be small, its strength will invariably be high.

Chapter 8 discusses individual liquid treatment options in detail.

Solids dewatering

Depending on the technology used for solids–liquid separation, further reduction in the solids water content may be required. The water content of sludge separated using sedimentation processes will normally be more than 90 per cent. It will thus require further drying before it can be handled as a solid. The solids content of the 'cake' produced by sludge presses is higher and the cake will normally behave as a solid. Nevertheless, further reduction of its volume may be desirable, particularly where the final disposal point is some distance from the treatment plant. Chapter 9 describes solids dewatering options in detail.

Additional treatment requirements for solids reuse

Further reductions in pathogen numbers and/or water content will be required to render biosolids suitable for use as a soil conditioner or solid fuel. When considering treatment options, it will be important to take account of their costs, particularly their operational costs, and their reliability in reducing pathogen numbers to safe levels. Reuse options will only be financially viable if:

$$R_{TP} = C_{TP} - C_{D}$$

where: R_{TP} is the revenue generated from the sale of treated products;

C_{TP} is the cost of the additional treatment required to render the products of treatment suitable for reuse; and

C_{D} is the cost of disposal if no treatment is provided.

The cost of treatment up to the point that the biosolids are of sufficient quality for disposal (for example, to landfill) is the same for both sides of the equation and therefore not included.

In most cases R_{TP} will not be greater than $(C_{TP} - C_{D})$ and thus there will normally be a revenue shortfall of $[(C_{TP} - C_{D}) - R_{TP}]$. In such cases, for the reuse of the biosolids to be financially viable, a subsidy will be needed, so that the equation becomes:

$$R_{TP} + S = C_{TP} - C_{D}$$

where: S is any subsidy that is available to promote the reuse of treated products.

Because of environmental costs, the economic cost of disposal to landfill may exceed its financial cost, so that some form of subsidy could be justified. However, when considering the use of subsidies, it will be important to ensure that government is willing to make a sustained commitment to the subsidy for the purposes of resource recovery. Revenue generation will depend on market conditions and the ability of the organization with responsibility for marketing the products of treatment to sell into the market. Chapter 10 examines options for end use of biosolids produced by faecal sludge and septage treatment processes. These include well-recognized, if not always widely implemented, approaches and those that are still at either the experimental or pilot stage.

Co-treatment with wastewater

Co-treatment of septage at wastewater treatment plants is the norm where almost all households have access to sewerage and the volume of septage is therefore small in comparison with that of wastewater. It is more challenging where sewerage coverage is limited and many households use on-site sanitation, as is the case in most lower-income countries. The high strength of septage and faecal sludge means that relatively small volumes of either can have a large impact on the organic, suspended solids, and nitrogen loads on a wastewater treatment plant. Possible consequences include an increase in the volume of screenings and grit requiring removal; increased odour emission at headworks; increased scum and sludge accumulation rates; increased organic loading, leading to overloading and process failure, and the potential for increased odour and foaming in aeration tanks. Because of their partly digested nature, septage and faecal sludge will usually degrade at a slower rate than municipal wastewater and their presence is likely to have an adverse impact on the efficacy of treatment processes. The intermittent nature of faecal sludge and septage loading will give rise to high instantaneous loads and so amplify the problems identified above. Despite these possible drawbacks, wastewater treatment facilities with spare capacity are a potential resource to be investigated. Even where co-treatment is not an option, existing wastewater treatment plants may provide land in strategic locations, close to areas of demand for septage management services.

Options for dealing with septage and faecal sludge through wastewater treatment processes include the following:

- Add septage to the wastewater stream at an upstream manhole or at the treatment plant headworks. This option treats the septage as a liquid effluent. It is most likely to be appropriate for weak septage with a water content exceeding 95 per cent. Pre-treatment will always be required for strong faecal sludges.
- Dewater faecal sludge in conjunction with the sludge produced in the course of the wastewater treatment process. For this option to be used without pre-treatment, the solids content of the faecal sludge should be at least 5 per cent.
- Pre-treat septage/faecal sludge so that the liquid fraction can be treated with the wastewater stream and the sludge dewatered with the sludge generated by the wastewater treatment process.

Potential risks associated with the addition of strong septage to much weaker municipal wastewater include the following:

- Effluent quality is reduced and no longer meets discharge standards, an issue that is likely to be particularly problematic where these include stringent ammonia standards.
- The volume of sludge generated increases and exceeds the capacity of the sludge handling arrangements at the treatment plant.

To reduce these risks, pre-treatment will always be desirable, regardless of where septage and faecal sludge are added to wastewater treatment streams. It should always include screening and, in the case of faecal sludge from pit latrines, removal of garbage and other gross solids. Solids–liquid separation will also be required for septage. It will reduce the organic and suspended solids concentrations in the liquid fraction of the septage and hence reduce the load on wastewater treatment facilities. After separation, the liquid fraction of the septage should be directed to the head of the wastewater treatment process while the solid fraction is directed to the treatment plant's sludge drying facilities.

It will normally be more appropriate to deal with faecal sludge as a sludge to be dewatered along with sludge generated by the wastewater treatment process. Prior biodigestion may be required for fresh faecal sludge from public toilets and CBS systems.

Choosing appropriate treatment processes and technologies

Choices relating to overall treatment processes and individual treatment technologies will depend on:

- the characteristics of the material to be treated;
- the proposed arrangements for end use/disposal of the products of treatment;
- the costs of the various options; and
- contextual factors such as land and power availability and the capabilities of the organization that will be operating the treatment process.

It will be best to take a stepped approach to choosing the most appropriate treatment processes. Suggested steps are listed and briefly explained below.

1. *Identify possible treatment facility sites.* Take account of the factors identified in Chapter 3 while bearing in mind the possibility that adoption of partly enclosed technology options, including those incorporating mechanical processes, may facilitate the use of relatively small sites relatively close to housing developments.
2. *Assess hydraulic, organic, and solids loadings.* Use the methods described in Chapter 3, taking account of both present and future loading conditions and making appropriate allowance for flow variations.

3. *Decide the approach to solids–liquid separation and select an appropriate technology.* This step is prioritized because the approach to solids–liquid separation and the technology chosen will influence both preliminary treatment and subsequent liquid treatment and solids dewatering needs. Chapter 7 examines the options for solids–liquid separation.

4. *Assess options for liquid treatment and select the most appropriate option.* Take account of the volume and characteristics of the material delivered to the facility, the selected approach to solids–liquid separation, the location, the required effluent quality, and the resource requirements of the various treatment options. In respect of resource requirements, operational and management requirements and funds to cover operational costs will be particularly important. Chapter 8 provides information on liquid treatment technologies and processes.

5. *Assess solids dewatering requirements and options.* Solids dewatering requirements will depend on the characteristics of the solids to be dewatered and the final solids content required. The arrangements made for solids–liquid separation will have a strong influence on the characteristics of the sludge delivered for dewatering while the required final solids content will depend on proposed disposal/end use arrangements. As for liquid treatment options, solids dewatering options should be assessed in relation to the location, their costs, and their resource and management requirements. Chapter 9 provides information on solids dewatering technologies and processes.

6. *Determine reception and preliminary treatment requirements and options.* The main purpose of preliminary treatment is to protect the subsequent treatment processes. This means that preliminary treatment requirements will depend on the technologies chosen for solids–liquid separation, liquid treatment, and solids dewatering. Assessment of preliminary treatment requirements and options should therefore follow technology selection for later stages in the treatment process. As with other stages in the treatment process, choices should reflect costs, location, and the availability of physical and institutional resources. Decisions on whether to include specific provision for grit and FOG removal, and stabilization of raw sludge will depend on the characteristics of the incoming sludge and institutional capacity to operate and maintain the required facilities. Chapter 6 provides information on preliminary treatment technologies and provides guidance on when they should be used.

7. *Determine additional treatment required to ensure that treated products are safe and suitable for any proposed end uses.* Where the intended end use is as an agricultural input, treated products must meet required pathogen standards. These will depend on the type of crop to be grown and whether or not the public has access to the area where treated products are to be used. The most stringent requirements are those relating to the presence of helminths. Sludge intended for use as a biofuel or animal feed must be dried to achieve the minimum solids content consistent with

the proposed use. Processes that rely on incineration and pyrolysis will only be financially viable if they include prior provision for reduction in water content. Chapter 10 provides further information on technologies to prepare biosolids for end use.

On occasion, there will be a need to revisit earlier steps in the light of decisions made regarding later steps in the process. With this in mind, readers should view the sequence set out above as a guide rather than a fixed sequence to be followed rigidly on every occasion.

Key points from this chapter

This chapter has introduced treatment technologies and has assessed options for combining individual treatment units into overall treatment processes. The following key points have emerged from the chapter.

- Many of the processes used in faecal sludge and septage treatment either derive from or use similar principles to those used in municipal wastewater treatment plants. However, the selection and design of treatment processes for faecal sludge and septage must take account of their high strength, variable composition, and partly stabilized nature.
- The low volume of faecal sludge and septage relative to that of wastewater may also influence technology choices.
- All treatment plants should provide for reception and coarse screening of influents. Where a plant receives both faecal sludge and septage, it will often be appropriate to make separate arrangements for each type of influent. Other preliminary treatment requirements will be dependent on local conditions and the technologies used at later stages in the treatment process.
- Where land availability is not a constraint and management capacity is limited, it may be appropriate to discharge screened septage directly to simple liquid treatment units such as anaerobic ponds. Screened faecal sludge may be discharged to sludge drying beds either directly or following treatment in a small-scale biodigester.
- In all other cases, provision of solids–liquid separation facilities prior to treatment of the separated liquid and solid fractions will be desirable. Solids–liquid separation will be particularly important where plans involve co-treatment of septage with municipal wastewater.
- Treatment requirements after separation will depend on the solids–liquid separation process adopted. The solids content of the cake from sludge presses may exceed 20 per cent while that achieved in gravity thickeners sedimentation is likely to be around 5 per cent. The solids content achieved using batch processes such as settling-thickening tanks and sludge drying beds will depend on the retention time in the unit.
- Because of the high strength of septage, even after solids–liquid separation, aerobic treatment of the liquid fraction will require a large

land area, significant energy costs, or both. Providing anaerobic treatment prior to aerobic treatment will reduce the loading on subsequent aerobic treatment units and so reduce the costs of and/or land requirement for liquid treatment.

- Additional specialized treatment will be required before the biosolids produced during the treatment process are suitable for end use. Treatment requirements will depend on the intended end use.

References

Bakare, B.F. Foxon, K.M., Brouckaert, C.J. and Buckley, C.A. (2012) 'Variation in VIP latrine sludge contents', *Water SA* 38(4) [online] <https://pdfs.semanticscholar.org/2e0e/a4ed1dae179c069acf4d9c22d0ba8a82ed3d.pdf> [accessed 6 November 2017].

Blumenthal, U., Mara, D.D., Peasey, A., Ruiz-Palacios, G. and Stott, R. (2000) 'Guidelines for the microbiological quality of treated wastewater used in agriculture', *Bulletin of the World Health Organization* 78(9), 1104–16 <www.who.int/bulletin/archives/78(9)1104.pdf?ua=1> [accessed 29 January 2018].

Government of South Africa (1996) *South African Water Quality Guidelines, Volume 2 Recreational Use* [pdf], Department of Water Affairs and Forestry <www.iwa-network.org/filemanager-uploads/WQ_Compendium/Database/Future_analysis/082.pdf> [accessed 4 November 2017].

Henze, M. and Comeau, Y. (2008) 'Chapter 3 – Wastewater characterization', in M. Henze, M. van Loosdrecht, G. Ekama and D. Brdjanovic (eds.), *Biological Wastewater Treatment: Principles Modelling and Design*, London: IWA Publishing <https://ocw.un-ihe.org/pluginfile.php/462/mod_resource/content/1/Urban_Drainage_and_Sewerage/5_Wet_Weather_and_Dry_Weather_Flow_Characterisation/DWF_characterization/Notes/Wastewater%20characterization.pdf> [accessed 13 January 2018].

Lopez-Vazquez, C., Dangol, B., Hooijmans, C. and Brdvanovic, D. (2014) 'Co-treatment of faecal sludge in municipal wastewater treatment plants', in L. Strande, M. Ronteltap, and D. Brdjanovic (eds.), *Faecal Sludge Management: Systems Approach for Implementation and Operation* [pdf], London: IWA Publishing <www.unesco-ihe.org/sites/default/files/fsm_ch09.pdf> [accessed 15 March 2017].

SPAN (National Water Services Commission) (2009) *Sewage Characteristics and Effluent Discharge Requirements*, Cyberjaya: SPAN <www.span.gov.my/files/MSIG/MSIGVol4/04_Sec._3_Sewage_Characteristics_and_Effluent_Discharge_Requirements.pdf> [accessed 21 November 2017].

World Health Organization (1989) *Health Guidelines for the Use of Wastewater in Agriculture and Aquaculture*, World Health Organization Technical Report Series 778, Geneva: World Health Organization <http://apps.who.int/iris/bitstream/10665/39401/1/WHO_TRS_778.pdf> [accessed 12 January 2018].

World Health Organization (2006) *Guidelines for the Safe Use of Wastewater, Excreta and Greywater, Volume 2 Wastewater Use in Agriculture*, Geneva: World Health Organization <www.who.int/water_sanitation_health/wastewater/wwuvol2intro.pdf> [accessed 12 January 2018].

CHAPTER 5

Planning and design for effective operation

The main focus of this book is on treatment processes. However, even the best process design will not guarantee effective operation unless operators are able to operate a plant. This chapter examines the ways in which designers can ensure that plants are operable. It stresses the need to match treatment capacity to the load on the plant, consider resource availability when choosing technologies, and design flexible processes that allow treatment to continue when treatment units are decommissioned for maintenance or repair. The need for effective management systems is emphasized and institutional arrangements to provide such systems are introduced. Information is given on design to ensure operator safety and facilitate good operational practice, and the operational importance of accurate, good quality construction is stressed. Finally, information is provided on the options for ensuring that operators understand and follow good operational procedures and practices.

Keywords: operational procedures, resources, capacity, safety, operator access

Introduction

The overall requirements for any treatment process are that it operates effectively and consistently achieves its design objectives. This is more likely to be the case if planners and designers assess and learn from previous and ongoing operational experience. It also requires that:

- treatment capacity matches the load on the plant;
- technology selection takes account of resource availability;
- the process design facilitates effective operation;
- management systems support and facilitate operational procedures;
- design details facilitate safe operator access to carry out those procedures;
- facilities are constructed accurately and to the minimum standards required to ensure effective operation; and
- both managers and operational staff have a sound knowledge of the operational requirements of the treatment process.

The last condition is more likely to be met if written standard operating procedures (SOPs) are available and are routinely followed by staff. The term 'operational procedures' covers all tasks required to operate and maintain facilities, monitor performance, and repair and replace system components when required.

http://dx.doi.org/10.3362/9781780449869.005

Assessment of operational experience

Questions to ask when assessing previous and ongoing operational experience include the following.

- What were the design assumptions for existing plants and in what ways does current operational practice diverge from those assumptions?
- Has operational experience revealed any problems and issues with previous designs?
- If so, what does operational practice suggest about the options for overcoming these problems and dealing with the issues they raise?

Observation of existing treatment plants and discussions with operators will provide a starting point for answering these questions. This may be done informally, but it will be better if systems are put in place to systematically monitor the performance of existing facilities and explore operator views on the operational challenges that these facilities pose. In addition to improving understanding of what does and does not work and the nature and cause of any problems, routine monitoring will provide local information on septage strength and system performance. This will inform the assumptions that are made for future designs.

Analysis of operational practice will be easier and more effective if actual operational procedures can be compared with those specified in written SOPs. These should be produced in any case because they provide the framework within which operators carry out the tasks assigned to them. They are particularly relevant when operators lack formal training and qualifications. However, unexamined operational procedures may prove to be unworkable or, worse, may result in outcomes that were not foreseen by the designer. This underlines the need for a reflective approach to design that learns from operational experience.

Where electromechanical equipment is installed at existing treatment plants, it will always be worthwhile to assess whether operators are using this equipment. For example, investigation may reveal that, in order to reduce electricity bills, aerators in aerated lagoons are operated only for limited periods, if at all. In many cases, anaerobic ponds with the same or slightly greater land requirement will work equally well.

All the above relates to technologies and practices that are already in existence so that there is operational experience to draw on. This will not always be the case. Faecal sludge and septage treatment is a developing field and some of the technologies described in this book have not been implemented at scale. Pilot-scale initiatives can provide information on the performance of these technologies and equip operational staff with experience of operating the technologies. It will be important to assess the challenges that will be faced in taking the technologies to scale and to monitor operational experience, adjusting approaches and designs in light of that experience.

Options for matching operational capacity to load

Treatment plant operation will be difficult if treatment capacity and the load on the plant are not in balance. Clearly, the plant will not function effectively if the load exceeds available treatment capacity, but there may also be operational difficulties if the operational treatment capacity greatly exceeds the load. The second situation will occur where existing demand for pit and tank emptying services is low but the treatment plant is designed for the much larger projected flow at the design horizon. In such circumstances, it is likely that operators will find it difficult to operate the plant as intended by its designers. For instance, the loading on anaerobic ponds may be insufficient to ensure fully anaerobic conditions, and flows through gravity thickeners and anaerobic baffled reactors may be insufficient to maintain design velocities, resulting in higher than designed sedimentation rates. Options for responding to this situation include:

- phase construction so that plant capacity increases incrementally as the load on the plant increases; and
- construct the plant with capacity to deal with projected loads at the design horizon but phase the commissioning of treatment units so that operational capacity matches load.

Phased construction is theoretically more cost effective. It incurs capital expenditure only when needed and so does not use scarce resources to fund non-productive assets. It also allows lessons learned from operation of the first units built to be incorporated into the design of later units.

In practice, funding for construction is often provided through programmes funded by central government and international agencies and is only available for time-bound initiatives. Where this is the case, the phased commissioning option may be more realistic, despite its theoretically greater financial cost.

Both phased construction and phased commissioning will benefit from a modular approach involving provision of a number of smaller treatment units rather than one large unit. Some technologies are more suited to a modular approach than others. For example, drying beds are inherently modular. The cost of constructing a larger number of smaller beds will not be significantly more than that of constructing a smaller number of larger beds with the same overall capacity. Indeed, providing more beds may facilitate operation. Other technologies, for instance mechanical presses, have minimum capacities and are more expensive and so offer less scope for modular implementation and commissioning. Even so, as explained in the section on process design below, it will always be advisable to provide enough individual units to allow alternative routes through the treatment process.

Even when construction, commissioning, or both are phased, there will be situations in which the load on an individual treatment unit will be less than the design load on that unit. SOPs should provide guidance on how operators should respond to this situation.

The influence of resource availability on technology choice

A treatment technology will only function effectively if the resources required for its continued operation are available. Technology choices should therefore take account of resource availability. If the resources required by a particular technology are not available, that technology will not be viable. The options then are to use a different technology or to take action to provide the resources required for successful long-term operation of the technology. Specific points to be considered in relation to resource availability are explored below.

Power availability

A reliable power source will be required for power-dependent technologies, such as pumps, mechanical screens, and activated sludge reactors. The best option will always be to draw power from a networked three-phase public supply. However, effective operation will only be possible if this supply is reliable, with few outages, and provides the design voltage. These conditions are not always met in lower-income countries. Frequent breaks in supply create a need for alternative power sources; furthermore low voltage in the supply system can result in high currents, leading to motor overheating and burn out. Alternative power sources include diesel generators and solar panels. Diesel generators are expensive to run and their running time may be restricted by the non-availability or unaffordability of fuel. Solar power may be an option for systems with low power consumption but will require battery storage and may be unable to meet the demand for power during prolonged cloudy periods. These points suggest that power-dependent technologies should not be considered unless a reliable and affordable power source is, or can be, made available. Box 5.1 describes an alternative to pumping for removing sludge from tanks that require frequent desludging.

Box 5.1 Use of hydrostatic pressure as an alternative to pumping

Pumps require a reliable power source, regular maintenance, and effective systems for the delivery of spare parts. These conditions may be difficult to guarantee in some locations. Hydrostatic pressure offers an alternative to pumping where sludge containing sufficient water to act as a liquid has to be removed from the bottom of a tank. Figure 7.5 shows how this principle is used to desludge hopper-bottomed tanks. Desludging takes place through a pipe, which extends to the bottom of the tank at its lower end and into a chamber below the liquid level in the tank at its upper end. A valve is provided on the connection to the chamber. Opening the valve leads to a pressure difference between the lower and upper ends of the pipe. This causes sludge from around the bottom of the pipe to flow through the pipe and into the chamber. European wastewater treatment plant designs routinely use this mechanism to remove sludge from sedimentation tanks, using small pressure differentials. A greater pressure differential may be required for the thicker sludges generated by septage treatment processes. The mechanism will only be effective where the lower end of the pipe is contained within a hopper with steeply sloping sides. As with pumping, regular sludge removal will be essential. Without it, consolidation of sludge in the bottom of the tank will lead to a situation in which it does not flow easily, at which point manual removal will be necessary.

Management and support systems

- *The availability of consumables and spare parts.* Uninterrupted operation of a technology or process is only possible if good supply chains exist to ensure the timely delivery of any consumables and spare parts required. When assessing the viability of technologies, it will be important to investigate the availability of the consumables and spare parts that they require. If the availability of either cannot be guaranteed, operational difficulties and breaks in service will be inevitable.
- *Manufacturer's after-sales services.* Good supply chains for manufactured parts are more likely to exist if the manufacturer either is local or has an in-country representative or agent with appropriate technical knowledge and the ability to procure replacement units and spare parts and deliver them to customers. Some manufacturers offer service contracts for a set period that can help guarantee the availability of spare parts and maintenance services. Even if this is not possible, preference should be given to equipment for which spare and replacement parts are locally available, provided that this can be done without sacrificing quality.
- *Management and operational resources.* No technology will continue to function if essential operation and maintenance tasks are neglected. Each technology option should therefore be assessed in terms of the ability of existing and possible future management systems to ensure that those tasks are undertaken both promptly and effectively. The section on management structures and systems below provides further information on assessing management structures and systems and the options for strengthening them is given later in this chapter.
- *Information and information systems.* When considering process options, it will be important to identify their information requirements and assess the ability of existing and possible future management systems to provide that information. For instance, efficient operation of activated sludge and extended aeration treatment processes requires information on the mixed liquor suspended solids in the reactor. Similarly, information on polymer dosing rates and sludge-cake water content will be required to optimize the performance of sludge presses.

Financial resources

It will be impossible to operate a process effectively if available funds are insufficient to cover its operational costs. When assessing technology options, it will therefore be necessary to assess the operational costs of each technology in relation to the funds that can realistically be expected to be available for operation and maintenance. There are two aspects to this: first, the availability of funds to cover routine operation and maintenance tasks; and second, the options for funding major repair and replacement requirements. Funding for routine operation and maintenance must cover the costs of labour, power, and any materials that are required for routine operation – for instance, the polymers that are essential to the effective performance of mechanical presses. Designers should discuss the availability of funds to cover these costs with the organization that will be responsible for operating the plant. The design report should include an assessment of the overall operational costs of preferred technologies, including an allowance for repair and replacement costs, and compare these costs with a best estimate of the operational budget. Where necessary, the need for an increased operational budget should be highlighted, and options for raising the required funds should be identified and assessed. When assessing potential equipment repair and replacement needs, the possibility that these may require foreign exchange should be considered.

Contracts for the supply of mechanical equipment should include a requirement for the manufacturer or his agent to provide instructional manuals in the local language and training for the client's staff. Where operational staff are unfamiliar with newly installed equipment, the contract should ideally provide for a lengthy handover period after commissioning, during which employees of the company that has supplied the equipment work alongside operational staff. This will serve both to identify and deal with any unforeseen operational problems, and to train operational staff in the correct operation and maintenance of the equipment.

Process design for effective operation

Continued operation of some technologies can only be guaranteed if they are preceded by units that protect them from potential damage. For instance, mechanical presses may be vulnerable to damage caused by small objects in the incoming sludge and so must be preceded by fine screening to remove such objects. Other technologies depend on some form of pretreatment. For instance, some dewatering technologies, including mechanical presses, will only be effective if the incoming sludge is first dosed with a polymer. These examples point to the need to consider treatment options as parts of an overall process rather than as self-contained technologies.

Planners and designers should also recognize that even the simplest technology will fail if essential operation and maintenance tasks either cannot be performed or are neglected. The overall process design should therefore take account of operation and maintenance needs. Points to be considered include:

- *The need to maintain flow while carrying out maintenance and repair tasks.* Wherever possible, parallel treatment streams should be provided so that at least one stream can continue to function while another is out of service for maintenance or repair. This is an essential requirement for facilities such as anaerobic ponds and anaerobic baffled reactors that must periodically be taken out of service for desludging. Similarly, standby units should be provided for mechanical components such as pumps, screens, and aerators.

- *The nature and timing of essential operation and maintenance tasks.* Operational staff are more likely to carry out frequently required but relatively easy tasks than infrequently required tasks that involve significant effort and/or difficulty. For example, the solids that accumulate in the hopper-bottomed tanks that are described in Chapter 7 must be removed several times a day. Sludge can be removed using hydrostatic pressure, thus removing the need to maintain pumps. Settling-thickening tanks, which are also described in Chapter 7, and anaerobic ponds require less frequent desludging, which will usually involve the use of mechanical equipment.
- *The consequences if essential operation and maintenance tasks are neglected.* Questions to be asked when assessing these consequences include 'how might this technology fail?' and 'how robust will it be in the event that routine operational tasks are neglected?'
- *The response of technologies to fluctuations in hydraulic and organic load.* Septage and faecal sludge treatment plants are more subject to short-term load fluctuations than wastewater treatment plants because of the great variability in the strength of the influent and the fact that loading is intermittent. Possible operational difficulties stemming from fluctuations in flow should be considered when selecting technologies, with preference given to technologies that are best able to deal with such fluctuations. As a general rule, the longer the hydraulic retention of a unit, the better will be its ability to deal with fluctuations in load.
- *The need to manage sludge and scum.* The solids content of septage is high and that of faecal sludge is often even higher. As already noted, this means that sludge and scum accumulate much more rapidly in ponds and tanks than would be the case for municipal wastewater. If sludge and scum are not removed, they will accumulate in treatment units, reducing the effective volume of these units. They may also block treatment unit inlets, outlets, and connecting pipework. If sludge removal is neglected indefinitely, sludge will fill the treatment units, leading to their complete failure. Neglect of scum removal may lead to pipe blockages, leading to system failure even earlier. Box 5.2 gives examples of problems arising from failure to manage sludge effectively and Photo 5.1 illustrates one of these problems.

Designers should be cautious when considering the options for automation. Labour costs in lower-income countries are usually much lower than those in industrialized countries, so one of the drivers for automation, the need to reduce staffing levels in order to reduce costs, has less force. Staff may face operational problems if automated systems break down. For instance, a site visit by the author revealed that expensive equipment at the Pula Gebang and Duri Kosambi septage treatment plants in Jakarta, while in good condition, was not functioning well because the automatic control system had broken down.

Box 5.2 Examples of problems arising because of neglected or delayed sludge removal

An investigation at the Achimota treatment plant in Accra, Ghana in the early 2000s found that sludge separation tanks were emptied every 4–5 months rather than the 7–8 weeks assumed in the design. Not surprisingly, this resulted in a significant reduction in solids–liquid separation performance (Montangero and Strauss, 2004).

In 2014, less than two years after commissioning, sludge and scum were already causing operational problems at the septage treatment plant serving Tegal in Central Java, Indonesia. Small shrubs had germinated on the scum layer on the anaerobic ponds and interconnecting pipes were blocked, leading tanker operators to discharge directly into the facultative ponds rather than via the discharge chamber (see Photo 5.1).

Operators in Indonesia report that it is often difficult to desludge Imhoff tanks. The high solids content of the incoming septage results in rapid sludge accumulation. Operators often have to add water to the tank contents to facilitate desludging, which defeats the treatment objective of separating solids from liquid. Investigation of upflow anaerobic sludge blanket (UASB) reactors installed in Latin America and under India's Ganga and Yamuma Action Plans concluded that failure to remove sludge that had accumulated in the reactors was significantly affecting reactor performance (Chernicharo et al., 2015; Khalil et al., 2006).

Photo 5.1 Sludge management problems in anaerobic pond, Tegal, Indonesia (note the lack of provision for operator access to the tanks)

As with other types of mechanical equipment, automatic control systems should only be considered if the manufacturer can guarantee the availability of local maintenance and repair systems at an affordable cost.

One important point, which is often overlooked, is the need to guard against theft and vandalism. Theft can be a problem for any items that might be sold or used elsewhere.

Management structures and systems for effective operation

Even the simplest technology will fail if it is ineffectively managed, a point that is illustrated by the findings of a review of wastewater treatment plant performance in India, which showed that simple waste stabilization ponds were among the worst performers. The probable explanation is that managers assumed that low maintenance meant no maintenance, with the result that ponds received very little operational attention (author's analysis based on Central Pollution Control Board, India, 2007). Existing management structures and systems should therefore be assessed at the planning stage in order to identify and address any weaknesses and constraints that might prevent effective operation and maintenance of the plant.

Questions to ask in relation to institutional structures and systems include:

- *Where do institutional responsibilities for faecal sludge management lie?* Municipal bodies often bear responsibility for septage and faecal sludge management but do not prioritize it. Decision-makers often treat it as an unimportant add-on to the activities of another municipal department (often the department with responsibility for solid waste management).
- *Who has official responsibility for operational decisions and who makes these decisions in practice?* Problems are likely if there is a wide gap between officially sanctioned and actual responsibilities.
- *Who has the power to approve expenditure on operation, maintenance, and repair?* In the event that an inadequate budget constrains the operating organization's capacity to carry out essential tasks adequately, what are the procedures to be followed to secure increased funding?
- Related to the last point, *what systems exist for ensuring timely procurement of materials, parts, and complete replacement of failed or worn-out units?* Do systems exist to ensure the availability of essential spare and replacement parts? Do the people with operational responsibilities have the executive and financial powers required to ensure that essential procurement tasks are carried out promptly? Box 5.3 identifies one option for facilitating prompt procurement.
- *Are there any institutional constraints on releasing the funds required for occasional repair and maintenance tasks?* In the event that spare parts must be imported, how effective are the systems for ordering and paying for those spare parts? Could customs procedures prolong the time required

---

Box 5.3 The use of framework contracts to facilitate prompt repairs

One option for facilitating timely responses to equipment breakdowns is to develop framework contracts with local suppliers and workshops to provide items and services against a costed list covering the repair and replacement activities that might be required. Items in the list would then be 'called down' as and when needed. This removes the need to undertake a detailed procurement process every time a repair or replacement part is needed. Adopting this approach does not remove the need for a good stores system, with stocks of all commonly required items and parts kept in stock.

to import the spare parts, and could these spare parts be subject to import duties that would increase their cost?

• *What scope is there within existing organizational systems to recruit and retain appropriately skilled staff?* This question is particularly important when considering options that involve sophisticated technologies and procedures.

The staff allocated to septage management tasks are often either low-grade employees or contract workers employed on a temporary basis. Many are daily-wage employees with no job security and no pension or sickness benefit rights. Such arrangements are not conducive to the employment and retention of staff members with the knowledge, experience, and skills to operate anything other than the simplest technologies. Where such arrangements exist, planners must make a realistic assessment of the steps that need to be taken to develop capacity before attempting to introduce new and improved treatment processes and technologies. These might include:

• *Creating new posts within the municipal structure.* The scope for doing this will depend on the division of powers between local and higher levels of government. If decisions about staffing are made at higher levels of government, the focus should be on introducing systems that apply to all municipalities.

• *Introducing new institutional arrangements* that provide increased scope for employing the required specialist staff. Institutional options include:
  – Setting up a semi-autonomous body within the municipality with specific responsibility for septage management. Indonesia follows this approach through its system of local technical implementation units (Unit Pelasana Teknis Daerah or UPTD in Bahasa Indonesian). The Indonesian experience shows the limitations of this approach, with UPTDs having limited financial and staff-hiring powers (Tayler et al., 2013).
  – Assigning operational responsibility to an existing specialist service-delivery organization, for instance an existing water provider.
  – Establishment of a public company with a remit to run septage management services on behalf of municipalities. This might be done throughout a whole state, province, or region, or at a more local level. Municipalities might be required to use the services of the public company or could voluntarily enter into contracts with it.
  – Employing private-sector companies to run septage management services through some form of public–private partnership arrangement. The private-sector companies might be responsible for all aspects of septage management or for specific aspects, including septage removal and collection, septage treatment, and the provision of laboratory services.

All but the first of these suggested institutional arrangements would expand the operating organization's remit, allowing it to bring in specialist equipment and personnel, a course of action that will rarely be feasible for municipal departments in all but the largest cities. When considering options involving new institutional arrangements, it will be necessary first to convince senior decision-makers that change is needed, and then to implement any changes in legislation required to facilitate implementation of the proposed institutional changes.

Designing with operators in mind

There are two aspects to designing with operators in mind. The first is to ensure the safety of operators, and indeed the public. The second is to ensure that designs facilitate the performance of operational tasks, not least in ensuring good operator access to carry out those tasks. With this in mind, design for operator safety and design to facilitate operational procedures are explored in turn below.

Designing for safety

Treatment plants should always be designed in ways that ensure the safety of both workers and the general public. This requires that:

- Treatment plants should be fenced, with fences designed to prevent, or at the very least deter, unauthorized access by members of the public.
- Facilities should be designed to minimize worker contact with faecal sludge and septage. Where contact cannot be avoided, workers should be provided with appropriate protective clothing and encouraged to use it.
- Enclosed spaces in which gases generated by anaerobic biodigestion might gather should be avoided wherever possible. Where the design requires an enclosed space, as is the case with domed biodigesters, the design should minimize the need for workers to enter the enclosed space. Where occasional entry cannot be avoided, the overall process design should provide time, preferably weeks, before workers have to enter an enclosed space such as a domed biodigester. Procedures for entry should be set out in SOPs. Appropriate safety equipment should be provided and workers should be required to use it.
- Electricity cables should be run in chases cut into walls or securely clipped to the wall. Hanging wires should be avoided, as should cable runs that pass through areas where there is a risk of flooding. All fittings should be securely fastened to a wall or ceiling.
- Railings or raised walls should be provided around tanks to a height of at least 1,067 mm (42 inches) above the level of the surrounding ground (based on US Department of Labor, undated). Where frequent access is required, railings and closable gates should be inserted, or chains should be provided.

- Anti-slip surfaces should be provided in areas, such as polymer handling areas, where spillages could result in slippery floors. Tiled surfaces can become slippery when wet and should be avoided.
- Warning notices should be provided where the formation of a scum layer and perhaps the growth of vegetation on a pond makes it difficult to distinguish between a scum-covered pond and hard ground.
- Where the size and depth of ponds justifies it, a small boat should be provided. Lifebelts should also be available where there is a danger that someone might fall into a pond.

Designing to facilitate operational procedures

Treatment units will perform poorly and eventually cease to function if operators neglect essential operation and maintenance tasks. The likelihood that operators will carry out these tasks in a timely manner will be greatly reduced if they find the task difficult, dangerous, or unpleasant. This means that designers should always review their designs from the operators' perspective. Some examples of what this might mean in practice, highlighting common operational challenges and design faults, and suggesting ways in which challenges might be met and design faults might be rectified, are given below.

Access for pond and tank desludging. Anaerobic and facultative ponds and tanks need periodic desludging, and the sludge will often be too thick to be pumped. Where this is the case, the only options will be to dig it out by hand or to remove it using a tractor fitted with a front-end loader. Both these options require access to the ponds after supernatant water has either been drained or pumped out of the pond. The normal arrangement for larger ponds is to provide ramps that allow vehicle access. For smaller ponds, which will be the norm at septage treatment plants, the design should provide for operator access by means of steps or a ramp. The designers of the tanks shown in Photo 5.1 have made no such provision. To desludge the tanks, operators will have to enter the pond using ladders leant against the walls and then pass sludge up to colleagues working at ground level, perhaps using buckets. This will be a slow and difficult task and it is likely that this has contributed to the neglect of desludging that is clearly evident in the photograph. Once the ponds are full of sludge, they will provide little or no effective treatment.

Screen design to allow access for raking. Photo 5.2 illustrates a common design fault, the provision of a vertical screen with no access, which makes raking the screen impossible unless the operator climbs into the tank. This is something that they will be reluctant to do, with the result that the task will almost certainly be neglected.

Photo 5.3 shows a screen at the wastewater treatment plant that serves the town of Naivasha in Kenya. This is a much better design. Note the gently

Photo 5.2 Vertical screen with no operator access

sloping screen, the slightly depressed area into which the operators can rake screenings and the platform to one side of the screen on which the operator can stand to rake the screen. This design could have been further improved by replacing the depressed area behind the stream with a trough leading to the side and allowing screenings to be pushed out into a waiting wheelbarrow. Chapter 6 gives more information on this arrangement.

Avoidance of settlement in places that are difficult to reach. Figure 5.1 is a longitudinal section through the discharge bays and connections to the solids separation chambers (SSCs) at the Tabanan septage treatment plant in Indonesia, which will be described in more detail in Chapter 7. Tankers discharge septage onto the apron shown at the left and it then passes through the screen under a baffle wall and through a series of pipes into the SSC proper. We have already noted the difficulties that operators will face in clearing a vertical screen. The other problem with the design relates to solids settlement. Solids will tend to settle at the point indicated by the arrow on the figure and will be difficult to remove. This is a specific example of the more general problem of unintended and unwanted solids settlement, often at inaccessible locations. Designers should always be aware of the possibility and design to minimize settlement, except where it is required as part of the treatment process. Where some settlement cannot be avoided, the design should ensure that operators have access to remove the settled solids.

Photo 5.3 Inclined screen with operator access

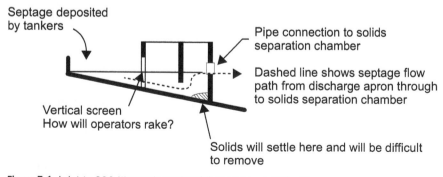

Figure 5.1 Inlet to SSC illustrating potential operational difficulties

Photo 5.4 Blocked connection pipework

Access to clear pipe blockages. Designers cannot ignore the possibility that pipes will block. The risk will be reduced if pipes are appropriately sized and laid at falls that are sufficient to ensure solids transport, but will be difficult to eliminate altogether. Blockages are most likely to occur at bends and changes in pipe direction, and designers should always consider how such blockages will be cleared. Photo 5.4, which shows a connection between two tanks, illustrates this point. A horizontal pipe, just visible in the photograph, provides the connection between the two tanks. This connects to vertical pipes on both sides, which extend down below the assumed maximum depth of the scum layer. The level in the pond on the upstream side has risen so that the pipe is almost submerged. This suggests that the pipe is at least partially blocked. The vertical pipes have been extended up to above the tank water level, allowing them to be rodded to clear any blockages that might occur in them. The photograph shows this being done. The detail is similar to the standard detail used for septic tank inlets and outlets. Its weakness lies in the fact that it is difficult to gain access to clear any blockages that occur in the horizontal pipe. A better detail would be an opening in the wall of the tank, protected on both sides by scum boards. This would reduce the length of the connection to the width of the wall and provide easier access in the unlikely event that the opening became blocked.

Access for delivery vehicles. The blockage shown in Photo 5.4 stemmed directly from a failure to adequately address vehicle access needs at the plant design stage. In theory, the connection shown is between a facultative pond and a maturation pond. In practice, tanker operators were discharging septage into the first pond, bypassing the anaerobic pond shown in Photo 5.1. This increased the load on the pond, resulting in the formation of a scum layer, which hastened the onset of the blockage problem. The problem could have been avoided or reduced by reducing the steep slope on the access ramp to the septage reception chamber and configuring the pond layout in way that made it impossible for tanker drivers to discharge their loads directly to the facultative pond. This example highlights the need to design to encourage good operational practice and discourage bad practice.

Other points to be considered by designers are listed and briefly explained below.

- Valves should be installed with sufficient clearance to allow easy operation of the lever or handwheel, and to allow clearance for wrench operation when the valve needs to be removed/replaced.
- Pipework should not be installed at or above ground level in locations that obstruct access. This is particularly important on routes along which operators will have to move wheelbarrows and bins.
- Access routes within the treatment plant, particularly those designed for vehicle access and to allow movement of wheelbarrows and bins, should be paved.
- Dismantling collars should always be provided on straight flanged pipe runs, particularly those located within pump houses and chambers.
- Buried valves should be installed with valve boxes or in chambers so they can be located and operated. Chambers are more expensive but are more visible and, for this reason, they will usually be the preferred option.
- Pumps and other equipment should be installed with sufficient clearances to allow for disassembly for maintenance and repair. Pump manufacturers can normally provide information on the spacing required between and around pumps.
- Points of lubrication or adjustment need to be easily accessible, or these tasks are likely to be neglected.
- Switches and controls should be easily accessible. They should be grouped together in control panels located in buildings with lockable doors. The function of each switch and control should be clearly identified. As far as is possible, the design should allow for power to be disconnected from some controls to allow for their maintenance and repair while other controls continue to function.
- Designs should include provision for safe access to take samples and assess processes. This will be particularly important for enclosed reactors such as anaerobic baffled reactors (ABRs) and UASBs.
- Ancillary equipment required to service mechanical equipment should be of an appropriate quality. For instance, sludge presses require a supply of high-pressure washwater. The simple washwater system installed

to serve the screw presses in the two Jakarta septage treatment plants proved to be inadequate, with the result that staff found it difficult to keep the presses clean. As a result, performance suffered (observation by Stantec team).

Actions to ensure accurate, good quality construction

The role of good contract documentation and effective site supervision

Poor construction can undermine operational performance. Contractors are directly responsible for construction but the quality of their work is strongly influenced by the information that is given to them and the quality of supervision during construction. Good quality construction depends on:

- clear definition of the duties, responsibilities, and rights of the parties to the contract;
- accurate drawings and specifications that provide all the information needed by the contractor to carry out the work;
- supervision of the contractor's work by experienced and knowledgeable staff, who attend site regularly so that they can point out mistakes and defects as soon as they occur;
- a contract requirement that the contractor makes good unacceptable materials and workmanship at his own expense.

The standard approach to supervision is for the client to appoint an engineer/project manager, who is given formal responsibility for all aspects of supervision, as set out in the contract documents (see, for instance, FIDIC (1999), which uses the term 'Engineer'). Where the design has been carried out by a consultant, the consultant's contract may also include the provision of the engineer/project manager and other supervisory staff. Regardless of whether this is the case, it will be advisable to make formal provision for inputs from the treatment plant designers and, where appropriate, equipment manufacturers at key stages in the construction process. This can be done by including appropriately worded clauses in the Special Conditions of Contract: the conditions of contract that apply only to the particular contract to which they relate.

The contract should include a defects liability period, covering at least six months, and preferably a year, from the formal completion of construction, during which the contractor or equipment supplier is responsible for making good or replacing any defective materials, equipment, and workmanship.

It will always be desirable for the organization with operational responsibilities to be involved in supervision, even where another organization is responsible for design and construction. This will help to avoid situations in which the operator refuses to take delivery of facilities provided by others because of construction defects.

Actions to ensure sound construction

Full consideration of good construction practice is beyond the scope of this book. However, points with particular relevance to the design of faecal sludge and septage treatment facilities are listed and briefly discussed below.

Dealing with corrosion. Treatment plant components are often exposed to highly corrosive conditions, which will lead to rapid rusting of steel components. Designs should take account of this, using other materials whenever possible. Where this is not possible, steel components should be coated with a suitable material to prevent corrosion. Galvanizing is one possibility, although it may be difficult to ensure that larger items are completely galvanized, particularly when some component assembly is required on-site. In many cases, a better option would be to apply an epoxy coating or bituminous paint.

Corrosion would be particularly problematic where hydrogen sulphide gas, produced during anaerobic treatment processes, can gather in enclosed spaces and combine with water to produce sulphuric acid. In such situations, sulphate-resistant cement should be used in concrete and mortar.

Leak-free construction. Concrete tanks will crack if they contain insufficient reinforcement and concrete will tend to spall if water penetrates to the reinforcement and causes it to rust. Reinforced concrete tanks should be designed in accordance with codes covering the construction of water-retaining structures. These require provision of a minimum amount of steel reinforcement, with a bar spacing of the order of 150 mm, minimum cover, and appropriately located contraction joints. It will usually be possible to combine the latter with construction joints. Expansion joints will not normally be required for the fairly small structures required at faecal sludge and septage treatment plants. All structures should be tested for leakage as soon as possible after construction and should only be accepted if leakage does not exceed specified limits which, in turn, should be based on relevant codes and guidelines. The Constructor: Civil Engineering Home (undated) provides further information on joints in liquid-retaining concrete structures.

Quality of concrete and other materials. Whenever possible, site supervisory staff should arrange for concrete cubes to be taken and tested to ensure that concrete quality is as set out in the specifications. Where a lack of testing facilities makes this difficult, supervisors should ensure that the concrete mix is as specified and that materials, in particular cement, are stored correctly. Samples of other materials, including sand, gravel, and bricks, should be inspected and, where necessary, sent for testing to ensure that they are in accordance with specifications.

The importance of accurate construction

Photo 5.5 shows part of an overflow weir on a clarifier at the Keputih septage treatment plant in Surabaya, Indonesia. Because of a slight variation in the weir height, there is no flow along the length of weir that is closest to the camera.

Photo 5.5 Unbalanced flow resulting from poorly levelled weir

Thus, a small construction error has resulted in imbalanced flow through the clarifier and will certainly affect its performance. This is a common problem for clarifiers and sedimentation tanks. The normal response to the problem is to fit a metal weir plate, fabricated with V-notches, to the inside of the concrete weir. This facilitates accurate levelling of the weir and reduces the effective length of the weir. This will increase the depth of flow through the V-notches, making it easier to ensure even flow. The Keputih weir is fitted with such a metal weir plate but, as is clear from Photo 5.5, it was not levelled correctly.

The levels of pipes and channels should be specified on drawings and site supervisors should check that the works are constructed to these levels. Backfalls should be avoided and levels should always allow free discharge. This will require that pumping station wet wells provide storage below the invert level of the lowest incoming pipe and that operators do not allow wet wells to surcharge.

Options for developing staff capacity and facilitating good operational practice

Training

Staff cannot operate treatment plants unless they have the knowledge and skills appropriate to their roles and the equipment that they are required to operate. Training for managers should cover both treatment processes and the logistics of ensuring safe and effective operation of the treatment processes. It should also cover the information needs of the technologies deployed, and the implementation of systems for collecting, recording, analysing, and using the required information. In-house resources may be limited. For instance, smaller treatment plants are unlikely to have laboratory facilities for the measurement of chemical oxygen demand (COD), biochemical oxygen demand (BOD), total suspended solids (TSS), and faecal coliform concentrations. In such cases, managers should be provided with knowledge of the external resources that are available to them and have clear procedures for obtaining services from external organizations.

Operators need to have sufficient knowledge of treatment processes to understand what they are required to do and why they are required to do it. However, the main focus of operator training should be on ensuring that they have adequate knowledge and skills to carry out all the tasks required for effective treatment plant operation. Where a treatment process involves mechanical or electrical equipment, it will be advisable that the contract for the supply of that equipment should include provision for the manufacturer to provide training for all operational staff who will be concerned with its operation and maintenance. Guidance should be provided on the procedures to be followed following unplanned events such as unscheduled power cuts.

Training for both managers and operators should cover all aspects of safety, including the avoidance of hazardous situations, the safe use of mechanical and electrical equipment, the use of protective clothing, accident prevention, and, where appropriate, responding to fires and other emergencies. First aid training should also be provided, with special emphasis on responding to injuries and conditions associated with the work environment. To ensure that this training can be put into practice, appropriate equipment, including fire extinguishers and first aid supplies, should be available. Where chemicals are used in the treatment process, training should be provided in dealing with chemical spills.

Training materials should be as simple as possible, using visual aids wherever possible. They should clearly explain what constitutes good and bad practice, and warn trainees against adopting the latter. The Department of Water Affairs and Forestry (2002) of South Africa provides an example of a well laid out training manual. This is intended for wastewater treatment plant operators, but its style and some of its contents could provide a template for developing a similar guide for septage and faecal sludge treatment plant operation.

The sections on screening, grit channels, anaerobic ponds, and drying beds are particularly relevant to the technologies discussed in this book. Training materials should be linked to SOPs, and training courses should be based on the procedures set out in SOPs.

It may be possible to conduct practical training on existing plants that use technologies and procedures similar to those that are to be used at the plants where operators are to be deployed. Whether or not this is possible, practical operator training should also be provided at the plants where operators are deployed as soon as those plants are operational. This practical training should be viewed as a way to assess the relevance and appropriateness of the SOPs. If necessary, the SOPs should be revised in the light of lessons learned during training.

As far as is possible, training should be conducted by those with operational experience. Where good operational experience is lacking in a country, it may be necessary to bring in trainers from outside, but it will always be better if training capacity can be developed in-country. This means that training programmes should initially focus on training in-country trainers and monitoring their ability to convey what they have learned to others. Training initiatives should be periodically assessed to ensure that the training has not become formulaic and divorced from the realities of the situations in which operational staff find themselves.

Managers with responsibility for septage and faecal sludge treatment should keep a record of all training that has been carried out. Staff records should include details of all training courses attended by each staff member.

Standard operating procedures

Overview. SOPs are sets of written instructions that identify and describe the regularly recurring tasks required to ensure effective operation of a treatment process. They provide operators with the information required to carry out those tasks and so help to ensure that they are carried out correctly and produce consistent results. SOPs should be available for all routine operation and maintenance tasks and should also provide guidance on the procedures to be followed in the event of critical equipment breakdown.

It is important that SOPs provide information that is correct. This might seem obvious, but there are many examples of SOPs and guidance materials that give incorrect information. There is a danger that, once produced, such materials will be widely replicated and used by those with limited knowledge who assume that they are correct. It is also important that SOPs reflect operational experience. Terms of reference produced for consultants charged with designing treatment plants usually include a requirement to produce SOPs. If the consultants lack direct experience of the operation of treatment plants, the SOPs that they produce may prove to be unworkable or, worse, may result in outcomes that were not foreseen by the designer. The important lesson to learn from this is that SOPs should be produced by, or at the very least in consultation with, those who have first-hand knowledge of the operational procedures that the SOPs describe.

SOPs must be accessible to the individuals charged with performing the activities that they describe. This requires that they are understandable to their intended users and that they are available in the places where those users carry out their work. To ensure that they are understandable, they should be written simply in the language normally used by operators. They should be specific to the facility where they are to be used, and should provide information in a step-by-step manner that is both unambiguous and uncomplicated. Flow charts, photographs, and diagrams should be used rather than text wherever possible. Each operation should have its own SOP. To ensure their availability to operators, SOPs relating to specific tasks should be either kept or displayed at the places where those tasks are to be carried out. It will be best if SOPs describing specific tasks are available in the form of laminated sheets.

In practice, those charged with writing SOPs are often engineers with theoretical knowledge of processes but relatively little operational experience. Where this is the case, the SOP writer should spend time with operators of similar technologies in order to learn from their experience, and should search for examples of SOPs for similar technologies online.

SOP structure and content. Overall SOPs covering all the operations to be undertaken at a treatment plant should be structured as follows:

Title page

Table of contents

Definitions

Brief description of the overall treatment process, including diagram to show treatment units and flows through the system.

A brief statement on the regulations that govern the operation of the plant and the standards that it is required to meet.

A brief overview of roles and responsibilities as they relate to operation, maintenance, and repair. These roles and responsibilities should normally be defined in relation to job titles/descriptions rather than named individuals.

A statement on health and safety issues as they relate to the plant as a whole.

Information on each treatment technology included in the overall treatment process, including a brief description of the technology, a statement of its purpose, an explanation of its relationship to other treatment units, and a listing of the tasks required to operate and maintain the technology. For each task listed, the SOP should include:

• Information on when and how often the task should be carried out.

- A statement on responsibilities (defined in terms of job titles rather than named individual) for carrying out and overseeing the task.
- A step-by-step description of the operational procedures to be followed, including information on methods, materials, and the equipment required to carry out the task. Where appropriate, the description should cover start-up procedures.
- Information on standard maintenance procedures. As with operational procedures, this information should be provided in the form of a step-by-step guides.
- Where appropriate, information on procedures to be followed to shut down or bypass facilities.
- If appropriate, a list of materials and spare parts to be kept in stock.
- A statement on safety concerns related to the task and the action to be taken to ensure operator and public safety.
- Samples of checklists and any forms that the operator is required to fill out as part of standard operational practice.
- A list of potential problems, including step-by-step instructions on the action to be taken to resolve the problems.

Photographs, diagrams, and short instructional videos, stored on DVD, should be used to support written task descriptions.

In addition, the information provided to operations managers should include:

- Information on the expected influent volume and characteristics, and a list of design criteria for each treatment unit process.
- A list of contact details for suppliers, manufacturers, other skilled operators from reference facilities, or any other useful contacts that may be able to help the operator.
- Copies of technical manuals, drawings, and other technical guidance material provided by equipment suppliers.
- Information on systems and activities for monitoring plant performance.

Style. Writers of SOPs should endeavour to write as though they were talking to the person who will carry out the procedures. They should have a clear idea of who that person will be and an understanding of their likely level of education and background knowledge. Guidance on procedures to be followed should be written in the active voice, with instructions relating to each operational step starting with an active verb such as 'lift', 'turn on', or 'open'. Plain language should be used throughout. The aim should be to include only facts that are relevant to the operational tasks to be carried out. Supplementary material can be included, as necessary, in training manuals. Where a task or procedure involves several steps, it may be appropriate to represent each step as a separate bullet point.

A common mistake when writing both SOPs and training materials is to assume that the reader has the same underlying knowledge as the writer.

This will rarely be the case. When writing SOPs, it will therefore be important to ensure that all concepts, ideas, and terms are fully explained when they are first introduced.

Steps in preparing a set of SOPs. As already noted, the first step when preparing a set of SOPs for a given facility should always be to collect and analyse information on the performance of similar facilities. A good next step will be to prepare a rough flow chart setting out the procedures to be followed and identifying responsibilities for carrying out those procedures. This flow chart can then be used as a guide when producing a first draft of the SOPs.

The process description part of the SOPs should be developed alongside the detailed design and should be subject to the same technical review process as drawings, specifications, and calculations.

Before finalizing SOPs, it will be advisable to ask one or more potential users to read them and explain in their own words what they think that the SOPs are asking them to do. Any incompleteness or inaccuracy in their explanation will provide an indication that further work is required to ensure that the SOPs cover all the steps to be undertaken to complete a task or procedure, and can be understood by their intended readers.

SOPs should be periodically reviewed and revised as necessary to take account of the lessons learned during operation. The first review should take place as soon as possible after a technology or process has been commissioned. This will normally be when all treatment units are functioning as intended and operational staffing is stable, with permanent staff occupying key posts. US EPA (2007) provides further information on preparing SOPs.

Key points from this chapter

Designers should always take account of the operational consequences of their designs. Key points regarding design for effective operation are summarized below.

- Designs should draw on operational experience with existing treatment plants. Designers should visit operational plants and talk to their operators about their experience and the operational problems that they face. Where relevant operational experience is lacking, small-scale pilot initiatives can provide useful operational information.
- Where possible, designs should be modular. This will allow plant capacity to be increased by phased construction and commissioning of additional units in response to increases in load.
- Technology choices should take account of the ways in which resource availability might affect the viability of each technology. Electricity supply, the capacity of the operating organization to manage and operate, and financial capacity to meet ongoing operation and maintenance

costs are particularly important in this respect. When considering mechanized systems, the availability of spare parts and consumables and manufacturers' after-sales services should be taken into account.

- Institutional constraints should be taken into account when determining the likelihood that the operational needs of technology options can be met. If institutional systems to support a particular technology cannot be implemented, that technology should not be considered a viable option.
- Technology choices should take account of the implications of those choices for the types of technology used in other stages in the process.
- Designs should take account of the need to ensure the health and safety of workers while facilitating access to carry out essential operation and maintenance tasks.
- Some treatment units will need to be taken out of service from time to time for maintenance, repair, and the performance of essential operational tasks such as desludging. Alternative paths through the treatment process must be provided to cater for the times when these units are out of service. To allow for this, it will normally be advisable to provide two or more treatment streams so that flow can continue around units that have been temporarily taken out of service.
- Similarly, standby pumps and bypass channels will be required to allow continued operation when treatment units and mechanical devices must be taken out of commission so that essential operation, maintenance, and repair tasks can be carried out.
- Good operator access is essential because operators will tend to neglect tasks that are difficult to carry out. When developing proposals, designers should always ask the questions, 'what operation and maintenance tasks are required for this facility?' and 'does the design facilitate worker access?' Conversely, design layouts and details should make it difficult to adopt practices that might adversely affect plant performance.
- Accurate, good quality construction is a basic requirement for successful operation. Comprehensive contract documentation and good site supervision are essential for a good standard of construction. It will always be advisable for representatives of the organization with operation and maintenance responsibilities to be involved in design decisions and construction supervision.
- The organization charged with preparing treatment facility plans and detailed designs for a treatment plant will normally be required to prepare SOPs for the plant. These should include brief technology descriptions, but their main focus should be on operation, maintenance, and repair tasks, their requirements and their timing.
- SOPs should provide guidance on the action to be taken if operating conditions, in particular the loading on the plant, differ from those assumed in the design.

References

Central Pollution Control Board, India (2007) *Evaluation of Operation and Maintenance of Sewage Treatment Plants in India*, Delhi: CPCB.

Chernicharo, C., van Lier, J., Noyola, A. and Ribeiro, T. (2015) 'Anaerobic sewage treatment: state of the art', *Reviews in Environmental Science and Bio/Technology* 14(4): 649–79 <http://dx.doi.org/10.1007/s11157-015-9377-3> [accessed 17 May 2018].

Department of Water Affairs and Forestry (2002) *An Illustrated Guide to Basic Sewage Treatment Purification Operations* [online], Pretoria <www.dwaf.gov.za/Dir_WQM/docs/sewage/BasicSewageGuide2002_1.pdf> [accessed 1 January 2018].

Fédération Internationale des Ingénieurs-Conseils (FIDIC) (1999) *Conditions of Contract for Construction for Building and Engineering Works Designed by the Employer* [online], 1st edition, Geneva: FIDIC <http://site.iugaza.edu.ps/kshaath/files/2010/12/FIDIC-1999-RED-BOOK.pdf> [accessed 15 February 2018].

Khalil, N., Mittal, A., Raghav, A. and Rajeev, S. (2006) 'UASB technology for sewage treatment in India: 20 years' experience', *Environmental Engineering and Management Journal* 5(5): 1059–69 [online] <www.academia.edu/7422241/UASB_TECHNOLOGY_FOR_SEWAGE_TREATMENT_IN_INDIA_20_YEARS_EXPERIENCE> [accessed 4 March 2017].

Montangero, A. and Strauss, M. (2004) *Faecal Sludge Treatment* [online], Dübendorf, Switzerland: Eawag/Sandec <www.sswm.info/sites/default/files/reference_attachments/STRAUSS%20and%20MONTANEGRO%202004%20Fecal%20Sludge%20Treatment.pdf> [accessed 4 March 2017].

Tayler, K., Siregar, R., Darmawan, B., Blackett, I. and Giltner, S. (2013) 'Development of urban septage management models in Indonesia', *Waterlines* 32(3): 221–36 <http://dx.doi.org/10.3362/1756-3488.2013.023> [accessed 17 May 2018].

The Constructor: Civil Engineering Home (undated) 'Joints in liquid retaining concrete structures' [online] <https://theconstructor.org/structural-engg/joints-concrete-water-tanks/6723/> [accessed 16 February 2018].

US Department of Labor (undated) 'Occupational Safety and Health Administration: Fall protection systems criteria and practices', Clause 1926.502(b)(1), [online] <www.osha.gov/pls/oshaweb/owadisp.show_document?p_table=STANDARDS&p_id=10758> [accessed 15 February 2018].

US EPA (2007) *Guidance for Preparing Standard Operating Procedures (SOPs)* [online], Washington, DC: Office of Environmental Information, United States Environmental Protection Agency <https://nepis.epa.gov/Exe/ZyPDF.cgi/P1008GTX.PDF?Dockey=P1008GTX.PDF> [accessed 28 December 2017].

CHAPTER 6

Faecal sludge and septage reception and preliminary treatment

This chapter examines options for reception and preliminary treatment of faecal sludge and septage. The term preliminary treatment refers to processes designed to remove gross solids, grit, and fats, oil, and grease (FOG) in order to guarantee trouble-free operation of later treatment processes. After a brief introduction, the chapter provides guidance on arrangements for delivery and reception of incoming material. It explores the possibility of designing reception units to attenuate peak flows. The importance of coarse screening is emphasized. Other preliminary treatment requirements, including fine screening, grit removal, partial digestion, and FOG removal, are then discussed. Guidance is given on when to include provision for each of these requirements and the options for making that provision. Each technology is then described and appropriate design guidance is provided.

Keywords: access, reception, preliminary treatment, screening, stabilization

Introduction

Faecal sludge and septage reception facilities provide the interface between faecal sludge and septage delivery vehicles and the treatment plant. They should:

- allow for faecal sludge and septage transport vehicle access, providing adequate space for vehicles to discharge their contents and exit the treatment facility;
- contain septage/faecal sludge during discharge so that it does not splash and overflow; and
- direct it to the next treatment unit.

Where a facility receives both faecal sludge and septage, it will often be appropriate to provide each with its own receiving facility.

Following the reception facility, preliminary treatment is required to protect subsequent treatment processes and, in some cases, improve the effectiveness of those processes. It should always include coarse screening to remove rags and bulky objects that might cause blockages or otherwise disrupt subsequent treatment processes. Other possible preliminary treatment functions include grit removal, removal of FOG, and stabilization of fresh sludge in order to reduce its odour and make it more easily treatable. Where the performance of subsequent treatment units may be adversely affected by flow variations, preliminary treatment should also include provision for attenuation of peak flows.

http://dx.doi.org/10.3362/9781780449869.006

Figure 6.1 is a diagrammatic representation of the relationship between these requirements. It distinguishes between treatment processes that will always be required and those that may be required depending on the size of the plant, the characteristics of the material to be treated, and the follow-up treatment processes to be adopted.

For loads that originate from septic tanks serving businesses such as restaurants that generate large quantities of FOG, it may be appropriate to provide a separate reception tank with a baffle and high-level outlet. The baffle will retain FOG, which can then be skimmed off. The remaining contents of the tank can then be directed back into the main septage flow, preferably by gravity or perhaps using the suction pump of a suction tanker.

The information provided in this chapter is applicable to both stand-alone faecal sludge/septage treatment plants and municipal wastewater treatment plants. In the case of the latter, it is possible to discharge septage to an upstream manhole but, for reasons that have already been explained, it will always be better to provide separate receiving and preliminary treatment facilities for faecal sludge and septage prior to solids–liquid separation and co-treatment of the separated solid and liquid streams.

Faecal sludge and septage reception

Vehicle access and traffic flow

Good vehicular access is the first requirement for any faecal sludge or septage treatment plant. Chapter 3 noted the importance of location, emphasizing the desirability of centrality and proximity to the main road network. Beyond these requirements, planners must ensure that on-site access is safe and adequate for the types of vehicle that transport sludge to the facility. This requires avoidance of steep gradients, adequately paved access roads with sufficient width to carry septage delivery vehicles, and a layout at the septage reception point that allows vehicles to either pull through after discharging their load or reverse up to the discharge position. For larger plants, access to vehicle washing facilities and vehicle parking facilities should be considered. Where faecal sludge is delivered in hand- or animal-drawn carts, avoidance of steep gradients will be particularly important.

Where septage is delivered by vacuum tanker, the road from the public highway to the septage treatment plant should ideally be wide enough to carry two septage tankers travelling in opposite directions. This requires a minimum of 6.8 metres paved width, although the preferred practice is to provide two lanes, each 3.65 m wide, giving a total width of 7.3 m (See for example UK Government, 2012). For smaller plants, it may be appropriate to provide single lane access with passing places. Single lane access requires a 3.5 m minimum paved width with inter-visible passing places provided at intervals of no more than 200 m.

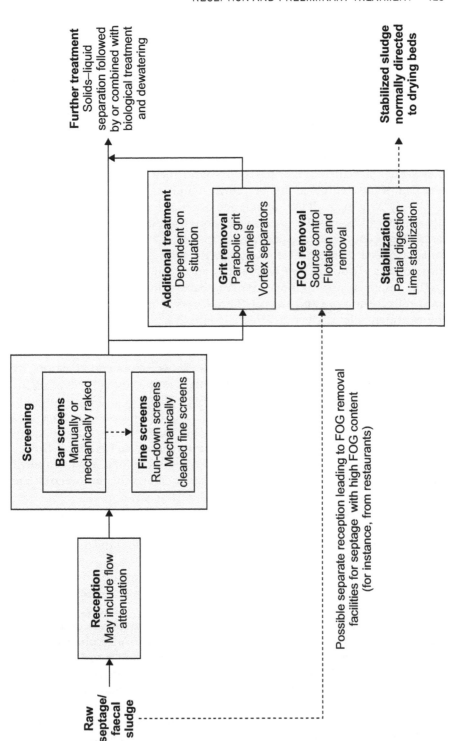

Figure 6.1 Overview of reception and preliminary treatment requirements

The gradient should not normally exceed 8.33 per cent (1 in 12) although short lengths with gradients up to 6 per cent (1 in 16.7) may be allowable (see, for example, East Sussex County Council, undated). The septage discharge area should be flat for at least the length of the longest truck expected, and the transition from the ramp to the flat discharge area should consist of a vertical curve rather than an abrupt change in slope. The layout should include barriers and separation zones to discourage discharge at locations other than the designated discharge point.

A barrier and a small office should be provided at the site entrance so that details of vehicles entering the site and their estimated loads can be recorded. If a weighbridge can be provided and information is collected on the empty weights of all the tankers and other conveyance vehicles entering the site, it will be possible to arrive at a precise estimate of the volume of faecal sludge and/or septage delivered to the plant. The estimate can be based on an assumed septage/faecal sludge specific gravity of 1. The office should incorporate a washbasin for handwashing and a toilet.

The design of turning areas, parking bays, and septage discharge bays must reflect the type and size of the vehicles that will deliver septage to the treatment plant. Overall vehicle lengths vary from about 7.5 m for a 3,000-litre capacity truck to around 10 m for a 10,000-litre capacity truck. Widths vary up to a maximum of about 2.6 m. Based on these figures, a standard truck parking bay should measure between 8 m and 11 m long by 3.5 m wide, the length depending on the length of the largest truck using the facility. AASHTO (American Association of State Highway and Transportation Officials) standards suggest an inside turning radius of at least 8.6 m for a fixed wheelbase truck (AASHTO, 2004). Based on this, the minimum internal radius of turning bays should be 10 m. Using this internal radius, Figure 6.2 shows a possible tanker turning and discharge area arrangement for a small treatment plant. The 5 m width at the top of the diagram allows for the sweep of the vehicle's front wheels as it backs up to the discharge point.

The road surface at the discharge point should slope towards the septage reception facility so that spilled septage can be washed back into the treatment stream. Low bunds should be provided as necessary around the discharge area to prevent run-off of spillage.

The access road and turning area should have a hard surface. Gravel and water-bound macadam cost less than hard surfacing but will deteriorate rapidly under the wheels of heavily loaded tankers. Bituminous surface treatment over a rolled granular base and sub-base will tend to deteriorate under heavy traffic loading and will require periodic replacement. An asphalt concrete carpet laid over a granular base and sub-base will therefore always be the best option. The carpet depth should be at least 50 mm and preferably 100 mm. It will be advisable to take advice from a road and/or structural engineer, particularly where the sub-grade is weak. Concrete is another option but is relatively expensive. The extra expense of concrete surfacing might be justified for any lengths of the approach road that are subject to regular flooding.

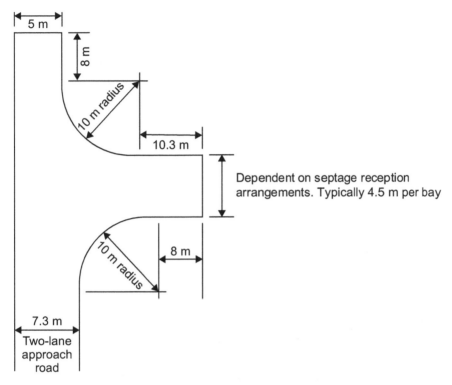

Figure 6.2 Typical tanker turning and discharge area layout

Where electricity is available, it will be advisable to provide lighting at the vehicle reception area to facilitate discharge of loads that arrive after dark.

Reception facilities

As noted in the introduction to this chapter, reception facilities must contain faecal sludge and septage during discharge and convey it on to the next stage in treatment in a controlled manner without spillage and splashing. Prevention of splashing and spillage will be especially important where faecal sludge is manually handled. Possible configurations for receiving faecal sludge and septage include:

- screens incorporated into the first unit in the treatment process;
- chambers with side walls and benching;
- flat aprons, surrounded by a low protective wall; and
- pipework with specialized couplings, designed to take the quick-release coupling at the end of a vacuum tanker discharge hose.

The first option is simple but does not prevent overflow and splashing during septage discharge. Photo 6.1, which shows overflowing septage during direct discharge through a screen into an Imhoff tank, illustrates this point. Another weakness of this arrangement is that the pressure from the falling

Photo 6.1 Direct discharge to an Imhoff tank: an unsatisfactory arrangement resulting in spillage

septage may force solids through the screen. For these reasons, this option should not be used.

Chamber with sidewall and benching. Photo 6.2 is an example of a reception chamber with sidewalls. The depth of the walls is about 1 m, which should be sufficient to prevent splashing beyond the chamber limits. The outlet pipe to subsequent treatment units is in the right-hand sidewall. The floor of such chambers should be benched (sloped) to direct flows to the outlet pipe and provide sufficient slope to avoid sludge accumulation on the flat chamber floor. As explained later, coarse screening should be provided. One option for doing this would be to lengthen the chamber sufficiently to allow installation of a screen, as shown in Figure 6.5. Alternatively, if flow attenuation is required, a chamber with a larger plan area and a small diameter pipe outlet followed by a screening chamber could be provided, as shown in Figure 6.4.

Flat apron with low protective wall. Photo 6.3 shows an example of the flat apron reception option. In this arrangement, septage is discharged onto an apron, which slopes towards an outlet incorporating a coarse screen. In the example shown,

Photo 6.2 Septage reception chamber, Tegal, Indonesia

Photo 6.3 Flat apron receiving unit that could be improved by adjusting the levels so that the apron is lower than the road, Gaborone, Botswana

septage is flowing out of the receiving apron through the openings in the low surrounding wall. These openings have a purpose in that they allow spillage and water used to wash the reception area to flow onto the apron. The problem of outflow during discharge could easily be overcome by adjusting the levels so that the apron is lower than the road on which the tanker stands. A height difference of 150 mm should be sufficient. The surrounding wall should extend a further 150–200 mm above the road surface. The side walls should extend to the same height and the height of the back wall should be 600 mm or more.

Photo 6.4 Reception arrangement with hinged plastic cover, Dumaguete, Philippines
Source: photo by Isabel Blackett

Photo 6.4 shows an arrangement for preventing splashing during septage discharge, requiring insertion of the tanker hose into an opening in a hinged plastic cover, which protects the operator from back splashing. It would be possible to modify the chamber shown in Photo 6.2 to incorporate a similar arrangement. The arrangement could have been improved by lowering the level of the reception point relative to the tanker so that the tanker hose does not sag. With the levels as shown, it will not be possible to drain the hose completely. Spillage will inevitably result when the hose is removed from the reception point, causing a nuisance and increasing the risk that the tanker operator will come into contact with septage.

Pipework with specialized coupling. Photo 6.5 shows a quick-release coupling arrangement installed at the Pula Gebang septage treatment plant in Jakarta, Indonesia. The tanker backs up to the pipe, connects its hose to the coupling and discharges its septage load. The pipe conveys the septage to mechanized screening and grit removal facilities, which will be described later in this chapter. The Pula Gebang arrangement provides two discharge points for each screening/grit removal unit, with the flow path from one or other of the discharge points selected by operating manually controlled valves.

In this arrangement, the discharge point should be at a height that allows gravity flow from the tanker through the screening/grit removal unit. In the Indonesian units, gravity flow was not possible when the septage level in the tanker dropped, creating a need to pump the septage. Operators suggested that this had caused problems with the screening/grit removal units. To save time and fuel, tanker drivers were discharging septage into a channel that bypassed the screens, allowing material which should have been screened out to pass to the downstream treatment processes. In Manila, both Manila Water and Maynilad Water Services are using systems that combine a coupling pipe with an automated data entry unit into which information about the load can be entered. Such systems might be appropriate for large cities, provided

Photo 6.5 Septage reception pipe with quick-release coupling, Pula Gebang, Indonesia

that systems exist for using the information collected and maintaining the automated data entry system. For smaller treatment plants and where the support systems for an automated data entry system cannot be guaranteed, simpler manual entry systems will normally be a more appropriate data recording option.

This section has described several options for receiving septage and faecal sludge. Points to consider when choosing between these options include site conditions, the topography, the characteristics of faecal sludge or septage being discharged, and the type of delivery vehicle. The design must:

- ensure that discharged material is contained;
- minimize spillage;
- allow for washing the discharge area and directing washwater back into the treatment stream;
- have adequate slopes to direct flow to an outlet fitted with a coarse screen;
- be at a height that allows gravity flow from the bottom of a truck; and
- minimize contact between workers and the material discharged.

Of the arrangements described, only that shown in Photo 6.3 will allow spillage to be directed back into the reception facility. Where this is not possible, the design should include provision to collect spillage water and direct it via a series of open drains or shallow pipes to a later stage in the treatment process. Points to consider when choosing an appropriate receiving facility option are as follows:

- Discharge to an apron will often be the best option for septage discharged from large tankers.

- The discharge chamber option should be considered for smaller flows, including those from tankers with up to 4 m³ capacity.
- When the discharge chamber option is chosen, the possibility of amending the design to include an anti-splashing arrangement similar to that used in Dumaguete (Photo 6.4) might be considered.
- Discharge via a pipe fitted with a quick-release coupling will be required for some mechanical screening/grit removal devices. Where suitable pipes and quick-release couplings are available, this option could also be used to direct flow to a discharge chamber.

Sizing flow reception facilities

Flow reception facilities must be sized to accommodate the peak instantaneous flow delivered to the plant without overflowing. This requires that either:

- the reception facility has capacity to temporarily store the liquid that accumulates because the tanker discharge rate is greater than the rate at which flow can exit the facility; or
- its outlet is large enough to carry the peak flow.

The first arrangement has the advantage that it results in some attenuation (reduction) in the peak flow to following treatment units. This point is considered in more detail in the sub-section on flow attenuation later in this chapter.

Peak flow and discharge time estimation. Reception facilities must be designed to deal with the peak flow rate, which will normally occur when a tanker starts to deliver its load. For larger plants with provision to receive flow from more than one tanker at a time, the peak flow will be some multiple of the peak flow from a single tanker, depending on the number of tankers that can deliver at the same time.

Where no hose is attached to the tanker delivery pipe, as shown in Photos 6.1 and 6.3, the situation will approximate to the theoretical case of discharge through a submerged orifice with a short tube outlet. This situation is represented by the equation:

$$Q = 1000\, C_d A_{pipe} \sqrt{2gh}$$

where: Q = flow rate (l/s)

C_d = discharge coefficient (empirically determined; see Dally et al., 1993)

A_{pipe} = area of the discharge pipe (m²)

g = acceleration due to gravity (9.81 m/s²)

h = height of the water in the tanker above the discharge pipe (m)

The value of C_d given in standard texts for a submerged orifice with a short tube outlet, with no downstream surcharge, is 0.8 (Dally et al., 1993). The head on the outlet is dependent on the depth of liquid in the tanker, varying from a maximum when the tank is full to zero when the tank is empty. The diameter of the holding tank on a vacuum tanker is typically 1–2 m, depending on the

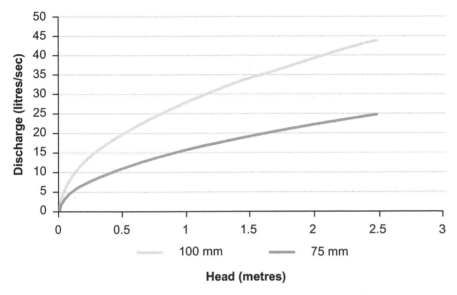

Figure 6.3 Flow–head relationship for discharge from a vacuum tanker by discharge pipe diameter

capacity of the tank. Figure 6.3 plots the flow rates predicted by the equation for 75 mm and 100 mm diameter discharge pipes that are typical of smaller and larger tankers, respectively.

If discharge from a tanker is through a short length of hose, as shown in Photo 6.4, friction will result in slightly reduced flow as liquid travels through the hose. Conversely, the head at the outlet, and hence the flow, will increase if the hose discharges below the bottom level of the tank. The net impact on flow will be limited. In practice, tanker operators often reduce the discharge rate by only partially opening the valve on the outlet pipe. It will be difficult to allow for this theoretically. In view of this, the best approach will usually be to measure the discharge rate directly and to check it against the predicted discharges given by Figure 6.3. The simplest way to measure discharge is to direct the flow from the tanker into a container or chamber of known capacity and plan dimensions, measure the rate at which the septage level rises in the container, and use this information to calculate the discharge rate. This will give information on the flow rate at a specific head. Actual flow will reduce as the liquid level in the tanker drops, as shown by Figure 6.3.

One option for calculating the time required for a tanker to discharge is to integrate theoretically calculated flow rates over time as the level in the tanker drops. A simpler option will be to record the time taken for a tanker to discharge. The author's observation of a 4,000 litre tanker with a 75 mm diameter hose revealed a total emptying time of about 200 seconds, giving an average discharge rate of 20 l/s. This is in line with the discharge rates indicated by Figure 6.3, although direct comparison is not possible because discharge was through a hose extending below the tanker outlet into a sewer manhole.

Responses to a discussion topic on the Sustainable Sanitation Alliance (SuSanA) web forum (SuSanA, 2016) suggest that actual discharge times are often longer than suggested by the calculations. The likely explanation for this, as noted in the previous paragraph, is that tanker drivers do not open the discharge valve fully when discharging to tank or chamber in order to avoid splashing.

Flow attenuation

The flow to faecal sludge and septage treatment plants is confined to the period, typically spanning 8–10 hours, when the plant is open to receive loads. Within that period, flow is intermittent, peaking when tankers start to discharge and reducing to zero at other times. The resulting flow variations may adversely affect the performance of treatment units. In theory it would be possible to equalize flows by storing incoming flows after screening and grit removal and ahead of the main treatment units, releasing it slowly for treatment. This is sometimes done at large municipal wastewater plants, using pumps to forward flow from the storage tank to later treatment units (Ongerth, 1979). Another option is to use a float-controlled constant head draw-off arm to allow liquid to be drawn off at a constant rate regardless of the depth of liquid in the tank. Unfortunately, both pumps and constant head draw-off arms are vulnerable to blockages, particularly at the small sizes that will be required to equalize the low flows received at most faecal sludge and septage treatment plants. For this reason, full flow equalization over a 24-hour period is unlikely to be feasible, except perhaps for the largest treatment plants. A better option will be to aim to achieve some attenuation (reduction) of peak flows, using relatively simple methods.

Some flow attenuation through a chamber like that shown in Photo 6.2 will occur if the diameter of the outlet pipe is equal to or smaller than that of the tanker outlet. However the effect will be limited unless the size of the chamber is increased to minimize the liquid depth in the chamber. Figure 6.4 shows a possible arrangement for modifying the discharge chamber to attenuate flows. This arrangement should be considered for discharge from tankers. It will be

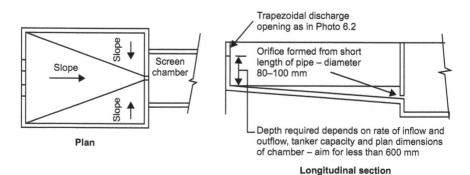

Figure 6.4 Simple arrangement for attenuating discharge flows

less appropriate when faecal sludge from pit latrines is delivered in barrels and unloaded manually since this material is likely to contain bulky objects that might block the outlet. The key features of the design are (a) the increased plan dimensions of the reception chamber, which provides storage, and (b) the small diameter pipe at the outlet, which restricts flow out of the chamber. The diameter of this should not be less than 75 mm. The large plan dimension of the chamber will reduce the depth of septage, so restricting the head and hence the flow rate through the orifice.

A suggested procedure for designing a flow attenuation chamber of the type shown in Figure 6.4 is as follows:

1. Determine the maximum discharge volume to the chamber at any one time. This will normally be equal to the capacity of the largest tanker that will use the facility. For larger plants, it may be necessary to allow for the possibility that more than one tanker will discharge at the same time.
2. Calculate the attenuation chamber area required to contain this flow while limiting the liquid depth in the chamber to a maximum of 0.5 m. At this depth, Figure 6.3 shows that, for a chamber outlet that is the same diameter as the tanker outlet pipe, reducing the maximum depth in the chamber to 0.5 m will reduce the peak flow rate to less than 50 per cent of the discharge rate from a tanker discharging at a head of 2 m.
3. Select chamber dimensions that will provide the required area, typically choosing a length to width ratio of between 2 and 3 to 1.
4. Determine floor levels that allow sufficient longitudinal and transverse fall to direct flows to the outlet point. Falls should typically be about 1 in 40, possibly rather more for thick sludges.
5. Recalculate the required depth at the upstream and downstream ends of the chamber, allowing for the variations in floor level. It may be appropriate to recalculate the plan dimensions at this point to keep the maximum liquid depth at the outlet below the 0.5 m figure.
6. Ensure that the opening or pipe through which tankers discharge is at least 200 mm above the calculated top liquid level.
7. Ensure that the side walls are high enough to prevent splashing during discharge.
8. Provide a water connection and hosing arrangements to allow the chamber to be washed down after use.

This procedure will overestimate the maximum depth in the chamber since it does not allow for outflow while the tanker is discharging. More accurate assessment is possible using computer simulation of inflows and outflows as the liquid level in the chamber rises; however, the simple procedure described here will provide a good initial idea of the size of chamber needed. The suggested 0.5 m depth is an arbitrary figure. If greater flow attenuation is required, the plan dimensions could be further increased.

Screening

Screening overview

Screening needs depend on both faecal sludge and septage composition and the requirements of subsequent treatment processes. The composition of the material to be treated is strongly influenced by toilet type. Faecal sludge from direct-drop pit latrines may include hard items used for anal cleansing, for instance corn cobs, and items thrown into the pit through the squatting hole. One study in Malawi found old clothes, shoes, bottles, plastic carrier bags, maize cobs, menstrual cloths, and medicine bottles in pits, together with gravel, stones, and even large rocks that had fallen from pit walls (WASTE, undated). Pit emptiers may separate bulky items prior to transport to the septage treatment plant but some objects are likely to remain in the faecal sludge delivered to the plant. It is much harder for bulky objects to pass through water seals, so septage from systems incorporating pour-flush and cistern-flush water closets (WCs) should be mostly free of bulky solids. However, it is possible that plastic bags and other materials will be contained in such waste. Removal of bulky solids is essential since they would otherwise block pipes and disrupt treatment processes. Smaller solids may be compatible with non-mechanized processes while adversely affecting the performance of some mechanized processes. Taken together, these points suggest the following:

- Coarse screens to remove rags and large solids from the septage flow should be provided for all treatment plants.
- Racks to catch rags and large solids may be desirable for faecal sludge removed from direct-drop pit latrines. These should be used prior to screening.
- Fine screening may be required where treatment processes include mechanical equipment that may be susceptible to damage by solids that can pass through a coarse screen. This may follow coarse screening, but some mechanical fine screens receive influent direct from tankers.

Where end use of biosolids is planned, screening will also improve the quality of the final biosolid product by removing non-organic items from the waste stream.

Coarse screening

Coarse screening options include manually raked screens, run-down screens, and various types of mechanical screen, some of which also remove grit. Because of their simplicity, robustness, and relatively low cost, manually raked coarse screens will normally be the best option for smaller septage treatment plants serving small to medium-sized towns with design populations up to around 400,000. For larger plants, mechanical screening may be appropriate. However, it will always be advisable to assess operation and maintenance requirements and costs before opting for a mechanical option. A manual bypass should always be provided for mechanical screens. The basic design principles are similar for manually and mechanically raked screens.

Manually raked bar screens. To facilitate raking, manually raked screens should consist of parallel bars rather than a grid. The clear spacing between the bars should not be less than 25 mm and should normally be between 40 and 50 mm. Figure 6.5 shows a recommended arrangement for a manually raked bar screen set within a concrete or blockwork septage reception chamber. This screening arrangement could be incorporated into a reception unit of the type shown in Photo 6.2, although this would limit the scope for flow attenuation.

Mechanically raked bar screens. Mechanically raked bar screens are an option for large treatment plants, for which manually raked screens will have high labour requirements. They are more expensive than manually raked screens, but the main challenges that they present are operational. Mechanically raked screens have low power requirements; nevertheless they will be ineffective if the power source is unreliable. Their performance is also dependent on the existence of adequate maintenance systems and reliable supply chains for spare parts and replacement components. To allow for the possibility of screen breakdown, a bypass channel fitted with a manually raked screen should always be provided for mechanical screens.

Photo 6.6 shows a mechanically raked screen, installed at a wastewater treatment plant in Chandigarh, India. The screen is curved, with a rotating rake powered by a small motor. The rake moves material caught on the screen upwards and into a trough at the top of the screen. The mechanism is simple and the main operational issue is likely to be failure of the drive system from the motor to the rotating rake.

Operational and design considerations for raked screens. Key design considerations, many of which are illustrated by Figure 6.5, are as follows:

- *At least two screens should be provided in parallel.* This will allow plant operation to continue when one screen is out of service for repair or maintenance.
- To avoid ponding of stagnant faecal sludge or septage, *the floor of the screening chamber should slope longitudinally towards the outlet.* In addition, benching should be provided to prevent ponding in the corners of the screening chamber.
- *The screen bars should run from top to bottom,* providing openings over the whole depth of the screen.
- *Screens should never be vertical* since this makes raking very difficult. Crites and Tchobanoglous (1998) recommend a slope between 45° and 60° to the horizontal. However, this criterion relates to screens on the inlets to wastewater treatment plants, which often have to be deep because of the depth of the incoming sewer. This is not a factor for septage treatment

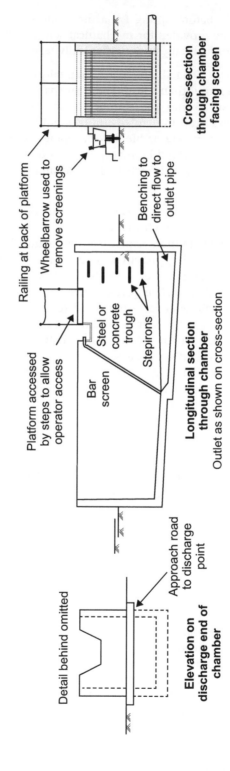

Figure 6.5 Typical manually raked screen arrangement

Photo 6.6 Curved screen with rotating raking mechanism

plants, since tankers discharge to a chamber at or above ground level, allowing the use of screens with flatter slopes.

- *Screens are subject to a corrosive environment.* Materials that are resistant to corrosion, such as cast iron and stainless steel, are expensive. The most cost-effective approach to minimizing corrosion will normally be to use steel with a suitable paint or coating, possibly tar or epoxy-based.
- Tapering the bars slightly inwards from front to back will reduce the likelihood of solids becoming jammed between the bars.
- *The bars of manual screens should be bent over at the top*, as shown by Figure 6.5. This will allow screenings to be raked into a trough, from which they can be pulled or swept out and deposited in a wheelbarrow or portable bin. For this to be possible, the screen chamber must be

raised above ground level. Small holes in the bottom of the trough will allow excess water to drain back into the treatment process.

- The wheelbarrow or portable bin will be used to transport the screenings to a location where they can be handled and disposed of as solid waste. These bins and wheelbarrows are heavy when filled with screenings, and therefore *an unobstructed paved path should be provided between the screening chamber and the screenings disposal site* to facilitate their movement.

- *A platform should be provided behind the screen* to allow the operator easy access to rake the screen. This is an important, but often neglected, design feature. Figure 6.5 shows a platform behind the screen, accessed by steps and with railings provided at the back and sides. The railings at the steps are replaced by a removable chain. Removable chains could also be provided at the front of the platform, immediately above the screens.

- *Operators will require access to the chamber to clear blockages.* For deeper chambers, this can be provided by step irons, as shown on Figure 6.5, a ladder or steps leading down to the top of the benching in the chamber.

- *A water point with a hose connection should be provided close to the screen* to allow the screens and chamber floor to be washed down at the end of the working day.

Design criteria for bar screens. Bar screen design calculations should be based on the peak flow generated when the tanker discharges, modified as necessary to take account of any flow attenuation arrangements provided prior to screening. As already indicated, the peak discharge rate from a single tanker may be measured directly or may be calculated theoretically. Where the design provides for two or more tankers to discharge their contents, the design should be based on the discharge from the maximum number of tankers that can discharge simultaneously.

Design parameters for coarse screens include the approach velocity, the bar width and depth, the clear spacing between the bars, the screen angle to the horizontal, and the allowable head loss through the screen. Table 6.1 sets out recommended values for these parameters. These recommendations apply to coarse screens protecting wastewater treatment processes.

The approach velocity recommendation assumes reasonably steady flow in a channel upstream of the screen. This assumption does not apply

Table 6.1 Coarse bar screen design criteria

Item	Unit	Manually cleaned	Mechanically cleaned
Bar width	mm	5–15	5–15
Bar depth	mm	25–40	25–40
Clear spacing between bars	mm	25–50	15–75
Angle to horizontal	degrees	45–60	60–90
Approach velocity	m/s	0.3–0.6	0.6–1
Allowable head loss	mm	150	150

Source: Crites and Tchobanoglous (1998)

to the situation normally found at faecal sludge and septage treatment plants, where the flow enters the system immediately upstream of the screen and flow conditions are highly variable. Because the total width of the screen openings is less than that of the chamber within which the screen is situated, the flow velocity through the screens must be greater than the approach velocity. This, in turn, means that the velocity head through the screen is greater than that of the upstream flow. Conservation of energy requires that there is a drop in the top liquid level through the screen. Head losses occur at entry to and exit from the screen. Standard texts such as Metcalf and Eddy represent the head loss through the screen by the equation:

$$H_{loss} = \frac{1}{0.7}\left(\frac{v_s^2 - v_a^2}{2g}\right)$$

where: H_{loss} = head loss (m);
v_s = flow velocity through the openings in the screen (m/s);
v_a = approach velocity (m/s); and
g = acceleration due to gravity (9.81 m/s²)
0.7 is an empirical coefficient to account for turbulence and eddy losses for a clean screen. The suggested coefficient for a partially blocked screen is 0.6 (Crites and Tchobanoglous, 1998; Metcalf and Eddy, 2003).

In practice, this equation is not determinate because the relationship between v_s and v_a is dependent on the head loss through the screen. The situation is further complicated by the intermittent and variable nature of discharges to the treatment plant. When a tanker starts to discharge, the liquid level upstream of the screen rises until an equilibrium level is reached, at which point the flow through the screen equals the discharge. The level then starts to drop as the flow from the tanker reduces. The equilibrium level may be influenced by downstream conditions. Clogging of the screen will reduce the area available for flow through the screen and so increase the head loss across the screen.

Given the relatively small discharge flows received at most plants, it will normally be sufficient to use the following criteria to size screening chambers:

- width: minimum 300 mm, preferably 450 mm to allow easy access;
- depth: minimum 500 mm, preferably 750 mm;
- floor slope: 1 in 80 (1.25 per cent).

These criteria may result in higher flow velocities through the screen than suggested by standard texts. The simplest way to reduce the flow velocity would be to reduce the floor slope but a slope of at least 1 in 80 is desirable to allow any settled material to be washed through the screen and out of the screen chamber.

The 150 mm maximum allowable head loss through the screen stated in Table 6.1 is a conservative figure. Other texts allow a larger head loss. For instance, Escritt (1972), suggests that a maximum differential of up to 750 mm is acceptable. Regardless of this, SOPs should stress the need for regular screen raking. For further information on screens and grit channels see US EPA (1999).

Fine screens

Fine screens are now routinely used to screen the influent to municipal wastewater treatment plants and there are also examples of their use to screen septage. They remove a higher proportion of solids than coarse screens and many also remove grit. This sub-section provides an introduction to types of fine screen that are already in use at septage treatment plants in East Asia. It first examines run-down screens, which have the advantage that they have no mechanical components, and then describes the mechanical screens that have been installed in sludge treatment plants in Indonesia and the Philippines.

Run-down screens. Run-down screens are designed to allow water to flow through the screen while solids slide down to the bottom of the screen, from where they can be manually removed. Run-down screens are simple, with no moving parts, and are sometimes used in place of raked coarse screens. They are normally manufactured from stainless steel with a wedge wire screen, giving a much finer aperture size than raked coarse screens. The fine aperture size means that the screen should remove significant amounts of sand and grit in addition to coarse solids. Photo 6.7 shows a run-down screen installed at Jakarta's Pula Gebang septage treatment plant.

Run-down screens require much more head than conventional raked screens. This will create a need for pumping unless the treatment plant site has a good

Photo 6.7 Run-down screen at Pula Gebang septage treatment plant

slope. The performance of the Pula Gebang screen highlights another problem. Some septage flows down rather than through the screen and is allowed to join the flow that has passed through the screen, providing a route for screened solids to re-enter the flow downstream of the screen. This could have been avoided by directing this flow back to the head of the screen, but this would require pumping and so increases system complexity and cost. In most situations, a simple manually raked screen is a better option than a run-down screen.

Mechanically cleaned fine screens. At both Duri Kosambi and Pula Gebang septage treatment plants in Jakarta, screening is provided by Huber ROTAMAT Ro3.3 units, which are designed to deal with septage. Other manufacturers provide similar equipment. For the facilities in Jakarta, each unit incorporates an integrated screenings press and an unaerated grit trap with grit classifier. The integration of these components within a single unit reduces the required footprint while the enclosed nature of the unit ensures that odour problems are minimized. The two tubular inclined extensions enclose rotating screws, which lift solids while allowing liquid to fall back into the enclosed horizontal section of the screen unit. The clearance on the first screw is slightly larger, allowing grit-sized particles to fall back into the liquid flow while retaining larger waste particles. The clearances on the second screw are smaller and ensure that this screw lifts grit. Screenings and grit emerge at the top of the screw tubes and fall into the two plastic waste containers positioned as shown in Photo 6.8. Septage is delivered

Photo 6.8 Combined mechanical screening and grit removal, Jakarta

to the screening system at the Jakarta treatment plants from trucks via pipework with a quick-release coupling, as also shown in Photo 6.8.

Because of their relative complexity and need for a reliable supply chain for replacement parts, mechanically raked fine screens should only be considered where there is a need to protect sensitive mechanical equipment from damage.

Operational and design considerations for mechanical screens. Most of the points already made regarding the operational and design requirements of hand-raked screens also apply to mechanically raked screens. However, mechanical screens are more likely to fail than static manually operated units due to their reliance on moving parts, some of which are installed in a corrosive environment. Although mechanical screens can reduce daily labour requirements, they require skilled mechanics for maintenance and repair. They are reliant on reliable supply systems for spare parts and replacement components, and these in turn depend on adequate budgeting and procurement systems. Costs and procurement difficulties will be greater if replacement parts are only available from overseas suppliers.

Like other mechanical equipment, mechanical screens require a reliable electricity supply. They also require a reliable water supply, capable of delivering washwater at high pressure. Precise requirements should be confirmed with the screen manufacturer but the required pressure is typically around 4 bar (400 kPa). Where the pressure in the public water system is low, it will be necessary to either install a booster pump or provide the treatment plant with its own borehole-based supply.

Most mechanical screens are intended for use with wastewater. When considering the use of a mechanical screen to screen faecal sludge or septage, it will be important to ensure that it can deal with the high solids loading to be expected in the influent. High FOG content may also be an issue if faecal sludge is collected from restaurants or kitchens. The possibility that modifications will be required to deal with high solids and/or FOG content should be discussed with manufacturers after obtaining information on typical characteristics of the material to be screened. Possibilities to be discussed include the use of hot washwater to remove FOG, shorter cycle periods to prevent blinding from higher solids, and channel modifications or additional protection for the lower portion of the screens to better resist impacts from larger items.

Disposal of screenings

Options for disposal of screenings should be considered during the planning stage. Where a suitable sanitary landfill facility is available close to the treatment plant site, the preferred option will be to temporarily store screenings on-site and then to remove them to the landfill. In the frequently encountered situation that a suitable controlled landfill is not available, alternative arrangements for disposal of screenings will be required. One option would be to reserve an area within the treatment plant site for their disposal. This should be provided with a suitable impermeable liner and leachate drainage and removal system, and protected from storm run-off in the same way as a solid waste landfill. Collection and treatment of leachate will be the biggest challenge. One response to this challenge is to elevate the screening disposal site sufficiently to allow leachate to drain to the plant liquid treatment facilities. If this is not possible, separate treatment for the leachate will be required, perhaps in a series of small ponds.

Screen manufacturers produce equipment for compacting and washing screenings but such equipment is only appropriate for large faecal sludge/septage treatment facilities. Experience with manual washing of screenings is limited but it is difficult to rinse all faecal material from soft materials such as cloth. It is arguably more important to ensure that screenings are dry before disposal to landfill (Thompson (2012) summarizes UK requirements on this). The simplest way to dry screenings will be to store them under cover for several weeks.

Operators who handle screenings will be exposed to pathogens, particularly when the screened material includes items such as diapers. Screens should be designed to minimize the need for direct operator contact with screened material but it will be difficult to avoid contact altogether. In view of this, operators should be encouraged to wear gloves and other protective clothing when working with screenings. Regulations in some countries may require that operators who transport screenings to a landfill are licensed. This will help to ensure that the operation is safe for operators and the general public but may lead to some increase in costs. The possibility of introducing licensing systems for operators who transport screenings and other potentially hazardous materials to landfills should be considered. Of course, such systems will only be effective if they can be enforced.

Grit removal

Faecal sludge and septage may contain high concentrations of grit, particularly when removed from pits or tanks with unlined walls or floors. This high grit content will increase the rate at which sludge accumulates in tanks, ponds, pipes, and channels, and may also damage mechanical equipment. The options for responding to the presence of grit are to either:

- accept the higher rate of sludge accumulation that will occur if grit removal is omitted; or
- provide for grit removal during preliminary treatment.

Because of the highly varying loading on faecal sludge and septage treatment plants, grit removal is not a simple task. Accordingly, as already indicated in Chapter 4, it will often be advisable to accept a higher rate of sludge accumulation and make no provision for grit removal. This option will be appropriate for small to medium-sized plants that use non-enclosed technologies, such as sludge drying beds, anaerobic ponds, settling-thickening tanks, and gravity thickeners, that have no enclosed tanks or mechanical equipment. Grit will then be removed along with other solids that settle in the ponds or tanks. To ensure that grit does not settle in the pipes that connect reception and screening facilities to treatment units, the aim should be to lay pipes to gradients that allow periodic flushing flows with a velocity of at least 1 m/s. Where the site topography does not allow this, channels should be provided, rather than pipes, as these will be easier to clean.

Grit removal should be considered in the following situations:

- at treatment plants designed for a hydraulic loading of greater than around 250 m³/day;
- where subsequent treatment units include either enclosed tanks, for instance, biodigesters, or mechanical equipment that might be affected by the presence of grit;
- where investigation shows that the influent contains large quantities of grit, as might be the case with faecal sludge removed from unlined pit latrines.

It will be advisable to assess the amount of grit at the start of the treatment plant design process. Assessment should be carried out for several composite samples taken from tanker loads taken from representative pits and tanks within the planned treatment plant area. The grit content of the composite samples can be roughly estimated by allowing the sample to settle in a settling device such as an Imhoff cone. Experience at the Kanyama sludge treatment plant in Lusaka, Zambia suggests that dilution and stirring may be necessary for thicker sludges (Jeannette Laramee, Stantec, personal communication, November 2017). Grit removal requirements should be discussed with the manufacturers of the mechanical equipment.

Where grit removal is required, the simplest option will be to provide parabolic channels controlled by Parshall flumes. These are simple, and the fact that they are designed to maintain a roughly constant flow velocity regardless of flow should help them to deal with the variation in flow that will occur as a tanker discharges. Vortex grit separators are another option. Both should be more appropriate for septage than for thick sludge. Since neither option has been used for grit removal from septage, both require further investigation. Square horizontal-flow grit chambers, a common grit removal option at wastewater treatment plants, do not handle rapid flow variations well, and so are unlikely to be suitable for use at faecal sludge and septage treatment facilities.

System description

Parabolic grit channels. Parabolic grit channels are now rarely used for wastewater treatment plants because they require a large land area relative to other technologies. However, they are an option for the relatively low flows received at septage treatment plants. They have no moving parts and are easy to maintain. The combination of the parabolic shape with appropriate downstream flow control ensures that the velocity through the channel remains at about 0.3 m/s, the velocity required to settle grit while keeping organic solids in suspension, over a range of flows. The channel has to have sufficient length to allow grit to settle. Two channels are normally provided in parallel so that operation can continue while grit is being removed from one channel. Downstream control is normally provided by a Parshall flume. Photo 6.9 shows a grit channel at a wastewater treatment plant in Naivasha, Kenya.

Vortex separators. Vortex separators are cylindrical units arranged round a vertical axis, into which flow enters tangentially, creating a vortex flow pattern. Lighter particles are pushed to the side of the separator by centrifugal forces and exit with the liquid outflow at the top of the tank. Grit settles by gravity and is collected in a hopper at the bottom of the tank, from where it is removed by a grit pump or an air lift pump. Vortex separators are simple and the only mechanical component is the pump that removes the settled grit. Air lift pumps have the advantage that they are powered by air compressors: a common technology, for which repair and maintenance services may be available locally. Vortex separators are proprietary items, only available from specialist manufacturers. Most are only available in sizes that are larger than will be required for most septage treatment plants. More research is required to determine how they would perform under the unsteady flow regime created by intermittent tanker discharge. For these reasons, they require further investigation before they can be recommended

Photo 6.9 Grit channel at wastewater treatment plant, Naivasha, Kenya

for use to remove grit from septage. The same reservations apply to aerated grit chambers, another grit separation technology commonly used at wastewater treatment plants.

Operational and design considerations – parabolic grit channels. Parabolic grit channels require regular removal of grit. The frequency with which this task will be required should be determined empirically since it will depend on the flow and the grit content of the septage. Grit removal will be required when grit that has previously settled in the channel starts to obstruct flow through the channel.

Constructing an exact parabolic cross-section for a channel is difficult in practice. Grit channels are therefore normally constructed with a cross-section that approximates the parabolic section.

Design criteria and procedure – parabolic grit channels. The flow through a parabolic grit channel can be controlled using a Parshall flume (Crites and Tchobanoglous, 1998). The flume must be constructed to provide specific relationships between the various dimensions, information on which is available in standard texts. Provided there is sufficient fall downstream of the flume to prevent any backwater effect, the equation for flow through a Parshall flume is:

$$Q = kbh^n$$

where: Q is the flow (m³/s);
$\quad\quad$ b is the flume throat width (m);
$\quad\quad$ h is the depth of flow above the floor of the flume, measured upstream of the flume (m);
$\quad\quad$ k is a constant, which varies depending on the flume throat width; and
$\quad\quad$ n is a constant which varies depending on the flume throat width but lies in the range 1.5 to 1.6
The equation can be rewritten as:

$$h = \left(\frac{Q}{kb}\right)^{\frac{1}{n}}$$

For information on Parshall flumes, including the constants and dimensions to be used for a range of flume throat widths, see OpenChannelFlow (undated).

If the equation is simplified to assume that the value of n is 1.5, it can be shown that the velocity upstream of the flow control device remains constant, regardless of depth, if the channel is parabolic in shape.

From standard mathematics theory, it can be shown that the area of a parabola is equal to two thirds of its height multiplied by its width. Thus, the width of parabolic grit channel required at any depth h is given by the equation:

$$w = 1.5\left(\frac{A}{h}\right)$$

where: w = width of grit channel (m); and
$\quad\quad A$ = cross-sectional area of flow (m²)
This equation can then be rewritten as:

$$w = 1.5\left(\frac{Q}{vh}\right)$$

where: v = velocity through the grit channel (m/s)

To maintain a constant velocity of 0.3 m/s, which is sufficient to ensure that organic solids remain in suspension while grit settles, this equation becomes:

$$w = 5\left(\frac{Q}{h}\right)$$

For a given flume throat width, these equations can be used to plot the required width of the grit channel over the anticipated range of flows and depths. First, the depth of flow at the maximum anticipated flow is calculated using the equation:

$$h = \left(\frac{Q}{kb}\right)^{1/n}$$

Table 6.2 gives the dimensions required for grit channels controlled by flumes with throat widths of 152 mm (6″) and 228 mm (9″). The values of k and n used to calculate the flow depths are taken from standard texts and are stated in the table.

The figures shown in Table 6.2, in conjunction with the calculated discharge rates shown in Figure 6.3, suggest that a Parshall flume with a 228 mm throat will be the appropriate choice where the tankers discharging have a 100 mm outlet pipe and there is limited flow attenuation. The grit channel must have sufficient length to allow grit to settle.

The required channel length ($L_{channel}$) may be calculated using the equation:

$$L_{channel} = h\left(\frac{v_h}{v_s}\right)$$

where: h = flow depth (m);
$\quad\quad v_h$ = horizontal flow velocity (m/s); and
$\quad\quad v_s$ = settling velocity (m/s)

The challenge when applying this equation is to determine an appropriate settling velocity. It is commonly assumed that grit channels should be designed to settle particles of 0.2 mm diameter and larger. Using Stokes' Law and assuming a particle specific gravity of 2.65, the settling velocity at 0.3 m/s horizontal velocity is 0.016 m/s, (Environmental Protection Agency 1995, pages 52–55) giving a required channel length of 18.75h. This is commonly rounded up to 20h. The length should be increased by

Table 6.2 Channel dimensions for 152 mm and 228 mm Parshall flume throat widths

Flow (l/s)	152 mm throat width k = 2.06, n = 1.58		228 mm throat width k = 3.07, n = 1.53	
	Flow depth (mm)	Width at surface (mm)	Flow depth (mm)	Width at surface (mm)
10	113	442	62	803
20	175	570	98	1,021
30	227	662	128	1,175
50	313	798	178	1,403

approximately 50 per cent to allow for end turbulence and the possibility that some grit particles will have settling velocities lower than 0.016 m/s. However, care should be taken to avoid making the grit channel too long to avoid the settling of other solids if that is not desired.

FOG removal

FOG are present in faecal sludge and septage to varying degrees depending upon the source. They may accumulate on screens and coat the inside of pipes, increasing the likelihood of blockage. Washing with water that has been heated to at least 60°C is an option for removing FOG from screens, and it will be useful to provide a source of hot water at larger treatment plants (based on statement in Brown and Caldwell (undated) that temperatures in excess of 140°F, equivalent to 60°C, will dissolve grease). However, the main problems are likely to occur later in the treatment process. Because of its density, FOG tends to float to the surface of sludge and form a layer of scum with other floatables. It can affect treatment processes, disrupting microbiological activity in aerobic biological treatment processes, and reducing evaporation and blocking percolation from drying beds. The need for FOG removal will depend on the amount of FOG present in the incoming material and its potential effect on downstream treatment processes.

Ideally, FOG problems at the treatment plant should be mitigated by using source control in the form of grease traps installed in homes and businesses, especially restaurants and fast-food outlets. Additionally, as already noted in the introduction, it may be appropriate to provide separate discharge and FOG removal facilities for loads with a high FOG content to facilitate FOG removal before further treatment.

FOG removal at a treatment plant requires a process or arrangement that facilitates flotation and then removes the FOG that accumulates at the surface of the sludge. The simplest option is to provide a tank or pond with a scum board or baffle around the outlet to prevent the escape of floating material. Where the first treatment unit after screening is an open pond or tank, the design will include provision for retaining scum. Where the first treatment unit after screening is a drying bed or enclosed unit such as a biodigester, any problems caused by FOG could be mitigated by inserting a tank equipped with scum boards after screening. The 'settler' compartment of an anaerobic baffled reactor (ABR) fulfils this role. The challenge with this arrangement will be to periodically remove the scum. Chapter 7 provides further information on this.

Stabilization

Septage taken from septic tanks and wet leach pits will normally offer limited scope for further digestion. In contrast, material taken from container-based sanitation (CBS) systems and frequently emptied cesspits and public toilet vaults is likely to be poorly stabilized, with the result that it smells unpleasant and has poor settling characteristics. For such material, stabilization will be desirable to reduce odours, control vectors, improve settleability, and reduce the unpleasantness associated with handling fresh waste in subsequent treatment processes. Stabilization will be particularly important if either a treatment plant is located within or near a community or downstream treatment steps require a high amount of handling by operators. Stabilization options include lime stabilization, aerobic digestion, and anaerobic digestion.

Lime stabilization

Lime stabilization involves the addition of hydrated lime, $Ca(OH)_2$ (also known as calcium hydroxide or slaked lime), to faecal sludge or septage. This raises the pH of the faecal sludge or septage sufficiently to kill pathogens. Chapter 10 explores this aspect of lime stabilization. The focus here is on its potential role in stabilizing sludge, improving settleability, and reducing odours. Experimental work in the USA in the 1970s established that adding lime did not greatly increase the settleability of poorly settling septage. The focus of the work then turned to mixing lime with the septage, prior to dewatering on sand drying beds (Feige et al., 1975). Bubble aeration was used to effect mixing. With lime dosing, solids concentrations of 20–25 per cent were achieved in less than one week. The research revealed that the recurrent cost of lime dosing was higher than the amortized capital cost of providing dosing facilities.

More recent investigation of the potential role of lime dosing in stabilizing sludges with greater than 11 per cent dry solids found that stabilization did not occur within 24 hours with lime doses capable of producing a pH of 12. Minimal reduction in volatile solids occurred over the 24-hour period of lime stabilization (Anderson, 2014).

Taken together, these findings cast doubt on the value of lime stabilization for preliminary treatment of poorly stabilized faecal sludge. More research is required to ascertain its effects and its viability, and this book does not consider its use at the preliminary treatment stage further. For further information on practical aspects of small-scale lime stabilization in a lower-income country see USAID (2015).

Aerobic digestion

Aerobic digestion presents difficulties as a preliminary treatment step in lower-income countries because it has a high energy requirement, which means that it has a high operational cost and is dependent on a reliable power source. In addition, air transfer to liquids is inhibited by the presence of solids and is dependent on adequate mixing (Henkel, 2010). For these reasons, aerobic digestion is not considered in this book.

Anaerobic digestion

During *anaerobic digestion*, microorganisms break down organic material and convert it to biogas, which consists mainly of methane and carbon dioxide. Depending on the technology used for this process, the biogas can be recovered and reused as a fuel source. In industrialized countries, large-scale anaerobic digesters are commonly used at centralized wastewater treatment plants to stabilize solids. These systems require mechanical mixing, external heating to maintain required temperatures, and large tank volumes to provide the retention time required to achieve pathogen inactivation. Because of their complexity and high capital and operational costs, they are not a good option for faecal sludge and septage treatment in lower-income countries and are not discussed in depth in this book. Small-scale biodigesters have been used for both faecal sludge and septage treatment in lower-income countries and their use is now explored in more detail.

Small-scale biodigesters

System description. Biodigesters have been used for faecal sludge and septage treatment in several countries. There are two basic designs: domed biodigesters and geobag biodigesters. Because biodigesters are simple and do not require power, they can be used in situations where there is no reliable electricity supply and operational capacity is limited. They are most appropriate for the treatment of thicker sludges with a total solids (TS) content exceeding 4 per cent and a volatile solids content in excess of 50 per cent. For septage with a low solids content, a preceding solids–liquid separation step would in theory be useful to minimize the digester volume while maintaining an adequate retention time. However, septage will usually be well stabilized and will not require further stabilization. Benefits of biogas digesters include partial stabilization of volatile solids, homogenization of sludge, and improved sludge dewaterability. Some reduction in total solids load is also possible. Biogas recovery is another potential benefit, although production will be limited where material has already undergone digestion during on-site storage. Vögeli et al. (2014) provide a good general introduction to small-scale anaerobic digestion.

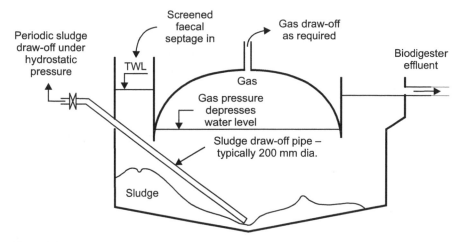

Figure 6.6 Section through fixed-dome biodigester

Fixed-dome digester. Small-scale, fixed-dome digesters are normally constructed with concrete, bricks, and cement plaster to create a gas-tight dome. Volumes typically range from 6 m³ to 100 m³, although systems as large as 200 m³ have been constructed (BORDA, personal communication, November 2017). Historically, fixed-dome digesters have mostly been used for treatment of animal wastes and energy production at the household level. Figure 6.6 is a diagrammatic cross-section of a fixed-dome digester used for treatment of faecal sludge in Kanyama, Zambia. In Kanyama, faecal sludge from pit latrines is delivered to the plant in 60 litre barrels. After screening, it enters the biodigester through the inlet chamber shown on the left side of the figure. Biogas is collected at the top of the dome, pushing the water level down as the gas volume expands, and is piped to nearby cooking facilities. Liquid passes through the digester and exits through the outlet shown to the right.

Geobag digester. A geobag (or geotube) digester is a flexible bag or tube typically fabricated from polyethylene with a length about five times its width. Volumes generally range from 4 m³ to 40 m³. Geobag digesters were initially developed to treat animal wastes. The Mexican organization Sistema Biobolsa has developed systems for partial digestion of human waste. The material in this sub-section draws on experience with two Sistema Biobolsa geobag digester systems, the first an experimental system in Kumasi, Ghana and the second a recently installed system in Antananarivo, Madagascar. For faecal sludge applications, screened sludge is discharged into an inlet pipe at one end of the geobag digester; the sludge is then pushed along the length of the geobag by incoming sludge and exits at the other end through an outlet pipe. Depending on treatment volumes and the desired retention period, several geobag digesters can be connected in series, as shown by Figure 6.7, which is based on the four-geobag configuration of the Antananarivo

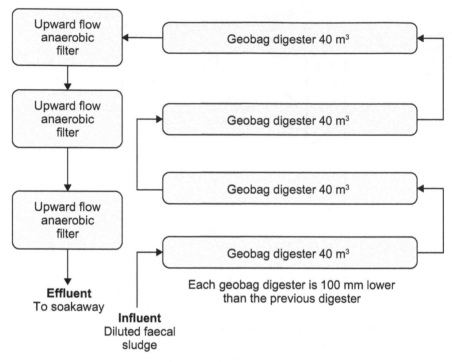

Figure 6.7 General arrangement of geobag digester plant in Antananarivo, Madagascar

system. Biogas collects at the top of the geobags, each of which is fitted with a valved pipe to allow gas to be drawn off and used. Geobags are typically placed in a shallow excavation or at ground level so that they are partially above ground, where they should benefit from natural solar gain. This will increase the internal operating temperature, which should lead to increased reaction and pathogen inactivation rates. However, diurnal temperature fluctuations may also adversely affect microbial activity by methanogens, which are sensitive to changes in temperature. Another possible disadvantage of the arrangement is that the relatively short lifespan of geobag digesters will be further reduced by exposure to ultra-violet light.

Photo 6.10 shows the Antananarivo plant under construction. The geobags are behind the workers. The excavations in the foreground will be filled with gravel to form anaerobic upflow filters to provide secondary treatment. Note the interconnecting pipework, which allows rodding to clear blockages. The Antananarivo biodigester plant is located in a residential area. Geobag biodigesters are closed systems, with sludge exposed to the atmosphere only at the inlet and final outlet points. This should allow them to be used closer to residential areas than technologies that leave a large surface area exposed to the atmosphere. Operational experience with the Antananarivo biodigester should throw further light on this point.

Photo 6.10 Geobag digester, Antananarivo, Madagascar
Source: photo by Georges Mikhael

Input requirements and performance range. Factors that affect the performance of biodigesters include the following:

- *The solids content of the incoming sludge.* This will influence the rate at which sludge accumulates. Small-scale, unmixed biodigesters work on the principle that organics remain in suspension at high solids contents. Sasse (1998) states that stirring will not be required to prevent settling of solids when the TS content of the incoming material is more than 6 per cent, implying that it will be required at lower TS contents. WEF (2010) recommend a dry solids content in the range of 4–6 per cent for large-scale digesters, while Nelson and Lamb (2002) report a wider range of 3–10 per cent solids content as suitable for mixed digesters. If no external mixing is provided, it will be necessary to provide an effective method for desludging of accumulated solids. At the higher solids content of thick slurries, most organics remain in suspension. This is the premise on which small-scale digesters treating livestock manures operate – for such systems, material which enters the digester, other than that which is digested, is assumed to exit the system. Nelson and Lamb (2002) report that a minimum of 11–15 per cent dry solids content is necessary to prevent settling for plug-flow systems treating animal manures. Solids cannot stay in solution and will tend to settle at lower solids concentrations. This suggests that long geobag digesters, which function as plug-flow reactors, may be more suitable for thicker slurries. However, further investigation to substantiate this and the applicability of these operational assumptions to systems treating human faecal sludge is required.

- *The carbon to nitrogen (C:N) ratio of the incoming sludge.* For optimum performance, this should be in the range 16–25:1 (Deublein and Steinhauser, 2011). At the lower C:N ratios of faecal sludge, ammonia accumulation may increase the pH of the reactor contents and lead to reduced performance (Verma, 2002).
- *Solids retention time. Solids retention time (SRT) is the primary parameter used for design of biodigesters treating thick organic wastes.* For such wastes, sedimentation is theoretically minimal and the SRT and hydraulic retention time (HRT) are assumed to be equal. If the SRT is too short, methanogenesis will not occur and the reactor contents will acidify. Depending on the extent of fresh waste expected at the treatment facility, an SRT of 15–30 days at a minimum temperature of 25°C should provide sufficient time for methanogenesis, sufficient hydrolysis, and acidification of lipids to occur (De Mes et al., 2003). PennState Extension (undated) suggests that to achieve effective odour reduction, the SRT should be at least 20 days.
- *Organic load and solids reduction.* Small-scale fixed-dome digesters used as settlers for primary treatment of wastewater are reported to achieve 25–60 per cent biochemical oxygen demand (BOD) removal (Mang and Li, 2010). BOD removal for faecal sludge or septage is likely to be considerably lower as significant digestion will already have occurred during retention in pits and septic tanks. The potential for organic load reduction through a biodigester will depend on the extent to which the incoming material has already undergone digestion in a pit or tank. The few available studies show chemical oxygen demand (COD) removal in the range of 20–40 per cent for faecal sludge applications (see Table 6.3). WEF (2010, Figure 25.2) states that volatile solids reductions of around 50 per cent after 17 days and 55 per cent after 18 days can be expected at temperatures of 20°C and 25°C, respectively.
- *Gas production.* Biogas consists mainly of methane (typically 55–70 per cent) and carbon dioxide (typically 35–40 per cent) (Cecchi et al., 2003). The methane can be stored and used as a fuel. If this option is not available, it should be flared as it is a potent greenhouse gas. Biogas production depends on the amount of undigested material in the faecal sludge or septage to be treated. Specifically, the volatile solids content of sludge represents the fraction of solid material that may be transformed into biogas. The biogas production from sludge stored in pit latrines and septic tanks will be limited because digestion of organics has already taken place. Production from fresh sludge, the only type of sludge for which biodigestion should be considered, will be greater. One study found average methane production figures of around 50 and 275 l/kg volatile solids destroyed for pit latrine sludge and fresh waste from portable toilets, respectively (Rose et al., 2014). For the portable toilet waste, most methane production occurred in the first 10 days. Other studies recorded a median yield of 200–250 l total biogas/kg COD (quoted in Forbis-Stokes et al., 2016). Biogas production can be inhibited by the presence of ammonia. One study found little effect at total

ammoniacal nitrogen (TAN) contents of up to 3 g/l but 66, 86, and 90 per cent reductions in biogas production for samples with TAN contents of 5, 8, and 10 g/l, respectively (Colón et al., 2015). This brief discussion suggests that, given the relatively small volume of gas produced, gas production should not be the main driver for providing biodigester treatment.

The limited available data on treatment performance of small-scale biogas digesters treating faecal sludge and septage are summarized in Table 6.3. The figures for biogas production are consistent with the Rose et al. (2014)

Table 6.3 Small-scale biogas digester characteristics and treatment performance

Location and source of information	System type and volume	Influent source	Influent characteristics	HRT[2]	Treatment efficiency and biogas production
Kanyama, Lusaka, Zambia (BORDA, personal communication, 2017)	Fixed-dome digester (brick): 58 m³ volume; (53 m³ liquid volume)	Faecal sludge from dry, unlined household pit latrines	1.2 m³ of faecal sludge per day, dry solids 12–20% and COD typically 80,000 mg/l[1] (plus 1–2 m³ water per day for solid-waste separation and cleaning equipment)	20 days	20–25% COD removal[1] 63 l biogas/kg dry solids
Devanahalli, Bangalore, India (CDD, personal communication 2017)	Fixed-dome digester (pre-fabricated fibreglass) 6 m³ volume in parallel (4.4 m³ liquid volume each)	Septage from household leach pits (wet) and septic tanks (Note: figures are for solid stream after solids–liquid separation)	1.1 m³ inflow per day Dry solids = 4–6% COD = 20,000–60,000 mg/l	8 days	<5% COD removal[1] 19 l biogas/kg dry solids
Kumasi, Ghana (Sarpong, 2016)	Geobag digester 8 m³ volume in series	Fresh faecal material from containerized toilets (emptied 2–3 times per week)	0.4 m³/day (for 21 days per month) COD = 35,500 mg/l (range: 20,000–40,000 mg/l) Dry solids = 5–10%	90 days	39% COD removal No biogas information available

Notes: [1] Influent COD and treatment efficiency calculated using a mass balance.
[2] Hydraulic and sludge retention times are theoretically equal for thick slurries. In practice, some sludge will settle out.

findings that biogas production is much lower for well-digested pit latrine sludge than for fresh material taken from portable toilets.

Operational and design considerations. Field experience in Lusaka shows that solids accumulation presents significant operational problems for domed biodigesters treating faecal sludge from pit latrines. The Kanyama biodigester design includes a draw-off pipe, which extends to the centre of the biodigester, as shown in Figure 6.5. The intention of the designers was that sludge would be drawn off from this under hydrostatic pressure. In practice, the arrangement was not effective and sludge remained in the bottom of the biodigester, necessitating periodic manual removal (WSUP, 2015). The reason for this lies in the phenomenon known as piping: the tendency for channels to form through the sludge, resulting in removal of relatively clear supernatant water rather than sludge. The important point here is that sludge that settles on a gently sloping surface will not move to a central withdrawal point unless it is directed to that point by a scraper. In the absence of a mechanical scraper system, a hopper with side slopes of 60° to the horizontal (45° for circular hoppers) will be required to ensure that sludge will move to a draw-off point at the bottom of the hopper (Institute of Water Pollution Control, 1980). This principle might be applicable to a domed biodigester but it would involve a fundamental change in design and cannot be recommended without field testing. Chapter 7 includes information on the design of hopper-bottomed tanks. Grit removal and screening prior to biodigestion will have some effect on solids accumulation rates but problems with sludge accumulation will remain. Possible responses to these problems include the following:

- *Periodic manual sludge removal.* This response requires provision of at least two biodigesters in parallel to enable continued operation while a biodigester is being desludged. The workers who desludge the biodigester will have to work in a confined space that contains anaerobic sludge and may contain methane. This poses a serious risk to workers. Ideally, operators should only enter a fixed-dome digester with breathing apparatus and protective equipment. If this is not possible, the contents should be left to digest for several months before manual desludging is attempted. Even then, extreme care should be taken when working in the biodigester. Only one worker should enter the confined space at a time, and a rope should be attached to his waist so that the other workers can pull him out if he is overcome by gas.
- *Periodic sludge removal using a tanker suction hose.* This response will require that the sludge remains sufficiently liquid to be moved by the suction available with the tanker. It will be necessary to move the hose around within the tanker and it may be difficult to reach all the points within the biodigester. It will be best if this option is used in conjunction with manual removal. After withdrawal of as much sludge as possible using the suction hose, the contents of the biodigester should be left for several days or even weeks before manual emptying to remove the

remaining sludge commences. This will reduce the risk from dangerous gases. Regardless of this, extreme caution should be exercised when entering the biodigester, as explained above.

- *Mechanically driven agitation to keep solids in suspension.* This is standard practice in large anaerobic digesters. However, mixing increases complexity and cost, requires a reliable source of power and, because of its reliance on mechanical equipment operating in a difficult environment, is likely to break down. Hoffman (2015) suggested the use of a 'biogas pump' to move sludge around a fixed-dome biodigester. His proposed system was based on the Vaughan Rotamix system, a proprietary mixing system, as described by the Marmara University Environmental Biotechnology Group (2011). This involves the use of pumps to deliver recirculated flow into the biodigester through a series of nozzles. The Rotamix system uses 'chopper' pumps to reduce the size of solids in the flow through the nozzles. The likelihood of failure is reduced by the fact that the system has no moving parts inside the biodigester. However, it has not been tested in the field for septage. It requires a reliable electricity supply, good pump maintenance systems, and a reliable supply chain for spare parts. Even with mixing, grit and condensed sludge will accumulate over time and digesters will eventually need to be manually emptied. It would be possible to pilot this approach for larger treatment plants but it is unlikely to be feasible for smaller plants with limited technical resources.

Advocates of the use of geobag biodigesters claim that they solve or at least reduce the problem of sludge accumulation. Box 6.1 summarizes the procedures recommended by Sistema Biobolsa to reduce problems with sludge accumulation. These methods were developed for small biodigesters used to treat animal wastes and monitoring is required to determine how well they will work at the larger scale that will normally be required at faecal sludge treatment plants. However, it is unlikely that deposition and accumulation of sludge can be entirely eliminated.

The operators of the geobag biodigester in Antananarivo dilute the incoming sludge and septage in the ratio one part of faecal sludge/septage to two parts of clean water to reduce the solids content of the influent from 11–15 per cent to 4–5 per cent. The secondary information summarized in the paragraph on the solids content of the incoming sludge on page 155 suggests that the dilution is not necessary and may lead to increased sludge accumulation. Further field research is required to confirm or modify this conclusion.

To allow for continued treatment plant operation when domed biodigesters are being desludged and geobags are being removed and replaced, small-scale biodigesters should be deployed in parallel. This will allow one unit to continue to function while the second unit is out of service.

Biodigesters will only collect gas if they are air-tight. To ensure that this condition is met, masons tasked with constructing fixed-dome digesters require specialized training to ensure gas-tight dome construction. Alternatively, prefabricated fixed-dome digesters and geobag digesters would generally be

---

Box 6.1 Preventing and removing sludge accumulation in geobag digesters: Sistema Biobolsa's standard operating procedure

The Mexican social enterprise organization Sistema Biobolsa has developed a geobag digester for partial digestion of human wastes. The organization Water and Sanitation for the Urban Poor (WSUP) has facilitated implementation of faecal sludge treatment schemes in Kumasi, Ghana and Antananarivo, Madagascar using the Sistema Biobolsa approach (Table 6.3). The standard operating procedures (SOPs) summarized below were developed by Sistema Biobolsa to reduce sludge accumulation in geobag digesters treating animal manure. It is possible that greater problems will be encountered when dealing with faecal sludge and septage from poorly constructed pits and tanks which will likely have a high grit content.

Sistema Biobolsa recommends daily agitation of the geobag digester contents to prevent sludge accumulation in 'dead' areas and the formation of a scum layer. Agitation should be performed each day before fresh sludge is added, in the morning or the evening when the geo-membrane is not very hot, and when there is little or no gas in the digester. Agitation is applied progressively along the geobag digester, with the intention of generating waves that move settled solids along and eventually out of the digester. The digester should be 'purged' at intervals of two to three years to remove settled solids. Water is added to the digester through the inlet pipe while the digester contents are agitated. The water flows along the digester and carries solids that have been lifted into suspension by the agitation out through the outlet pipe of the digester. Reactivation is required at intervals of 8–20 years or whenever operators notice a significant but unexplained drop in biogas production. The objective of reactivation is to remove sediments that have built up over the years despite purging of the digester contents. As with purging, water is added and the digester is agitated. A sludge pump is used to remove sludge from the bottom of the digester. The digester is then washed out with a high-pressure hose, after which it is replaced in its original position.

Source: based on Sistema Biobolsa (undated)

---

purchased from specialized suppliers. Gas piping and appliances are susceptible to corrosion due to trace amounts of hydrogen sulphide contained in biogas and will need to be repaired or replaced more frequently than the main digester structure. Sasse (1998) estimates a six-year lifespan for these components. Personnel who are required to work on the maintenance of gas infrastructure should be provided with training on safety considerations and procedures.

Biodigester design. The most important points to be considered in biodigester design are the reactor volume and dimensions. The reactor volume is given by the equation:

$$V_{reactor} = Q_{T,BD} \; R_{BD}$$

where: $V_{reactor}$ = total reactor volume (m³)

$Q_{T,BD}$ = design hydraulic flow rate (m³/day)

R_{BD} = retention time in the biodigester (days)

The retention time should be in the range 15–30 days. The total reactor volume should be split into at least two biodigesters, with additional capacity provided to allow continued treatment when one biodigester has been decommissioned for desludging and repair.

The volume of fixed-dome digesters typically consists of the sum of the gas volume at the top of the dome, the dome volume below the maximum gas storage level, and the volume in a gently sloping conical base section. Only the second and third of these are included in the reactor volume.

$$V_{reactor} = \frac{2\pi r^3}{3} - \frac{\pi h^2(3r - h)}{3} + \frac{\pi r^2 d}{3}$$

where: r = dome radius (m);
   h = maximum gas volume height (typically 0.8–1.2 m); and
   d = depth of conical base (m)

This calculation is somewhat conservative as the gas volume at the top of the dome will decrease during use and, therefore, the gas volume will not always be at maximum storage capacity. Designs for other biodigester types will have different geometries, but should similarly consider only the liquid and sludge volume, and not the gas volume, when calculating the biodigester reactor volume.

Key points from this chapter

This chapter has dealt with the design of facilities to receive faecal sludge and septage and provide the preliminary treatment required to ensure that the forward flow is compatible with the needs of later treatment facilities. Key points made in the chapter are as follows:

- Reception facilities should be designed to facilitate easy access and quick turn-around times for septage and faecal sludge transport vehicles. Provision of separate reception facilities for septage and faecal sludge should be considered where both are delivered to the treatment facility.
- Reception facilities should be designed for the maximum rate of discharge from the vehicles used to transport faecal sludge and septage. For conventional tankers, this will depend on the size of the tanker discharge hose. Designing reception facilities to include flow attenuation will reduce the hydraulic load on subsequent treatment units.
- Flow attenuation will often be advisable. Flow attenuation facilities should be simple and designed with slopes that can be washed down to prevent accumulation of sludge and grit.
- Coarse screening, which may be combined with septage reception, should always be provided. In most cases, manually raked screens will be the best option. These should be bar screens, sloping at an angle of not more than 60° to the horizontal and with good access to allow operators to rake and remove screenings.
- Mechanical screening systems may be appropriate for larger plants if their substantially higher capital cost can be justified and effective maintenance systems and spare/replacement part supply chains can be provided.

- Removal of FOG will be advisable where it is possible that FOG will adversely affect follow-up treatment processes. The simplest option will be to use scum boards to capture the scum that rises to the surface of tanks and ponds and periodically remove FOG with the scum.
- Mechanical fine screening and grit removal may be required to protect mechanical presses from damage. Grit removal should also be considered when subsequent treatment units include enclosed tanks and reactors.
- The arrangements for grit removal must take account of the fact that flows from tankers and other delivery vehicles will be intermittent and variable. Parabolic grit channels are a good grit removal option, combining simplicity with the ability to separate grit from organic material.
- Stabilization may be required when the material to be treated is fresh and so poorly digested. Lime stabilization is possible but most systems installed to date rely on partial digestion, using either fixed-dome or geobag biodigesters. Biodigestion is not required for septage, pit latrine sludge, and other wastes that are already well-digested.
- Both types of digester are susceptible to sludge and grit accumulation. Grit removal upstream of biodigesters will have some effect on the rate of accumulation but will not remove the need to either prevent sludge accumulation or remove accumulated sludge. Safety is a key consideration for enclosed reactors, particularly for anaerobic reactors such as domed biodigesters. To avoid the need for workers to enter spaces filled with digesting sludge, which may produce dangerous gases, at least two biodigesters should be provided in parallel.

References

American Association of State Highway and Transportation Officials (AASHTO) (2004) *A Policy on Geometric Design of Highways and Streets*, 5th edn, Washington, DC: AASHTO.

Anderson, K. (2014) *Treatment of Faecal Sludge, with Hydrated Lime: Small Scale Experiments*, The Netherlands: WASTE <www.janspitcsdelft.nl/downloads/150/file_block/93480f8b0e432d03a6d94e27876a50f9> [accessed 18 November 2017].

Brown and Caldwell (undated) *Fats, Oil and Grease Best Management Practice Manual* [online], prepared for the Oregon Association of Clean Water Agencies <www.klamathfalls.city/sites/www.klamathfalls.city/files/Recycling/FOG-manual-english.pdf> [accessed 21 November 2017].

Cecchi, F., Traverso, P., Pavan, P., Bolzonella, D. and Innocenti, L. (2003) 'Characteristics of the OFMSW and behaviour of the anaerobic digestion process', in J. Mata-Alvarez (ed.), *Biomethanisation of the Organic Fraction of Municipal Solid Wastes*, London: IWA Publishing.

Colón, J., Forbis-Stokes, A.A. and Deshusses, M.A. (2015) 'Anaerobic digestion of undiluted simulant human excreta for sanitation and energy recovery in less-developed countries', *Energy for Sustainable Development* 29: 57–64 <https://doi.org/10.1016/j.esd.2015.09.005> [accessed 17 May 2018].

Crites, R. and Tchobanoglous, G. (1998) *Small and Decentralized Wastewater Management Systems*, Boston, MA: WCB McGraw Hill.

Dally, J.W., Riley, W.F. and McConnell, K.G. (1993) *Instrumentation for Engineering Measurements*, 2nd edn, New Delhi: Wiley India Pvt.

Deublein, D. and Steinhauser, A. (2011) *Biogas from Waste and Renewable Resources: An Introduction*, Weinheim: Wiley-VCH Verlag GmbH & Co. KGaA.

East Sussex County Council (undated) *Design Standards for Industrial Roads* <www.eastsussex.gov.uk/media/1768/design_standards_for_industrial_roads.pdf> [accessed 21 February 2018].

Environmental Protection Agency (2005) *Wastewater Treatment Manuals: Preliminary Treatment,* Environmental Protection Agency Ireland, Ardvacan, Wexford <https://www.epa.ie/pubs/advice/water/wastewater/EPA_water_treatment_manual_preliminary.pdf> [Accessed 25 June 2018].

Escritt, L.B. (1972) *Public Health Engineering Practice, Volume II: Sewerage and Sewage Disposal*, London: Macdonald and Evans.

Feige, W., Oppelt, E. and Kreiss, J. (1975) *An Alternative Septage Treatment Method: Lime Stabilization/Sand-Bed Dewatering* [online], Cincinnati, OH: Municipal Environmental Research Laboratory, Office of Research and Development, US Environmental Protection Agency <https://nepis.epa.gov/Exe/ZyPDF.cgi/9100SNQA.PDF?Dockey=9100SNQA.PDF> [accessed 8 March 2018].

Forbis-Stokes, A.A., O'Meara, P.F., Mugo, W., Simivu, G.M. and Deshusses, M.A. (2016) 'On-site fecal sludge treatment with the anaerobic digestion pasteurization latrine', *Environmental Engineering Science* 33(11): 898–906 <http://dx.doi.org/10.1089/ees.2016.0148> [accessed 17 May 2018].

Henkel, J. (2010) *Oxygen Transfer Phenomena in Activated Sludge* [online], PhD thesis, Department of Civil Engineering and Geodesy, Darmstadt Technical University, Germany <http://tuprints.ulb.tu-darmstadt.de/3008/1/Henkel-2010-Oxygen_Transfer_Phenomena_in_Activated_Sludge.pdf> [accessed 3 March 2018].

Hoffman, T. (2015) 'Innovative faecal sludge (FS) treatment: appropriate decentralised treatment system design', presentation from *FSM3, 3rd International Faecal Sludge Conference, Hanoi, Vietnam*.

Institute of Water Pollution Control (1980) *Manuals of British Practice in Water Pollution Control: Unit Processes, Primary Sedimentation*, Maidstone, Kent: IWPC.

Mang, H.-P. and Li, Z. (2010) *Technology Review of Biogas Sanitation (Draft) Biogas sanitation for blackwater, brown water, or for excreta and organic household waste treatment and reuse in developing countries*, Eschborn, Germany: GIZ <www.susana.org/_resources/documents/default/2-877-gtz2010-en-technology-review-biogas-sanitation-july.pdf> [accessed 3 March 2018].

Marmara University Environmental Biotechnology Group (2011) 'Lectures 1, Anaerobic digester mixing systems', Marmara University, Turkey [online] <http://mebig.marmara.edu.tr/Enve737/Chapter1-Mixing.pdf> [accessed 8 January 2018].

De Mes, T., Stams, A., Reith, J. and Zeeman, G. (2003) 'Methane production by anaerobic digestion of wastewater and solid wastes', in J. Reith, R. Wijfells, and H. Barten (eds), *Status and Perspectives of Biological Methane and Hydrogen Production*, pp. 58–94, The Hague: Dutch Biological Hydrogen Foundation.

Metcalf & Eddy (2003) *Wastewater Engineering Treatment and Reuse*, 4th Edition, New York: McGraw Hill.

Nelson, C. and Lamb, J. (2002) *Final Report, Haubenschild Farms Anaerobic Digester* [online], St Paul, MN: The Minnesota Project <www.build-a-biogas-plant.com/PDF/HaubenshchildCaseStudy.pdf> [accessed 3 March 2018].

Ongerth, J.E. (1979) *Evaluation of Flow Equalization in Municipal Wastewater Treatment* [online], Cincinnati, OH: US EPA Municipal Environmental Research Laboratory <https://nepis.epa.gov/Exe/ZyPDF.cgi/300007H3.PDF?Dockey=300007H3.PDF> [accessed 17 November 2017].

OpenChannelFlow (undated) 'Parshall flumes' [online], <www.openchannelflow.com/flumes/parshall-flumes> [accessed 19 February 2018].

PennState Extension (undated) 'Anaerobic digestion for odour control' [online] <https://extension.psu.edu/anaerobic-digestion-for-odor-control> [accessed 19 February 2018].

Rose, C., Parker, A. and Cartmell, E. (2014) *The Biochemical Methane Potential of Faecal Sludge* [online], Cranfield University, UK <www.cce.edu.om/iwa2014/Presentations/06BMP.pdf> [accessed 21 February 2018].

Sarpong, D. (2016) *Treating Container Toilet Waste in Kumasi, Ghana*, MSc thesis, School of Water, Energy and Environment, Cranfield University, UK.

Sasse, L. (1998) *DEWATS Decentralised Wastewater Treatment in Developing Countries*, Bremen, Germany: BORDA <www.sswm.info/sites/default/files/reference_attachments/SASSE%201998%20DEWATS%20Decentralised%20Wastewater%20Treatment%20in%20Developing%20Countries_0.pdf> [accessed 13 March 2018].

Sistema Biobolsa (undated) *Manual de Usuario: Uso y mantenimiento del biodigester* [online] <http://sistemabiobolsa.com/wp-content/uploads/2016/07/Manual-de-usuario_-Biodigestor_-Sistema-Biobolsa.pdf> [accessed 14 March 2017].

SuSanA (2016) 'Time taken for faecal sludge tankers to discharge?' [online] <http://forum.susana.org/99-faecal-sludge-transport-including-emptying-of-pits-and-septic-tanks/18932-time-taken-for-faecal-sludge-tankers-to-discharge> [accessed 8 March 2018].

Thompson, B. (2012) *The Treatment and Disposal of Sewage Screenings and Grit* [online], Technical Note TRPM TN005, Stockton on Tees, UK: ThompsonRPM <http://79.170.44.80/thompsonrpm.com/wp-content/uploads/2012/02/website-techhnical-note-5-v2.pdf> [accessed 3 March 2018].

UK Government (2012) *Design Approach Statement – Roads: Appendix A HS2 Rural Road Design Criteria* [online] <www.gov.uk/government/uploads/system/uploads/attachment_data/file/405938/HS2_Rural_Road_Design_Criteria.pdf> [accessed 3 March 2018].

USAID (2015) *Implementer's Guide to Lime Stabilization for Septage Management in the Philippines* [online], Manila: USAID <http://forum.susana.org/media/kunena/attachments/818/ImplementersGuidetoLimeStabilizationforSeptageManagementinthePhilippines.pdf> [accessed 3 March 2018].

US EPA (1999) *Wastewater Technology Fact Sheet: Screening and Grit Removal* [online] <www.3.epa.gov/npdes/pubs/final_sgrit_removal.pdf> [accessed 3 March 2018].

Verma, S. (2002) *Anaerobic Digestion of Biodegradable Organics in Municipal Solid Wastes*, Master's thesis, Department of Earth & Environmental Engineering

Fu Foundation School of Engineering and Applied Science, Columbia University, USA.

Vögeli, Y., Lohri, C.R., Gallardo, A., Diener, S. and Zurbrügg, C. (2014) *Anaerobic Digestion of Biowaste in Developing Countries: Practical Information and Case Studies*, Dübendorf, Switzerland: Swiss Federal Institute of Aquatic Science and Technology (Eawag) <www.eawag.ch/fileadmin/Domain1/Abteilungen/sandec/E-Learning/Moocs/Solid_Waste/W3/Anaerobic_Digestion_Biowaste_2014.pdf> [accessed 3 March 2018].

WASTE (undated) *Testing and development of desludging units for emptying pit latrines and septic tanks: Results of nine months field-testing in Blantyre – Malawi* [online] <www.speedkits.eu/sites/www.speedkits.eu/files/Summary%20field%20testing%20pit%20emptying%20Blantyre.pdf> [accessed 3 March 2018].

WEF (2010) *Design of Municipal Wastewater Treatment Plants, WEF Manual of Practice no. 8*, 5th edn, Alexandria, VA: WEF Press.

WSUP (2015) *Introducing Safe FSM Services in Low-income Urban Areas: Lessons from Lusaka* [online], Topic Brief <http://thesff.com/system/wp-content/uploads/2017/01/Introducing-safe-FSM-services.pdf> [accessed 7 January 2018].

CHAPTER 7
Solids–liquid separation

Solids–liquid separation is an essential aspect of faecal sludge and septage treatment. It may be combined with either treatment to reduce organic loads or dewater sludge. However, it will often be advisable to separate the solids and liquid fractions before dealing with each fraction separately. This chapter explores the options for solids–liquid separation. It identifies technologies that are currently in use and suggests technologies that might be used in the future. Technologies that combine solids–liquid separation with organic load reduction and sludge dewatering are introduced early in the chapter, but the main focus is on technologies whose sole purpose is solids–liquid separation. Technologies that rely on physical sedimentation are considered first, followed by those that rely on pressure. This chapter deals mainly with septage, which is more likely to require solids–liquid separation than thicker faecal sludge.

Keywords: solids–liquid separation, septage, technologies, design parameters, separation mechanisms

Introduction

Context

All wastewater treatment processes involve solids–liquid separation. The sole function of some technologies, for instance, sedimentation tanks, is to separate solids from the liquid flow. Other technologies, for instance, septic and Imhoff tanks and ponds, combine solids–liquid separation with biological treatment. It is possible to proceed directly from preliminary treatment to treat the whole of the faecal sludge/septage flow as either liquid or sludge. Many existing treatment plants adopt this approach, utilizing either anaerobic ponds or drying beds to separate solids in conjunction with biological treatment and sludge dewatering, respectively. This approach may be appropriate for small treatment plants in towns where land is available and operational skills are limited. In other situations, as indicated in Chapter 4, specific provision for separation of solids from liquid prior to treatment of the separated fractions will normally be advisable unless the incoming material has a solids content of 5 per cent or more. This chapter identifies and describes the options for achieving solids–liquid separation. It includes brief references to technologies that combine solids–liquid separation with either biological treatment or dewatering, but the main focus is on technologies whose main function is solids–liquid separation.

http://dx.doi.org/10.3362/9781780449869.008

Objectives

Solids–liquid separation serves to:

- Reduce the organic and suspended solids loads in the liquid fraction of the septage and faecal sludge, so reducing the area and/or power required for its subsequent treatment and reducing problems with solids accumulation.
- Reduce the water content of the separated solids and so reduce the volume and bulk of solids to be handled, thereby reducing the space and/or power requirements for subsequent dewatering and drying technologies. The technologies described in this chapter all reduce the water content to 95 per cent or less.

Solids–liquid separation should always be considered for septage. It is less likely to be appropriate for fresh faecal sludge from frequently emptied public toilets and container-based systems. Material removed from such facilities is likely to have a water content of less than 95 per cent and to have poor settling characteristics. Lime stabilization or biodigester treatment followed by dewatering on a sand drying bed may be a better option for this type of material. Material removed from dry pit latrines is mostly well-digested but its high solids content may mean that separate provision for solids–liquid separation is not necessary.

Separation mechanisms

Mechanisms suitable for achieving solids–liquid separation include:

- physical, gravity-driven settlement;
- pressure;
- filtration;
- evaporation and evapotranspiration, which combines evaporation with transpiration from plants; and
- use of the centrifugal movement created by rapid rotation.

Sedimentation tanks and gravity thickeners use physical settlement mechanisms. Mechanical presses use a combination of pressure and filtration through a cloth attached to a filter plate. Sludge drying beds rely on complex settlement, filtration, and evaporation processes. Planted drying beds use evapotranspiration in addition to the mechanisms that occur in unplanted drying beds. Centrifugal movement is a result of inertia, which results in a body continuing in a straight line and hence away from the centre of rotation. This is often described in terms of centrifugal force, which is commonly viewed as an apparent force, equal and opposite to the centripetal force, drawing a rotating body away from the centre of rotation. Centrifuges use centrifugal movement to throw denser material to the outside of a rotating flow, as do vortex separators, which are mainly used for grit separation.

Sedimentation and filtration separate readily separable free water. In addition to free water, centrifugal movement, pressure, and evaporation remove some of the water that is bound to the solids in the faecal sludge (Bassan et al., 2014). Chapter 9 lists and briefly describes the various types of bound water.

Overview of technologies

Technologies currently used in lower-income countries for solids–liquid separation include:

- *sludge drying beds,* which separate solids and liquid through evaporation, settling, and filtration;
- *anaerobic ponds,* which combine solids–liquid separation with reduction of the organic loads;
- *Imhoff tanks,* which are designed to combine solids–liquid separation in an upper compartment with digestion of settled solids in a lower compartment;
- *settling-thickening tanks (STTs),* rectangular batch-loaded tanks that allow solids to settle while supernatant water continues to liquid treatment facilities;
- *mechanical presses,* which use pressure to force liquid out of the sludge and through a filter cloth or fine sieve. Common types include belt filter presses, which use filter cloth attached to filter plates to retain sludge, and screw presses, which retain sludge within a cylindrical sieve.

Other technologies with the potential to be used for solids–liquid separation of septage in lower-income countries include:

- *gravity thickeners,* which rely on the same settling mechanisms as Imhoff tanks and STTs; and
- *decanting drying beds* from which water is removed by decanting as well as evaporation.

Imhoff tanks are used in Indonesia and some other countries. The Imhoff tank consists of two interconnected compartments, located one above the other. The two-compartment design separates digesting solids from the flow through the tank, thus reducing the possibility of sludge resuspension and carry-over. Sedimentation takes place in the upper compartment and solids that settle to the bottom of the upper compartment drop through the openings between the compartments and digest in the lower compartment (for further information, see Tilley et al., 2014). Imhoff tanks have a proven track record for the treatment of dilute wastewater, but they are a poor treatment choice for septage, which has a much higher solids content than municipal wastewater. This high solids content leads to rapid sludge accumulation, necessitating desludging at intervals of weeks rather than the six to nine months recommended for tanks treating municipal wastewater. This limits the time for digestion to the point that the rationale for including the lower digestion tank is undermined. For this reason, this book does not recommend the use of Imhoff tanks and they are not considered further. However, the sedimentation mechanism used in the upper compartment is the same as that used in gravity thickeners, leading to the conclusion that simple sedimentation gravity thickeners may be an option for solids–liquid separation. This possibility is further explored below.

Centrifuges are used to thicken sludge in wastewater treatment plants and there is no technical reason why they should not be used for solids–liquid separation of septage and faecal sludge. However, they have high power costs and are mechanically complex and expensive. For these reasons, they are not considered to be suitable for use in developing countries and are not considered further in this book. Similarly, membrane bioreactors and rotary drum thickeners are not considered because of their high capital and operational costs and need for highly skilled operators.

Figure 7.1 summarizes the other solids–liquid separation options introduced above, indicating where they are considered in subsequent chapters.

Key points to consider when comparing options are:

- the solids concentration of separated solids, which will influence follow-up solids dewatering requirements;
- the organic load and solids concentration in separated liquid, which will influence follow-up liquid treatment requirements;
- the land required for the option: calculated surface overflow rates can be used to compare the land requirements of solids–liquid separation technologies that rely on physical sedimentation.

Table 7.5 at the end of this chapter provides a comparison of the various options considered in the chapter in relation to the points identified above.

Sludge drying beds

Sludge drying beds consist of a layer of sand, underlain with gravel, contained within low walls and with an underdrain system to pick up liquid that percolates through the bed. Wet sludge is discharged onto a bed to a depth of 200–300 mm. It is then left on the bed to allow water to percolate through the bed and evaporate from the surface until the material on the bed has dried sufficiently to allow its removal using spades or other suitable equipment. Their main function is to dewater sludge and, in doing so, they separate solids from liquid.

Many existing treatment plants rely on sludge drying as their main treatment process. Incoming faecal sludge and septage is discharged to the beds, with or without preliminary screening. Dried sludge is removed and either disposed of locally or removed to a landfill. In many but not all cases, percolating liquid is treated in ponds. This system has the virtue of simplicity. Its disadvantage is that it needs a large land area, particularly

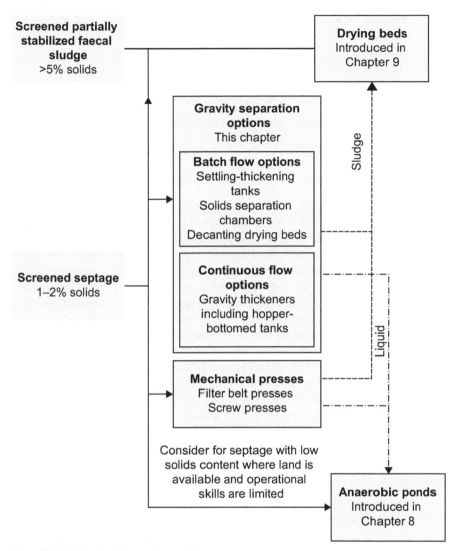

Figure 7.1 Solids–liquid separation options

when the material to be treated has a low solids content, as is likely to be the case for septage.

Consider sludge drying beds as an option for combined solids–liquid separation and sludge dewatering where the following conditions are met:

- The material to be treated has a high solids content, typically over about 3 per cent. Where the material to be treated is fresh faecal sludge, prior biodigestion will be advisable.
- The volume to be treated is low. Most existing treatment plants that rely solely on drying beds for solids–liquid separation and dewatering are

designed for less than 20 m³/day. Where land is available, it should be possible to consider this option for larger hydraulic loads, up to perhaps 50 m³/day.

- Land is available.
- The management capacity, knowledge, and skills required for more complex treatment processes are lacking.

Chapter 9 provides more information on the planning and design of sludge drying beds.

Anaerobic ponds

As their name suggests, anaerobic ponds are ponds that are loaded sufficiently heavily for them to operate in purely anaerobic mode. Those used for municipal wastewater treatment are typically 3–5 m deep. There are arguments, which are further explained in Chapter 8, for the depth of ponds used for septage treatment to be at the lower end of this range. Like sludge drying beds, anaerobic ponds are simple, requiring few specialist operational skills. They are widely used as the first stage in septage treatment with separate solids–liquid separation facilities either omitted or bypassed. They require more land than the technologies described later in this chapter but their main disadvantages are operational. Solids settle in anaerobic ponds, reducing the pond volume and creating a need for periodic sludge removal. If sludge removal is neglected, the performance of a pond will deteriorate and it will eventually fail. The desludging interval for anaerobic ponds that treat municipal wastewater is typically measured in years, but the high solids content of septage and faecal sludge means that the desludging interval for ponds that are not preceded by other forms of solids–liquid separation is likely to be measured in months.

Consider anaerobic ponds for combined solids–liquid separation and the first stage in biological treatment where:

- the material to be treated is septage with a low solids content, preferably 1 per cent or less;
- the volume to be treated is low – typically up to around 50 m³/day although there may be situations in which anaerobic ponds will be an option for higher flows;
- land is available; and
- the management capacity, knowledge, and skills required for more complex treatment processes are lacking.

The challenge when using ponds will be to ensure that they are regularly desludged. One way to achieve this will be to design ponds to allow periodic decanting of liquid, either by gravity or using pumps, leaving the sludge to dry. Solids–liquid separation and sludge dewatering functions will thus be separated in time rather than by location. This is a simpler version of the principle underlying the operation of sequencing batch reactors. This approach will require sufficient units to allow some to function as ponds while others are functioning as drying beds. The section on decanting drying beds, below, develops this concept further, while Chapter 8 provides guidance on the planning and design of anaerobic ponds.

Settling-thickening tanks and solids separation chambers

System description

Settling-thickening tanks are rectangular concrete units, typically 2–3 m in depth with a floor that slopes from one end to the other. There are two rather different tank configurations, one developed at the Rufisque and Cambérène faecal sludge treatment plants (FSTPs) in Dakar, Senegal and the other at the Achimoto FSTP in Accra, Ghana. The solids separation chambers (SSCs) used in Indonesia are similar to the Dakar tanks but include provision for percolation through a permeable sand bed. In all three designs, faecal sludge or septage enters the tank at one end and flows out over a weir at the other end. Solids settle along the length of the tank, as in a conventional rectangular sedimentation tank. Unlike sedimentation tanks, STTs operate in batch mode, with each tank loaded for several days and then allowed to rest before sludge is removed. During this period, discharge continues to a second tank. The Indonesian SSCs share some design and operational features with the West African STTs and so the three technologies are considered together.

Achimota. Two tanks were installed in the late 1980s, each 24 m long by 8.3 m wide, with a floor sloping from ground level at the inlet end to a depth of 3 m at the outlet end to provide a total volume of just under 300 m³. The tanks received septage and public toilet sludge, mixed at a ratio of approximately 4 to 1 to give typical influent concentrations in the range 15,000–20,000 mg/l. The tanks were loaded sequentially at a rate of about 150 m³ per day. Loading continued for a period of 4–8 weeks with excess liquid overflowing into a downstream pond system. Loading was then switched to the other tank while the accumulated solids in the first pond were left to dry and consolidate. The dried solids were then removed from the tank using front-end loader tractors. Loading of this tank then recommenced while the other tank was left to dry and consolidate. Smell and odour problems during the extended retention period were reduced by the formation of a stable scum layer a few days after commissioning (Heinss et al., 1998).

Rufisque and Cambérène. The Dakar tanks were constructed in the 1980s and have a similar configuration to conventional rectangular sedimentation tanks, as shown in Figure 7.2. The capacity of each of the two Cambérène tanks is 155 m³ (Dodane and Bassan, 2014). The influent is septage with a mean solids content of less than 1 per cent. It enters the tanks at one end and exits over a weir at the other end. At 8.6 hours, the design hydraulic retention time (HRT) of the Cambérène tanks is significantly less than the two-day HRT of the Achimota

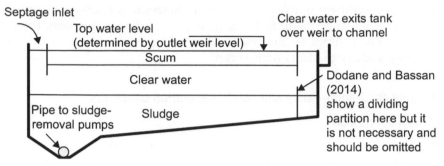

Figure 7.2 Longitudinal section through Dakar-style STT

tanks and around four times the HRT of conventional sedimentation tanks. In practice, the reported loading was much higher than the design loading so that the actual HRT in the mid-2000s was only 1.7 hours (Badji et al., 2011). Information on the depth of the tanks is not available but, based on the information provided in Dodane and Bassan (2014), it is reasonable to assume an average depth of about 2.2 m. At this depth, the surface overflow rates at the design and peak hydraulic loading rates are as given in Table 7.1. As with the Achimota tanks, the Dakar tanks are operated in batch mode, but the cycle is shorter. The two tanks are loaded alternately with septage delivered to one tank for about a week. Loading is then switched to the second tank while the contents of the first tank are allowed to settle and consolidate. At the end of each two-week cycle, vacuum tanker suction pumps are used to remove sludge and scum from the tank that has completed the cycle.

Table 7.1 Summary of STT and SSC design parameters

Design parameter	Unit	Achimota FSTP	Dakar FSTPs	Tabanan SSC
HRT	hours	48, reducing as sludge accumulates	8.6 (designed) 1.7 (actual)	About 38
Surface overflow rate (SOR)	m³/m² d	0.75 (0.375 over complete loading cycle)	6–14 (3–7 over complete loading cycle)	About 1
Solids loading rate	kg TS/m² d	3.75–5 over complete loading cycle	2.25 (designed) 5.5 (actual) over complete loading cycle	Not known

Note: The solids loadings rates for Achimota and Dakar are calculated using information from Heinss et al. (1998) and Dodane and Bassan (2014) on tank sizes, loading rates, and influent TSS concentrations. Dodane and Bassan (2014), quoting personal experience provided by Pierre-Henri Dodane, suggest a surface overflow rate of 0.5 m/h or 12 m³/m² d for rectangular settling tanks treating faecal sludge with a sludge volume index of less than 100.

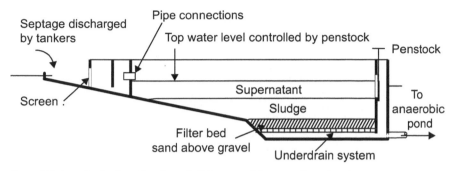

Figure 7.3 Longitudinal section through Tabanan solids separation chamber

Indonesian solids separation chambers. The Indonesian SSCs are similar in some respects to the West African STTs. Like the Achimota STTs, they slope away from the discharge point, but access is blocked by the discharge and screening arrangement at the inlet end of the chamber. Portable pumps are used to remove sludge, in the same way as vacuum tanker suction pumps are used to desludge the Dakar STTs. They differ from the West African STTs in the inclusion of a filter bed above the floor of the chamber, which allows some liquid to percolate through to an under-drainage system, and the provision of a penstock at the far end of the chamber, which can be lowered to allow supernatant water to be decanted from the tank. Figure 7.3 shows the arrangement serving Tabanan in Bali.

All the Indonesian SSCs have a similar basic layout but design details vary from plant to plant. Earlier units, such as that at the Keputih plant in Surabaya, omit the filter bed detail, and others make no provision for lowering the water level before sludge is pumped out of the chamber. Designs for individual plants show either four or five chambers arranged in parallel. The unpublished standard operating procedures for the Tabanan plant specify that each chamber should be loaded for four days. The contents should then be left to settle for a further three days. Supernatant water should then be decanted and sludge pumped to drying beds using a portable submersible pump. A draft design manual for Indonesian septage treatment plants prepared by the Indonesian Ministry of Public Works, states that the 'drying time' of the sludge should be between 5 and 12 days, with one additional day allowed for sludge retrieval. Another source says that each chamber is loaded for five days, after which water is decanted and the bed is left to dry for 10 to 15 days before sludge is removed to a drying area for further dewatering (Joni Hermana, personal communication, 2017).

Performance

The performance of the Achimota tanks was assessed in 1994 (Heinss et al., 1998, 1999). Information from an assessment of the Dakar tanks is based on information from Badji et al. (2011, quoted in Dodane and Bassan, 2014). Box 7.1 summarizes the findings of these assessments. They show that

---

Box 7.1 Summary of findings on operation of Achimota, Accra and Cambérène, Dakar tanks

The assessment on the Achimota tanks found that the material retained in the tanks divided into four layers: lower and upper sludge layers, a central 'clean water' layer, and a top scum layer. Average solids concentrations of 140 g/l (14 per cent) and 200 g/l (20 per cent) were recorded in the bottom sludge layer and scum layer, respectively. In parallel laboratory investigations in 1000-ml cylinders, the maximum concentrations in the sludge layer reached 60–85 g/l after nine days and more than 100 g/l after 30 days (Heinss et al., 1999). Despite the difference in the average influent solids concentrations, 12 g/l for Accra and 5 g/l for Dakar, these figures compare well with recorded sludge solids concentrations of 60–70 g/l (6–7 per cent) after one week in the Dakar tanks (Dodane and Bassan, 2014). The results obtained from field tests were not as good as those obtained from laboratory cylinder tests, which suggests that laboratory tests tend to overestimate settling performance. No quantitative information is available on the material removed from the Tabanan SSC but observation suggests that its solids content was low.

The 1994 investigations also assessed the performance of the tanks in removing five day biochemical oxygen demand (BOD_5) and total suspended solids (TSS) from the liquid flow. BOD_5 and TSS removal during the first five days averaged 55 per cent and 80 per cent, respectively. After this, performance deteriorated with TSS removal falling to about 40 per cent after 20 days and BOD_5 removal dropping below 20 per cent after 10 days. Overall, mass balance calculations showed reasonably good solids removal over the full operating cycle with 57 per cent TSS removal and 48 per cent volatile suspended solids (VSS) removal. Organic load reduction in the liquid effluent was poor, amounting to only 12 per cent for unfiltered BOD_5 and 24 per cent for unfiltered chemical oxygen demand (COD). The COD/BOD ratio dropped from an average of 9 at the inlet to 5.6 at the outlet, suggesting that poorly biodegradable material was settling out in the sludge, leaving more easily biodegradable material to exit the tanks in the effluent (Heinss et al., 1998, 1999).

---

extending the loading period from one week to four weeks results in some increase in the solids content of the settled sludge, but also leads to a significant reduction in organics and suspended solids removal. The solids content of the sludge in the Dakar tanks was higher than that to be expected from gravity thickening.

Design parameters

Table 7.1 summarizes calculated STT and SSC design parameters, based on available information on actual sizes and reported loading rates.

These figures show that:

- The design HRT of the Achimota tanks is towards the lower end of the range recommended for anaerobic waste stabilization ponds (see Table 8.3)
- The surface overflow rates for the Dakar tanks are under half the 15.5–31 m³/m² d recommended for gravity thickeners treating primary sewage works sludge (Metcalf & Eddy, 2003). The design HRT of these tanks is greater than the 2–3 hours at maximum flow recommended by British practice for primary clarifiers, although actual overflow rates at Cambérène are similar to those recommended for primary clarifiers.

- The solids loading rates on the Dakar tanks are similar to the 4–6 kg/m² h loading rates recommended by Metcalf & Eddy (2003) for gravity thickeners treating primary sludge.

Operational considerations

All three systems described in this section operate in batch mode, with one tank or chamber being loaded while sludge in the other is allowed to settle. This requires provision of at least two tanks or chambers.

The Dakar design includes a sump at one end with a pipe for sludge withdrawal. This arrangement is also a feature of rectangular sedimentation tanks at wastewater treatment plants. Sedimentation tanks are fitted with a scraper mechanism to push sludge that settles along the length of the tank back to the sump. Without a scraper mechanism, the pipe will only remove sludge from the sump. In Dakar, sludge is removed using sludge tanker suction pumps. The operational procedure for the Tabanan SSC, where a small submersible pump is moved around in the SSCs to remove sludge, is similar. In both cases, the likely result will be removal of a mixture of bottom sludge and supernatant water. Evidence for this is available from the reported experience with desludging a similar rectangular tank with gentle floor slopes at a displaced persons camp in Sittwe, Myanmar. Pipes were provided at intervals along the tank to allow sludge to be discharged by gravity to drying beds. A report on experience with desludging states that 'During the first few minutes after opening the valve, a thick liquid can be removed. After this, only a highly liquid fluid can be withdrawn' (Kraehenbuehl and Hariot, 2015).

These points lead to an important conclusion: *for tanks with a flat or gently sloping floor, it will not be possible to remove sludge using portable pumps or suction hoses without removing some supernatant water.* This must lead to a reduction in the effectiveness of the solids–liquid separation process.

Sludge pumping will become more difficult if sludge is left for a long period in the tanks. In the absence of site-specific information, standard operating procedures should require that sludge is removed at intervals of no more than two weeks. Access should be provided to allow manual sludge removal in the event that sludge has consolidated to the extent that it can no longer be removed by pumping. As noted in Chapter 5, strict safety procedures should be followed when working in tanks containing digested or digesting sludge.

The use of a front-end loader, as in Achimota, will require that supernatant water has evaporated and that the solids concentration of the material that remains is of the order of 15 per cent. This will only be possible with the long operational cycle adopted for Achimota.

There is no quantitative information on percolation through the SSC filter bed. Visual inspection during a visit to the Tabanan plant suggested that the amount of liquid percolating is relatively small compared with the combined volume removed by decanting and pumping to drying beds.

To ensure that scum does not either escape with the effluent or block the flow to the outlet weir, the depth of the baffle protecting the outlet weir must be deeper than the greatest depth of accumulated scum. Based on experience in Dakar, Dodane and Bassan (2014) suggest a scum depth of 0.4 m and a baffle wall depth of 0.7 m below the liquid surface.

Based on these points, it can be concluded that STTs and SSCs provide a simple but effective means of separating and settling solids. However, their gently sloping floors make it difficult to remove settled solids without also removing a significant amount of supernatant water. The Achimota tanks overcame this difficulty by extending the loading–resting cycle sufficiently to allow the sludge to dry so that it could be removed as a solid. This increased the land requirement and resulted in a gradual deterioration in liquid quality. As implemented at Achimota, the STT option relied on front-end loaders to remove dried sludge, an option that is unlikely to be available for smaller plants. The section on decanting drying beds later in this chapter examines the possibility of adapting the Achimota design to provide for initial gravity settlement in a relatively shallow basin, decanting of the supernatant, and drying of the sludge that remains after decanting.

The performance of Accra-style STTs and the SSCs could be improved by increasing the floor slope sufficiently to allow solids to settle by gravity to a sludge removal point. This will be difficult and expensive for the rectangular shaped tanks used by both of these technologies. A better approach will arguably be to replace the rectangular horizontal flow tanks with tanks that are either circular or square in plan and rely on either radial or vertical flow, as in conventional wastewater treatment plant sedimentation tanks and gravity thickeners. The next section explores this option.

Gravity thickeners

System description

Conventional gravity thickeners with mechanical scrapers. Gravity thickeners are used to thicken the sludge produced in wastewater treatment plants prior to digestion and dewatering. They are normally circular in plan, sloping to a central hopper and fitted with a rotating mechanism that moves sludge towards the hopper. The tank bottom slopes towards the central hopper at 1 in 6 or more and the central hopper sides should be at 60° to the horizontal (US EPA, 1987). Mechanically powered scrapers push settled sludge towards the hopper, from which it is removed through a desludging pipe, either under hydrostatic pressure or by pumping. A device is provided on the top of the thickener for the removal of scum. Figure 7.4 shows a typical motorized gravity thickener.

When used to thicken primary sludge in wastewater treatment, gravity thickeners typically increase the solids content of sludge from 2–6 per cent to 4–10 per cent dry solids (Metcalf & Eddy, 2003) and similar or better performance can be expected with well-digested septage. However, there

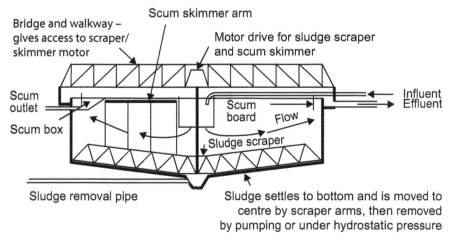

Figure 7.4 Conventional gravity thickener

are few examples of their use in septage treatment plants. In 2017, a gravity thickener was commissioned at a septage treatment plant in Bali, Indonesia, but no details of the design or performance are available.

Conventional gravity thickeners are mechanically complex and require good supply chains for spare parts and operators with the knowledge and skills required for maintenance and repair of the mechanical scraper/scum skimmer assembly and the motor that drives it. Failure to remove sludge regularly will lead to sludge accumulation in the tank, which will increase the load on the scraper drive mechanism and quickly lead to bearing failures and complete plant breakdown. These points suggest that circular gravity thickeners with mechanically driven scrapers should only be considered for large septage treatment plants with appropriately skilled mechanical maintenance staff available in-house or through the local market.

Hopper-bottomed tanks. Conventional gravity thickeners are similar to the circular plan clarifiers that are used to settle solids in many wastewater treatment plants. The main differences lie in the increased side-wall depth and slightly lower surface overflow rates recommended for gravity thickeners. The similarities between gravity thickeners and sedimentation tanks suggest the possibility of using hopper-bottomed tanks for solids–liquid separation. Historically, hopper-bottomed sedimentation tanks were used for primary and secondary sedimentation at small and medium-sized septage treatment plants. They have no moving parts and are thus simple to operate – features that make them an attractive proposition in situations lacking a reliable power supply and highly trained staff. Influent enters the tank through a central feed pipe, flows down through the stilling box and then up through the main body of the thickener, exiting the tank over the peripheral weir. The up-flow velocity must be less than the settling velocity of solids so that settleable solids sink to the bottom of the tank. Figure 7.5 shows a typical hopper-bottomed tank.

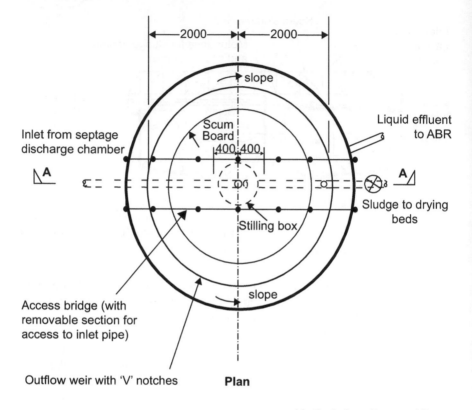

Plan

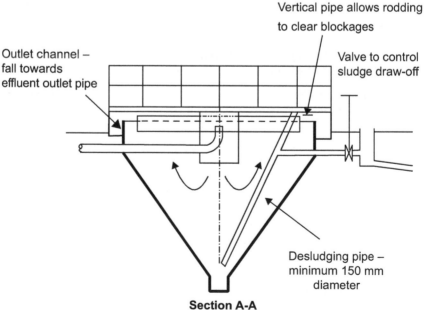

Section A-A

Figure 7.5 Plan and section of typical hopper-bottomed sedimentation tank

Hopper-bottomed tanks rely on gravity rather than a mechanized scraper to move sludge towards the sludge removal pipe. This simplifies operation but will only be possible if the sides of the tank slope steeply. The slope should be at least 60° to the horizontal for tanks that are square in plan and 45° to the horizontal for tanks that are circular in plan (Institute of Water Pollution Control, 1980). At lower slopes sludge will tend to adhere to the sides of the tank while relatively clear water flows to the inlet of the desludging pipe. The requirement for steeply sloping sides means that the depth and hence the cost of hopper-bottomed tanks increases rapidly with size. This limits the plan size of hopper-bottomed tanks to about 9 m across, which means that they are only appropriate for use in sewage treatment plants serving small communities. This should not be an issue for the much smaller flow received at septage treatment plants.

Hopper-bottomed tanks in Britain are desludged using hydrostatic pressure through a pipe that extends from the bottom of the hopper to a chamber alongside the tank. Figure 7.5 shows this arrangement. The outlet of the pipe is set sufficiently below the water level in the tank to provide the hydraulic gradient required to generate sludge flow through the pipe when the valve that controls flow through the pipe is opened. An adjustable bellmouth weir can be used to vary the hydrostatic head. Hydrostatic head is used to desludge a hopper-bottomed tank at a plant treating septage from a camp for internally displaced people at Sittwe in Myanmar. Desludging is required several times a day, which means that the sludge has not had time to consolidate. Another option will be to pump the sludge out of the hopper but this requires mechanical equipment and will fail if the pump breaks down or cannot be operated because of power cuts.

Photo 7.1 Hopper-bottomed gravity thickener, Sittwe, Myanmar
Source: photo by Solidarités International

Operational and design considerations

The high solids content of septage means that the sizing of gravity thickeners will usually be governed by the solids load rather than the hydraulic load. The result will often be a surface overflow rate that is less than the minimum rate recommended by standard texts. In wastewater treatment plants, low hydraulic loading rates can result in septic conditions, which cause problems with floating solids and odours. This problem is overcome by recycling effluent to maintain aerobic conditions, but this requires a reliable power source and will increase both operational costs and the hydraulic load on downstream units. The reliance on a reliable power source and mechanical equipment means that it will be unwise to rely on recirculation at smaller septage treatment plants. It is probable that low surface overflow rates will not be a problem for septage because the septage to be treated is already well-digested and so unlikely to experience significant biological change during the time that it is in the gravity thickener. If this is the case, it will be possible to design gravity thickeners to meet organic loading criteria and accept low velocities that drop to zero overnight and at other times when there is no discharge to the plant. Support for this view is given by the fact that the recommended surface overflow rate (equivalent to the upward flow velocity for vertical flow tanks) for the Dakar STT is 0.5 m^3/m^2 h or 12 m^3/m^2 d, below the 15.5–31 m^3/m^2 d range recommended for conventional gravity thickeners. The 0.5 m^3/m^2 h rate is a maximum rate and the mean flow rate through the Dakar tanks over a 24 hour period will be less than a third of this rate, falling to zero overnight.

Gravity thickeners should be sized to deal with the estimated peak-hour flow, based on the maximum rate at which tankers discharge their loads to the plant, adjusted as necessary to allow for any flow attenuation through the septage reception and preliminary treatment facilities.

Regular sludge removal is critical to the successful operation of gravity thickeners. Without it, excessive solids accumulation will occur, preventing the operation of mechanical scrapers and blocking sludge removal pipes. The high solids content of the influent septage means that desludging will be required much more frequently than for tanks treating municipal wastewater. Experience with a small hopper-bottomed tank used for solids–liquid separation at the Sittwe plant in Myanmar is that solids removal is required several times each day (Solidarités International, personal communication). Failure to remove sludge regularly from conventional gravity thickeners will lead to excessive sludge accumulation in the thickener, leading to increased load on the scraper drive mechanism and, eventually, premature bearing failure.

The incoming septage will contain floating solids, fats, oil, and grease, which will float to the surface of tanks and form a scum. Provision must be made to retain this floating material and periodically remove it. To retain scum, a baffle or scum board must be provided, typically located about 0.3 m inside the peripheral weir and extending at least 200 mm below the

Photo 7.2 Arrangement for scum removal, Sittwe hopper-bottomed tank

water surface. Provision is also required for periodic scum removal. One option will be to provide an adjustable weir, leading to a box from which a pipe controlled by a valve gives access to the sludge removal pipework. The adjustable weir should be located within the scum board and preferably close to the walkway across the tank to allow operator access. The first step in removing scum will be for operators to push it across the tank surface to the vicinity of the adjustable weir, using a 'raking' tool consisting of a long flat plate attached to a handle. The adjustable weir can then be lowered and the valve opened to allow a mixture of scum and liquid to be drawn off from the top of the tank. Photo 7.2 shows the simpler arrangement installed to allow removal of scum from the Sittwe hopper-bottomed tank: a chute with a handstop.

Design criteria and procedure

To allow for continued operation while a unit is decommissioned for repair and maintenance, at least two units should be provided, arranged in parallel. The units should be operated on a duty–standby basis and each should provide sufficient capacity to deal with the full hydraulic and suspended solids loads when the other has been taken out of service for repair or maintenance.

Table 7.2 Gravity thickener design criteria

Parameter	Symbol	Units	Recommended range/value	Notes	References
Solids loading rate	SLR	kg/m² h	4–6	Range is for primary solids (in wastewater treatment)	WEF (2010)
Surface overflow rate	SOR	m³/m² d	15.5–31	Range is maximum overflow rate for primary solids (in wastewater treatment)	WEF (2010), Metcalf & Eddy (2003)
Hydraulic retention time	HRT	h	2–6	Recommended range	WEF (2010)
Depth	Z	m	2–4		WEF (2010)

Table 7.2 summarizes recommended design criteria for circular plan gravity thickeners with mechanically powered scrapers. With the exception of the depth, these criteria are also appropriate for hopper-bottomed tanks receiving septage.

The design procedure is set out below:

1. Calculate the design loading using the equation:

$$L_s = \frac{Q_i P_d TSS_i}{(t_{op})}$$

   where L_s = the design loading in kg/h

   TSS_i = the mean suspended solids content of the influent in g/l (kg/m³)

   Q_i = the mean flow to the plant (m³/d)

   P_d = an assumed or assessed peak day factor; and

   t_{op} = the time for which the plant is operated in hours per day (h/d)

2. Calculate the total surface area (SA_T) (in m²) required by dividing the solids loading (L_s) by the allowable solids loading rate (SLR):

$$SA_T = \frac{L_s}{SLR}$$

3. Calculate the surface area of individual gravity thickeners. As already indicated, at least two units should be provided and the combined capacity of the operational units should be sufficient to deal with the design load when one unit is taken out of service for maintenance or repair. This will require that:

$$SA_{tank} = \frac{SA_T}{(n-1)}$$

where: SA_{tank} = the surface area of one unit; and

n = the number of units.

4. Calculate the tank volume. The volume (V_{tank}) of a circular gravity thickener is given the equation:

$$V_{tank} = SA_{tank}Z$$

where Z is the average depth of the tank. That for a circular plan hopper-bottomed tank is given by the equation:

$$V_{tank} = \pi\left[r^2d + r^3\tan\theta/3\right]$$

where r = the plan radius of the tank;

d = the depth from the top water level to the top of the hopper section; and

θ = the angle of the hopper sides to the horizontal.

5. Calculate the surface overflow rate (SOR) and the hydraulic retention time (HRT) using the equations:

$$SOR = 24\,\frac{Q_iP_d}{t_{op}SA_T}$$

$$HRT = 24\,\frac{(n-1)\,V_{tank}}{Q_i}$$

The SOR is calculated for the peak flow to the tank experienced when a tanker is discharging. The calculated HRT is that under mean design flow conditions. It will be shorter at times of peak daily flow but even then is likely to exceed the range given in Table 7.2.

6. Calculate the solids accumulation rate in the thickener and determine an appropriate desludging frequency.

$$DS_a = Q\,(TSS_i)\left(\frac{\%TSS_{rem}}{100}\right)$$

where DS_a = solids accumulation rate in kg/day

Q = daily flow in m³/d (will vary up to maximum of Q_iP_d)

TSS_i = the suspended solids concentration in the influent in g/l (kg/m³), If TSS_i remains constant, DS_a will increase with increased daily flow, reaching a peak when $Q = Q_iP_d$ and

$\%TSS_{rem}$ = the percentage of solids removed in the thickener.

The sludge accumulation rate is given by the equation:

$$Q_{sludge} = \frac{100DS_a}{\%DS \times \rho_{sludge}}$$

where Q_{sludge} = the volumetric sludge accumulation rate in m³/d,

$\%DS$ = the percentage dry solids content of the sludge withdrawn from the bottom of the tank, and

ρ_{sludge} = the density of the sludge.

The density of sludge can be taken as 1,000 kg/m³. The dry solids content of the sludge withdrawn from the bottom of the tank will depend on the nature and solids content of the influent sludge. Figures given for wastewater treatment plant sludge vary from 2–3 per cent for activated sludge, through 5–10 per cent for primary sludge, to 12 per cent for anaerobically digested primary sludge from primary digesters (Metcalf & Eddy, 2003). The most relevant figure for septage is the 6–7 per cent range recorded for the STT in Dakar, as described in Box 7.1. Based on these figures, the solids content of sludge removed from gravity thickeners is likely to lie in the range 6–10 per cent. A figure in this range should be assumed for design. The actual figure under operational conditions should be checked and design recommendations for the sludge accumulation rate and desludging frequency should be adjusted accordingly.

The desludging interval will depend on the solids content and settling characteristics of the influent. The operational staff should decide a suitable desludging regime based on operational experience at the plant. The mass and volume of sludge removed during each desludging event are given by the equations:

$$m_w = \frac{DS_a}{f_{desludging}}$$

and:

$$V_{sludge} = \frac{m_w}{\%DS \times \rho_{sludge}} = \frac{DS_a \times 100}{f_{desludging} \times \%DS \times \rho_{sludge}}$$

where $f_{desludging}$ = the number of times that the tank is desludged during a typical day

m_w = mass of sludge removed during each desludging event

V_{sludge} = volume of wet sludge removed during each desludging event

It is possible to first decide the desludging interval and then use these equations to calculate the mass and volume of sludge removed. For hopper-bottomed tanks, the better option will be to determine the desludging interval required to remove a defined volume of sludge. In this case, the second equation is rearranged to give:

$$f_{desludging} = \frac{DS_a \times 100}{V_{sludge} \times \%DS \times \rho_{sludge}}$$

Regardless of the desludging interval, the critical factors for the design of subsequent dewatering facilities will be volume of sludge removed in a day and the solids content of that sludge.

As already noted, at conventional wastewater treatment plants, the normal practice when the HRT exceeds the recommended range is to recirculate flow in order to increase the flow through the gravity thickener and so reduce the HRT. For septage treatment, this will only be appropriate for larger plants, where the resources required to manage recirculation are available. Given that septage will normally be well-digested, increased retention time should not lead to increased septicity. It should therefore be possible to omit recirculation, even when the HRT is less than the minimum recommended figure given in Table 7.2. Further research is required to confirm this view.

Where it is decided that recirculation is both necessary and possible, the procedure for calculating the recycle flow rate is as follows:

- Choose an HRT (HRT*) at the lower end of the range recommended in Table 7.2.
- Determine the total flow rate (Q_T) required to achieve this HRT for the tank volume calculated in Step 4 above, using the equation:

$$Q_T = \frac{V_{tank} \times 24}{HRT^*}$$

- Calculate the recycle flow rate (Q_R) by subtracting the influent flow rate as the influent flow rate will vary through the day (Q) from Q_T,

$$Q_R = Q_T - Q$$

A design example for a hopper-bottomed tank is given below. It reveals a need for frequent desludging, confirming the experience with the hopper-bottomed tank installed at the septage treatment plant serving internally displaced person (IDP) camps around Sittwe in Myanmar, which is desludged around 12 times per day.

Design example: Hopper-bottomed gravity thickener

A gravity thickener is to be designed to treat a mean septage flow of 100 m³/day with a mean influent solids concentration of 20,000 mg/l. The peak day discharge to the plant is 1.5 times the mean discharge. The assumed loading figures and design parameters assumed are listed below.

Parameter	Symbol	Value	Units
Mean flow	Q_i	100	m³/d
Peak day factor	P_d	1.5	–
Influent solids concentration	TSS_i	20,000	mg/l
Solids loading rate	SLR	6	kg/m²h
Desired HRT	HRT	6	h
Depth to top of hopper section	d	1	m
% TSS removal	$\%TSS_{rem}$	60	%
Desludging frequency	$f_{desludging}$	to be calculated	events/d
Operating hours	t_{op}	12	h/d
Number of units	n	2	–
Sludge % dry solids content	%DS	6	%
Density of sludge	ρ_{sludge}	1,000	kg/m³

1. Calculate the design loading (L_s):

$$L_s = 100 \text{ m}^3/\text{d} \times 1.5 \times 20{,}000 \text{ mg/l} \times \frac{1{,}000 \text{ l}}{1 \text{ m}^3} \times \frac{1 \text{ kg}}{1{,}000{,}000 \text{ mg}} \times \frac{1 \text{ d}}{12 \text{ h}}$$

$$= 250 \text{ kg/h}$$

2. Calculate the required surface area:

$$SA_T = \frac{250 \text{ kg/h}}{6 \text{ kg/m}^2 \text{ h}} = 42 \text{ m}^2$$

3. Determine the number and diameter of thickeners.
   Design for two duty thickeners and one standby thickener, each providing 50 per cent of the required capacity at peak design flow.
   Radius of each thickener = $\sqrt{[42/(2\pi)]}$ = 2.58 m, say 3 m.
4. Calculate the volume of the tank:
   Assume hopper-bottomed tanks, circular in plan, with 1 m vertical side wall above the hopper and the hopper sides sloping at 45° to horizontal:

$$V_{\text{tank}} = 2 \times \pi \times \left(3^2 \times 1 + 3^3 \tan 45°/3\right) = 113 \text{ m}^3$$

5. Calculate and check the overflow rate and hydraulic retention time:

$$\text{SOR at peak daily flow} = \frac{100 \times 1.5 \text{ m}^3/\text{d}}{42 \text{ m}^2} = 3.6 \text{ m/d}$$

$$\text{HRT} = \frac{113 \text{ m}^3 \times 24 \text{ h}}{150 \text{ m}^3 \text{ d}} = 0.75 \text{ d} = 18 \text{ h}$$

The HRT is higher and the SOR is lower than those recommended for gravity thickeners treating sludge from a wastewater treatment plant.
   For an HRT of 6 hours (0.25 d), (The HRT will be even higher at the mean daily flow) the total flow Q_T would have to be:

$$Q_T = \frac{113 \text{ m}^3 \times 24}{6} = 452 \text{ m}^3 \text{ d}$$

The recirculation flow required (Q_R) at the mean daily flow would be (452 – 100) m³/d = 352 m³/d or an average of about 4 l/sec. Given the digested nature of the septage, it is unlikely that septicity will be a problem and so no recirculation has been assumed.
6. Calculate the mass and volume of solids accumulated at the bottom of the thickener:
   If 60 per cent of the solids entering the gravity thickeners settle out, the dry solids accumulation rate at peak flow will be:

$$DS_a = \left(150 \text{ m}^3/\text{d} \times 20 \text{ kg/m}^3 \times 60/100\right) = 1800 \text{ kg/d}$$

At a dry solids content of 6 per cent, the daily sludge production will be:

$$V_{\text{sludge}} = [(1800 \text{ kg/d})(10^{-3} \text{ m}^3/\text{kg})]/6/100 = 30 \text{ m}^3/\text{d}$$

This will be divided between two hopper-bottomed tanks, so 15 m³ of sludge must be removed from each tank each day. If the tanks are desludged when the sludge depth in the hopper reaches 1.25 m, the volume to be removed each time a tank is desludged will be $(1.25^3\pi)/3 = 2.04$ m³. Each tank will therefore need to be desludged between seven and eight times each day, at intervals of about 1.5 hours for a 12-hour working day.

Decanting drying beds

As already noted, conventional drying beds are simple and easy to operate but their land take is much higher than that of other solids–liquid separation technologies. Decanting drying beds offer one possible option for combining the simplicity of conventional drying beds with reduced land requirement (US EPA, 1987). Figure 7.6 is a diagrammatic section through a decanting drying bed, as used in the USA. The decanting bed is paved so that liquid is removed by evaporation and decanting rather than by percolation through a porous sand and gravel bed. The sludge is stirred to prevent the formation of a crust at the liquid surface that would inhibit evaporation. Sludge is delivered through a vertical pipe located in the centre of the bed. From this highest point in the bed, the floor slopes down to the edges of the bed at a rate of 0.2–0.3 per cent. Excess supernatant water is drawn off through pipes located in each corner of the bed. This arrangement requires adjustable-height telescopic valves that can be lowered to allow the supernatant water to be decanted. A series of handstops will provide a simpler alternative.

The US EPA suggests that for sludge with good settling characteristics, it is possible to decant 20–30 per cent of its liquid fraction. Given the generally good settling characteristics of digested septage, it is possible that a greater proportion of its liquid fraction can be decanted. Several fill-and-decant cycles are possible before the partly dewatered sludge is left to evaporate. The retention time on the bed will depend on climate conditions and the provision made for mixing. EPA reported a design loading rate of 244 kg TSS/m² year for decanting drying beds in Roswell, New Mexico, which has a hot and dry climate (US EPA, 1987). Like the STTs and SSCs described above, the decanting drying bed approach incorporates the idea of repeated loading of a single unit, followed by a period during which the sludge is allowed to dewater. The hydraulic overflow rate of the Ghanaian STTs and the Indonesian SSCs, though significantly lower than that of gravity thickeners, is typically 50 or more times greater than the rate of liquid removal in conventional drying beds. This suggests that decanting drying beds should require a smaller footprint than conventional drying beds. They may thus provide a simple but effective alternative to drying beds where sufficient land for these is not available and the management systems required to operate more sophisticated technologies do not exist. Figure 7.7 shows a possible arrangement for a shallow decanting bed arrangement, incorporating features from the Achimota STTs, and Box 7.2

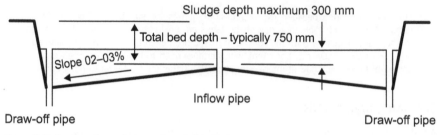

Figure 7.6 Section through decanting drying bed

Box 7.2 Possible operating procedure for decanting drying beds

Loading phase – three days. Septage discharged to a single drying bed, which would have to have sufficient capacity to take all the septage delivered during this period. For 40 m³/d, the capacity for 3 days' retention would be 120 m³. If the depth of septage is to be limited to 600 mm, this would require a total area of 120/0.6 = 200 m², say 20 m × 10 m.

Settling phase – one day should be sufficient, at the end of which supernatant could be drawn off down to a level of 200–250 mm. This might be done by using a series of handstops set at a range of heights.

Drying phase – the length of this would depend on the rate of drying but in hot climates is likely to lie in the range 7–15 days.

Desludging phase – this will depend on the availability of tools and labour but should typically take around two days.

Based on these timings, the total cycle for a single drying bed would be between 13 and 21 days, requiring between five and seven drying beds.

The TS loading rate for a TS concentration of 10,000 mg/l and a 21-day loading cycle would be 104 kg TS/m² year. For a conventional bed with a sludge depth of 200 mm and a shorter 12-day loading cycle, the TS loading would be 61 kg/m² year. The bed area required would increase from 1,400 m² to 2,400 m². This would be at the expense of reduced quality of the combined supernatant/percolate liquid fraction taken from the bed.

---

sets out a possible loading cycle and includes approximate calculations and loading rates.

Further investigation, including field trials, is required to assess and quantify the potential benefits of decanting drying beds and establish design and operational guidelines. Points to be investigated include the length of the operational cycle to be used, the solids loading rates that can be achieved, the depth to which supernatant water can be decanted without entraining a large amount of solids, the optimum depth of beds/ponds, and the likely quality of decanted supernatant water. Because of the lack of operational evidence, no detailed design guidelines are given here. The most appropriate use for decanting drying beds is likely to be to achieve an increased solids loading rate, as compared with that achieved using conventional drying beds for septage with a low solids content.

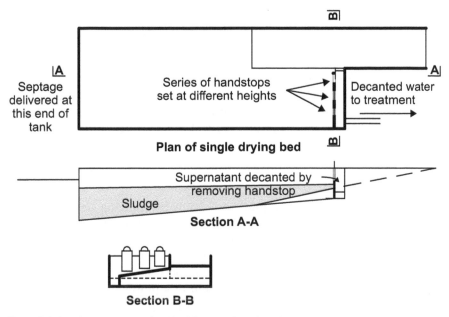

Figure 7.7 Possible shallow solids–liquid separation chamber arrangement

Mechanical presses

Overview

Mechanical dewatering devices have been used for many years for dewatering sludge from wastewater treatment plants. They require less land than other solids–liquid separation processes, but require a reliable electricity supply, skilled labour, an expensive chemical polymer, and an effective supply chain for spare parts. These requirements must be considered at the planning stage.

Two types of press are considered here, the screw press and the belt filter press, both of which have been used for septage and faecal sludge treatment in lower-income countries. They are normally deployed immediately after screening and grit removal and this book considers them as a solids–liquid separation technology, although they may also be used for dewatering of separated solids as explained in Chapter 9. Mechanical presses have low energy costs compared with centrifuges, the other mechanical solids–liquid separation and dewatering option. Other operating costs to be considered when assessing mechanical dewatering options include expenditure on periodic maintenance, replacement parts, and polymer. The cost of polymer will normally be the largest operating cost, and financial projections should also take account of the possibility of occasional expenditure on major repairs and replacement of failed and worn-out components. Mechanical presses will require trained operators with the knowledge required to monitor performance and adjust polymer dosing rates to optimize performance. Continued performance will be dependent on the availability of maintenance staff with appropriate knowledge and skills and effective supply chains for replacement spare parts.

Mechanical press manufacturers should be involved in the planning and design process. The usual procedure is to specify the performance required from the press and ask for quotes from several manufacturers. Once a preferred supplier has been selected, that supplier will normally be closely involved in the detailed design of the equipment.

System description

Mechanical presses separate liquid from solids by applying pressure to the sludge to separate liquid and force the separated liquid through a filter or fine mesh which retains the dewatered sludge. The addition of chemical polymer upstream of the press is required to precondition the sludge and improve dewatering effectiveness. A dilute solution of polymer (typically 0.5 per cent or less) is made up from either an emulsion or a powder and is mixed with the sludge in a flocculation tank. Sludge is pumped into the flocculation tank, from where it flows into the press. Dewatered sludge is moved on to a conveyor belt while the liquid drains out and is collected separately. Further information on screw and belt presses is given below.

Screw press. Screw presses separate liquid from solids by forcing sludge through a screw or auger contained within a perforated screen basket. The screw diameter increases with distance along the shaft while the gap between its blades decreases so that the gap between basket, shaft, and flights continuously decreases and sludge is squeezed into a progressively smaller space. This results in an increase in pressure along the press. Pressure probes are used to control and monitor the pressure to ensure treatment performance. The inclined press includes a pneumatic or manually adjusted counter-pressure cone that maintains a constant sludge pressure at the discharge end of the press. The water squeezed from the sludge drops into a collector channel at the bottom of the press, which conveys it to the next stage of treatment. The dewatered cake drops out of the end of the press for storage, disposal, or further drying on a drying bed or in a thermal dryer. High-pressure water is used periodically inside the press for cleaning. Photo 7.3 shows the screw press at Duri Kosambi Septage Treatment Plant in Jakarta.

Belt filter press. Belt filter presses separate liquid from solids, using gravity and applied pressure between fabric belts. The process typically involves four steps: preconditioning, gravity drainage, low-pressure linear compression, and high-pressure roller compression (and shear). After preconditioning, sludge passes through a gravity drainage zone where liquid drains by gravity from the sludge. It is then moved on to a low-pressure zone (sometimes referred to

Photo 7.3 Screw press at Duri Kosambi, Jakarta

as a wedge zone), where two belts come together to squeeze out liquid from the solids, forcing liquid through the fabric belts. In most cases, the sludge is then subjected to higher pressure as it is forced between a series of rollers, which create shearing forces and compression to further dewater the sludge. The dewatered sludge cake is then scraped off the belts for conveyance to the next stage of treatment or disposal. The belts are cleaned with high-pressure washwater after each pass. Figure 7.8 and Photo 7.4 show a schematic view of a belt filter press and a picture of an installation for septage treatment, respectively.

Performance

Mechanical presses can receive sludge with a solids content of as low as 1 per cent, although a solids content of 2 per cent or more is preferable. Sludge with a lower solids content will require more time to dewater, so that the sizing of presses will be determined by hydraulic rather than solids loading when the material to be treated is septage with a low solids content. The final solids content of dewatered sludge typically lies in the range of 15–25 per cent for both types of press. Performance depends upon the sludge characteristics, polymer dosing, and equipment characteristics and operation (e.g., for belt presses: gravity drainage configuration, belt speed, applied pressure, etc.). Stabilized or digested sludge, including most types of septage, can be dewatered to a greater solids content than fresh faecal sludge or waste-activated sludge. Both types of press can remove 85–95 per cent of the solids contained in

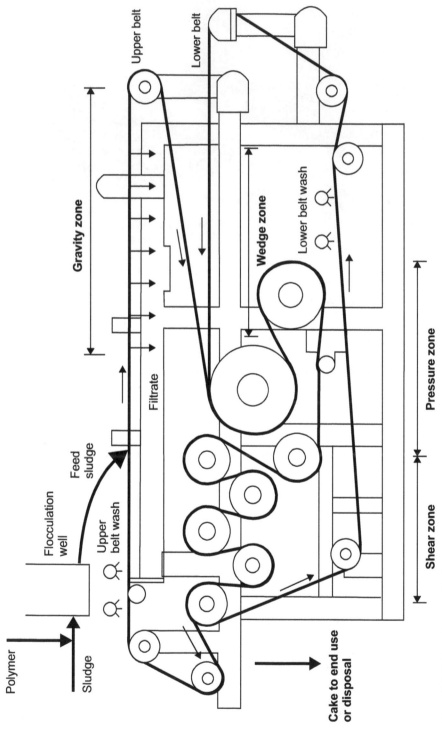

Figure 7.8 Schematic view of belt press
Source: WEF (2010)

Photo 7.4 Belt filter press at Duri Suwung Septage Treatment Plant, Denpasar, Indonesia
Source: Chengyan Zhang of Stantec

the raw sludge (WEF, 2010). Table 7.3 provides a summary comparison of the screw press and belt filter press. Additional information is given by Gillette et al. (2009).

Operational and design considerations

Many operational and design considerations apply to both belt filter and screw presses and so the two are discussed together here, with differences noted where appropriate. Points to be considered when assessing options include manufacturer design support, pre- and post-treatment requirements, ancillary system and support requirements, operation and maintenance considerations, and environmental and safety considerations.

Manufacturer support during selection and design. This is necessary because of the differing performance, specifications, set-up needs, and ongoing operational needs of different models. Before discussing options with manufacturers, it will be important to have gained some understanding of the characteristics of the material to be treated and be able to assess how their products would deal with these characteristics. For example, some belt press manufacturers have presses with three belts, which allows the gravity drainage zone belt to be controlled independently of the pressure zone belts, which is particularly valuable for dilute sludges.

Pre-treatment and post-treatment requirements for effective operation. Pre-treatment requirements for mechanical presses include the following:

- *Removal of grit and gross solids.* This is particularly important for belt filter presses, since unscreened solids, especially glass and hard materials,

Table 7.3 Summary comparison of mechanical dewatering equipment

Technology	Operation	Maintenance	Dewatering performance	Cost
Screw press	Intermittent medium-pressure washwater (<10% sludge flow rate) Simpler operation Enclosure keeps surrounding environment clean and safe Low energy consumption	Fewer parts to maintain	Can receive sludge with low solids (<1%) 15–25% final dry solids Less sensitive to non-homogeneous sludge characteristics	Higher capital costs Slightly lower operating cost
Belt filter press	Continuous washwater (50–100% sludge flow rate) Unenclosed units are messy to operate, allow visibility of process performance, but present health hazard from harmful gases and aerosols Low energy consumption	Simple equipment to maintain (rollers, bearing, belt) More parts to monitor/inspect and maintain	Receive as low as 0.5% solids (3-belt press best) 15–25% final dry solids Can be provided with greater capacity for single unit	Lower capital cost Slightly higher operating cost

might damage the belts. It is best if this is done using mechanically cleaned fine screens, designed to remove both grit and larger solids.

- *Flow balancing and mixing.* These are desirable to smooth out the variations in flow resulting from intermittent sludge delivery and the highly variable characteristics of tanker loads. Simple flow-balancing options were considered in Chapter 6. Mixing to homogenize incoming flows might be carried out in a tank, using aeration to agitate the tank contents and effect mixing.
- *Conditioning with polymer.* As already noted, the normal arrangement is to mix polymer with sludge in a flocculation tank located ahead of the press. Operators must be trained to monitor performance and adjust the polymer dose as required in response to changing sludge characteristics. Manufacturers should be asked to provide advice on the design of systems to add polymer to their presses.

Post-treatment, dewatered sludge must be moved away from the presses to storage or further treatment. Separated sludge typically drops from the press onto a conveyor belt, which carries it to a storage area.

Depending on the intended end use of the solids, they may require further treatment. Dewatering and drying options are described in Chapters 9 and 10. Liquid separated in mechanical presses will need further treatment to meet typical effluent discharge standards, as described in Chapter 8. A well-operated mechanical press should achieve reductions in the organic and suspended solids content of separated liquid that are comparable to those achieved by sand drying beds and significantly higher than those achieved by simple settling.

Sludge press manufacturers will normally be able to provide a complete treatment package, including grit and solids removal, flow mixing as necessary, provision for polymer addition and mixing, the sludge presses themselves, and subsequent provision for removal of pressed sludge and liquid.

Many manufacturers offer integrated systems that combine pre-treatment, sludge presses, and conveyance of treated sludge. For example, the septage treatment plants at Duri Kosambi and Pulo Gebang in Jakarta use inclined screw presses, installed as elements in an integrated treatment system comprising:

- mechanical screening and grit removal;
- polymer dosing;
- screw press dewatering; and
- conveyor belt transport to covered storage/drying areas.

Mechanical press operation requires a reliable source of clean, pressurized washwater. It is possible to clean belt filter presses using compressed air but this method is not widely used. A strainer may be used on the washwater supply piping to prevent debris from clogging the spray nozzles. Washwater is provided intermittently, typically several times per hour for screw presses, and continuously for belt filter presses. The washwater will require subsequent treatment and this needs to be taken into account when designing the downstream liquid treatment process. Typical washwater requirements for screw and belt presses are as follows:

- *Screw presses*. The instantaneous washwater flow rate may range from 70 to 450 litres per minute, typically at a pressure of at least 4 bar (400 kPa). The total average washwater flowrate ranges from 2 to 9 per cent of solids feed flow rate (based on WEF, 2010).
- *Belt filter presses*. The instantaneous washwater flow rate may range from 70 to 450 litres per minute, typically at a pressure of up to 8 bar (800 kPa). The total average washwater flowrate ranges from 50 to 100 per cent of the solids feed flow rate (WEF, 2010).

Mechanical press performance should be continuously monitored. This is required so that the polymer dose can be adjusted as necessary in response to changes in the characteristics of incoming sludge. It also facilitates early detection of any problems. This type of monitoring will not be possible unless staff have received appropriate training. Supply chains must cover both consumables, in particular the supply of polymer, and spare and replacement parts. To ensure prompt supply of spare and replacement parts, it may be advisable to require that the manufacturer has a local presence, preferably directly but, failing that, through an authorized agent.

The design should take account of the need for maintenance and repair. At least two presses with their associated polymer dosing and washwater systems should be installed so that treatment can continue if one press is out of service. To allow for periods when presses are decommissioned for maintenance and repair, the total capacity provided should exceed the estimated peak sludge flow. Ideally, one or more duty presses and a standby press should be provided, with standby polymer dosing and washwater systems as appropriate. The option of reducing capital costs by extending the operating period of the remaining presses when one press is decommissioned might be considered. This option is only likely to be viable where supply chains are good so that maintenance and repair time is minimized.

Belt filter presses have more maintenance requirements than screw presses, since they have more moving parts and components, including belts, rollers, and bearings. Operator attention is required for both types of equipment to inspect for bearing failures and keep the spray nozzles clean and effective. Operators should also monitor belt condition and keep the gravity sludge drainage area free of blockages and sludge build-up.

Designs should take account of environmental and health concerns. Screw presses are compact and enclosed so that they do not create an environmental nuisance. Belt filter presses can be either open or enclosed. An open arrangement is cheaper, allows inspection of the dewatering process and facilitates access. The layout should provide for good airflow around presses in order to minimize potential health and environmental concerns arising from aerosols, pathogens, and harmful gases released into the area around the presses. Enclosed belt filter pressures are available, but add cost, can be prone to corrosion, limit visibility, and will typically require an odour-handling system to be provided with it to convey and/or treat the hazardous gases and odours mentioned. Because mechanical presses have moving parts, operator safety training should cover the need to take appropriate precautions when working near moving equipment. Box 7.3 provides information on experience with screw presses in Greater Jakarta, Indonesia. This illustrates some of the points identified above.

Design criteria and procedures

Mechanical press selection and sizing are based primarily on solids loading and hydraulic loading. Other parameters that will influence the design include the number of hours for which the presses will operate each day and, in the case of belt presses, the width of the belt. Table 7.4 summarizes the recommended design criteria for screw and belt filter presses.

Box 7.3 Experience with screw presses in Greater Jakarta, Indonesia

The Duri Kosambi and Pulo Gebang septage treatment plants in Jakarta, and the nearby Bekasi septage treatment plant, provide useful case studies of the operation of screw press dewatering systems. Operators at the Jakarta plants do not adjust the amount of polymer added to the septage as it was programmed by the manufacturer when the presses were commissioned. Significant problems at the Jakarta plants, particularly at Duri Kosambi, were leakage from the presses and, at times, poor quality of the filtrate. The tiled floor was dangerously slippery because of the leakage from the press. The leakage may have been a consequence of malfunctioning pressure sensors and/or wearing of seals caused by poor grit and solids removal upstream of the presses. (At Duri Kosambi, the mechanical screens were bypassed because of the problems noted in the caption to Figure 8.8.) The poor filtrate quality was generally related to poor polymer dosing because the water supply to the polymer systems and some sensors controlling the polymer makeup had failed, resulting in an ad hoc mixing of polymer that provided variable concentrations of polymer to the presses.

Despite these deficiencies, both plants were producing sludge suitable for transport by conveyor belt to large covered areas, described as 'sludge drying areas'. In practice, these functioned as storage areas and no further drying was necessary. Dried sludge has accumulated over the years that the screw presses have been operational. At both Duri Kosambi and Pulo Gebang, the water pressed out of the sludge is treated in a series of ponds. At both locations, aeration is available for the ponds, through surface aerators at Duri Kosambi and bubble aeration at Pulo Gebang, but is used only intermittently.

The absence of effective supply chains can compromise the long-term performance of screw presses and other mechanical dewatering devices. The first screw press at Pulo Gebang, installed in 2010, was not operational in 2014. The reason given by staff was the unavailability of replacements for failed components, which were only obtainable from Germany. Similarly, it seems that delays in replacing malfunctioning pressure sensors occurred because replacements were either unaffordable or unobtainable. Since the manufacturer had a local agent company in Jakarta, it seems that the problem may have been caused by the lack of funds to purchase the parts rather than inability to have them shipped to Indonesia.

Bekasi, also in Greater Jakarta, provides a more recent and, to date, trouble-free example of the use of screw presses. The presses are installed at a new 100 m³/day septage treatment facility operated by a recently formed sludge treatment utility. To ensure effective operation of the facility, the utility recruited and trained appropriately skilled staff, involving them in implementation from the time when equipment was selected so that they were aware of key design decisions and were able to develop a close relationship with the screw press manufacturer.

The loading rates given in Table 7.4 are compatible with the solids and hydraulic loading rates on the larger septage treatment plants where mechanical presses are most likely to be deployed. For example, the hydraulic loading rate on a treatment plant receiving 400 m³/d of septage over an eight-hour period will be 50 m³/h. If the solids content of the septage is 1.5 per cent, the solids loading rate over the 8-hour period will be 750 kg/h. In this case, hydraulic loading will be critical. For septage with a solids content greater than about 3 per cent, solids loading is likely to be critical.

Mechanical press design procedure. Mechanical press equipment should be selected and designed in consultation with equipment suppliers since design

Table 7.4 Summary of mechanical press design criteria

Parameter	Symbol	Screw press – recommended range	Belt filter press – recommended range	Notes on supplier role in design
Solids loading rate (Tchobanoglous et al., 2014)	λ_s	15–1,900 kg/h	180–1600 kg/h m	Confirm with equipment supplier – may vary with sludge characteristics
Hydraulic loading rate	λ_1	0.3–48 m³/h (WEF 2010)	6–40 m³/h m (Tchobanoglous et al., 2014)	Confirm with equipment supplier
Belt width	W_b	Not applicable	0.5–3.0 m (typically 1–2 m)	Confirm with equipment supplier
Polymer dose	C_p	3–17.5 g polymer/ kg dry solids (WEF, 2010)		Depends on sludge characteristics and type of polymer
				Confirm with polymer supplier and equipment manufacturer after bench testing with sludge samples
Operating time per day	t_{op}	4–12 hours/day (normally the same period that sludge is received from tankers)		Provide this information to the equipment supplier

parameters are specific to each manufacturer and model. Information provided to suppliers should include the following: hydraulic loading, including information on average and maximum rates of flow, proposed operating period, sludge characteristics (TSS and VSS), and sludge source, which may influence sludge characteristics and hence press performance. Based on this information, the supplier will normally propose a system to meet the purchaser's requirements, giving information on the size and number of screw presses, solids loading rate (design and maximum capacity), hydraulic loading rate (design and maximum capacity), polymer system size and capacity (pump and storage tank size), polymer dose and consumption, and washwater requirement.

The steps in an approximate calculation to determine basic design parameters and the likely scale of polymer use are summarized below.

1. Determine the peak and average daily volumetric loadings and calculate the peak daily mass loading:

$$m_{sp} = Q_{sp} \times TSS$$

$$m_{sm} = Q_{sm} \times TSS$$

where Q_{sp} = peak daily volume of septage delivered for treatment in m³/d,

Q_{sm} = mean daily volume of septage delivered for treatment in m³/d

TSS = suspended solids concentration of the incoming septage in g/l (kg/m³),

m_{sp} = peak daily dry solids loading in kg/d.

m_{sm} = mean daily dry solids loading in kg/d.

2.   Calculate the peak hourly hydraulic and solids loadings on the presses:

$$Q_{sph} = Q_{sp} / t_{op}$$

$$m_{sph} = Q_{sph} \times TSS$$

where Q_{sph} = peak-hour flow to be treated (m³/h),

m_{sph} = peak-hour dry solids loading to be treated (kg/h),

t_{op} = number of hours for which presses will operate during a normal working day.

3.   Determine number of units required:

Compare the calculated mass and hydraulic loading with information on equipment capacity provided by equipment manufacturers. For screw presses, choose units that provide at least enough capacity to deal with peak-hour hydraulic and solids loadings. A minimum of two units should be provided and the calculations should indicate the proposed strategy for dealing with periods when one press is out of commission for repair and maintenance.

For a belt filter press, the capacity per unit width should be calculated and used to assess the belt width required. This will be the larger of the values obtained from the equations:

$$w_b = \frac{m_{sph}}{\lambda_s}$$

$$w_b = \frac{Q_{sph}}{\lambda_1}$$

where w_b = total belt width required (m),

λ_s = rated dry solids capacity of the belt press model being considered (kg/m h), and

λ_1 = rated hydraulic capacity of the belt press model being considered (m³/m h).

4.   Calculate polymer dosing requirement:

An assessment of the annual polymer requirement will be required when comparing the operational costs of different solids–liquid separation options. The peak daily and mean annual polymer requirements are given by the equations:

$$m_{polymer, day} = \frac{m_{sp}C_p}{1000}$$

$$m_{\text{polymer, year}} = \frac{m_{\text{sm}} C_\text{p} D}{1000}$$

where $m_{\text{polymer, day}}$ = maximum daily polymer requirement (kg),
$m_{\text{polymer, year}}$ = yearly polymer requirement (kg),
C_p = polymer requirement (g polymer/kg solids in septage),
and
D = number of days in year for which plant is operational (d/year).

The polymer dose depends on the specific polymer used and the characteristics of the sludge. The polymer supplier or equipment manufacturer may indicate the likely required dosage, but the dosage should always be confirmed by performing jar tests.

Screw press design calculation example

Consider a screw press requirement to provide solids–liquid separation for a treatment plant designed to receive 150 m³ of septage for 5 days per week for 52 weeks of the year.

Parameter	Symbol	Value	Units
Operation time	t_{op}	8	h/d
Peak hydraulic load	Q_{sp}	150	m³/d
Mean hydraulic load	Q_{sm}	100	m³/d
Influent solids content	TSS	20	kg/m³
Polymer requirement	C_p	10	g/kg dry solids

1. Calculate the peak and average dry mass loading:

$$m_{sp} = 150 \text{ m}^3/\text{d} \times 20 \text{ kg/m}^3 = 3000 \text{ kg/d}$$

$$m_{sm} = 100 \text{ m}^3/\text{d} \times 20 \text{ kg/m}^3 = 2000 \text{ kg/d}$$

2. Calculate peak hourly hydraulic and dry mass loading:

$$Q_{sph} = \frac{150 \text{ m}^3/\text{d}}{8 \text{ h/d}} = 18.75 \text{ m}^3/\text{h}$$

$$m_{sph} = (18.75 \text{ m}^3/\text{h})(20 \text{ kg/m}^3) = 375 \text{ kg/h}$$

3. Determine the number of units required.
    Both hydraulic and solids loadings are within the design range of a single screw press, as given in Table 7.4. Given the relatively low solids content of the incoming septage, it is likely that hydraulic loading will be critical, but this should be checked with manufacturers of suitable screw presses. To allow for continued operation at least two screw presses should be provided. Provide either two screw presses, each rated at 18.75 m³/h to operate in duty/standby mode or two duty screw presses, each rated at at least 9.4 m³/h, with a standby unit to give three presses in total.

Alternatively, determine requirements if belt filter presses are provided.

Based on available equipment (to be confirmed with suppliers), assume a solids loading rate of 400 kg/m h and hydraulic loading rate of 15m³/m h.

4. Based on solids loading:

$$w_b = \frac{375 \text{ kg/h}}{400 \text{ kg/m h}} = 0.9375 \text{ m}$$

5. Based on hydraulic loading

$$w_b = \frac{18.75 \text{ m}^3/\text{h}}{15 \text{ m}^3/\text{m h}} = 1.25 \text{ m}$$

The required belt width is governed by the hydraulic loading rate. Provide two units with at least a 1.25-m belt width to operate on a duty/standby basis. Most manufacturers provide belt filter presses in a range of standard widths, typically multiples of 0.5 m. Providing two presses with a 1.5-m belt width will provide some additional capacity to cater for varying sludge characteristics.

6. Calculate daily and annual polymer requirement:

$$m_{polymer, \, day} = 3000 \text{ kg solids/d} \times \frac{10 \text{ g polymer}}{\text{kg solids}} \times \left[\frac{1 \text{ kg}}{1000 \text{ g}} \right]$$

$$= 30 \text{ kg/d}$$

$$m_{polymer, \, year} = 2000 \text{ kg solids/d} \times \frac{10 \text{ g polymer}}{\text{kg solids}} \times \left[\frac{1 \text{ kg}}{1000 \text{ g}} \right]$$

$$\times \frac{52 \text{ weeks} \times 5 \text{ days}}{1 \text{ yr}}$$

$$= 5,200 \text{ kg polymer/year}$$

Note that the annual dry polymer requirement is based on the mean loading over the year rather than the peak loading.

Key points from this chapter

Table 7.5 summarizes the information given in this chapter on the performance of the various solids–liquid separation options. It includes information on surface overflow rates for technologies that rely on gravity settling.

Key points made in this chapter include the following:

- Mechanisms for solids–liquid separation include sedimentation, pressure, filtration, and evaporation. Sludge presses use less land than systems that rely on sedimentation and these, in turn, require significantly less land than those that rely on filtration and evaporation.
- Where land is available and operational skills are limited, drying beds are a good option for combined solids–liquid separation and sludge dewatering. They should be considered where the sludge or septage to be treated has a solids content of 5 per cent or more, preferably after partial digestion if the sludge is fresh.

Table 7.5 Comparison of main solids–liquid separation options considered in this chapter

Solids–liquid separation option	Typical solids content of separated sludge	Percentage reduction in liquid strength		Surface overflow rate (m³/m² d)
		TSS	BOD	
Unplanted drying beds	At least 20% (more possible in hot dry climates and with longer retention time)	95%[1]	70–90%[1]	0.005–0.015
Anaerobic ponds	Typically 10%	Perhaps 80%	Depends on temperature – around 60% at 20°C	Typically around 0.6 depending on retention
Belt presses	Typically 12–35% depending on type of sludge	95%		Not applicable
Gravity thickening in hopper-bottomed tanks	4–10% Typical 6%	30–60%	30–50%	Up to 30
Dakar SSTs[2]	6%	50% (but dependent on length of cycle)	65–80%	12
Achimota STTs[3]	Up to 15%	50% or more	10–20% after 4 weeks loading	0.25–0.5

Notes: [1] See Chapter 9 for further information
[2] Information on Dakar-style STTs based on Dodane and Bassan (2014).
[3] Information on Achimota-style STTs based on Heinss et al. (1998). Similar performance might be achieved with decanting drying beds.

- Where operational resources are limited and the septage to be treated has a low solids content, solids–liquid separation may be combined with biological treatment in anaerobic ponds. This option will only be viable if effective systems are in place to ensure that the ponds are regularly desludged.
- In all other situations, solids–liquid separation prior to treatment of separated solid and liquid fractions is desirable.
- STTs are a recognized solids–liquid separation technology. There are two distinct types of tank: the Ghanaian design, which has an eight-week operating cycle with sludge allowed to dry to a solid state, when it is removed using front-end loaders; and the Senegalese design, which uses a shorter operating cycle, with sludge pumped out at the end of each cycle. Both are batch processes.
- The Ghanaian STT design has some similarities to the decanting drying bed concept described by the US EPA. Supernatant water is allowed to flow

through the tank for around four weeks, after which the contents are left to dry for four weeks before being removed using front-end loaders. The design could possibly be modified to use shallower tanks, provision for decanting supernatant water and perhaps a reduced operating cycle. This option, which combines initial sedimentation in a pond with subsequent drying in what is in effect a drying bed, could be developed for use at small treatment plants where management resources are limited.

- The Senegalese STTs are similar in outline to rectangular gravity thickeners, but they have no scraping mechanism to move accumulated sludge to a sump, from where it can be removed by hydrostatic pressure or a pump. In the absence of such an arrangement, sludge removed from the tank is likely to be mixed with supernatant water, which will increase its water content. There is also a danger that sludge will accumulate in the tank over time.
- An alternative to STTs for medium-sized plants would be to provide hopper-bottomed tanks for solids–liquid separation, with sludge withdrawn from the bottom of the hopper at frequent intervals. The sludge will not have had time to consolidate, but this arrangement will make it much less likely that supernatant water is drawn off along with sludge. The key to the success of such tanks will be active management of the sludge removal process, without which sludge accumulation will lead to system failure. Calculations and operational experience suggest that sludge removal will be required several times a day.
- Sludge presses are an option for larger plants. They typically produce sludge with a solids content in the range 15–25 per cent, significantly higher than the 5–10 per cent that might be achieved by most forms of gravity separation. Their energy requirement is low, but good performance depends on the addition of polymers. They should be considered for larger plants if the appropriate operation and maintenance systems and effective supply chains for polymer and replacement parts exist or can be instigated.
- In the past, Imhoff tanks have been used as a solids–liquid separation technology. Unfortunately, the rapid sludge accumulation rate arising from the high solids content of septage leads to a need for frequent desludging, which undermines the rationale for a system incorporating solids digestion. For this reason, this book does not recommend the use of Imhoff tanks.

References

Badji, K., Dodane, P-H., Mbéguéré, M. and Koné, D. (2011) *Traitement des boues de vidange: éléments affectant la performance des lits de séchage non plantés en taille réelle et les mécanismes de séchage,* Dübendorf: EAWAG/SANDEC <https://www.pseau.org/outils/ouvrages/eawag_gestion_des_boues_de_vidange_optimisation_de_la_filiere_2011.pdf> [accessed 24 March 2018].

Bassan, M., Dodane, P-H. and Strande, L. (2014) 'Treatment mechanisms', in L. Strande, M. Ronteltap, and D. Brdjanovic (eds), *Faecal Sludge Management: Systems Approach for Implementation and Operation*, London: IWA Publishing <https://www.un-ihe.org/sites/default/files/fsm_book_lr.pdf> [accessed 24 March 2018].

Dodane, P-H. and Bassan, M. (2014) 'Settling-thickening tanks', in L. Strande, M. Ronteltap, and D. Brdjanovic (eds), *Faecal Sludge Management: Systems Approach for Implementation and Operation*, London: IWA Publishing <www.un-ihe.org/sites/default/files/fsm_ch06.pdf> [accessed 3 April 2018].

Gillette, R., Swanbank, S. and Overacre, R. (2009) *Improved Efficiency of Dewatering Alternatives to Conventional Dewatering Technologies*, 2009 PNCWA Webinar, Recent Developments in Biosolids Management Processes, <http://www.pncwa.org/assets/documents/Alternative%20Dewatering%20Technologies%20Gillette%20200908%20pncwa.pdf> [accessed 8 March 2018].

Heinss, U., Larmie, S.A. and Strauss, M. (1998) *Solids Separation and Pond Systems for the Treatment of Faecal Sludges in the Tropics: Lessons Learnt and Recommendations for Preliminary Design*, 2nd edn (SANDEC Report No. 05/98), Dübendorf: Eawag/Sandec <https://www.sswm.info/sites/default/files/reference_attachments/HEINSS%201998%20Solids%20Separation%20and%20Pond%20Systems%20For%20the%20Treatment%20of%20Faecal%20Sludges%20In%20the%20Tropics.pdf> [accessed 24 March 2018].

Heinss, U., Larmie, S. and Strauss, M. (1999) *Characteristics of Faecal Sludges and their Solids–Liquid Separation*, Dübendorf: Eawag/Sandec <https://www.sswm.info/sites/default/files/reference_attachments/HEINSS%20et%20al%201994%20Characteristics%20of%20Faecal%20Sludges%20and%20their%20Solids-Liquid%20Seperation.pdf> [accessed 24 March 2018].

Institute of Water Pollution Control (1980) *Manuals of British Practice in Water Pollution Control: Unit Processes, Primary Sedimentation*, Maidstone, Kent: IWPC.

Kraehenbuehl, M. and Hariot, O. (2015) *Assessment of latrine desludging, transport of human waste and treatment at the sludge treatment station (STS) in Sittwe Camp, Myanmar*, Myanmar: Solidarités International (unpublished report).

Metcalf & Eddy (2003) *Wastewater Engineering Treatment and Reuse*, 4th edn, New York: McGraw Hill.

Strande, L., Ronteltap, M. and Brdjanovic, D. (2014) *Faecal Sludge Management: Systems Approach for Implementation and Operation*, London: IWA <www.sandec.ch/fsm_book> [accessed 17 November]

Tchobanoglous, G., Stensel, H.D., Tsuchihashi, R. and Burton, F. (2014) *Wastewater Engineering: Treatment and Resources Recovery*, New York: McGraw Hill Education.

Tilley, E., Ulrich, L., Lüthi, C., Reymond, P. and Zurbrügg, C. (2014) *Compendium of Sanitation Systems and Technologies*, 2nd edn, Dübendorf: Eawag/Sandec <http://www.iwa-network.org/wp-content/uploads/2016/06/Compendium-Sanitation-Systems-and-Technologies.pdf> [accessed 25 March 2018].

US EPA (1987) *Innovations in Sludge Drying Beds: A Practical Technology*, Columbus, OH: EPA <https://nepis.epa.gov/Exe/ZyPDF.cgi/200045M2.PDF?Dockey=200045M2.PDF> [accessed 8 March 2018].

WEF (2010) *Design of Municipal Wastewater Treatment Plants, WEF Manual of Practice no. 8*, 5th edn, Alexandria, VA: WEF Press.

CHAPTER 8
Liquid treatment

This chapter examines the options for treating liquid septage and the separated liquid fraction of faecal sludge and septage produced by solids–liquid separation. Treatment proposals must take account of the high strength of the liquid to be treated and the need to produce an effluent that can be safely used or discharged to the environment, meeting discharge standards where necessary. This means that more than one treatment stage will normally be required, with aerobic treatment often following anaerobic treatment. The relatively low volume and higher solids content of faecal sludge means that it will often be treated as a slurry rather than a liquid and so this chapter focuses on septage treatment. The chapter is mainly concerned with technologies that are suitable for use in stand-alone septage treatment plants, but information is also given on the points to be taken into account when considering options for co-treatment with municipal wastewater.

Keywords: liquid fraction, high strength, anaerobic treatment, aerobic treatment, discharge requirements, end use requirements

Introduction

Liquid-stream treatment objectives

As noted in earlier chapters, the main objectives of faecal sludge and septage treatment processes are to ensure that the products of treatment cause no harm to either public health or the environment. When liquid effluent is discharged to a natural watercourse, the main objective will be to reduce the organic and suspended solids loads to levels that comply with the relevant discharge standards and do not adversely affect the water quality, especially the dissolved oxygen concentration, in the receiving water body. Depending on the nature, uses, and quality of the receiving watercourse, it may also be necessary to remove nutrients (principally nitrogen and phosphorus). If there is a possibility that treated liquid will be used to irrigate crops or public spaces, it will also be necessary to reduce pathogen concentrations to safe levels to protect public health. Most lower-income countries have discharge standards for effluent organic and suspended solids concentration, expressed in terms of either five day biochemical oxygen demand (BOD_5) or chemical oxygen demand (COD) and total suspended solids (TSS). Some also set standards for nutrients, including phosphorus, nitrate, and ammonia, as illustrated by the Malaysian standards summarized in Table 4.1. The 1989 WHO guidelines summarized in Table 4.2 recommend acceptable pathogen concentrations for treated liquid used to irrigate crops and public spaces.

http://dx.doi.org/10.3362/9781780449869.008

This chapter deals with treatment options to reduce effluent organic and suspended solids loads. Information on simple, low-cost options for removing pathogens is also included. Treatment options that focus explicitly on nutrient removal are not covered. Phosphorus can be removed by using either metal salts or lime to precipitate phosphate and so remove it from the liquid stream. The most commonly used nitrogen removal method in wastewater treatment plants is to add an anoxic stage to activated sludge processes (Metcalf & Eddy, 2003; WEF, 2010). These processes are more complex than the relatively simple options for BOD and TSS removal described in this chapter and will incur much higher capital and operational costs. For this reason, nutrient removal should only be considered where effluent is to be discharged to a water body that is at risk of eutrophication. Where such situations do arise, it will often be better to seek an alternative effluent disposal option, for instance use of the effluent in restricted irrigation.

Many of the treatment technologies described in this chapter are suitable for both stand-alone treatment of the liquid portion of faecal sludge and septage, and their co-treatment with municipal wastewater. Issues to be taken into account when considering co-treatment are addressed at appropriate points in the chapter, in a sub-section and at the end of the chapter.

Treatment challenges and options

The BOD, COD, and ammonia concentrations in faecal sludge and septage are much higher than those in municipal wastewater. This remains true of their liquid fraction after solids–liquid separation. Other factors to be considered when assessing treatment options are the characteristics of the material to be treated and the likelihood that faecal sludge and septage treatment plants will be subjected to wide variations in loading. With regard to the first, septage removed from infrequently emptied leach pits, wet pit latrines, and septic tanks will normally be uniformly well digested and the potential for further organic reduction will be lower than that for municipal wastewater. The two measures of the treatability of any wastewater are its volatile solids (VS) content which is normally expressed as a percentage of total solids (TS), and its COD to BOD_5 ratio. TS is measured by evaporating the water from a 1 litre sample of wastewater and measuring the weight of the residue. TS consists of both total dissolved solids (TDS) and total suspended solids (TSS). The TSS content of wastewater is measured by determining the dry weight of the residue left when a 1 litre sample of wastewater is passed through fine-pored filter paper. The TDS content is then obtained from the fact that TS = TSS + TDS. The distinction between TDS and TSS is rather arbitrary in that the measured TSS content depends on the pore size of the filter paper. TDS can include mineral salts that are present in the water from which the wastewater derives. Both TDS and TSS include a volatile solids fraction (VDS and VSS respectively), which, as with VS, is normally expressed as a fraction of either TDS or TSS as appropriate. The VS percentage

Table 8.1 Varying volatile solids content of wastewater and septage sources

Liquid source	VS content %	Source
Untreated wastewater	76–79 (VSS)	Metcalf & Eddy (2003)
	40 (VDS)	
Septage from around 50 pits and tanks in Kampala, Uganda	65 (VSS) 60 (VS)	Author's analysis of data presented in Schoebitz et al. (2016)
Public toilet sludge	68 (VS)	Koné and Strauss (2004)
Septage	47–73 (VS)	Koné and Strauss (2004)
Septage (Hanoi, Vietnam)	66–83	Schoebitz et al. (2014)
Septage and contents of wet-pit latrines in Ouagadougou, Burkina Faso	60–72 (VSS) 53–61 (VS)	Bassan et al. (2013)

is a proxy for organic content and a high VS to TS value indicates potential for further biological treatment. The VSS content of untreated wastewater typically lies in the range 75–80 per cent of TSS (Metcalf & Eddy, 2003, Table 3-15). The figures given in Table 8.1 suggest that the VSS of septage and faecal sludge will normally be lower. They also show a tendency for the VSS content of faecal sludge and septage samples to be slightly higher than the VS content of those samples. One possible explanation for this is that septage and well-digested faecal sludge contain a high proportion of well-digested fine particles, which do not settle easily and so remain in the liquid fraction, reducing its VS content and hence its treatability. Regardless of this, the figures given in Table 8.1 suggest that there is significant scope for biological treatment of septage and faecal sludge.

As noted in previous chapters, both the strength of the material to be treated and the hydraulic loading on faecal sludge and septage treatment plants can be highly variable. Some reduction in short-term variations in strength and hydraulic load will take place during preliminary treatment and solids–liquid separation. However, as noted in Chapter 5, flow equalization will be very difficult to achieve for the relatively small flows received at septage and faecal sludge treatment plants. The result will be that most of the loading on these plants will occur during the working day, which will be longer than 8–10 hours. At other times, there will be no flow. Technologies with a long retention time, for instance waste stabilization ponds, aerated lagoons, and constructed wetlands, will be best suited to cope with flow variations. Treatment processes such as upflow anaerobic sludge blanket (UASB) reactors, which depend on maintenance of a sludge blanket, will be very difficult to operate if there are extended periods with no flow. Similarly, long interruptions in flow will affect the performance of trickling filters and may result in problems with odours and insects. For this reason, this chapter does not describe either UASBs or trickling filters in detail. It does briefly explore their potential role in co-treatment with municipal wastewater.

Overview of liquid stream treatment processes and technologies

Even after solids–liquid separation, the high strength of septage creates a need for more than one treatment stage if an acceptable effluent standard is to be achieved. If there is a possibility that treated liquid will be used to irrigate crops or public spaces, the design must aim to reduce pathogen concentrations to safe levels. Anaerobic processes do not require power and work better with relatively strong influents, particularly in hot climates. In this respect, they are a very good option for the first stage of treatment. Their main disadvantage is their long start-up time, which is a consequence of the time required for anaerobic processes to become established. It may take several weeks for an anaerobic treatment unit to achieve its design performance, after which a well-managed anaerobic process can remove over 70 per cent of the organic load. Follow-up aerobic treatment will be required to meet discharge standards, but the inclusion of a first-stage anaerobic process will reduce the oxygen, and hence power and/or land, requirements of subsequent treatment processes. Figure 8.1 shows how various liquid treatment options can be linked together in series, with anaerobic treatment often providing the first stage, followed by aerobic treatment and pathogen reduction or additional polishing steps. While not suitable for stand-alone septage treatment, UASB reactor treatment may be an option for co-treatment with municipal wastewater. Activated sludge and extended aeration are aerobic options for co-treatment, but designers should take account of the impact that the increased loading associated with septage will have on their power costs.

When assessing treatment options, attention should be paid to the challenges created by the high solids content of the liquid to be treated. While prior solids–liquid separation will have reduced the solids concentration in the influent, it will still be high enough to lead to rapid sludge accumulation in tanks and ponds, and the options for dealing with this sludge should be considered at the design stage. Sludge removed from the anaerobic and aerobic/biological treatment units will require dewatering, as explained in Chapter 9. Figure 8.1 shows the possibility of disinfecting treated water intended for agricultural use. This will normally only be required when treated effluent is to be used for unrestricted irrigation. Given the relatively small volume of effluent produced at faecal sludge and septage treatment plants, it will normally be best to avoid the need for chemical disinfection by using treated effluent for purposes other than unrestricted irrigation.

Anaerobic treatment options

All the anaerobic treatment processes considered in this book rely on a combination of sedimentation and mesophilic digestion processes. They are strongly temperature-dependent, which means that they will normally perform well in hot climates. Much of the literature on anaerobic treatment options relates to the treatment of municipal wastewater and the design parameters presented here are drawn from this literature. Further research is needed to determine appropriate design parameters for septage and it is likely that the

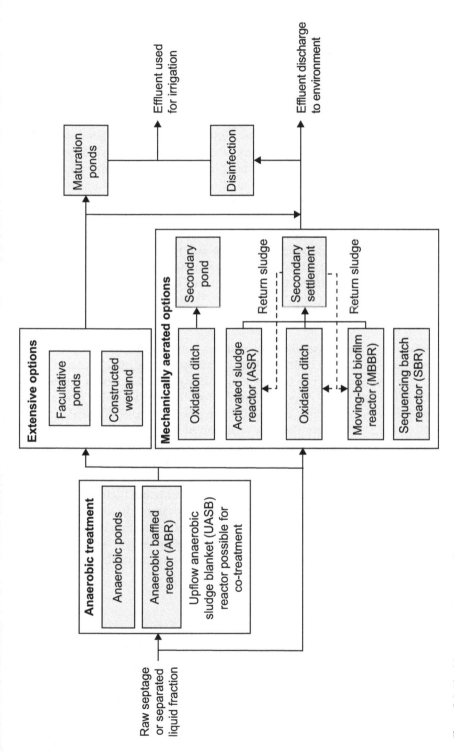

Figure 8.1 Liquid stream treatment options

rate constants for anaerobic digestion of partly digested septage will be lower than those for undigested domestic wastewater. For instance, studies at the Khirbit-as-Samra wastewater treatment plant in Jordan showed that the biodegradation rate for septage was lower than that for both domestic wastewater and primary sludge from a wastewater treatment plant (Halalsheh et al., 2011).

Wastewater contains nitrogen as both ammonium (NH_4) and ammonia (NH_3). NH_4 predominates when the pH is neutral, typically accounting for around 95 per cent of total ammoniacal nitrogen (TAN). At high concentrations, NH_3 is toxic to anaerobic bacteria and will inhibit methanogenesis. The available evidence suggests that the threshold for inhibition occurs at an NH_3 concentration of around 1,000 mg/l (see for example, Moestedt et al., 2016; Hansen et al., 1998). Total nitrogen concentrations in faecal sludge and septage vary from typical values of less than 500 mg/l for digested septage to over 5,000 mg/l for fresh faecal sludge (Strande et al., 2014, Table 9.2). At neutral pH levels, most of this nitrogen will be in the form of ammonium which, unlike ammonia, will not inhibit anaerobic processes and so should not present problems unless the treatment process results in a significant increase in pH.

Anaerobic ponds

Anaerobic ponds are the simplest form of anaerobic treatment. As their name suggests, they are ponds, typically (but not always) rectangular in shape with an inlet for the wastewater to be treated near one end and an outlet for treated effluent at the diagonally opposite corner. They must be loaded at a rate that ensures anaerobic conditions throughout the pond depth. Solids settle to the bottom of the pond where the lack of dissolved oxygen facilitates anaerobic processes that degrade the settled solids. The separated liquid flows through the pond for further treatment, which is often provided in facultative and maturation ponds. The land requirement of anaerobic ponds is significantly less than that of facultative ponds and constructed wetlands, but higher than that of anaerobic baffled reactors. Their retention time is measured in days rather than hours with the result that they are reasonably good at dealing with variations in flow. Anaerobic ponds are an option for co-treating septage with municipal wastewater, provided that the process design takes account of the high organic and solids loads contributed by the septage.

Design and operational considerations

Dimensions. Most anaerobic ponds are 2–5 m deep and have a length to breadth ratio of not more than 2:1 (Tilley et al., 2014; Mara, 2004). Deeper ponds are possible and will increase the storage available for settled solids. However, increasing the pond depth will increase construction costs, particularly where the water table is close to the surface, and make sludge removal more difficult. For all but the largest septage treatment plants, the relatively small pond volume required will mean that it will be more practical to provide less depth and rely on more frequent desludging.

As already noted in Chapter 5, the probability that a task will be undertaken will tend to be higher for those tasks that require less effort at more frequent intervals. The required desludging interval will depend on the solids load and the size of the pond but will usually be much shorter than the 3–5 years typically required for anaerobic ponds treating municipal wastewater. Where ponds are used for solids–liquid separation, the desludging interval is likely to be measured in months rather than years.

Inlet and outlet arrangements. The inlet and outlet should be at diagonally opposite corners of the pond. To prevent sludge accumulation around the inlet, it will be advisable to carry the influent to ponds with sloping sides through a pipe or channel to a point some distance from the edge of the pond. Where grit is expected, the pond can be deepened beneath the inlet pipe to accommodate it. The inlet should deliver influent vertically downwards since this will reduce the possibility that the discharge will induce circulation in the pond, leading to short-circuiting. A scum board should be provided at the outlet to contain scum. Where land is available, ponds are normally constructed with 1:2 internal side and end slopes. This reduces construction costs and facilitates access, but has a significant effect on the area required for the relatively small ponds that will normally be required for septage treatment. For this reason, it may be appropriate to construct ponds at smaller plants with vertical concrete walls. The sides and base of anaerobic ponds are normally lined. While a waterproof membrane may be used for the base, the normal practice is to line the sides with concrete, precast concrete slabs, or bricks. In all cases, a sloping ramp should be provided to allow worker access for desludging. Further information on design details for all types of waste stabilization pond is available in Arthur (1983) and Mara (2004).

Design for operational continuity during desludging. The design should provide for at least two anaerobic ponds, arranged in parallel. Sufficient capacity should be provided to deal with the design loading when one pond is taken out of service for desludging. Where there is a large annual variation in ambient temperature, the pond volume required will be reduced if it can be guaranteed that pond desludging will always take place during the warm months of the year, when the allowable loading on the pond will be at its highest.

Gas production will occur, particularly at high loading rates. This may lead to odours, as methane and hydrogen sulphide are generated and escape into the atmosphere. Another point to be considered is the inhibitory effect of free ammonia on anaerobic digestion processes. Both these effects are discussed further below.

Design criteria and procedure

Anaerobic ponds are designed using empirically derived design criteria, the most important of which is the organic load per unit volume. Recommended organic loadings for municipal wastewater treatment range from 100 to 400 g BOD_5/m^3 d, depending on temperature. Mara (2004) suggests the more specific relationships between ambient temperature (T), allowable volumetric organic loading rate (λ_v), and percentage BOD_5 removal given in Table 8.2.

Table 8.2 Anaerobic pond relationship between volumetric BOD loading rate, BOD removal, and temperature

Temperature, T (°C)	λ_v (g BOD_5/m^3 d)	BOD removal (%)
<10	100	40
10 to <20	$20T - 100$	$2T + 20$
20 to <25	$10T + 100$	$2T + 20$
≥25	350	70

Table 8.2 gives a maximum volumetric loading rate of 350 g BOD_5/m^3 d, reflecting experience that odours are likely at higher loading rates. As will become clear from the equations given below, the retention time in an anaerobic pond equals the BOD concentration in the influent divided by the volumetric loading rate. This means that the required retention time for an influent BOD of 3,000 mg/l and a volumetric loading rate of 350 mg/l is 8.57 days. This compares with the recommended retention times of 1–7 days for municipal wastewater (Mara, 2004; von Sperling, 2007; Tilley et al., 2014). In practice, there are examples of anaerobic ponds with loading rates considerably higher than 350 g/m³ d. For instance, a 700 g BOD_5/m^3 d design figure was adopted for loading on an experimental septage treatment anaerobic pond system at Maximo Paz in Argentina with an average influent BOD_5 of 2,800 mg/l. A review of the pond performance revealed that actual loading increased from 533 to 800 g BOD_5/m^3 d as sludge accumulated and reduced the effective pond volume. The reported reductions in BOD_5, TSS, and VSS were 90 per cent, 82 per cent, and 91 per cent, respectively (Fernández et al., 2004). The BOD_5 removal figure compares with the 70 per cent BOD_5 removal rate suggested by Mara (2004) and the 75–84 per cent BOD_5 removal rate given by Arthur (1983), both for ponds treating municipal wastewater. Based on these results and with a view to avoiding excessive ammonia production, Fernandez et al. recommended the adoption of a design loading of 600 g BOD_5/m^3 d (2004). Box 8.1 provides evidence taken from one study in New Zealand that supports the view that the scum layer that forms over heavily loaded anaerobic ponds may reduce odour problems. If the results of this study are corroborated for ponds treating septage, there will be a strong case for adopting a maximum loading rate of 600 g BOD_5/m^3 d. In the meantime, it will be best to adopt the more conservative figures given in Table 8.2 until investigation of pond performance under local conditions confirms that it is possible to adopt an increased loading rate.

Table 8.3 summarizes recommended design criteria for anaerobic ponds. The design procedure for anaerobic ponds is summarized below.

1.   Calculate the pond volume required (m³):

$$V_A = \frac{L_i Q}{\lambda_v}$$

Box 8.1 Investigation of the scum layer impact on odour emissions

Investigations at a treatment plant serving a meat-processing facility in Moerawa, New Zealand found that a continuous scum cover effectively stopped emission of unpleasant odours. Gas detector tests carried out 100 mm above the surface showed a typical hydrogen sulphide concentration of 0.35 mg/l above the 25 mm thick scum layer as compared with concentrations of 2–15 mg/l over scum-free areas (Rands and Cooper, 1966 reported in Milner, 1978). Postulated reasons for the low hydrogen sulphide concentration over the scum layer included physical retention by the scum cover and sulphide oxidation as the gases passed through the porous scum mat. The tests did not cover methane, although the report of the investigations states that 85 per cent of the gas collected in a bell jar over a clear section of pond was methane.

Table 8.3 Summary of anaerobic pond design criteria

Parameter	Symbol	Units	Value/Range
Organic loading rate	λ_v	g BOD/m³ d	350 – consider possibility of increasing to 600 where some odour is acceptable
Hydraulic retention time	θ_A	days	Dependent on influent strength and λ_v
Depth	D_A	m	2–5
Length-to-width ratio	L/W	–	Typically 1–2:1
Side slope	S	–	1:2 or vertical, depending on pond size

Where: V_A = pond volume (m³)
  L_1 = Influent BOD (mg/l)
  Q = flow through the pond (m³/d)

2. Calculate the pond retention time (days):

$$\theta_A = \frac{V_A}{Q} = \frac{L_1}{\lambda_v}$$

3. Decide the depth for the anaerobic pond (D_A, m) and calculate the surface area (SA_A, m²).

The depth selected should normally be in the range indicated in Table 8.3 and should take account of the available land area and ease of construction. Deeper ponds require a smaller surface area but may be difficult to construct, particularly in areas where the ground is rocky or the water table is high. For the relatively small flows received at many septage treatment plants, it will usually be more practical to limit the pond depth to ≤3 m. For ponds with vertical sides, the required surface area of the pond is given by the equation:

$$SA_A = \frac{V_A}{D_A}$$

For a pond with a length-to-width ratio of 2:1, this can be rewritten as:

$$\frac{L^2}{2} = \frac{V_A}{D_A}$$

where L is the length of the pond (m). In practice, it will be necessary to provide at least two ponds, arranged in parallel and the area of a single pond must be adjusted to allow for this.

For ponds with sloping sides, the relationship between the pond volume, areas, and depth is given by the equation (Alberta Agriculture and Forestry, 2012):

$$V_A = \left(A_T + A_B + 4A_M\right)\left(\frac{D_A}{6}\right)$$

where: L = surface length of the pond (m);
$\quad W$ = surface width of the pond (m);
$\quad A_T$ = area of the pond surface = LW (m²);
$\quad A_B$ = area of the pond base = $(L - 2sD_A)(W - 2sD_A)$ (m²);
$\quad A_M$ = mid-depth area of the pond $(L - sD_A)(W - sD_A)$ (m²);
$\quad V_A$ = pond volume (m³);
$\quad D_A$ = pond depth (m);
$\quad s$ = embankment slope (horizontal/vertical).

With the volume and depth known and a length-to-width ratio assumed, this expression becomes a quadratic equation, which can be solved for either length or width. Alternatively, the exact dimensions of the top and bottom surfaces of the pond can be found using the online pond-volume calculator given by Alberta Agriculture and Forestry (2012). The pond embankment length and width will be equal to $(L + 2sF)$ and $(W + 2sF)$, respectively, where F is the freeboard (the vertical distance from the top of the pond embankment to the pond water level).

4. Estimate the effluent BOD and TSS concentrations:

$$L_e = L_i\left(1 - \frac{\%BOD_{rem}}{100}\right)$$

$$TSS_e = TSS_i\left(1 - \frac{\%TSS_{rem}}{100}\right)$$

where: L_e = effluent BOD (mg/l);
$\quad L_i$ = influent BOD (mg/l);
$\quad \%BOD_{rem}$ = percentage BOD removal in the pond;
$\quad TSS_e$ = effluent TSS (mg/l);
$\quad TSS_i$ = influent TSS (mg/l); and
$\quad \%TSS_{rem}$ = percentage TSS removal in the pond.

In the absence of information from local pond systems, use the BOD removal figures given in Table 8.2 to estimate BOD_{rem}.

5. Estimate the sludge accumulation rate and the required desludging frequency.

$$DS_a = Q \times \frac{TSS_i}{1000} \times \frac{\%TSS_{rem}}{100} \times \left(1 - \frac{\%TSS_d}{100}\right)$$

where: DS_a = dry sludge accumulation rate (kg/d);

Q = flow through the pond (m³/d);

$\%TSS_{rem}$ = percentage TSS removal through the pond; and

$\%TSS_d$ = percentage solids destruction rate (assume 20 per cent if no data are available).

The wet sludge volume accumulation rate ($Q_{sludge, wet}$, m³/d) in the settled zone can be calculated based on the solids accumulation rate and an assumed TS content of the sludge. In the absence of data, assume an average sludge TS content of 10 per cent. The density of the wet sludge ($\rho_{sludge, wet}$, kg/m³) is assumed to be approximately equal to the density of water. Thus:

$$Q_{sludge, wet} = \frac{DS_a}{(\%TS/100)\,\rho_{sludge, wet}}$$

The required desludging frequency ($f_{desludging}$, days) can then be calculated based on the anaerobic pond volume and desludging when sludge accumulation is about one-third of the pond volume. Thus:

$$f_{desludging} = \frac{\frac{1}{3}V_A}{Q_{sludge, wet}}$$

The volume and solids content of the sludge removed during each desludging event will influence the design of subsequent sludge dewatering facilities.

Anaerobic pond design example

Consider the design of anaerobic ponds to treat the liquid effluent from a solid–liquid separation module. The influent characteristics and process assumptions are summarized below:

Parameter	Symbol	Value	Unit
Flow rate	Q	40	m³/d
Average daily temperature	T	25	°C
Influent BOD concentration	L_i	2,000	mg/l
Influent TSS concentration	TSS_i	5,000	mg/l
Depth	D_A	3	m
L:W ratio	–	2:1	–
Number of ponds	N	2	–
Assumptions			
% TSS removal	$\%TSS_{rem}$	55	%
% solids destroyed	$\%TSS_d$	20	%
% TS of wet sludge	$\%TS$	10	%
Density of sludge	ρ_{sludge}	1,000	kg/m³

1. *Calculate the total pond volume required:*
   The maximum recommended organic loading rate at 25°C, as recommended in Table 8.2, is 350 g BOD/m^3 d. Thus:

   $$V_A = \frac{2000 \text{ mg/l} \times 40 \text{ m}^3}{350 \text{ mg/l}} = 229 \text{ m}^3$$

   Where the BOD of the influent is significantly higher, it might be appropriate to use a higher loading rate, up to (but not above) the 600 g/m^3 d figure suggested following the Maximo Paz investigations.

2. *Calculate the retention time in the pond:*

   $$\theta_A = \frac{229 \text{ m}^3}{40 \text{ m}^3/\text{d}} = 5.7 \text{ d}$$

3. *Determine the surface area, dimensions, and configuration of pond(s):*

   $$SA_A = \frac{229 \text{ m}^3}{3 \text{ m}} = 76 \text{ m}^2$$

   Assume two ponds in parallel, each with an area of 38 m^2 and receiving 20 m^3/d. These ponds are too small to incorporate a side slope, so the sides will have to be vertical. For a length:width ratio of 2 the dimensions of each pond are 4.4 m × 8.8 m to give a pond area of 38.72 m^2.

4. *Calculate the effluent BOD and TSS concentrations:*
   Assume 70 per cent BOD removal:

   $$L_e = 2,000 \text{ mg/l} (1 - 0.7) = 600 \text{ mg/l}$$

   Assume 55 per cent TSS removal:

   $$TSS_e = 5,000 \text{ mg/l} (1 - 0.55) = 2,250 \text{ mg/l}$$

5. *Calculate the desludging frequency, and mass and volume of sludge removed during each desludging event:*
   Calculate the solids accumulation rate in each pond, assuming a solids destruction rate of 20 per cent:

   $$DS_a = \left(0.5 \times 40 \text{ m}^3/\text{d}\right) \times 5,000 \text{ mg/l}$$

   $$\times \left[\frac{1,000 \text{ L}}{1 \text{ m}^3}\right] \times \left[\frac{1 \text{ kg}}{1,000,000 \text{ mg}}\right] \times \frac{55}{100} \times \left(1 - \frac{20}{100}\right)$$

   $$= 44 \frac{\text{kg}}{\text{d pond}}$$

   Calculate the wet sludge volume accumulation rate in the settled zones of the two ponds, assuming a 10 per cent TS content in the sludge:

   $$Q_{\text{sludge, wet}} = \frac{44 \text{ kg/d}}{0.10 \times 1000 \text{ kg/m}^3} = 0.44 \text{ m}^3/\text{d}$$

   Calculate the required desludging frequency for each pond:

   $$f_{\text{desludging}} = \frac{\frac{1}{3} \times 229 \text{ m}^3/2}{0.44 \text{ m}^3/\text{d}} = 87.8 \text{ d (i.e. } \sim 3 \text{ months)}$$

Volume to be removed at each desludging event is one-third of the pond volume:

38 m² (pond area) × 3 m (pond depth) × ⅓ = 38 m³

The timing of the desludging of the two ponds should be staggered so that one pond is operational at all times.

The calculation reveals a need for frequent desludging. In doing so, it highlights the desirability of solids–liquid separation to reduce the solids content of the liquid fraction of separated septage before it is treated.

Anaerobic baffled reactor

Anaerobic baffled reactors (ABRs) are concrete, masonry, or prefabricated fibreglass tanks consisting of several compartments in series (Figure 8.2). They remove organic material through anaerobic digestion and settling of particulate matter. Pipes or baffles direct waste liquid from an opening just below the water surface of each compartment to the bottom of the next compartment, thereby directing wastewater through a layer of settled sludge and providing intensive contact between organic pollutants and active biomass. ABRs used for wastewater treatment usually incorporate a settler compartment similar to the first compartment of a septic tank, followed by between four and six upflow compartments, with one or more anaerobic filter (AF) chambers provided after the up-flow compartments (Sasse, 1998). Because of the compartmentalization, acidogenesis and methanogenesis are separated longitudinally along the reactor, with acidogenesis predominant in the first compartment and methanogenesis predominant in later compartments. This separation allows different bacterial groups to develop under favourable conditions. Advocates of ABRs claim that this allows the reactor to behave as a two-phase system without the associated high cost and control problems normally associated with two-phase operation. The result is a significant increase in acidogenic and methanogenic activity. Reynaud and Buckley (2016) suggest another benefit of compartmentalization: they state it is a strongly stabilizing factor in that it evens out feed fluctuations across reactor chambers.

The settler compartment serves to separate large solids ahead of the up-flow compartments (Sasse, 1998). It does not have to be attached to the up-flow compartments, and could perhaps be omitted when ABR treatment is preceded by solids–liquid separation, as will almost always be the case for plants treating septage. However, given that the influent solids concentration is likely to be high, even after solids–liquid separation, it will normally be advisable to include a settler compartment to retain solids and so reduce the rate of solids accumulation in subsequent up-flow compartments. Because of its relatively large plan area, the settler compartment will also tend to attenuate peak flows and so reduce hydraulic load fluctuations on subsequent up-flow compartments.

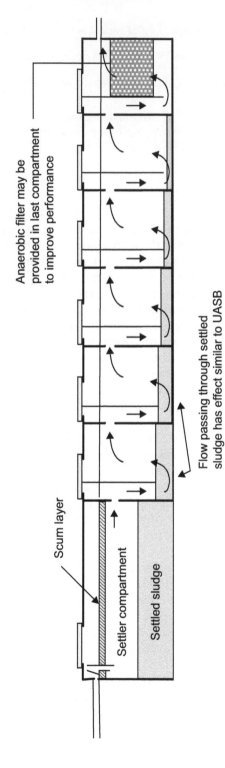

Figure 8.2 Typical ABR arrangement

Figure 8.2 shows a typical ABR arrangement, including both a settler compartment and an up-flow anaerobic filter in the last compartment.

ABRs have a relatively small footprint, are not reliant on electricity, and require only limited technical skills for operation (Gutterer et al., 2009). They require less land than anaerobic ponds and the fact that they are enclosed means that it may be possible to use them in locations where anaerobic ponds cannot be used because of odour problems. Because they are enclosed, desludging an ABR will be more difficult than desludging anaerobic ponds and, because of the presence of methane and other gases, it will be potentially hazardous.

Performance

Much of the information on ABR performance is based on laboratory and pilot-scale studies. While most of these studies report a COD removal rate of more than 80 per cent, laboratory studies do not take account of important aspects of field operation, including diurnal flow variations, the need to allow an adequate start-up period, and the influence of chamber outlet design. Another factor to be considered when assessing likely performance is the high non-biodegradable content of septage compared with that of wastewater. This is likely to result in lower COD removal rates than those recorded for the treatment of wastewater. Table 8.4 summarizes the findings of selected studies that provide information on ABR performance under field conditions and, in one case, a laboratory-scale investigation of the treatment of pit latrine sludge.

These findings confirm that ABR performance in the field is unlikely to match that achieved under controlled laboratory conditions. Factors contributing to the poor performance of the ABRs treating communal wastewater are likely to have included low organic loading rates and hydraulic surges resulting from stormwater intrusion. Performance will also be adversely affected by the presence of illegal chemicals in the septage and accumulation of sludge in the up-flow compartments. The Bwapwa study supports the view that the higher non-biodegradable content of faecal sludge and septage will also affect ABR performance.

Until further information on full-scale ABRs treating liquid from septage and faecal sludge is available, it seems appropriate to assume 50 per cent COD removal for systems meeting the design criteria set out later in this chapter. BOD removal is likely to be higher than COD removal as BOD includes a higher proportion of readily degradable material. Little information is available on TSS removal for ABRs treating liquid from either faecal sludge or septage. In the absence of specific information, it seems reasonable to assume that the removal rate for TSS will be similar to that for COD. Generally it will be appropriate to assume conservative values for design parameters until additional operating information is available.

Design and operational considerations

Reactor resilience. Some studies have found that ABRs are resilient, recovering well from hydraulic and organic shock loading (Barber and Stuckey, 1999).

Table 8.4 ABR treatment performance in selected studies

Influent source	System description and location	Influent characteristics	Up-flow velocity	Treatment efficiency	Notes and references
Septage from pit latrines serving internally displaced persons (IDP) camp	12 ABR compartments following separate settler compartment (Sittwe, Myanmar)	Influent COD: 6,200 mg/l Organic loading rate 2.55 kg COD/m³ d (entire ABR) Hydraulic retention time (HRT): 5 h per compartment	Peak: 0.9 m/h (over 8 h inflow period) Average: 0.3 m/h (over 24-h period)	55% COD removal	Unpublished report, Solidarités International, cited in de Bonis and Tayler (2016)
Communal wastewater	4–12 ABR compartments 50–156 m³ reactor volume (4 systems studied in India and Indonesia)	COD influent: 350–510 mg/l	Peak: 0.4–1.3 m/h	37–67% COD removal	Poor performance may be due to low organic loading rate (Reynaud, 2014)
Pit latrine sludge	4 compartment laboratory-scale ABR preceded by 'feed tank' (220 l feed tank and 20 l per ABR compartment)	Influent COD 1,000–3,000 mg/l	Not given	52–80% COD removal, mainly in feed tank	Bwapwa (2012) Only 28% of COD reduction by biological degradation
Liquid portion of septage from household pits (wet) and septic tanks	1 settler, 4 ABR, 2 AF prefabricated ABR 12 m³ reactor volume (Devanahalli, India)	COD influent: 1,500 mg/l	Peak: 0.10 m/h (over 8 h inflow period) Average: 0.03 m/h (over 24-hour period)	58% COD removal 64% TS removal (including AF treatment)	Personal communication, CDD – Consortium for DEWATS Dissemination, Bangalore, India
Liquid portion of faecal sludge from household pits (wet)	5 ABR, 1 AF compartments; 14 m³ reactor volume (Dar es Salaam, Tanzania)	COD influent: 950 mg/l	Peak: 0.36 m/h (over 8 h inflow period) Average: 0.12 m/h (over 24-hour period)	58% COD removal (including AF treatment)	Personal communication, BORDA Tanzania

However, high peak flows can result in sludge washout, which leaves little active biomass for treatment (Reynaud, 2014). When designing ABRs, it is therefore necessary to assess the impact of upstream treatment units on the peak flow passed forward to the ABR. The aim should normally be to attenuate flow sufficiently to ensure that the peak flow to the ABR can be taken as the average flow over the hours when the treatment plant is receiving flow, typically 8–10 hours each day.

Start-up. As with other anaerobic processes, ABR performance depends on the availability of active microbial mass and takes time to reach an optimal level. Gutterer et al. (2009) note that inoculation with old sludge from septic tanks will shorten the start-up phase and suggest that it is advantageous to start with only a quarter of the daily flow and to slowly increase the loading rate over the first three months of operation.

Desludging needs. ABR performance will be adversely affected by sludge accumulation in the reactor compartments. It is therefore essential that provision is made for regular desludging. Periodic scum removal may also be required depending on the fats, oil, and grease (FOG) content and upstream treatment modules. Gutterer et al. (2009) recommend that ABRs treating domestic wastewater should be desludged at intervals of between six months and three years. ABRs treating septage will require more frequent desludging. Operators of the ABR treating separated liquid at the septage treatment plant serving IDP camps around Sittwe in Myanmar reported that sludge accumulated quickly in the first four compartments of the 12-compartment ABR and had to be removed at frequent intervals (de Bonis and Tayler, 2016). Where the outflow from ABRs is regularly monitored, a rise in the solids content of the outflow will provide an indication that desludging is required. Some active sludge should be left in each compartment to maintain anaerobic activity (Sasse, 1998).

Desludging options. Desludging may be carried out using small submersible pumps and vacuum trucks. Manual desludging involves significant health risks and should be avoided. It might be possible to shape the floors of individual ABR compartments as hoppers and to provide for sludge draw-off from the bottom of the hopper. Sludge could be pumped or removed using hydrostatic pressure. This option requires field-testing, which could be carried out on pilot ABR facilities.

Provision of parallel treatment streams. To ensure flexibility of operation during maintenance events, the design should include at least two baffled reactor streams in parallel. To ensure good mixing and avoid high structural costs, individual streams should not be more than 2.5–3 m wide.

Number of compartments. The available information suggests that increasing the number of compartments improves solids retention. An investigation of the performance of ABRs with a 14-day retention time and between two and five compartments found a positive relationship between solids retention and the number of compartments (Boopathy, 1998). Based on this finding, Foxon and Buckley (2006) suggested that repeated passes through the sludge bed have a greater beneficial effect on treatment performance than maintaining a low up-flow velocity. However, they also noted that COD reduction occurs almost exclusively in the first three chambers.

Allowance for continued operation during desludging and major repair activities. Where submersible pumps or tanker suction hoses are used to desludge ABR compartments, desludging can be carried out without taking a treatment stream out of service. The main concern will then be to provide continuity of service during any major ABR repairs. One option will be to accept higher loading rates on the remaining ABR units on the rare occasions when one stream is out of service for repair. Alternatively, an additional stream can be provided to allow continued operation while one of the treatment streams is out of service for desludging and/or repair. Where each treatment stream is designed to take 50 per cent of the design flow, this will require a total of three streams giving a total capacity of 150 per cent of the peak flow. Where there are four streams, their combined capacity will be 133 per cent of the peak flow.

Design details and the need for accurate levelling. To minimize the possibility of blockages and retain scum in ABR compartments, the outlet from each compartment, apart from the last one, should be located approximately 20 cm below the water surface, as shown on Figure 8.2. Where the outlet connection is to a pipe, it should be via a T-junction rather than bend, with the vertical pipe extended above water level to allow rodding to remove any blockages. Outlet pipes should be carefully levelled to ensure equal distribution of flow across the entire width of the reactor. Manhole access should be provided to each compartment. A vertical vent pipe and vent holes between chambers above the top water level should be provided to allow the release of gases produced during digestion.

Design criteria and procedure

Settler compartment. Existing ABR design guidelines provide little information on the design of settler compartments. The simplest design approach is to assume that the settler performs in a similar way to the first compartment of a two-compartment septic tank. The Brazilian code (Associação Brasileira de Normas Técnicas, 1993) recommends a linear reduction in retention, from 24 hours for a flow of 6 m³/d, to 12 hours for flows of 14 m³/d and more (Franceys et al., 1992). Since the first compartment of a two-compartment septic tank usually accounts for about two-thirds of the septic tank volume, the settler compartment retention time will typically lie in the range 8–16 hours, depending on flow. Additional allowance, equivalent to 50–100 per cent of the calculated retention time, should be made for sludge storage. The depth and width should be the same as those of the baffled up-flow compartments. The length-to-depth ratio of the settler compartment should be about 1.5.

ABR up-flow compartments. Current design guidelines provide recommendations on the maximum up-flow velocity through the individual compartments and minimum retention time through all the ABR up-flow compartments. Temperature will influence ABR performance. Existing design equations are based on operational experience at ambient temperatures of 20°C and higher, and there is a need for further research on ABR performance at lower temperatures.

Organic loading also influences performance, although Reynaud and Buckley (2016) suggest that the limiting factor is the hydraulic rather than the organic loading rate. Sasse (1998) recommends a maximum loading of 3 kg COD/m³ d, based on the whole ABR volume, but laboratory-scale studies have demonstrated that higher loadings are possible when the loading is gradually increased over several months (Boopathy, 1998; Hui-Ting and Yong-Feng, 2010, referenced in Hassan and Dahlan, 2013; Chang et al., 2008). Nguyen et al. (2010) compared available information on the relationship between organic loading rate and COD removal. Their findings suggest that there is little change in performance for loading rates up to about 15 kg COD/m³ d and that performance deteriorates at higher loading rates. It appears that some of these results are based on laboratory-scale studies, which often produce better results than are achievable in the field. In view of this, this book suggests a maximum COD loading rate of 6 kg COD/m³ d but recognizes the need for further research in this area.

Given the separation of acidogenesis and methanogenesis along the length of the ABR, there is a theoretical argument for defining loading in terms of the loading on a single up-flow compartment. It is possible that this would lead to variation in the size of up-flow compartments along the length of the ABR. Further research is required to investigate this possibility. Suspended solids loading is also likely to be important for ABRs treating septage, but is not covered by existing design criteria. Again, there is a need for further research to define appropriate design parameters.

Table 8.5 summarizes recommended ABR design criteria.

The steps in ABR design are as follows:

1. Determine the loading on the plant.

    The design hydraulic loading will normally be the peak daily flow to the plant at the design horizon. The organic and suspended solids loadings should be calculated by multiplying the peak daily flow by the estimated COD and TSS concentrations in the influent. These should be based on the characteristics of septage delivered to the treatment plant, with appropriate allowance made for the reductions in COD and TSS concentrations effected by solids–liquid separation.

2. Calculate the peak flow rate through the baffled reactors, using the equation:

$$q_P = \frac{Q_p}{t_p}$$

Table 8.5 Summary of anaerobic baffled reactor design criteria

Parameter	Symbol	Units	Value/range	Notes/Reference
Up-flow velocity	v_{up}	m/h	1	At peak flow (Gutterer et al., 2009).
Hydraulic retention time	θ_{ABR}	h	48–72	Figure given by Tilley et al. (2014). Foxon and Buckley (2006) give 20–60 hours, with 40–60 hours during start-up.
Organic loading rate	λ_{ABR}	kg COD/m³d	6	Maximum allowable loading (Hui-Ting and Yong-Feng, 2010; Chang et al., 2008, quoted in Hassan and Dahlan, 2013). Sasse gives a figure of 3 kg COD/m³ d. The approach to organic loading should be reviewed in the light of further research.
Number of compartments	N_c	–	4–8	Most treatment occurs in first three compartments. Additional compartments will reduce likelihood of sludge washout (Gutterer et al., 2009; Reynaud and Buckley, 2016).
Depth of compartment	z_c	m	Typically 1.8–2.5 m	Depending on site conditions and excavation cost (Foxon and Buckley, 2006; BORDA, personal communication).
Length of compartment	L_c	m	Minimum of 0.75 m between wall and baffle and up to half of compartment depth ($z_c/2$)	To ensure good flow distribution over entire area of reactor compartment (Gutterer et al., 2009).

where q_p = peak flow rate (m³/h);

Q_p = peak daily flow (m³/d); and

t_p = the number of hours per day over which the plant is open to receive flow (h/d).

3.   Calculate the total ABR compartment width:

$$w_c = \frac{q_p}{L_c v_{up}}$$

where w_c = total ABR width (m);

L_c = baffled reactor compartment length (m). This should be the greater of 0.75 m and half the compartment depth (z_c);

v_{up} = peak up-flow velocity (m/h).

4. Determine the number of treatment streams and the width of each treatment stream

    To ensure good flow distribution and minimize structural costs, the width of individual treatment streams should not normally exceed 3 m. The number of treatment streams (N_s) is then given by the whole integer above the value of $w_c/3$.

5. Calculate the retention time in the ABR

$$\theta_c = \frac{24N_sN_cV_p}{Q_p} = \frac{24N_cw_cz_cL_c}{Q_p}$$

where: θ_c = HRT in the ABR (h);

N_s = number of treatment streams;

N_c = number of up-flow compartments in series;

V_p = volume of single compartment (m³) = $w_cz_cL_c/N_s$;

z_c = selected compartment depth (which should be in the range 1.8–2.5 m).

If the retention falls below 48 hours, options for increasing it are to reduce v_{up}, increase z_c, and increase N_c. More research is needed to determine which combination of these options will be the best for high loadings such as those experienced by ABRs treating the liquid fraction of septage.

In common with the other design approaches quoted in the literature, the design equations given above make no allowance for the reduction in reactor volume resulting from sludge accumulation. This is justified by the fact that flow passes through the sludge layer at the bottom of each ABR compartment so that the sludge layer does not greatly reduce the effective volume of the compartment.

6. Calculate the organic loading rate and compare it with the recommended maximum organic loading rate:

$$\lambda_{ABR} = \frac{COD_iQ_p}{1,000N_sN_cV_c} = \frac{24COD_i}{1,000\theta_c}$$

where λ_{ABR} = the organic loading rate on the ABR (kg COD/m³ d);

COD_i = influent COD (mg/l).

The value of COD_i should take account of COD reduction through any settler compartment provided ahead of the up-flow compartments. In practice, this reduction is likely to be limited and can be ignored for preliminary calculation purposes. Assumptions can be revised once relevant field data are available.

Designs should be based on the conservative assumption that λ_{ABR} should not exceed 6 kg COD/m³ d when the reactor is working at its full design capacity but it is possible that this figure will be amended in the light of further research. When the ABR is commissioned or individual streams are brought back into use after decommissioning for repair purposes, the loading should be increased to this level over several months.

7. Calculate effluent COD concentration (COD_e) based on the influent COD concentration (COD_i) and an assumed percentage COD removal. In the absence of other information, assume a 50 per cent COD removal rate. Thus:

$$COD_e = COD_i (1 - 0.5)$$

In the absence of other information, assume that TSS removal is also 50 per cent, so that:

$$TSS_e = TSS_i (1 - 0.5)$$

Calculation of the required desludging interval requires information on both the overall sludge accumulation rate and the distribution of settled sludge between ABR compartments. At present, information on these factors for ABRs treating influents with a high solids content is limited. In view of this, this book does not suggest a design approach to assessing the sludge accumulation rate and desludging interval. Rather, operators should determine desludging requirements by constant monitoring of sludge accumulation rates in individual ABR compartments. Further research on the desludging requirements of ABRs is required.

ABR design example

Consider the design of anaerobic baffled reactors to treat the liquid effluent from a solid–liquid separation module. The influent characteristics and process assumptions are summarized below:

Parameter	Symbol	Value	Unit
Peak daily flow rate	Q_p	40	m³/d
Time of flow	t_p	8	h/d
Mean COD influent concentration	COD_i	5,000	mg/l (= g/m³)
Mean TSS influent concentration	TSS_i	4,000	mg/l (= g/m³)
Depth of ABR reactor (liquid depth)	z_c	2	m (based on assessed site conditions)
Hydraulic retention time	θ_c	48	h
Maximum up-flow velocity	v_{up}	1	m/h

1. *Determine loading:*
   The design hydraulic loading is based on the peak daily flow rate to the treatment plant of 40 m³/d.

2. *Calculate the peak flow rate:*

$$Q_p = \frac{40 \text{ m}^3/\text{d}}{8 \text{ h/d}} = 5 \text{ m}^3/\text{h}$$

3. *Determine reactor dimensions based on maximum upflow velocity:*
Calculate the compartment length. This is subject to a minimum value of 0.75 m and a maximum value of $0.5z_c$. In this example $z_c = 2$ and the compartment length is therefore $(0.5 \times 2) = 1$ m.
Calculate the total ABR width required based on the maximum upflow velocity:

$$w_c = \frac{5 \text{ m}^3/\text{h}}{1 \text{ m} \times 1 \text{ m/h}} = 5 \text{ m}$$

4. *Decide number of parallel treatment streams required and width of each stream:*
For a maximum stream width of 3 metres, two parallel treatment streams will be required, each 2.5 metres wide. Other than routine desludging, which can be carried out without taking units out of service, only minimal maintenance should be required and so no standby capacity is assumed.

5. *Calculate the retention time in the ABR*
Calculate total reactor volume of ABR, assuming six compartments in each of the two parallel treatment streams:

$$V_{ABR} = 6 \times (2 \text{ m} \times 1 \text{ m} \times 5 \text{ m}) = 60 \text{ m}^3$$

Calculate the hydraulic retention time:

$$\theta_{ABR} = \frac{60 \text{ m}^3}{40 \text{ m}^3/24 \text{ h}} = 36 \text{ h}$$

This is less than the recommended 48 hours' retention. Options for providing the required retention are:
- Increase N_c from 6 to 8.
- Increase the total width and so reduce the upflow velocity. The total width required to give 48 hours retention is given by $48 \times 40/(24 \times 6 \times 2 \times 1) = 6.67$ m.

The second option provides more operational flexibility. Provide three treatment streams, each with six 2.25 m wide up-flow compartments. Each compartment is 2 m deep × 1 m long, giving a total volume of $3 \times 6 \times 2.25 \times 2 \times 1 = 81$ m³.

6. Check maximum organic loading rate (λ_{ABR}):

Design COD loading $= 40 \text{ m}^3/\text{d} \times 5{,}000 \text{ g/m}^3 \times \left(\dfrac{1 \text{ kg}}{1{,}000 \text{ g}} \right) = 200 \text{ kg/d}$

Recognizing that influent COD 5,000 mg/l is equivalent of 5,000 g/m³

$$\lambda_{ABR} = 5{,}000 \text{ g/m}^3 \times 40 \text{ m}^3/\text{d} \times \frac{1 \text{ kg}}{1{,}000 \text{ g}} \times \frac{1}{81 \text{ m}^3} = 2.47 \text{ kg COD/m}^3 \text{ d}$$

This is less than the maximum value of 6 kg COD/m³ d and therefore satisfactory.

7. *Determine COD and TSS effluent concentrations*
Assuming a 50 per cent reduction of both COD and TSS, the effluent concentrations are:

$$COD_e = 0.5 \times 5{,}000 \text{ mg/l} = 2{,}500 \text{ mg/l}$$
$$TSS_e = 0.5 \times 4{,}000 \text{ mg/l} = 2{,}000 \text{ mg/l}$$

Further treatment will be necessary to meet most national effluent standards and, where required, reduce effluent pathogen concentrations.

Upflow anaerobic sludge blanket reactor

Background and system description

Upflow anaerobic sludge blanket (UASB) reactors were first used for wastewater treatment in Brazil and Colombia in the early 1980s. Since then, they have been widely used in Latin American countries, including Brazil, Colombia, Chile, the Dominican Republic, Guatemala, and Mexico (Noyola et al., 2012). Many were installed under the Ganga and Yamuna action plans in India. A review of the literature on the performance of UASBs treating municipal wastewater in Latin America, India, and the Middle East found COD, BOD$_5$, and TSS removal to be in the range of 41–79 per cent, 41–84 per cent, and 34–69 per cent, respectively (Chernicharo et al., 2015).

UASBs separate wastewater into three phases: sludge, liquid effluent, and gas. The wastewater to be treated is introduced at the bottom of the tank and rises through a suspended sludge blanket. Anaerobic bacteria in the sludge blanket break down organic material in the influent, converting it into biogas which rises up through the reactor. Baffles separate the gas from the liquid flow and direct it into one or more gas hoods, from which it is drawn off and either used or flared. Water rises to weirs located on either side of the hood and the solids remain in the blanket or settle. Together, the gas hood and baffle arrangement is referred to as the GLS (gas–liquid–solids) separator. Good contact between sludge and wastewater is achieved through even distribution of the inflow across the bottom of the UASB and the agitation caused through the production of biogas. Figure 8.3 shows a typical UASB reactor.

Design and operational considerations

UASBs require operators who have a basic understanding of the processes that take place in the UASB reactor and know and follow the practices required to

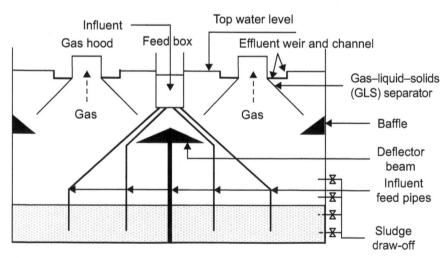

Figure 8.3 Typical UASB reactor
Source: adapted from van Lier et al. (2010)

ensure good reactor performance. Successful operation of UASBs depends on regular monitoring of sludge levels and suspended solids concentrations and withdrawal of excess sludge from the reactor. To facilitate sludge withdrawal a series of valves should be provided at intervals of about 50 cm across the height of the sludge blanket, with the first valve positioned 15–20 cm above the reactor floor. These valves can also be used to take samples, although the valves will be prone to wall effects so that the samples may not be representative of conditions in the reactor as a whole. There is also a danger that rapid opening of a valve may create a vortex, which may lead to errors in assessing the sludge qualities at the sampled level. A better alternative for sampling is to provide an opening in the top part of the GLS separator device, suitable for introduction of a simple sampling device, which can be lowered to the required depth and opened to take the sample. To prevent gas escape, the opening must have a secure cap, which should only be removed for sampling. A hydraulic seal should be provided to prevent gas escape while sampling (van Lier et al., 2010).

Most UASBs have volumes in the range 1,500–3,000 m³, giving a capacity range of 6,000–12,000 m³/d for a 6-hour retention period. UASBs have been constructed with volumes as low as 65 m³, giving a capacity of the order of 260 m³/d, but these have usually been pilots for larger installations (van Lier et al., 2010). These figures suggest that the normal flow range for UASBs is above that at most septage treatment plants. A more serious drawback is the impossibility of maintaining an effective sludge blanket with influent flows varying from over three times the average flow during the working day to zero at night. This problem might be overcome by flow equalization but, as already indicated in Chapter 6, it will be difficult to manage flow equalization effectively at the hydraulic loadings received by most septage treatment plants.

These points suggest that anaerobic ponds and ABRs will almost always be better anaerobic treatment options than UASBs for stand-alone treatment plants. UASB treatment is, however, a possible co-treatment option, particularly in situations in which municipal wastewater is weak, containing a relatively low concentration of organic solids. For detailed guidance on UASB design, see van Lier et al. (2010).

Aerobic and facultative biological treatment options

Facultative ponds

Facultative ponds are the simplest form of secondary treatment. Their main purpose is to remove organic material and solids but they can also remove ammonia that is incorporated into biomass (Mara, 2004). When used in faecal sludge and septage treatment, they will normally follow anaerobic ponds. If the treated effluent is to be used to irrigate crops, further treatment in maturation ponds will be required. Maturation ponds will be discussed as an option for pathogen removal later in this chapter.

The upper layers of facultative ponds are aerobic, with oxygen introduced through atmospheric oxygen diffusion and algal photosynthesis. Anaerobic conditions prevail near the bottom of ponds while intermediate levels may be intermittently aerobic and anaerobic, depending on the time of day and whether or not photosynthesis is occurring.

Their long hydraulic retention time enables anaerobic ponds to deal well with variations in hydraulic and organic load, but also means that they require more land than most other technologies. This apparent disadvantage is mitigated by the fact that the hydraulic loading on a septage treatment plant is much lower than that on a wastewater treatment plant serving the same population. Land requirements will therefore be relatively low, despite the much higher strength of septage and faecal sludge.

Facultative ponds are an option for co-treatment of septage with municipal wastewater but should be preceded by solids–liquid separation of the septage. Where the treatment plant serves a relatively small catchment area and a high proportion of the population uses on-site sanitation, the load exerted by septage may comprise a large part of the total load on the plant and this will have to be taken into account in the design.

When treating municipal wastewater, correctly sized, configured, and operated facultative ponds can remove 70–90 per cent of the influent BOD (Mara, 2004). The algae that are present in the ponds contribute to relatively high BOD and TSS levels in the effluent compared with other treatment processes – the suspended solids from facultative ponds are approximately 60–90 per cent algae (Mara, 2004). Facultative ponds treating wastewater have reported TSS removal efficiencies of 70–80% (von Sperling, 2007).

Design and operational considerations

Pond geometry and depth. Facultative ponds should be between 1.0 and 2.5 m deep in order to maintain aerobic conditions on the surface and anaerobic conditions at the bottom (Tilley et al., 2014). In practice, most ponds are 1.5–2 m deep. Their length-to-width ratio should be at least 2:1 and preferably 3:1 to prevent short-circuiting and so ensure maximum retention time.

Ponds can be constructed with vertical concrete walls, but the normal practice is to provide sloping sides, typically with internal and external slopes of 1:3 and 1:2, respectively. Whichever construction method is used, it is essential to provide worker access to remove scum and sludge since it is likely that a pond that is difficult to desludge will never be desludged.

Avoidance of short-circuiting. Pond performance can be significantly reduced by short-circuiting, which occurs when some combination of flow and environmental conditions and pond geometry causes flow to move directly from the pond inlet to its outlet while other areas of the pond remain almost stagnant. Short-circuiting can be the result of winds or of forces created by the momentum of the inflow to the pond. They can be reduced by designing pond inlets to minimize the entry velocity and installing baffle walls inside ponds to lengthen the flow path and prevent direct flows from inlet to outlet.

Provision for occasional desludging. While desludging of facultative ponds will be required less frequently than that of anaerobic ponds, it will still be required from time to time. The normal configuration of two or more ponds operating in parallel allows one pond to be decommissioned and dewatered so that it can be desludged. The liquid removed from the pond will normally be pumped into another pond. Another option is to desludge using a raft-mounted sludge pump. This will avoid the need for dewatering but may leave some sludge in-situ, leading to an eventual requirement for pond decommissioning and dewatering to allow removal of consolidated sludge that cannot be pumped.

Pond appearance. When operating as intended, facultative ponds have a distinct green colour, caused by the presence of algae, as shown by the facultative pond in Tabanan, Indonesia in Photo 8.1. If the pond is overloaded, it will become red-brown in colour, scum will form on the pond surface and it may emit odours.

Design criteria and procedure
The primary design criterion for facultative ponds is the maximum allowable organic loading on the pond. Because the main oxygen-transfer processes

Photo 8.1 Facultative pond at Tabanan, Indonesia

occur at or near the surface, the allowable loading rate is defined in relation to pond area rather than pond volume. Empirical equations for calculating the allowable loading rate on facultative ponds include:

McGarry and Pescod (1970): $\lambda_s = 60(1.099)^T$

Mara (1987): $\lambda_s = 20T - 120$

Arthur (1983): $\lambda_s = 20T - 60$

Mara (1987, 2004): $\lambda_s = 350(1.107 - 0.002T)^{T-25}$

where λ_s is the loading rate in kg BOD$_5$/ha d; and

T is the mean temperature of the coldest month in °C.

Figure 8.4 represents these equations graphically. The McGarry and Pescod and Arthur equations predict the maximum loading that can be applied to a facultative pond before it becomes anaerobic, a key consideration for the design and proper functionality of a facultative pond. The two Mara equations are design equations that allow a factor of safety before the pond goes anaerobic. For temperatures in the range 10–17.5°C, the McGarry and Pescod and Arthur equations are in close agreement. At temperatures above 20°C, the predictions of the McGarry and Pescod equation diverge significantly from those of the other equations. With these points in mind, and bearing in mind the uncertainties regarding the performance of ponds when treating partly digested septage, it will be advisable to base designs on the second Mara equation. The temperature used for design purposes should be the mean temperature of the coldest month of the year.

Table 8.6 summarizes the recommended facultative pond design criteria. It does not include retention time, which is determined by the surface loading rate and pond depth and is therefore not an independent design criterion.

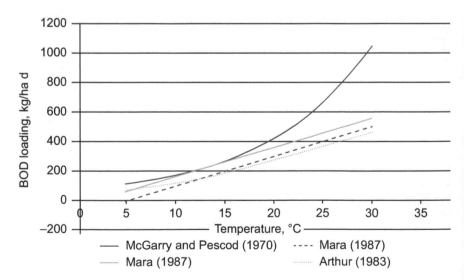

Figure 8.4 Comparison of permissible loading rate predictions for facultative ponds

Table 8.6 Summary of facultative pond design criteria

Parameter	Symbol	Units	Value/range	Notes/reference
Surface BOD loading rate	λ_s	kg BOD/ha d	Temperature-dependent. Calculate using appropriate equation	$\lambda_s = 350 \times (1.107 - 0.002T)^{(T-25)}$
Depth	D_f	m	1–2.5 m; commonly 1.5 m	Recommended range (Mara, 2004)
Length-to-width ratio	L/W	–	Commonly 2:1–3:1	(Mara, 2004)
Side slope	S	–	1:2	For ponds with sloping sides

The steps in facultative pond design are as follows:

1. Calculate the allowable organic loading on the pond (λ_s, kg BOD/ha d), using the equation:

$$\lambda_s = 350(1.107 - 0.002T)^{T-25}$$

where T = mean temperature of the coldest month of the year in °C.

2. Calculate the required mid-depth pond area using the equation:

$$A_f = \frac{10L_iQ}{\lambda_s}$$

where A_f = total facultative pond area at mid-depth (m²);
L_i = BOD of inflow in mg/l (commonly the BOD of the effluent from the anaerobic pond); and
Q = mean daily flow into the facultative pond (m³/d).

3. Choose a pond depth (D_f) within the range 1.5–2.5 m and use this and the pond area to calculate the pond retention time θ_f in days

$$\theta_f = \frac{A_f D_f}{Q}$$

4. Determine the number, plan area, and dimensions of ponds, allowing at least two treatment streams in parallel to provide operational flexibility. For a system with two parallel streams, the required pond area for each stream will be $A_f/2$. Using the calculated surface area for one pond, determine the pond dimensions, using a length-to-width ratio of 2:1–3:1. If necessary, the pond dimensions can be calculated using the methods suggested above for anaerobic ponds. In most cases, it will be sufficiently accurate to calculate the required pond area using the mid-depth pond dimensions.

5. Calculate the effluent BOD (L_e) using the equation:

$$L_e = L_i\left(1 - \frac{\%BOD_{rem}}{100}\right)$$

where: L_i is the influent BOD; and

$\%BOD_{rem}$ is the percentage BOD removal through the pond (assume a figure of 70 per cent unless data is available on BOD removal in ponds treating septage under similar conditions).

Facultative ponds should be desludged when sludge accumulation has reached 20–25 per cent of the pond volume. The sludge accumulation rate, desludging frequency, and sludge volume removed can be calculated using the approach already described for anaerobic ponds. The actual desludging interval should be determined using the actual sludge accumulation rate and may differ from the calculated interval. To ensure that this can be done, standard operating procedures should include guidance on monitoring the sludge accumulation rate.

Facultative pond design example

A facultative pond is to be designed to treat the liquid effluent from an anaerobic process. The influent characteristics and process assumptions are as stated in the table below.

Parameter	Symbol	Value	Unit
Flow	Q	40	m³/d
Influent BOD concentration	L_i	500	mg/l
Influent TSS concentration	TSS_i	500	mg/l
Depth	D	1.5	m
Temperature	T	20	°C
Assumptions			
% BOD removal	%BOD	70	%
% TS of wet sludge	%TS	10	%
% of pond as sludge	–	20	%
% DS content	%DS	10	%
Density of sludge	ρ_{sludge}	1,000	kg/m³

1. Calculate the allowable organic loading on the pond:

$$\lambda_s = 350[1.107 - (0.002 \times 20)]^{20-25} = 250 \text{ kg/ha d}$$

2. Calculate the required mid-depth pond area:

$$A_f = \frac{10 \times 500 \text{ mg/l} \times 40 \text{ m}^3/\text{d}}{250 \text{ kg/ha d}} = 800 \text{ m}^2$$

3. Decide the pond depth and calculate the retention time.
   Select 1.5 m pond depth. Pond volume $V_f = 800 \times 1.5 = 1,200 \text{ m}^3$

$$\text{Retention } \theta_f = \frac{1,200 \text{ m}^3}{40 \text{ m}^3/\text{d}} = 30 \text{ d}$$

4. Decide the number of ponds in parallel and calculate the pond plan dimensions
   Provide two ponds in parallel and assume a length-to-width ratio of 3:1. The required pond width approximates to the square root of [800/(3 × 2)], which equals 11.55 m. Rounding this to 11.5 m, the mid-pond dimensions become 11.5 m × 34.5 m.
   Assume a 1:2 side slope
   Top water level dimensions are 11.5 + (4 × 0.75) by 34.5 + (4 × 0.75) = 14.5 m by 37.5
5. Calculate BOD of the pond effluent, assuming 70 per cent removal:

$$L_e = (1 - 0.7) \times 500 \text{ mg/l} = 150 \text{ mg/l}$$

If information is available on TSS removal and solids destruction rate through the pond and the TSS content of the sludge, the sludge accumulation rate can be calculated using the methods already given for anaerobic ponds. For 80 per cent TSS removal through the ponds, 20 per cent solids destruction rate, and 10 per cent TSS content in the pond sludge, the calculated sludge accumulation rate is 0.064 m³/d per pond.

If the pond is desludged when the accumulated sludge equates to 20 per cent of the pond volume, required desludging interval is given by the equation:

$$f_{desludging} = \frac{0.2\left(\frac{1}{2} \times 1,200 \text{ m}^3\right)}{0.064 \text{ m}^3/\text{day}} = 1,875 \text{ days} - \text{ie. } \sim 5 \text{ years}$$

The volume of sludge to be removed from one pond (V_{sludge}) equals the pond volume divided by five:

$$V_{sludge} = \frac{\frac{1}{2} \times 1,200}{5} = 120 \text{ m}^3$$

Aerated lagoons

Some septage treatment plants serving cities in lower-income countries use aerated lagoons to treat the liquid fraction of septage. Aerated lagoons are simple, but their reliance on mechanical aeration means that they are a step up in complexity from passive facultative ponds. They may be either fully or partially mixed. Partially mixed aerated lagoons perform in facultative mode and contain both aerobic and anaerobic zones. They use less power than fully mixed lagoons but require much more land. For ponds operating in the warm south of the USA, US EPA (2011) gives estimated land area requirements for facultative waste stabilization ponds, partially mixed lagoons, and fully mixed lagoons to treat 3,785 m³ (1 million American gallons) of wastewater of 20, 13, and 1 hectares, respectively. This suggests that partially mixed lagoons require around two-thirds of the land required for facultative waste stabilization ponds. The relatively small land saving is unlikely to justify the increase in operational cost and complexity resulting from the provision of mechanical aeration. In view of this, the focus here is on fully mixed lagoons.

Fully mixed aerated lagoons require sufficient energy to maintain the solids in suspension and provide enough oxygen to maintain aerobic conditions in the whole pond. In these respects, they are similar to activated sludge reactors (ASRs) but differ from them in that there is no sludge return. As with

ASRs, effluents from fully mixed aerated lagoons have high TSS concentrations, which must be removed before final discharge. Sedimentation ponds are the simplest TSS removal option. The retention time in these ponds should normally be 2 days, which is short enough to prevent algal growth and the resultant increase in effluent solids concentration (Mara, 2004).

Aerated lagoons require a reliable electricity supply and some operator skills, although the skills required are not as great as those required for ASRs and their variants. For these reasons, they should only be considered where land availability is insufficient to allow the use of facultative waste stabilization ponds.

Aerated lagoons provide an option for co-treatment of the liquid fraction of separated faecal sludge and septage with municipal wastewater. As with other co-treatment options, the loading exerted by the separated liquid must be taken into account when sizing the lagoon. Since aerated lagoons will normally follow solids–liquid separation, grit and FOG will not normally be a problem.

Aerated lagoons treating wastewater can remove up to 70–90 per cent of the influent BOD, if properly designed and operated. The TSS removal efficiency of a well-maintained, partially mixed aerated lagoon treating wastewater is likely to be around 80 per cent (von Sperling, 2007).

Design and operational considerations

Air delivery options. Air may be provided either by surface mounted mechanical aerators or with compressed air delivered through diffusers located near the bottom of the lagoon. Surface aerators may be high or low speed and diffusers may deliver either fine or coarse bubbles. Table 8.7 provides basic information on the four aeration options.

Most aerated lagoons use high-speed surface aerators and some use coarse bubble aeration. Low-speed surface aerators are mainly used in ASRs at large

Table 8.7 Lagoon aeration options

Type of aeration	Oxygen transfer kg O_2/kWh	Design and maintenance issues
High-speed surface aerator up to 50 kW 900–1200 rpm	0.9–1.3	Direct drive from motor; can be brought to side of pond for maintenance
Low-speed surface aerator up to 150 kW 40–60 rpm	1.5–2.1	Requires supporting structure
Coarse bubble diffusion 5–12 mm diffusers	0.6–1.5	More robust than fine bubble diffusion
Fine bubble diffusion 1–3 mm diffusers	3.6–4.8 (Will deteriorate unless system is well maintained and regularly cleaned)	Requires regular cleaning, typically at intervals of between 6 months and 2 years

Source: based on Stenstrom and Rosso (2010)

wastewater treatment plants. The need for a supporting structure and a permanent access platform increases their installation cost and they are not normally used in aerated lagoons. Despite their superior oxygen transfer performance, fine bubble aerators are unlikely to be a good choice for septage treatment plants in lower-income countries. They are susceptible to problems with blocked diffusers and require regular cleaning, which will normally require complete dewatering of the lagoon: a difficult task that may be neglected, leading to complete system failure. Coarse bubble diffused air systems are much less susceptible to problems with blocked diffusers but lagoons will have to be drained to undertake major repair and maintenance tasks, such as clearing pipe blockages and repairing leaking pipe joints and corroded pipes. The use of plastic pipework, particularly polyethylene pipes with welded joints, should eliminate corrosion problems and greatly reduce the incidence of leaky joints. It will not eliminate problems with pipework blockages. Floating high-speed aerators avoid these problems and can be moved so that they are more flexible than diffused air systems. For these reasons, they will normally be the preferred option. Photo 8.2 shows a high-speed surface aerator at the Duri Kosambi septage treatment plant in Jakarta, Indonesia. The aerators are used intermittently and it appears that the lagoon is operating in partially mixed mode.

Lagoon geometry. Some standard texts advise the use of square lagoons (Crites and Tchobanoglous, 1998), but aerated lagoons are often rectangular in shape.

The need for parallel treatment streams and standby aeration capacity. For the reasons already explained for anaerobic and facultative ponds, it will be advisable to provide two treatment streams in parallel whenever the site geometry allows it. Standby aerators should be provided to meet calculated aeration requirements when one aerator is out of service

Surface aerator tethering and spacing requirements. Surface aerators should be installed in a way that allows them to be repositioned if needed and pulled

Photo 8.2 High-speed surface aerator at Duri Kosambi, Jakarta

into the side of the pond for maintenance and repair. This is usually done by tethering the aerators in place with ropes or wires, as shown in Photo 8.2. Floating aerators must be sized to ensure that the whole lagoon area is aerated but excessive turbulence, which could result in erosion of the lagoon bed, is avoided. The required spacing will typically be in the range 8–15 m, depending on the size and power of the aerator. Adjacent aerators should rotate in opposite directions. The spacing of aerators may be decreased, or more powerful aerators may be placed in the inlet zone, where there is higher oxygen demand, with fewer aerators placed in the outlet zone to allow some settling (von Sperling, 2007).

The need for reliable supply chains. Aerated lagoons depend on mechanical equipment and so reliable supply chains will be required for replacement parts. Staff should be trained in routine maintenance and simple repair tasks. It may be appropriate to contract out more complex repair tasks to local workshops. There will be need for access to laboratory services, either in-house or contracted, to allow collection of the information on influent and effluent parameters that is required to adjust operational practice in the light of operational experience.

Design criteria and procedure
The key design parameters for aerated lagoons are the lagoon size and dimensions, the retention time, and the amount of oxygen required to remove BOD and ammonia. Lagoon depths and hydraulic retention times are typically in the ranges 2–5 m and 2–6 days, respectively (Tilley et al., 2014; Arthur, 1983). Mechanical surface aerators are rated to have an oxygenation efficiency of 1.2–2.0 kg O_2/kWh (von Sperling, 2007). The recommended design criteria for an aerated lagoon are presented in Table 8.8.

Aerated lagoon design also requires information on the design temperature (typically the average ambient temperature during the coldest month of the year), the flow rate, the BOD and NH_3 concentrations of the influent, and their required concentrations in the effluent. The design steps are as follows.

Table 8.8 Summary of aerated lagoon design criteria

Parameter	Symbol	Unit	Value/range	Notes/reference
Depth	z_{AL}	m	2–5	Recommended (Tilley et al., 2014)
Hydraulic retention time	θ_{AL}	days	2–6	Recommended 4 days (Mara, 2004)
Length : width ratio	l : w	–	2 : 1–4 : 1	Recommended range (von Sperling, 2007)
Peak factor	PF	–	Typically 1.5	Use peak month factor for septage delivery to the treatment plant

1. Calculate the required BOD and ammonia removals:
   The required BOD removal is given by the equation:

   $$L_{\text{BODrem}} = \frac{Q(L_i - L_e)}{1,000 \text{ l/m}^3}$$

   where L_{BODrem} = required BOD removal (kg/d);
   $\quad\quad Q$ = flow to the aerated lagoons (m³/d);
   $\quad\quad L_i$ = influent BOD (mg/l);
   $\quad\quad L_e$ = required effluent BOD (mg/l).
   The required ammonia removal is calculated in the same manner.

2. Calculate the oxygen demand for BOD removal (OD$_{\text{BOD}}$, kg/d):

   $$OD_{\text{BOD}} = L_{\text{BODrem}} \times F_o$$

   where: F_o is the ratio of the weight of oxygen required to weight of BOD removed, 1.5 (i.e., 1.5 kg O$_2$ required per kg BOD removed).

3. Calculate the oxygen demand for ammonia removal (OD$_{\text{NH3}}$, kg/d) – if ammonia removal by nitrification is required:

   $$OD_{\text{NH3}} = L_{\text{NH3rem}} \times F_n$$

   where: F_n is typically 4.6 (i.e., 4.6 kg O$_2$ required per kg NH$_3$ removed) and L_{NH3rem} is the required NH$_3$ removal (kg/d).

4. Calculate the total actual oxygen requirement for the pond:
   To find the total oxygen required, calculate the average daily actual oxygen requirement (AOR$_{\text{avg}}$, kg O$_2$/d) by adding the oxygen requirements for BOD and ammonia. To find the peak daily AOR (AOR$_{\text{peak}}$), multiply AOR$_{\text{avg}}$ by an appropriate peak factor (PF). This will normally be the peak day factor for flow to the treatment plant. The average and peak oxygen requirements are then given by equations:

   $$AOR_{\text{avg}} = OD_{\text{BOD}} + OD_{\text{NH3}}$$

   $$AOR_{\text{peak}} = AOR_{\text{avg}} \times PF$$

   The first should be used when estimating the yearly power requirement and the second when assessing the required aerator power output.

5. Calculate the power requirement:
   This requires information on the efficiency of the equipment used to transfer oxygen to the liquid to be treated. To obtain this information, manufacturers should be contacted and their literature should be consulted. Manufacturer's data will typically state the oxygen per hour that an aerator can transfer to the water, the aerator spacing required to ensure that the lagoon is fully mixed, and the power requirement for the aerator. The actual power requirement (P, kW) can be found using the peak AOR and the oxygenation efficiency of the selected aerators (OE, kg O$_2$/kWh). The manufacturer's oxygenation efficiency (OE$_{\text{m}}$)

should be adjusted for field conditions using an empirical OE adjustment factor of 0.55–0.65 (von Sperling, 2007).

$$OE = OE_m \times 0.6$$

$$P = \frac{AOR_{peak}}{24 \ OE}$$

6. Determine the number and spacing of aerators and the pond dimensions:
   - *Number of aerators* = P/P_{aer}, where P_{aer} is the power rating of a single aerator. In most cases, the aerators selected for use at septage treatment plants will have a power output in the range 4–18 kW.
   - *Aerator spacing and lagoon dimensions.* The key dimension used to calculate the aerator spacing and pond dimensions is the influence diameter of the aerators. Table 8.9 provides information on this and other parameters required for preliminary design.
   For fully mixed lagoons the influence diameter must not exceed the mixing diameter. For square and rectangular lagoons, the critical dimension is the diagonal at 45° from the axes of the lagoon, which will define the point at which the influence zone either touches the corner of the lagoon or intersects with the influence zone of another aerator. The distance from any aerator to the side of the lagoon is then the mixing radius divided by the square root of two while the distance between in-line aerators is the mixing diameter divided by the square root of two. The lagoon dimensions are then defined by the equation:

$$L = nD/\sqrt{2}$$

where L = lagoon length in a given direction (m);
   n = number of aerators provided in line in that direction;
   D = the mixing diameter (m).

   Since surface aerators can be moved around in the pond, the normal procedure should be to place sufficient aerators in position to meet oxygen requirements with standby aerators available in store or tethered at the side of the pond. The standby aerators should be ready to be moved into position if one of the operational aerators has to be taken out of service for maintenance and repair.

7. Check the retention time in the lagoons
   The total lagoon area is given by the equation $A_{AL} = N(D/\sqrt{2})^2$
   where A_{AL} = total lagoon area (m²)
      N = total number of aerators
   Retention time (days) = $z_{AL}A_{AL}/Q$
   This will change slightly if pond dimensions are rounded up or down.

8. Determine the final sedimentation pond dimensions. Provide one pond for each treatment stream. For a two-day retention period, the area of each pond will be given by the equation:

$$A_p = 2Q/(nz_p)$$

Table 8.9 Design parameters for high-speed aerators

Aerator power		Operating depth (m)	Influence diameter (m)	
Horsepower (hp)	kW		Oxygenation	Mixing
5–10	3.70–7.35	2.0–3.6	45–50	14–16
15–25	11.0–18.4	3.0–4.3	60–80	19–24
30–50	22.00–36.75	3.8–5.2	85–100	27–32

Source: adapted from von Sperling (2007)

where A_p = area of one sedimentation pond (m³);
n = number of treatment streams;
z_p = pond depth (m).
Ponds should be either square or rectangular, with a length-to-width ratio not exceeding 2:1.

Further guidance on aerator sizing and positioning is available in Boyle et al. (2002).

Aerated lagoon design example

Separated liquid that has already been treated in anaerobic waste stabilization ponds is to be treated in a fully mixed aerated lagoon using mechanical surface aerators. The design parameters are as set out below.

Parameter	Symbol	Value	Unit
Peak flow rate	Q	100	m³/d
Influent BOD concentration	L_i	1,500	mg/l
Influent NH$_3$ concentration	N_i	180	mg/l
Target effluent BOD concentration	L_e	50	mg/l
Target effluent NH$_3$ concentration	N_e	50	mg/l
Mass O$_2$ required per mass BOD	–	1.5	–
Mass O$_2$ required per mass NH$_3$	–	4.6	–
OE factor	–	0.6	–
BOD load peak day factor	PF	1.5	–
Manufacturer's aerator oxygenation efficiency	OE$_m$	2	kg O$_2$/kWh

1. *Calculate required BOD and ammonia removals:*

$$L_{BODrem} = 100 \text{ m}^3/\text{d} \left(1,500 - 50 \text{ mg/l}\right)\left(1,000 \text{ l/m}^3\right)\left(1 \text{ kg}/10^6 \text{ mg}\right) = 145 \text{ kg/d}$$

$$L_{NH3rem} = 100 \text{ m}^3/\text{d} \left(180 - 50 \text{ mg/l}\right)\left(1,000 \text{ l/m}^3\right)\left(1 \text{ kg}/10^6 \text{ mg}\right) = 13 \text{ kg/d}$$

2. *Calculate oxygen requirement for BOD removal:*

$$OD_{BOD} = 145 \text{ kg BOD/d} \times 1.5 \left(\frac{\text{kg O}_2}{\text{kg BOD}}\right) = 217.5 \text{ kg O}_2/\text{d}$$

3. *Calculate oxygen requirement for ammonia removal:*

$$OD_{NH3} = 13 \text{ kg NH}_3/d \times 4.6\left(\frac{\text{kg O}_2}{\text{kg NH}_3}\right) = 59.8 \text{ kg O}_2/d$$

4. *Calculate the total actual oxygen requirement (AOR) for the aerated lagoon:*

$$AOR_{avg} = 217.5 + 59.8 = 277.3 \text{ kg O}_2/d$$

$$AOR_{peak} = 277.3 \times 1.5 = 416 \text{ kg O}_2/d$$

5. *Calculate the power requirement:*
Assume a manufacturer's oxygenation efficiency of 2 kg O_2/kWh, and an empirical field adjustment factor of 0.6. Thus:

$$OE = 2\left(\frac{\text{kg O}_2}{\text{kWh}}\right) \times 0.6 = 1.2\left(\frac{\text{kg O}_2}{\text{kWh}}\right)$$

$$P = \frac{416 \text{ kg O}_2/d}{1.2 \text{ kg O}_2/\text{kWh}} = 347 \text{ kWh per day}$$

Fully mixed ponds require continuous aeration. Total aerator power required = 347/24 = 14.45 kW
6. *Determine number and spacing of aerators and lagoon dimensions:*
Assume two treatment streams, each with a pair of aerators located in a rectangular lagoon, giving a total of four aerators.

$$\text{Power requirement of each aerator} = \frac{\text{Power requirement}}{\text{No. of aerators}} = 14.45/4 = 3.6125 \text{ kW}$$

This power requirement will be met by four 5 hp (3.73 kW) aerators.
    Based on Table 8.9, choose a lagoon depth and determine the required mixing diameter. Take these as 2 m and 14 m, respectively.

$$\text{Lagoon length } L \text{ (two aerators in line)} = \frac{2 \times 14 \text{ m}}{\sqrt{2}}$$

$$= 19.8 \text{ m}$$

$$\text{Lagoon width } W \text{ (one aerator in line)} = \frac{1 \times 14 \text{ m}}{\sqrt{2}}$$

$$= 9.9 \text{ m}$$

Hydraulic retention time (peak month flow)

$$= \frac{20(\text{lagoon length}) \times 10(\text{lagoon width}) \times 2(\text{lagoon depth})}{100(\text{design flow}) \times 1.5(\text{peak factor})} = 2.67 \text{ days}$$

This assumes that peak organic and ammonia nitrogen concentration remain constant over a range of flows so that loadings vary in proportion to flow.
7. *Determine final sedimentation pond dimensions.*
Provide two 1.5 m deep ponds in parallel, sized to provide two days' retention at design flow.

$$\text{Area required for each pond} = \frac{2(\text{days retention}) \times 150 \text{ m}^3/d}{2(\text{no. of ponds}) \times 1.5 \text{ m (pond depth)}} = 100 \text{ m}^2$$

Provide two 10 m × 10 m × 1.5 m deep sedimentation ponds.

Constructed wetlands

System description
Constructed wetlands are engineered systems that replicate the processes that occur in natural wetlands (Vymazal, 2010). They fall into three categories:

- horizontal free-surface flow systems (in which the flow is mainly above ground);
- horizontal sub-surface flow systems;
- vertical-flow systems.

Most operational systems in hot climates are of the horizontal sub-surface flow type. The preference for such systems stems from recognition of potential insect vector problems with free-surface flow wetlands and the difficulties involved in ensuring equal distribution of flow across vertical-flow wetlands. The impermeable sides and base of the wetland structure contain a gravel bed, typically 30–60 cm deep and planted with wetland plants. Wastewater enters at one end of wetland 'cells' and must be distributed across the full width of the wetland. It then flows through the gravel and exits the cell at the other end. As it does so, a combination of physical and aerobic, anoxic, and anaerobic microbial processes reduces the suspended solids, organic carbon, and nitrogen loads in the wastewater.

Unlike horizontal-flow wetlands, vertical-flow wetlands are loaded intermittently, typically 4–10 times a day for municipal wastewater (Tilley et al., 2014). When the bed is loaded, wastewater percolates down through the bed, drawing air into the filter media and so creating aerobic conditions. The wetland plants transfer a small amount of oxygen through their roots, but their main function is to maintain the permeability of the bed. Organisms are starved of food in the intervals between dosing events and this ensures that excessive biomass growth is avoided and that the porosity of the bed is maintained. The intermittent dosing regime allows vertical-flow constructed wetlands to be loaded at a higher rate than horizontal-flow wetlands. Unfortunately, it also makes operation of the wetlands more complex since intermittent dosing requires either pumping or the use of a siphon. The siphon option is simpler and should be used where the fall required for siphon operation is available.

To date, constructed wetlands have mainly been used to treat domestic wastewater, grey water (sullage), and run-off water. The high organic and suspended solids loadings associated with strong wastewaters such as septage may lead to plant die-off and a build-up of solids in the bed, resulting in reduced hydraulic capacity and eventual system failure. For this reason, constructed wetlands should only be considered for septage treatment after solids–liquid separation and anaerobic treatment in ponds or an ABR. Conversely, plants will die if the bed is grossly underloaded so that there is no liquid in the bed to support plant growth, so it is important to ensure that the bed area provided matches the expected inflow of septage both immediately and at the design horizon. This may require more beds to be planted and commissioned over time.

Design and operational considerations

The need for pre-treatment. Because they rely on flow through a gravel or sand medium with small pore spaces, constructed wetlands are susceptible to blockages. This is particularly true when they are used to manage septage, with its high suspended-solids concentration and potentially high FOG content. It is therefore important that upstream processes to remove solids and FOG are reliable.

System monitoring. Standard operating procedures should include a requirement for regular inspection of the wetland surface to look for surface ponding which is an indicator of blockages in the bed.

The need for multiple cells. The only way to clear blockages will be to remove the wetland plants and media and replace them with new plants and clean media. This is a fairly arduous task and requires that the whole of the cell be taken out of service. To minimize the disruption caused by such activities, the wetland should be divided into several cells with pipework designed to allow individual cells to be isolated and bypassed while they are undergoing maintenance.

Routine maintenance. Important maintenance tasks include removal of dead vegetation and undesirable plant species (for instance, tree saplings) from the bed, thinning out of wetland plants, and replacement of plants that have died.

Bed configuration. The length-to-width ratio of horizontal-flow constructed wetland should be at least 2:1, sufficient to create a long travel path for liquid travelling through the wetland and reduce the likelihood of short-circuiting. The length-to-width ratio of vertical-flow beds will be influenced by the method used to distribute the flow onto the bed. Beds that receive flow through vertical pipes should normally be approximately square in plan to reduce differential flows caused by head-losses in long lengths of pipework. Where flow is introduced through a channel along the side of the bed, a long, relatively narrow, configuration is likely to be a better option. The bed should have a longitudinal slope of around 1 per cent from inlet to outlet.

Design criteria and procedure
The simplest approach to the design of constructed wetlands is to size the wetland on the basis of an organic loading rate per unit of wetland area. Loading guidelines, based on European and North American practices, typically recommend organic loading rates for horizontal-flow constructed wetlands in the range 7–16 g BOD_5/m^2 d (see, for instance US EPA, 2000). This approach makes no allowance for either temperature or the amount by which the organic load is reduced through the constructed wetland. Research on pilot-scale beds in Thailand found higher removal rates for both horizontal and vertical-flow beds. In horizontal-flow wetlands, an organic removal rate of 33.9 g BOD_5/m^2 d was achieved at an average wastewater temperature of 27°C and a hydraulic loading rate of 20 cm/d (Kantawanichkul and Wannasri, 2013). This research also found that the removal rate increased with increased hydraulic loading and that horizontal-flow wetlands performed better than vertical-flow wetlands.

Various researchers have developed equations to model the performance of constructed wetlands, taking account of temperature and the influent and effluent concentrations. A widely accepted first-order rate equation for the design of horizontal-flow constructed wetlands is Kickuth's equation:

$$A = \frac{Q(\text{Ln } C_i - \text{Ln } C_e)}{k_{20}1.06^{(T-20)}dn}$$

where: A is the wetland area in m²;
Q is the average daily flow rate in m³/d;
C_i and C_e are the inlet and outlet BOD₅ concentrations in mg/l;
Ln denotes the natural logarithm;
k_{20} is a rate constant at 20°C in day⁻¹;
T is the design ambient temperature in °C;
d is the bed depth in m; and
n is the porosity of the substrate medium, expressed as a fraction.

Rearranging this equation and multiplying Q by C_i to give the loading, Kickuth's equation gives the following expression for permissible loading

$$L_{cw} = \frac{C_i Q}{A} = \frac{C_i\left(k_{20}1.06^{(T-20)}\right)dn}{(\text{Ln } C_i - \text{Ln } C_e)}$$

Where L_{cw} is the permissible loading expressed in g BOD₅/m² d

In the absence of site-specific information, assume a k_{20} of 1.1 day⁻¹ for horizontal-flow wetlands. Assuming a temperature of 10°C, and typical values of 40 cm bed depth and 40% for bed porosity, this equation gives a permissible loading of 12.8 g BOD₅/m² d on a bed designed to reduce a 300 mg/l influent BOD₅ to 30 mg/l. This is within the 7–16 g BOD₅/m² d range given above. The inclusion of the term 1.06⁽ᵀ⁻²⁰⁾ in the equation means that L_{cw} is highly temperature dependent, increasing by a factor of about 2.4 when the ambient temperature increases from 10°C to 25°C, to give an organic loading rate of 30.73 g BOD₅/m² d at 25°C. Since this is in broad agreement with the findings of the Thailand investigations, it seems reasonable to use Kickuth's equation to calculate the allowable loading on constructed wetlands. For further information on this and other aspects of the design of constructed wetlands see UN Habitat (2008).

Jiminez (2007) reports removal rates of 90–98 per cent for thermo-tolerant coliforms and 60–100 per cent for protozoa in horizontal-flow constructed wetlands, but suggests that follow-up treatment in a horizontal-flow gravel bed is required to ensure 100 per cent helminth egg removal. This suggests that constructed wetlands will not provide a stand-alone option for removing pathogens to allow effluent to be used for unrestricted irrigation.

The figures quoted above all derive from experience with constructed wetlands treating domestic wastewater. Few examples of the use of constructed wetlands for treatment of liquid from septage or faecal sludge exist and more work is needed to assess their suitability for this purpose. Regardless of this, a loading rate of about 30 g BOD₅/m² d at 25°C, equivalent to 300 kg BOD₅/ha d, is below the rate that can be achieved in a facultative pond at the same temperature. The possibility of deriving some income from the sale of harvested plants exists but this income will be small. Overall, facultative ponds will almost always offer a better option for simple secondary treatment than constructed wetlands. One exception might be the situation in which flows are low and the evaporation rate from open ponds is high so that the effluent from ponds has a high salinity. In this situation, constructed wetlands may be a better option where treated effluent is to be used for restricted irrigation. Further treatment or disinfection will be required to ensure that treated wastewater is safe for unrestricted irrigation. Given the relatively small volumes of treated water produced, the better option will normally be to explore options for using treated effluent for restricted irrigation.

Other aerobic technologies

Other aerobic treatment technologies include trickling filters, rotating biological contactors (RBCs), ASRs, sequencing batch reactors (SBRs), moving-bed biofilm reactors (MBBRs), and oxidation ditches, which are a form of extended aeration. There are few examples of the use of these technologies in lower-income countries to treat faecal sludge and septage, although all have potential for use in plants providing co-treatment. They are briefly introduced below and their potential for faecal sludge and septage treatment is examined.

Trickling filters

Trickling filters use microorganisms attached to a medium to remove organic matter from wastewater. The medium is typically about 2 m deep, consists of stones or plastic shapes with a high surface area, is contained within a circular structure, and is provided with a system of underdrains. The wastewater to be treated is applied to the top of the medium through holes in a rotating arm, which should preferably be driven by the force of the water ejected through the holes. The system requires either a pump or some form of siphon device to deliver the intermittent discharge that drives the rotating arm. The term 'filter' is misleading since trickling filters function mainly through microbiological growth attached to the filter medium as biofilm. Excess biofilm sloughs off and is carried through the filter, creating a need for secondary settlement in 'humus' tanks after filtration.

Trickling filters are unlikely to be a suitable technology for stand-alone treatment of the liquid fraction of septage and faecal sludge for the following reasons:

- The high organic content of the liquid means that the design is governed by the organic load rather than the hydraulic load. This results in a low hydraulic loading rate, which is unlikely to be sufficient to keep the filter media adequately wetted.
- The liquid flow is highly variable, dropping to zero for between 12 and 16 hours per day, depending on the opening hours of the plant.
- The solids content of septage and faecal sludge is high and will remain much higher than that of municipal wastewater after solids–liquid separation. High solids concentrations are likely to cause blockages in

trickling filter distribution arm nozzles, resulting in uneven flow distribution and poor filter performance.

All three of the effects listed above will result in odour and insect problems. Recirculation will deal with the first two effects but will require the installation and operation of pumps, which will increase operational cost and complexity. Fine screening might be used to remove the larger suspended solids particles that are most likely to block distributor arm nozzles, but this will also increase system complexity since fine screens will require mechanical cleaning.

When septage or faecal sludge is to be co-treated with municipal wastewater at a plant that includes trickling filters, it will be important to assess the effect of the increased loading on trickling filter operation. Solids–liquid separation of faecal sludge and septage should always be provided and it may also be desirable to provide fine screening of the separated liquid prior to the trickling filters. Because addition of strong faecal sludge and septage will have a greater effect on organic loading than hydraulic loading, recirculation rates will normally have to be increased to ensure that minimum recommended hydraulic loading rates are achieved.

Rotating biological contactors
RBCs are widely used to treat small wastewater treatment flows. An RBC consists of a series of discs mounted on a horizontally mounted shaft which runs just above the water surface over a rectangular tank so that the discs are partly submerged. Wastewater flows through the tank from one end to the other past the partly submerged discs, which rotate slowly as the shaft is turned by a small electric motor. Bacteria and other organisms grow on the surfaces of the discs, forming a biofilm that passes alternately through wastewater and air as the discs rotate. The biofilm adsorbs oxygen as it passes through the air and this oxygen is then available to support aerobic treatment processes as the biofilm passes through the wastewater. The biofilm thickens over time and eventually parts of it slough off, creating a need for sedimentation in humus tanks, in the same way as required for trickling filters. Typical daily hydraulic and organic loading criteria are 0.08–0.16 m^3/m^2 of disc surface (Arundel, 1999) and 10–15 g BOD/m^2 of disc surface although higher organic loading rates are possible (Hassard et al., 2015). Researchers have explored the possibility of using RBCs to treat stronger wastewaters, for instance those generated by dairies (Kadu et al., 2013).The main issue with RBCs is likely to be difficulty in maintaining aerobic conditions due to the high strength and highly variable flow of the influent. Further investigation of these difficulties is required before RBCs can be recommended as a treatment option for septage and faecal sludge. However, given their low energy requirement and relative simplicity, there is a case for exploring their use for secondary treatment.

Mechanically aerated options
Fully mixed aerated treatment options include ASRs, oxidation ditches, various forms of extended aeration, SBRs, and MBBRs. All of these technologies rely on suspended-growth processes that aerate the wastewater to be

treated along with sludge returned from final settling tanks. MBBRs also use attached-growth processes that take place on the surfaces of small plastic carriers suspended in the reactor.

SBRs are essentially ASRs that operate in batch mode, with aeration and sedimentation taking place as part of a time sequence in the same reactor rather than in separate treatment units as in a conventional ASR. SBR processes have the added advantage that adjusting their operating sequence allows them to be used to treat a wide range of influent volumes and strengths, which makes them more flexible than conventional activated sludge processes. Wilderer et al. (2001) provide detailed information on SBR technology. SBRs are installed at some treatment plants in the Philippines, and oxidation ditches provide treatment at Surabaya's Keputih septage treatment plant in Indonesia.

All activated sludge and extended aeration processes require that the solids concentration in the reactor, the mixed liquor suspended solids (MLSS), is kept within an optimum range, which is typically 2,200–3,000 mg/l for ASRs and 4,000–5,000 mg/l for oxidation ditches. If the MLSS is too high, bulking of solids may occur, leading to a drop in oxygen levels, poor sludge settleability and an increase in the amount of energy required to maintain the process. If the MLSS is too low, plant performance will deteriorate. Operators maintain the MLSS at an appropriate level by recirculating sludge from the clarifiers that follow the aerated stage of the treatment process. Effective aeration process performance is dependent on operators knowing how much sludge to return and this requires that they have information on MLSS levels on the reactor. An experienced operator may be able to estimate the MLSS level from the appearance of the reactor contents, but good operation normally requires that decisions on recirculation are based on information obtained from regular sampling of the MLSS concentration. To control the system, the operator must also have information on the dissolved oxygen concentration in the bioreactor and the effluent quality. Provision of this information requires access to reliable laboratory facilities. Mechanically aerated technologies have a high power requirement, which will often raise operational costs to unaffordable levels. This will be of particular concern for strong influents such as faecal sludge and septage. In view of the likely difficulty in meeting these requirements, mechanically aerated options should only be considered for large cities, where land availability constrains other options.

Information on design criteria and procedures for activated sludge systems is available in standard wastewater texts, for instance Metcalf & Eddy (2003) and WEF (2010).

Pathogen reduction

Overview

The purpose of the treatment technologies described in Chapter 7 and earlier in this chapter is to separate solids and reduce the organic and suspended solids loads in the liquid effluent. They will not produce an effluent that meets the WHO Category A and Category B requirements set out in Table 4.2. Further treatment to remove pathogens will therefore be required if the liquid effluent is to be used for irrigation and will also be desirable if effluent is to be discharged to a water body that is used for recreation or as a source of potable water.

Maturation ponds, deployed after facultative ponds and constructed wetlands, provide a simple pathogen reduction option. Their drawback is their large land take. Where this is an issue, other pathogen removal methods, including chlorination, ozone treatment, and ultraviolet radiation, are theoretically possible. All need good management systems and a reliable supply chain, and will only be effective for liquids with low suspended solids concentrations. Given that liquid discharges from septage treatment plants are small in comparison with flows from wastewater treatment plants, there will be few situations in which the benefits of producing an effluent suitable for use for unrestricted irrigation will justify provision of these more complex pathogen-reduction options. With these points in mind, the strategy for pathogen reduction should be as follows:

- Where land is available and previous treatment stages are to include either facultative pond or constructed wetland treatment, consider the possibility of using maturation ponds to reduce pathogen concentrations to the levels required for either restricted or unrestricted irrigation.
- Where these conditions do not apply, explore liquid effluent disposal options that require minimal worker access, for instance, irrigation of tree nurseries.
- Where the preferred treatment plant location is close to a water body that is used for recreation or as a water source, explore options for avoiding effluent discharge direct to the watercourse.

Maturation ponds

As indicated in the overview, maturation ponds normally follow facultative ponds and are designed for pathogen removal. Their shallow depth, typically 1–1.5 m, allows sunlight to penetrate to the bottom of the pond and inactivate pathogens. The sunlight also encourages photosynthesis, and aerobic bacterial and algal growth. Faecal coliform concentrations are normally used as a proxy for the presence of specific pathogens as they are relatively easy to measure.

Design and operational considerations

Place in treatment process. Since their main purpose is to remove pathogens rather than reduce the organic and suspended solids loads, maturation ponds must follow processes that have already removed BOD and TSS.

Pond configuration. Ponds should have a length-to-width ratio of at least 2:1 and up to 10:1. Higher ratios provide better model plug flow conditions (Mara, 2004). The 2:1 figure is appropriate when two or more ponds are provided in series. Ponds can be constructed with vertical concrete walls but the more normal practice is to provide sloping sides, as already described for facultative ponds. Baffles can be used to prevent short-circuiting, but the more normal procedure is to provide several ponds in series, since this maximizes pathogen removal.

At this stage in the treatment process, the solids content of the liquid to be treated will be low and sludge and scum accumulation will therefore be slow. In view of this, it is not essential to provide ponds in parallel although it will be advisable to design the interconnecting pipework to allow individual ponds to be bypassed so that they can be taken out of service for maintenance, repair, and occasional desludging. Options for facilitating sludge removal include provision of sloping access ramps at the side of ponds and installation of sludge pumps carried on floating rafts.

Design criteria and procedure
The reduction in faecal bacteria in anaerobic, facultative, and maturation ponds can be approximated assuming first-order kinetics. The equation for a single pond is:

$$N_e = \frac{N_i}{1 + K_b t}$$

where N_e = number of faecal coliforms per 100 ml in the effluent;
   N_i = number of faecal coliforms per 100 ml in the influent;
   K_b = first-order rate constant for faecal coliform removal (day^{-1}); and
   t = retention time in the pond (days).
When several ponds are arranged in series, the equation becomes:

$$N_e = \frac{N_i}{\left[(1 + K_b t_1)(1 + K_b t_2)...(1 + K_b t_n)\right]}$$

where t_1 to t_n are the retention times in the first to nth ponds. This equation is applied to all ponds, including anaerobic and facultative ponds.

The first-order rate constant (K_b) is temperature-dependent. In theory, the rate constant will vary slightly depending on the type of pond but for practical design purposes, it is approximated by the equation:

$$K_b = 2.6 \times 1.19^{(T-20)}$$

where T is the temperature of the pond (°C).
   The steps in design are as follows:

1. Calculate the value of K_b for the design temperature, which can normally be taken as the ambient temperature in the coolest month of the irrigation season.
2. Determine the values of N_i and N_e.
   To determine N_i, establish a value for the faecal coliform count in the untreated influent to the treatment plant and calculate the likely reduction through previous steps in the treatment process. Assume a 50 per cent reduction through gravity thickeners and settling thickening tanks and 90 per cent (1 log) reduction through mechanical presses. Use the equation for faecal coliform reduction through ponds arranged in series to calculate the faecal coliform reduction achieved in anaerobic and facultative ponds. This exercise will give a value for N_i.

Next, choose an appropriate value for N_e. Where effluent is to be used for unrestricted irrigation this will be 1,000 MPN (most probable number) faecal coliforms per 100 ml.

3. Select a retention time (θ, days) for a standard maturation pond, subject to a minimum value in warm climates of 3 days (Marais, 1974), and calculate the number of standard maturation ponds required.

    The basic equation for pathogen reduction through n equally sized maturation ponds is:

    $$\frac{N_e}{N_i} = \frac{1}{\left(1 + K_b \theta\right)^n}$$

    where n is the number of ponds.

    This equation can be rewritten as:

    $$n = \frac{\log\left(N_i/N_e\right)}{\log\left(1 + K_b \theta\right)}$$

    It can then be solved for n using the previously determined values of N_i, N_e, K_b and θ.

    Where the resultant value of n is slightly less than a whole number, it should be rounded up to that whole number. If it is slightly over a whole number, a better solution may be to increase the size of the ponds slightly to reduce n to below that whole number.

4. Select an appropriate pond depth, typically around 1.2 m, and calculate the required area of each of the equally sized maturation ponds, using the equation:

    $$SA_{MP} = \frac{Q\theta}{z_{MP}}$$

    where SA_{MP} is the surface area of each maturation pond in m²;
    Q is the flow rate in m³/d; and
    z_{MP} is the selected pond depth.

The length and width of the pond can be calculated from the surface area of the pond using a minimum length-to-width ratio of 2:1.

Design example: maturation pond in series of waste stabilization ponds

Calculate the number of ponds required to achieve the target 1,000 faecal coliforms/100 ml for a system that includes gravity thickening, an anaerobic pond with five days' retention, and a facultative pond with 15 days' retention.

Parameter	Symbol	Value	Units
Temperature	T	20	°C
Flow	Q	40	m³/d
Retention time in single maturation pond	θ_{MP}	3	days

Parameter	Symbol	Value	Units
Faecal coliform (FC) count in influent septage	FC_{sept}	10^8	per 100 ml
Length:width ratio	$L:W$	$3:1$	–
Depth of maturation ponds	z_{MP}	1.2	m

1. Calculate the first-order rate constant at the design temperature of 20°C:

$$K_b = 2.6 \times 1.19^{(T-20)} = 2.6 \ \text{day}^{-1}$$

2. Calculate the FC count at inlet to the maturation ponds.
   The FC count in raw septage is 10^8 per 100 ml
   Assume 50 per cent reduction through gravity thickening to give FC count at the inlet to the anaerobic pond of 5×10^7 per 100 ml.
   The FC concentration after the (assumed) 5-day anaerobic pond and the (assumed) 15-day facultative pond is given by the equation:

$$N_e = \frac{5 \times 10^7}{[1 + (2.6 \times 5)][1 + (2.6 \times 15)]} = 9 \times 10^4$$

3. Determine number of ponds required to reduce FC concentration in effluent to target level. Assuming a 3-day retention time in each pond, the number of maturation ponds required is given by the equation:

$$n = \frac{\log(9 \times 10^4 / 1000)}{\log[1 + (2.6 \times 3)]} = 2.07$$

   Providing two 3-day retention ponds will theoretically result in an FC concentration in the effluent slightly above the target faecal coliform count. If the pond retention is increased to 3.5 days, the value of n reduces to 1.95.
   Provide two maturation ponds, each providing 3.5 days' retention at the design flow.
4. Determine the pond dimensions:
   The volume of a single pond = 40 m³/d × 3.5 d = 140 m³
   Assume a 1.2-m pond depth. Required pond area = 140/1.2 = 116.67 m²

   For 3:1 length-to-width ratio, the required width will be √(116.67/3) = 6.23 m. Round up dimensions to give typical pond size of 18.75 m × 6.25 m. These are guideline dimensions and may need to be adjusted to fit the site geometry.

Co-treatment of faecal sludge and septage with municipal wastewater

This chapter has included references to the way in which the various technologies described might be used for co-treatment of separated liquid with municipal wastewater. However, its main focus has been on stand-alone treatment of faecal sludge and septage. This will normally be the preferred option when considering options for new treatment facilities. However, as noted in Chapter 4, there will be situations in which existing wastewater treatment plants have spare capacity, which could potentially be used for faecal sludge and septage treatment. Co-treatment might also be considered because it makes effective use of limited managerial and operational resources.

When considering the co-treatment option, it is important to be aware of its drawbacks and design to minimize the effect of those drawbacks. As already indicated in Chapter 4, these include the high strength of faecal sludge and septage relative to that of municipal wastewater, the potential effect of their partly digested nature and high ammonia content on treatment processes, and their highly variable delivery rate and the consequent variable loading on the plant.

Chapter 7 emphasized the point that solids–liquid separation is an essential first step in any scheme involving co-treatment. Separate reception facilities should be provided for faecal sludge and septage, incorporating screening, flow attenuation, and provision for other preliminary treatment processes as required. Chapter 6 provides information on these requirements. The liquid fraction resulting from solids–liquid separation will still exert high organic and suspended solids loads. The basic equations governing the hydraulic, organic, and suspended solids loads on a combined treatment plant are:

$$\text{Hydraulic load } Q_t = Q_w + Q_s$$

$$\text{Organic or suspended solids load} = Q_w c_w + Q_s c_s$$

where Q_t = total flow;

Q_w = wastewater flow;

Q_s = septage flow;

c_w = concentration of COD, BOD, NH_4 or TSS in the wastewater; and

c_s = COD, BOD, or TSS concentration in the liquid fraction of separated septage/faecal sludge.

These equations can be used to calculate either daily or hourly loadings. In the latter case, appropriate peak factors must be applied to both the wastewater and the septage flow. Flows should be expressed in m^3/d or m^3/h as appropriate. Concentrations should be given in kg/m^3, equivalent to g/l. The second equation can be used with each parameter in turn to calculate total COD, BOD, NH_4, and TSS loads.

Because of the high strength of septage and faecal sludge relative to wastewater, a relatively small volume in the septage/faecal sludge stream will result in a large increase in organic suspended solids, and nitrogen loads on the treatment plant. Increased solids accumulation can lead to a reduction in oxygen transfer efficiency and hence a decrease in treatment capacity. With these points in mind, US EPA (1984) recommended that the ratio of septage flow to total flow should not exceed 0.036 (3.6 per cent) for aerated lagoons, 0.0285 (2.85 per cent) for activated sludge preceded by primary treatment, and 0.0125 (1.25 per cent) for activated sludge without primary treatment. These recommendations are based on assumptions, unstated by US EPA, regarding the relative strengths of septage and sewage and refer to the plant's capacity to treat septage when there is no wastewater flow. If wastewater already contributes 50 per cent of the design loading, the allowable septage loading is only 50 per cent of the figures given above; similarly if wastewater contributes 75 per cent of the design loading, the allowable septage loading is reduced to 25 per cent.

More recent investigations suggest a need to revise these US EPA recommendations downwards for activated sludge plants designed to achieve biological nitrogen removal (Dangol et al., 2013, quoted in Lopez-Vazquez et al., 2014). For 'low strength' digested material with COD and TSS concentrations of 10,000 mg/l and 7,000 mg/l, respectively, Lopez-Vazquez et al. recommend that the faecal sludge volumes should not exceed 3.75 per cent and 0.64 per cent of total flow for steady state and 'dynamic' conditions, respectively. The meaning of 'dynamic' is not defined, but presumably refers to the intermittent nature of septage and faecal sludge discharges.

Both the US EPA recommendations and the Dangol research relate to aerobic treatment in an ASR. One option for improving co-treatment capacity would be to include an anaerobic stage ahead of aerobic treatment. When considering this option, it should be recognized that the addition of digested septage to the municipal wastewater flow is likely to reduce the anaerobic degradation rate. Studies in Jordan found that 86 per cent of the biodegradable fraction of the influent to a plant receiving only municipal sewage was digested after 27 days, compared with only 57 per cent of the biodegradable fraction for a plant receiving both municipal sewage and septage (Halalsheh et al., 2004, quoted in Halalsheh et al., 2011). Follow-up studies confirmed that the biodegradation rate for septage was lower than that for both domestic wastewater and primary sludge from a wastewater treatment plant (Halalsheh et al., 2011). The septage biodegradation rate approximates to a first-order reaction with a rate constant of 0.024 day^{-1} at 35°C. This compared with an estimated rate constant of 0.103 day^{-1} for domestic sewage and a reported rate constant of 0.113 day^{-1} for primary sludge. These findings related to a fairly weak septage with mean recorded COD of 2,696 mg/l in winter and 6,425 mg/l in summer and a COD to BOD ratio of 2.22, which suggested good biodegradability.

Overall, these points suggest that co-treatment should be approached with caution. If possible, designs and/or loading guidelines should be based on field studies, involving either pilot-plant studies or monitoring of the effect of septage loads on the performance of an existing wastewater treatment plant.

Key points from this chapter

- The liquid component of septage and faecal sludge must be treated to reduce organic, suspended solids, and pathogen concentrations to levels that are compatible with relevant national and international standards and ensure protection of both public health and the environment.
- Given the strength of the liquid, even after solids–liquid separation, more than one treatment stage will usually be required to achieve these objectives.
- Technologies for liquid treatment involve both anaerobic and aerobic processes and range from simple 'natural' systems to engineered systems that rely on mechanical equipment.

- Anaerobic processes do not require external energy and have a fairly small footprint. They therefore offer a good option for first-stage liquid treatment, reducing the land and/or power requirements of subsequent aerobic stages.
- Anaerobic treatment processes that are suitable for treatment of the liquid stream of separated faecal sludge and septage include anaerobic waste stabilization ponds and ABRs. Upflow UASB reactors should be considered for co-treatment with municipal wastewater, but they are unlikely to be a good option for stand-alone faecal sludge and septage treatment.
- Sludge accumulation will be an operational challenge for all anaerobic processes.
- Facultative ponds and constructed wetlands are simple but require a large land area in comparison with other treatment options. Facultative ponds will be an appropriate option for secondary treatment, following anaerobic treatment, where land is available and operational skills are limited. Because of their simplicity, they will normally be a better option than constructed wetlands, which require at least as much land as facultative ponds.
- Mechanized systems based on activated sludge, extended aeration and their variants can produce good effluent quality but are dependent on a reliable power supply, trained operators, and good performance-monitoring systems. Because of their power requirements, they may be expensive to operate and they are also subject to power outages. They may be considered for larger plants where knowledgeable managers, skilled staff, effective monitoring systems, and reliable supply chains are in place. Operating costs will be reduced if mechanized aerobic treatment is preceded by anaerobic treatment.
- Fully mixed aerated lagoons do not require recirculation and are thus simpler to operate than activated sludge systems. Like other mechanized systems, they are dependent on a reliable power supply and will incur high electricity costs. They should only be considered when there is no space for facultative ponds and, like other mechanized options, should normally follow anaerobic treatment.
- When flows are intermittent, trickling filters will experience fly and odour problems. Recirculation of treated effluent will help to reduce these problems, but this requires pumping and thus an increased reliance on mechanical equipment, resulting in higher operating costs. For this reason, trickling filters are not a suitable option for stand-alone septage treatment.
- Where land is available, maturation ponds can be provided to reduce effluent pathogen concentrations to levels that meet discharge and end use standards. Where it is not possible to meet these standards, other disposal/end use options – for instance, discharge to an area planted with trees – should be explored.

References

Alberta Agriculture and Forestry (2012) *Dugout/Lagoon Volume Calculator* <https://www.agric.gov.ab.ca/app19/calc/volume/dugout.jsp> [accessed 9 April 2018].

Arthur, J.P. (1983) *Notes on the Design and Operation of Waste Stabilization Ponds in Warm Climates of Developing Countries* World Bank Technical Paper Number 7, Washington, DC: World Bank <http://documents.worldbank.org/curated/en/941141468764431814/pdf/multi0page.pdf> [accessed 26 January 2018].

Arundel, J. (1999) *Sewage and Industrial Effluent Treatment*, 2nd edn, Oxford: Wiley Blackwell.

Associação Brasileira de Normas Técnicas (ABNT) (1993) *Projeto, construção e operação de sistemas de tanques sépticos*, NBR 7229, Rio de Janeiro: ABNT

Barber, W.P. and Stuckey, D.C. (1999) 'The use of the anaerobic baffled reactor (ABR) for wastewater treatment: a review', *Water Research* 33(7): 1559–78 <http://doi.org/10.1016/S0043-1354(98)00371-6> [accessed 19 July 2018].

Bassan, M., Tchonda, T., Yiougo, L., Zoellig, H., Maahamane, I., Mbéguéré, M. and Strande, L. (2013) 'Characterization of faecal sludge during dry and rainy seasons in Ouagadougou, Burkina Faso', paper presented at the *36th WEDC International Conference at Nakuru, Kenya* <https://wedc-knowledge.lboro.ac.uk/resources/conference/36/Bassan-1814.pdf> [accessed 7 February 2018].

de Bonis, E. and Tayler, K. (2016) *Latrine Sludge Management in the IDP Camps of Sittwe, Myanmar*, Unpublished report produced for Solidarités International, Paris.

Boopathy, R. (1998) 'Biological treatment of swine waste using anaerobic baffled reactors', *Bioresource Technology* 64: 1–6 <http://dx.doi.org/10.1016/S0960-8524(97)00178-8> [accessed 19 July 2018].

Boyle, W.C., Popel, H.J. and Mueller, J. (2002) *Aeration: Principles and Practice*, Boca Raton, FL: CRC Press.

Bwapwa, J.K. (2012) 'Treatment efficiency of an anaerobic baffled reactor treating low biodegradable and complex particulate wastewater (blackwater) in an ABR membrane reactor unit (MBR-ABR)', *International Journal of Environmental Remediation and Pollution* 1(1): 51–8 <http://dx.doi.org/10.11159/ijepr.2012.008> [accessed 19 July 2018].

Chang, S., Li, J., Liu, F. and Zhu, G. (2008) 'Performance and characteristics of anaerobic baffled reactor treating soybean wastewater', paper presented at the *2nd International Conference on Bioinformatics and Biomedical Engineering (ICBBE) Shanghai, China* <http://dx.doi.org/10.1109/ICBBE.2008.1030> [accessed 19 July 2018].

Chernicharo, C.A., van Lier, J., Noyola, A. and Ribeiro, T. (2015) 'Anaerobic sewage treatment: state of the art, constraints and challenges', *Reviews in Environmental Services and Bio/Technology* 14(4): 649–79 <http://dx.doi.org/10.1007/s11157-015-9377-3> [accessed 19 July 2018].

Crites R. and Tchobanoglous, G. (1998) *Small and Decentralized Wastewater Management Systems*, Boston, MA: WCB McGraw Hill.

Fernández, R.G., Inganllinella, A.M., Sanguinetti, G.S., Ballan, G.E., Bortolotti, V., Montangero, A. and Strauss, M. (2004) 'Septage treatment using WSP', paper presented at the *9th International IWA Specialist Group Conference on Wetlands Systems for Water Pollution Control* and to the *6th International IWA Specialist Group Conference on Waste Stabilization Ponds, Avignon, France, 27 September – 1 October 2004*.

Foxon, K.M. and Buckley, C.A. (2006) *Guidelines for the Implementation of Anaerobic Baffled Reactors for On-Site or Decentralised Sanitation*, Durban: University of KwaZulu-Natal <http://citeseerx.ist.psu.edu/viewdoc/downl oad?doi=10.1.1.568.378&rep=rep1&type=pdf> [accessed 20 June 2018].

Franceys, R., Pickford, J. and Reed, R. (1992) *A Guide to the Development of On-site Sanitation*, Geneva, Switzerland: World Health Organization <http://apps.who.int/iris/bitstream/handle/10665/39313/9241544430_eng.pdf?sequence=1&isAllowed=y> [accessed 29 March 2018].

Gutterer, B., Sasse, K., Panzerbieter, T. and Reckerzügel, T. (2009) *Decentralised Wastewater Treatment Systems (DEWATS) and Sanitation in Developing Countries*, Loughborough: Water, Engineering and Development Centre, University of Loughborough <https://wedc-knowledge.lboro.ac.uk/details.html?id=10409> [accessed 29 March 2018].

Halalsheh, M., Smit, T., Kerstens, S., Tissingh, J., Zeeman, G., Fayyad, M. and Lettinga, G. (2004) 'Characteristics and anaerobic biodegradation of sewage in Jordan', in *Proceedings of the 10th IWA World Conference on Anaerobic Digestion, Montreal, Canada*, pp. 1450–3.

Halalsheh, M., Noaimat, H., Yazajeen, H., Cuello, J., Freitas, B. and Fayyad, M.K. (2011) 'Biodegradation and seasonal variations in septage character-istics', *Environmental Monitoring and Assessment* 172(1–4): 419–26 <http://dx.doi.org/10.1007/s10661-010-1344-4> [accessed 19 July 2018].

Hansen, K.H., Angelidaki, I. and Ahring, B.K. (1998) 'Anaerobic digestion of swine manure: inhibition by ammonia', *Water Research* 32(1): 5–12 <http://dx.doi.org/10.1016/S0043-1354(97)00201-7> [accessed 19 July 2018].

Hassan, S.R. and Dahlan, I. (2013) 'Anaerobic wastewater treatment using anaerobic baffled reactor: a review', *Central European Journal of Engineering* 3(3): 389–99 <http://dx.doi.org/10.2478/s13531-013-0107-8> [accessed 19 July 2018].

Hassard, F., Biddle, J., Cartmell, E., Jefferson, B., Tyrrel, S. and Stephenson, T. (2015) 'Rotating biological contactors for wastewater treatment', *Journal of Process Safety and Environmental Protection* 94: 285–306 <http://dx.doi.org/10.1016/j.psep.2014.07.003> [accessed 19 July 2018].

Hui-Ting, L. and Yong-Feng, L. (2010) 'Performance of a hybrid anaerobic baffled reactor (HABR) treating brewery wastewater', paper presented at the *International Conference on Mechanic Automation and Control Engineering, Wuhan, China, 26–28 June 2010*.

Jiminez, B. (2007) 'Helminth ova removal from wastewater for agriculture and aquaculture use', *Water Science and Technology* 55(1–2): 485–93 <http://dx.doi.org/10.2166/wst.2007.046> [accessed 19 July 2018].

Kadu, P.A., Landge, R.B. and Rao, Y.R.M. (2013) 'Treatment of dairy wastewater using rotating biological contactors', *European Journal of Experimental Biology* 3(4): 257–60 <http://www.imedpub.com/articles/treatment-of-dairy-wastewater-using-rotating-biological-contactors.pdf> [accessed 20 January 2018].

Kantawanichkul, S. and Wannasri, S. (2013) 'Wastewater treatment perfor-mances of horizontal and vertical subsurface flow constructed wetland systems in tropical climates', *Songklanakarin Journal of Science and Technology* 35(5): 599–603 <http://rdo.psu.ac.th/sjstweb/journal/35-5/35-5-13.pdf> [accessed 21 January 2018].

Koné, D. and Strauss, M. (2004) 'Low-cost options for treating faecal sludges (FS) in developing countries: challenges and performance', paper presented at the *9th International IWA Specialist Group Conference on Wetlands Systems for Water Pollution Control and the 6th International IWA Specialist Group Conference on Waste Stabilization Ponds, Avignon, France, 27 September – 1 October* <https://www.eawag.ch/fileadmin/Domain1/Abteilungen/sandec/publikationen/EWM/Journals/FS_treatment_LCO.pdf> [accessed 7 February 2018].

Lopez-Vazquez, C., Dangol, B., Hooijmans, C. and Brdvanovic, D. (2014) 'Co-treatment of faecal sludge in municipal wastewater treatment plants', in L. Strande, M. Ronteltap, and D. Brdjanovic (eds.), *Faecal Sludge Management: Systems Approach for Implementation and Operation*, London: IWA Publishing <https://www.eawag.ch/fileadmin/Domain1/Abteilungen/sandec/publikationen/EWM/Book/FSM_Ch09_lowres.pdf> [accessed 15 March 2017].

Mara, D.D. (1987) 'Waste stabilization ponds: problems and controversies', *Water Quality International* 1: 20–2 <www.personal.leeds.ac.uk/~cen6ddm/pdf%27s%201972-1999/e9.pdf> [accessed 8 March 2018].

Mara, D.D. (2004) *Domestic Wastewater Treatment in Developing Countries*, London: Earthscan <www.personal.leeds.ac.uk/~cen6ddm/Books/DWWTDC.pdf> [accessed 8 March 2018].

Marais, G.V.R. (1974) 'Faecal bacterial kinetics in waste stabilization ponds', *Journal of the Environmental Engineering Division*, American Society of Civil Engineers, 100 (EE1): 119–39.

McGarry, M.G. and Pescod, M.B. (1970) 'Stabilization pond design criteria for tropical Asia', in *Proceedings of the 2nd International Symposium on Waste Treatment Lagoons*, pp. 114–32, Kansas City, KS.

Metcalf & Eddy (2003) *Wastewater Engineering Treatment and Reuse*, 4th edn, New York: McGraw Hill.

Milner, J.R. (1978) *Control of Odors from Anaerobic Lagoons Treating Food Processing Wastewaters*, Cincinnati, OH: Industrial Environmental Research Laboratory, US EPA <https://nepis.epa.gov/Exe/ZyPDF.cgi/9101KSIA.PDF?Dockey=9101KSIA.PDF> [accessed 7 April 2018].

Moestedt, J., Müller, B., Westerholm, M. and Schnürer, A. (2016) 'Ammonia threshold for inhibition of anaerobic digestion of thin stillage and the importance of organic loading rate', *Microbial Biotechnology* 9(2): 180–94 <http://dx.doi.org/10.1111/1751-7915.12330> [accessed 19 July 2018].

Nguyen, H., Turgeon, S. and Matte, J. (2010) *The Anaerobic Baffled Reactor: A study of the wastewater treatment process using the anaerobic baffled reactor*, Cape Town: Worcester Polytechnic Institute <http://wp.wpi.edu/capetown/files/2010/12/Anaerobic-Baffled-Reactor-for-Wastewater-Treatment.pdf> [accessed 13 May 2018].

Noyola, A., Padilla-Rivera, A., Morgan-Sagastume, J.M., Gureca, L.P. and Hernanndez-Padilla, F. (2012) 'Typology of municipal wastewater treatment technologies in Latin America', *Clean Soil Air Water* 40(9): 926–32 <http://dx.doi.org/10.1002/clen.201100707> [accessed 19 July 2018].

Rands, M.B. and Cooper, D.E. (1966) 'Development and operation of a low cost anaerobic plant for meat wastes', in *Proceedings of 21st Purdue Industrial Waste Conference, Lafayette, IN*.

Reynaud, N. (2014) *Operation of Decentralised Wastewater Treatment Systems (DEWATS) Under Tropical Field Conditions* (PhD thesis), Dresden: Faculty of Environmental Sciences, Dresden Technical University <www.qucosa.de/fileadmin/data/qucosa/documents/18556/Dissertation_Nicolas_Reynaud_Final.pdf> [accessed 9 April 2018].

Reynaud, N. and Buckley, C.A. (2016) 'The anaerobic baffled reactor (ABR) treating communal wastewater under mesophilic conditions: a review', *Water Science and Technology* 73(3): 463–78 <http://dx.doi.org/10.2166/wst.2015.539> [accessed 19 July 2018].

Sasse, L. (1998) *DEWATS: Decentralised Wastewater Treatment in Developing Countries*, Bremen: Overseas Research and Development Association (BORDA) BORDA <www.sswm.info/sites/default/files/reference_attachments/SASSE%201998%20DEWATS%20Decentralised%20Wastewater%20Treatment%20in%20Developing%20Countries_0.pdf> [accessed 13 March 2018].

Schoebitz, L., Bassan, M., Ferré, A., Vu, T.H.A., Nguye, A. and Strande, L. (2014) 'FAQ: faecal sludge quantification and characterization – field trial of methodology in Hanoi, Vietnam', paper presented at *37th WEDC International Conference, Hanoi, Vietnam* <https://www.dora.lib4ri.ch/eawag/islandora/object/eawag%3A11874/datastream/PDF/view> [accessed 2 May 2018].

Schoebitz, L., Bischoff, F., Ddiba, D., Okello, F., Nakazibwe, R., Niwagaba, C.B., Lohri, C.R. and Strande, L. (2016) *Results of Faecal Sludge Analyses in Kampala, Uganda: Pictures, Characteristics and Qualitative Observations for 76 Samples*, Dübendorf: Eawag, Swiss Federal Institute of Aquatic Science and Technology <www.eawag.ch/fileadmin/Domain1/Abteilungen/sandec/publikationen/EWM/Laboratory_Methods/results_analyses_kampala.pdf> [accessed 7 February 2018].

Stenstrom, M.K. and Rosso, D. (2010) *Aeration*, University of California <www.seas.ucla.edu/stenstro/Aeration.pdf> [accessed 12 April 2018].

Strande, L., Ronteltap, M. and Brdjanovic, D. (2014) *Faecal Sludge Management: Systems Approach for Implementation and Operation*, London: IWA Publishing https://www.un-ihe.org/sites/default/files/fsm_book_lr.pdf [accessed 20 June 2018].

Tilley, E., Ulrich, L., Lüthi, C., Reymond, P., Schertenleib, R. and Zurbrügg, C. (2014) *Compendium of Sanitation Systems and Technologies*, 2nd edn, Dübendorf: Swiss Federal Institute of Aquatic Science and Technology (Eawag) <http://www.iwa-network.org/wp-content/uploads/2016/06/Compendium-Sanitation-Systems-and-Technologies.pdf> [accessed 8 April 2018].

UN-Habitat (2008) *Constructed Wetlands Manual*, Kathmandu, Nepal: UN-HABITAT Water for Asian Cities Programme <https://sswm.info/sites/default/files/reference_attachments/UN%20HABITAT%202008%20Constructed%20Wetlands%20Manual.pdf> [accessed 27 November 2017].

US EPA (1984) *Handbook: Septage Treatment and Disposal*, Cincinnati, OH: Municipal Environmental Research Laboratory <https://nepis.epa.gov/Exe/ZyPDF.cgi/30004ARR.PDF?Dockey=30004ARR.PDF> [accessed 19 June 2018].

US EPA (2000) *Wastewater Technology Fact Sheet Wetlands: Subsurface Flow*, Washington, DC: US EPA <https://www3.epa.gov/npdes/pubs/wetlands-subsurface_flow.pdf> [accessed 20 June 2018].

US EPA (2011) *Principles of Design and Operations of Wastewater Treatment Pond Systems for Plant Operators, Engineers and Managers*, Cincinnati, OH: US EPA <https://www.epa.gov/sites/production/files/2014-09/documents/lagoon-pond-treatment-2011.pdf> [accessed 10 April 2018].

van Lier, J.B., Vashi, A., van der Lubbe, J. and Heffernan, B. (2010) 'Anaerobic sewage treatment using UASB reactors: engineering and operational aspects', in H.H.P. Fang (ed.), *Environmental Anaerobic Technology; Applications and New Developments* pp. 59–89, London: Imperial College Press <https://courses.edx.org/c4x/DelftX/CTB3365STx/asset/Chap_4_Van_Lier_et_al.pdf> [accessed 20 June 2018].

von Sperling, M. (2007) *Waste Stabilization Ponds, Biological Wastewater Treatment Series, Volume 3*, London: IWA Publishing <https://www.iwapublishing.com/sites/default/files/ebooks/9781780402109.pdf> [accessed 20 June 2018].

Vymazal, J. (2010) 'Constructed wetlands for wastewater treatment', *Water* 2: 530–49 <http://dx.doi.org/10.3390/w2030530> [accessed 19 July 2018].

Water Environment Federation (WEF) (2010) *Design of Municipal Wastewater Treatment Plants (WEF Manuals of Practice No. 8 and ASCE Manuals and Reports on Engineering Practice No. 76, 5th edn)*, Arlington, VA: Water Environment Federation Press <https://www.accessengineeringlibrary.com/browse/design-of-municipal-wastewater-treatment-plants-wef-manual-of-practice-no-8-asce-manuals-and-reports-on-engineering-practice-no-76-fifth-edition> [accessed 17 May 2018].

Wilderer, P.A., Irvine, R.L. and Goronszy, M.C. (2001) *Sequencing Batch Reactor Technology*, London: IWA Publishing.

CHAPTER 9

Solids dewatering

This chapter examines the options for dewatering sludge, either after or in conjunction with solids–liquid separation. Solids dewatering is required to reduce the water content of faecal sludge and septage sufficiently to reduce its bulk to manageable proportions and allow it to be handled as a solid, using spades or mechanical equipment such as front-end loaders. Depending upon the end use of the dewatered sludge (disposal or safe reuse), further solids treatment may be required after dewatering and this is discussed in Chapter 10. This chapter starts with a brief overview of relevant theoretical concepts, moves on to identify dewatering options, then examines each option in detail, providing information on design parameters and details, and concludes with a summary and comparison of the technologies examined.

Keywords: dewatering, sludge, water content, drying bed, loading cycle

Introduction

Solids dewatering is required to increase the solids content of sludge to at least the 20 per cent needed for the sludge to act as a 'cake' that can be handled using a spade or similar equipment. Drying to a solids content above 20 per cent reduces the volume of sludge to be handled and may be advantageous where sludge has to be transported to a remote site for disposal.

Solids dewatering mechanisms

The water content in wet sludge includes both free and bound water. Most of the water is free and is not bound to the solids contained in the sludge. The much smaller bound water component includes:

- *interstitial water*: found in the pore spaces between solid particles and bound to those particles by capillary forces;
- *colloidal water*: found on the surfaces of solids and bound to those solids by adsorption and adhesion; and
- *intracellular water*: contained within microorganism cells and thus impossible to remove except by mechanisms that break down those microorganisms.

Settling and filtration mechanisms remove free water while removal of bound water requires some combination of chemical dosing, centrifugation, pressure and evaporation. The proportions of free and bound water in the sludge will influence the approach to dewatering but in most cases removal of free water alone will be sufficient to produce a sludge that acts as a solid.

http://dx.doi.org/10.3362/9781780449869.010

Septic tank sludge usually has less bound water and is hence easier to dewater than fresh faecal sludge.

Overview of solids dewatering options

As already indicated, the main objective of sludge dewatering is to increase its solids content to the point at which it acts as a cake and can be handled as a solid. Further drying of solids may be necessary where a subsequent end use requires a solids content beyond the 20–40 per cent typically achieved through dewatering. Similarly, further treatment to reduce pathogens may be required, depending upon the reuse application. Chapter 10 covers additional treatment requirements for various end uses. Figure 9.1 shows the relation of solids dewatering to prior and subsequent treatment steps.

Figure 9.1 identifies three sludge dewatering options: unplanted drying beds, planted drying beds, and mechanical presses. As explained in Chapter 7, there is no hard dividing line between solids–liquid separation and sludge dewatering and the two are sometimes combined. As will be explained later in this chapter, the land requirement of unplanted drying beds tends to increase with increased sludge water content. This means that solids–liquid separation will normally be desirable prior to dewatering if the solids content of the material to be treated is less than about 5 per cent. Faecal sludge from frequently emptied containers, pits, and vaults may benefit from stabilization prior to dewatering on drying beds, as explained in Chapter 6. Mechanical presses can follow solids–liquid separation but, to date, all examples of their use for faecal sludge and septage treatment combine solids–liquid separation with sludge dewatering. For this reason, they were discussed in detail in Chapter 7 and are only briefly referred to in this chapter.

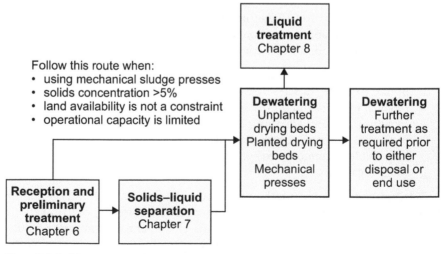

Figure 9.1 Solids dewatering in context

The design of dewatering units must take account of the characteristics of the liquid to be dewatered, its solids content, and the loading pattern. The loading pattern will depend on the technologies adopted for solids–liquid separation and liquid treatment, as explained below.

- Dewatering facilities that are loaded directly by faecal sludge/septage delivery vehicles will receive loads at frequent intervals throughout the day.
- Dewatering facilities loaded with wet solids separated in gravity thickeners will typically receive wet sludge at intervals of less than one day, usually several times per day.
- Dewatering facilities loaded with wet solids from settling-thickening tanks and decanting systems will receive sludge at intervals varying from about a week up to about four weeks, depending on the operating sequence of the preceding unit.
- Liquid treatment processes will generate solids that require dewatering. The volume and frequency of the loads generated will depend on the type of treatment and the operating regime. For example, anaerobic baffled reactors (ABRs) will generate sludge at intervals of several weeks or months while anaerobic ponds will generate larger quantities of sludge at intervals that are typically measured in months or years.

The implications of these points for the various dewatering options will be explored as each option is described and analyzed in more detail.

Unplanted drying beds

System description

Unplanted sludge drying beds are the longest established and simplest option for sludge dewatering. The operational principle is simple. Wet sludge is discharged onto a sand bed to a depth of 200–300 mm. It is then left on the bed until percolation through the bed and evaporation from the surface have increased its solids content to the point at which it can be removed using spades or other suitable equipment. Percolation of free water is the predominant mechanism during the early stages of dewatering, with evaporation assuming greater importance after removal of most of the free water. Heinss et al. (1998) stated that percolation typically accounts for 50–80 per cent and evaporation 20–50 per cent of the water removed. A study of the drying performance of pilot-scale beds loaded with wastewater sludge in Yemen revealed that percolation and evaporation accounted for 65 per cent and 35 per cent of the water removed, respectively, with over 70 per cent of the percolating water removed within the first two days (Al-Nozaily et al., 2013). Similarly, pilot studies in Dakar found that percolation ceased after 2–4 days for total solids (TS) loading rates of 100 kg TS/m^2 year and 6–8 days for loading rates of 150 kg TS/m^2 year (Seck et al., 2015).

To allow sludge to dry, several beds are required, with the number depending on the length of the drying cycle and the timing and volume of wet sludge delivery, as will be explained later in this chapter. Individual beds are typically 5–6 m wide and 10–20 m long and are usually arranged in parallel, with shared dividing walls. Sand beds consist of up to 300 mm of sand overlying 200–450 mm of gravel, all enclosed within a watertight 'box' constructed from some combination of concrete, blockwork, and brickwork. The sand should have an effective size in the range 0.3–0.75 mm and a uniformity coefficient of no more than 3.5 (Crites and Tchobanoglous, 1998). Sand should be washed to remove fines, which might otherwise clog the bed and prevent effective drainage. The side walls of the bed should have sufficient freeboard to contain the design depth of wet sludge applied to the bed. Open-jointed clay tiles placed below the gravel, or perforated pipes placed within the gravel, collect percolating water and convey it to the mid-point of the bed, where it flows into a channel or perforated pipe. The normal practice is to provide several drying beds alongside one another within one shallow box structure. Figure 9.2 is a cross-section of a typical drying bed, showing part of an adjoining bed.

Photo 9.1 shows a drying bed under construction at Samarinda, East Kalimantan, Indonesia. The drying bed structure is in place, together with the central collector channel but the gravel and sand layers have yet to be placed.

Photo 9.1 illustrates several important points regarding drying bed arrangements.

- Ramps allow access for removal of dried sludge. They are rather steep and it would have been better to have provided a flatter gradient.
- The influent, in this case separated sludge, is distributed to the drying beds by a channel, which runs along the near side of the drying beds. Penstocks control septage flow into the drying beds.
- The transverse slope of the beds is greater than the 1 in 20 recommended in Figure 9.2. This will increase the volume of gravel required.

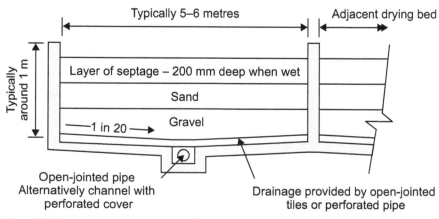

Figure 9.2 Cross-section of typical drying bed

Photo 9.1 Drying beds under construction

- Stub columns with embedded bolts are located at intervals around the drying beds. These will anchor a covering structure that will keep rainwater from the beds.

A hard concrete or blockwork splash pad should be provided below the inlet to each drying bed to ensure that incoming sludge does not scour the sand bed. To achieve this objective, it is suggested that the splash pad should extend at least 0.5 m on either side of the inlet pipe and at least 0.75 m beyond it.

Performance

Factors affecting performance. Dewatering on unplanted drying beds can produce sludge with a dry solids content of 20 per cent or more within 7–10 days in hot, dry climates, rising to 75 per cent or more if the conditions are favourable and sufficient drying time is allowed. Factors that influence dewatering performance include:

- *Temperature, humidity, and wind strength.* The evaporation rate increases with increased temperature and wind strength and decreases with increased humidity. In hot, dry climates, dewatering to produce a solids content exceeding 20 per cent may take less than a week while several weeks may be required to achieve the same result in a wet, temperate climate.

- *Rainfall.* In areas that experience periods of heavy rainfall, the drying time increases significantly during the wet season unless the drying beds are covered. Indeed, drying on uncovered beds may be impossible for extended periods in places that experience a pronounced rainy season.
- *Sludge dewaterability.* This is dependent on the sludge characteristics, which in turn depend on the origin of the sludge. Studies have shown that fresh undigested sludges take longer to dry than digested sludges, probably because of the high intracellular water content. For instance, trials in Accra, Ghana (Heinss et al., 1998) gave the following results over an 8-day drying period:
  - Primary pond sludge, presumably fairly well digested, dried to 40 per cent total solids.
  - Public toilet sludge gave erratic results, ranging from almost no settleability to 29 per cent total solids.

The dewaterability of fresh sludge can be improved by mixing it with digested sludge. During the Accra trials, a mixture of one part public toilet sludge to four parts septage dried to 70 per cent total solids. Another option is stabilization, which is described in Chapter 6.

The best way to assess sludge dewatering performance for a specific location will be to carry out field trials on existing drying beds or small pilot installations. Field results obtained in one location may be applicable to other sites in the same region with similar climatic conditions and sludge characteristics.

Percolate quality. Unplanted drying beds remove organics and suspended solids from the drained liquid stream. Studies show that total suspended solids (TSS) concentrations in the percolate from unplanted drying beds can be less than 5 per cent of those in the wet sludge. Tests in Accra, Ghana reported ≥95 per cent removal of TSS (Heinss et al., 1998), and tests in Kumasi, Ghana reported 96 per cent average TSS removal (Cofie et al., 2006). Organic load removal will normally be lower. The Accra and Kumasi studies reported chemical oxygen demand (COD) removal from the liquid filtrate of 70–90 per cent and 85–90 per cent, respectively. Biochemical oxygen demand (BOD) removal was reported as 86–91 per cent (Cofie et al., 2006). Despite these high removal rates, the percolate will still have a high suspended solids concentration and exert a high oxygen demand. For example, assuming that the TSS and COD concentrations of the raw sludge are both 20,000 mg/l, and that the TSS and COD are reduced by 95 per cent and 85 per cent, respectively, the TSS and COD concentrations in the percolate will be 1,000 mg/l and 3,000 mg/l, respectively.

Both the percolate and the dewatered sludge will have a high pathogen content after dewatering. Further treatment will be required prior to discharge of the percolate to a surface water body (covered in Chapter 8). Similarly, the sludge cake may require further treatment, depending on any intended end use. This point will be particularly relevant if the intention is to use dried sludge as a soil conditioner. Investigations in Accra, Ghana found that dewatering on drying beds did not inactivate all helminth eggs. Helminth egg numbers were recorded over two operational cycles each comprising dewatering on drying beds followed by composting. The recorded egg count in the raw sludge used for the first operational cycle was 60 eggs/g TS. The egg count in the raw sludge used for the second operational cycle was not recorded. Helminth (*Ascaris* and *Trichuris*) egg counts in the dewatered sludge were 38 after the first cycle and 22 after the second cycle, of which 25–50 per cent were viable (Koné et al., 2007). In the latter case, the egg count in the raw sludge was 60 eggs/g TS. The exact numbers will vary, depending on the number of helminth eggs in the raw sludge. However, the results show that dewatering on unplanted drying beds cannot be guaranteed to deactivate helminth eggs. Options for reduction of pathogen numbers in dried sludge to levels that allow its safe end use as an agricultural soil conditioner are identified and described in Chapter 10.

Operational and design considerations

Covering drying beds to improve utilization. Providing a roof over drying beds will allow them to be used throughout the year, regardless of rainfall. This will remove the need to provide additional drying bed capacity to treat sludge that has had to be stored during rainy periods. Studies in Lusaka, Zambia and Dakar, Senegal showed that covered beds performed significantly better than uncovered beds during the wet season (Lusaka Water and Sewerage Company, 2014; Seck et al., 2015). Photo 9.2 shows an example of a drying bed protected by a transparent sheet covering.

Key points to note about the arrangement shown in Photo 9.2 include the following:

- The translucent covering does not extend to the top of the drying bed side walls and so allows for cross-ventilation.
- The support structure is constructed from metal sections. It should be well anchored and strong enough to withstand the maximum predicted wind forces.
- To prevent rain penetrating the gap between the roof covering and the walls of the bed during windy weather, some roof overhang is desirable.
- The roof configuration directs rainwater run-off away from the bed.

Where several beds are located alongside each other, guttering will be required to catch water that runs off sloping roofs and direct it clear of the bed. Without cross-ventilation, condensation will occur on the inside of the covering material, humidity above the bed will increase, and little or no increase in drying performance will occur under dry season conditions (Seck et al., 2015). This problem can be overcome by providing fans and mechanical ventilation, but this increases mechanical complexity. Further information on this option is given in the section on solar drying in Chapter 10.

Photo 9.2 Drying bed cover arrangement, Jombang, Indonesia

Depth of wet sludge. As already indicated, unplanted drying beds are normally operated with wet sludge depths of 200–300 mm. Early investigations by Pescod (1971) found that drying performance was best at a loading depth of 200 mm. Higher overall solids loading rates are possible if the wet sludge depth is further reduced, but the increased desludging frequency required will result in increased labour requirements.

The effect of stirring. Stirring wet sludge while it is dewatering increases the dewatering rate and shortens the time needed to reach a given solids content. The Dakar research referred to above (Seck et al., 2015) found that daily mixing of the sludge reduced the dewatering time by about 6 days from the 19 ± 1 days and 26 ± 2 days required without mixing at loading rates of 100 kg TS/m^2 and 150 kg TS/m^2, respectively. These reductions in drying time represent 31 per cent and 23 per cent of the dewatering times required without mixing for the respective loading rates. The research involved observation of the performance of twelve 2 m × 2 m drying beds, which were clearly easier to mix than full-scale drying beds. Manual mixing will become progressively more difficult as the water content of the sludge reduces and, for this reason, mixing normally involves mechanical equipment, which is likely to pose significant cost and operational challenges. It is required for solar drying as explained in Chapter 10.

Pumping should be avoided whenever possible. Pumping requires a reliable power supply, and effective provision for mechanical maintenance, including a reliable spare parts supply chain. It should therefore be avoided where possible, particularly at small treatment plants. Where the topography allows, the design should allow for percolate from drying beds to flow to the liquid treatment units by gravity. Where this is not possible, the possibility of avoiding pumping by discharging percolated liquid to a soakaway should be explored.

Labour requirements. Few drying beds at faecal sludge and septage treatment plants will be large enough to justify the use of front-end loaders and other mechanical equipment to remove dried sludge. Manual removal will therefore normally be required. This is a labour-intensive process. One study found that it took one worker about two days to remove 7 cm of dried sludge from a 130 m² bed, suggesting a removal rate of about 4.5 m³ of dried sludge per worker per day (Dodane and Ronteltap, 2014). Another study found that manual sludge removal required 2–4 hours of labour per tonne of dried sludge, suggesting a sludge removal rate of up to about 4 m³ per worker per day (Nikiema et al., 2014). Sequential loading of relatively small beds will result in a fairly constant need for labour but peaks in demand will occur when large amounts of sludge require drying, for instance, when anaerobic ponds are desludged. This is likely to result in a need for additional casual labour.

The need for periodic sand replacement. Some sand is lost each time dried sludge is removed, so that the bed sand thickness gradually reduces over time. Replacement of the sand is required once its overall thickness reduces to about 100 mm. The cost of sand replacement must be taken into account when assessing the operating costs of sludge drying beds.

Design criteria and design procedure

Most design guidelines for sludge drying beds specify the allowable solids loading on the bed in kilograms of total solids per square metre per year (kg TS/m² year). Metcalf & Eddy (2003) recommend design figures of 120–150 kg dry solids/m² year for primary sewage-works sludge and 90–120 kg dry solids/m² year for sludge from humus tanks. These figures are intended for use in temperate climates. Referring to conditions in tropical countries, Strande et al. (2014) state that loading rates typically vary between 100 and 200 kg TS/m² year, while noting the possibility of achieving higher loading rates. In practice, various researchers have reported loading rates higher than 200 kg TS/m² year, as indicated in the examples listed below.

- Experiments in Bangkok with sludge total solids content varying from 1.7 per cent to 6.5 per cent and different dosing depths achieved loading rates of between 70 and 475 kg TS/m² year (Pescod, 1971).
- Monitoring of the performance of unplanted drying beds in Accra, Ghana over eight loading cycles revealed loading rates ranging from 196 to 321 kg TS/m² year (Cofie et al., 2006).

- Bench-scale investigations in Kumasi, Ghana achieved loading rates up to 467 kg TS/m² year for a 3:1 septage to public-toilet sludge mixture. The organic matter content of the dried sludge was 334 kg total volatile solids (TVS)/m² year. With the addition of sawdust, the loading rate reached 525 kg TS/m² year (Kuffour, 2010).
- Another study in Ghana found effective sludge loading rates of 300 and 150 kg TS/m² year for sludges with 60 g TS/l and 5 g TS/l, respectively (Badji et al., 2011, quoted in Strande et al., 2014, pp. 145).

The findings of the Pescod and Badji studies revealed an increase in solids loading with increased wet sludge solids content, suggesting that designs that are based on an assumed solids loading, without reference to wet sludge solids content, may be incorrect. This point is illustrated by experience at the Cambérène faecal sludge treatment plant in Dakar, Senegal. The drying bed design assumed 200 kg TS/m² year loading and a 200 mm sludge layer. Subsequent analysis of operational practice showed that the loading rate achieved was actually around 340 kg TS/m² year, so that only 6–7 beds were required, instead of the 10 beds assumed in the design (Box 7.2; Dodane and Ronteltap, 2014).

Box 9.1 summarizes research on the relationship between the wet sludge solids content and the solids loading rate. The findings of this research relate to conditions in temperate climates and cannot be used directly to assess loading rates on drying beds in places with hot climates. However, they do support the view that the achievable solids loading rate is influenced by the wet sludge

---

Box 9.1 Results of research into relationship between wet sludge solids content and gross bed solids loading

Haseltine (1951) used data from different treatment plants to derive a straight line relationship between gross bed solids loading and wet sludge solids content. Using regression analysis on the same data, Vater (1956) derived the equation:

$$Y = 0.033S_o^{1.6}$$

where Y is the gross loading on the bed in kg/m²/d and S_o is the percentage solids content of the sludge discharged to the bed.

The Vater equation is for wastewater sludge in a temperate climate and so is not directly applicable to the dewatering of faecal sludges in warmer climates. Its relevance here lies in its prediction that the achievable loading rate increases with wet sludge solids content. Other researchers came to different conclusions. For instance, Vankleeck (1961, quoted in Wang et al., 2007, pp. 410) reported a doubling of drying time for an increase in sludge solids content from 5 per cent to 8 per cent, figures that suggest that the solids loading rate decreases rather than increases with increasing sludge solids content. Later researchers have produced detailed mathematical models to predict the way in which various parameters, including initial solids content, affect drying bed performance (Adrian, 1978). Laboratory experiments suggest that the drainage time to reach a given solids concentration is roughly proportional to the initial sludge solids concentration (Wang et al., 2007). If drainage were the only mechanism contributing to drying, this would suggest that initial sludge solids content would have very little effect on achievable loading rates. In practice, evaporation plays a big part in drying, particularly in warmer climates.

solids content. If this view is accepted, calculations that are based on an assumed solids loading rate, regardless of wet sludge solids content, will be unreliable. A better approach to the design of unplanted drying beds will be to:

- Determine the achievable hydraulic loading loading rate, which is the product of the depth of wet sludge at the beginning of each dewatering cycle and the number of dewatering cycles in a year and is expressed as m^3/m^2 year.
- Calculate the achievable solids loading rate by multiplying the hydraulic loading rate by the mean solids content of the wet sludge.

The time required for sludge dewatering, and hence the length of the dewatering cycle, depends on a range of factors including the depth of wet sludge applied to the bed, the climate, the sludge characteristics, the measures taken to exclude rainfall from the drying bed, and the required solids content of the dewatered sludge. It should be assessed by either monitoring sludge drying times achieved on pilot-scale beds or obtaining information from existing drying beds operating under similar climatic conditions.

The achievable solids loading for wet sludge with a low solids content is likely to be lower than the 200 kg TS/m^2 year commonly assumed in drying bed design. Where calculations indicate a high solids loading rate, say higher than 300 kg TS/m^2 year, it will be advisable to check that the time required for sludge dewatering has been accurately assessed by either evaluating the performance of an existing drying bed or constructing a small pilot drying bed and monitoring its performance.

Recommended ranges for the design criteria for unplanted drying beds are discussed and summarized in Table 9.1.

Table 9.1 Summary of unplanted sludge drying bed design criteria

Parameter	Symbol	Units	Recommended/ typical range	Notes
Sand effective size	De	mm	0.3–0.75	Sand should be washed to remove fines and prevent clogging. River sand will typically be too small to be suitable.
Sand uniformity coefficient	UC	–	<3.5	
Loading depth – wet sludge	Z	mm	200–300	Achievable loading rate increases with decreased loading depth.
Dewatering time	t_d	days	4–15 days (hot/arid climate with covered beds) 15–30 days (temperate/wet climate with covered beds)	The times given are guide figures to achieve ~15–30% solids. Actual drying times will depend on the characteristics of the sludge and local climatic conditions. Longer times will result in a higher TS content.
Solids loading rate	λ_s	kg TS/ m^2 year	Not used in initial design	Check assumed drying time if greater than 300 kg TS/m^2 year.

The steps in the design procedure for unplanted drying beds are as follows:

1. Determine the volume of sludge to be dried and the intervals at which it will be delivered for drying.
    Possible scenarios include:

    -   *Sludge to be dewatered is delivered to beds daily or more frequently.* This will be the situation for drying beds that receive raw faecal sludge and septage, sludge separated in gravity thickeners, and solid cake produced by sludge presses.
    -   *Sludge to be dewatered is delivered to beds at intervals of more than a day but less than the dewatering cycle time.* This is likely to be the situation for Dakar-style settling-thickening tanks.
    -   *Sludge to be dewatered is delivered at intervals of weeks or months.* This will be the situation for Achimota-style settling-thickening tanks, anaerobic ponds and ABRs. The desludging interval will normally be longer than the length of the drying cycle.

    Where septage is discharged directly to drying beds, the design loading on the beds will be the average daily loading during the month during which the highest loading occurs (the peak month loading), calculated using the methods described in Chapter 3. For processes involving solids–liquid separation, the frequency of sludge production and the volume of sludge produced should be calculated using the methods described in Chapter 7. Sludge production volumes and frequency for anaerobic and facultative ponds and ABRs should be calculated using the methods described in Chapter 8.

    In the likely event that the initial loading is lower than the projected loading at the design horizon, the options are to:

    -   commission, and perhaps build, beds as needed to match the load;
    -   use all the beds but reduce the depth of wet sludge;
    -   use all the beds but increase the dewatering time.

    In the short term, the second and third options will result in increased solids content in the dewatered sludge.

2. Assess the dewatering cycle time, using the equation:

$$t_{dc} = t_L + t_d + t_{ds}$$

where: t_{dc} = dewatering cycle time (d);
t_L = sludge loading time (d);
t_d = dewatering time (d); and
t_{ds} = sludge removal time (d).

For frequently loaded beds, the loading time will normally be one day, extending to perhaps two days for lightly loaded drying beds. Where sludge originates in anaerobic ponds and other treatment facilities, the loading time will be longer. Use Table 9.1 and information from existing installations in similar climatic conditions to make an initial estimate of t_d, the dewatering time. Assume a desludging rate of 2–4 m³ per worker per day to calculate the time required for dewatered sludge removal.

3. Assess the bed area required per day or, in the event of discharges at intervals of less than a day, per wet sludge discharge event.

    The area required is given by the equation:

$$SA = \frac{V_s}{Z}$$

    where: SA = required surface area in m²;
    V_s = volume of wet sludge delivered in m³; and
    Z = wet sludge loading depth in m.

    For sludge delivered at intervals of a day or less, V_s is the volume of sludge delivered during a day and may be referred to as V_d. The corresponding bed area, SA_d, will normally be provided by one bed, although it could be divided between two beds at large treatment plants. At small plants, the size of one bed might be $2SA_d$, with the bed loaded over two days.

    For sludge removed from ponds and tanks at intervals of more than one day, V_s is the volume of sludge delivered during one desludging event and may be referred to as $V_{s\text{-event}}$. Depending on the volume of sludge removed, this area might be provided by two or more beds.

4. Determine the number of drying beds required.

    The number of dewatering beds required will depend on the dewatering cycle time, the quantity of wet sludge to be dewatered and the intervals at which wet sludge is delivered for treatment. Figure 9.3 provides a graphical representation of the loading cycle for a set of drying beds showing a situation in which sludge is delivered daily and the total dewatering cycle time is 10 days, of which one day is for loading, seven days for dewatering and two days for sludge removal. A five-day working week is assumed. Sludge dewatering can continue over weekends but sludge loading and removal can only take place during the working week. Using these assumptions, loads are plotted, with a new row added each time a new drying bed

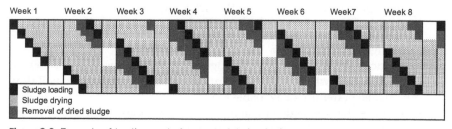

Figure 9.3 Example of loading cycle for a set of drying beds

is required. The graph shows that by day 11, the first bed is clear and can be loaded again.

Where sludge is discharged to a separate bed each day, the number of beds required will normally be given by the expression:

$$n = t_{dc} - D_{we}$$

where: n = number of beds required;

t_{dc} = dewatering cycle time (days); and

D_{we} = minimum number of non-working days over the length of the dewatering cycle.

This is reflected by Figure 9.3, which shows that eight beds are required for a 10-day dewatering cycle with a two-day non-working weekend. An additional bed should be provided to allow beds to be taken out of service for repair and maintenance. This will also provide some back-up capacity to deal with disruptions in the loading schedule resulting from short breaks in delivery on holidays and other non-working days.

A similar approach can be used for tanks that are desludged at intervals of more than a day but less than the dewatering cycle time. Take, for example, the case of sludge settling-thickening tanks that are desludged at intervals of 7 days with an 18-day dewatering cycle time. In this case, the effect of weekends can be ignored since the operational cycle can be adjusted to ensure that bed loading and sludge removal always take place on the same days of the week. Three beds will be required, with loading returned to the first bed during the fourth loading cycle. In theory, it would be possible to optimize the use of the beds by increasing the sludge loading depth slightly and reducing the drying bed area by a proportionate amount so that the dewatering cycle time could be increased to 21 days. In practice, such fine adjustment of the loading regime may not be practical.

Additional beds will be required to dewater sludge from anaerobic and facultative ponds, Achimota-style settling-thickening tanks, and ABRs, all of which will be desludged at intervals that exceed the dewatering cycle time. This may result in situations in which the available drying time exceeds the time required to achieve the desired sludge cake solids content. Possible responses to this situation are:

- Extend the dewatering time and so produce a sludge cake with a high solids content.
- Increase the depth of wet sludge. This will increase the dewatering cycle time while reducing the number of beds required and will thus make better use of available space.
- Store the wet sludge in sludge-holding lagoons, from which it can be released at intervals to the drying beds.

It may be appropriate to implement a scheme that combines two or more of these options.

5. Determine the total dewatering bed area required.

The total drying bed area required is the sum of the areas required for the sludge from the various treatment units. The total surface area required by hydraulic loading is the sum of the surface areas required to accommodate regular and intermittent sludge loading:

$$SA_h = nSA_d + \Sigma SA_{event}$$

where SA_h = total bed area required in m²;

SA_d = bed area required for a single day's regular sludge loading (direct from tankers or from a regularly desludged facility such as a gravity thickener) in m²;

n = number of beds required to accommodate regular loading; and

SA_{event} = bed area, in m², required for occasional desludging of facilities such as anaerobic ponds and ABRs. The summation symbol indicates the possibility that drying bed area may be required to cater for sludge from more than one type of facility.

Systems that use settling-thickening tanks or anaerobic ponds to separate solids will have no regular daily sludge loading.

6. Determine the number of dewatering cycles in a year.

For daily loaded beds, the first step in determining the number of dewatering cycles in a year is to plot a series of consecutive drying cycles for the first bed, starting from the first day of the working week. When plotting the drying cycles, no wet sludge loading and removal of dewatered sludge should be shown on non-working days. After several weeks, the cycle will repeat itself with the bed again being loaded with wet sludge on the first day of the working week. In the example shown in Figure 9.3, the dewatering cycle repeats itself from week 9 onwards, with five dewatering cycles taking place over an 8-week period. This cycle repeats itself for all the beds. Once the number of complete cycles in a given period has been determined, the number of loading cycles in a year can be calculated using the equation:

$$N_c (\text{cycles per year}) = \left(\frac{\text{cycles completed in } x \text{ weeks}}{x \text{ weeks}} \right) \times 52 (\text{weeks/year})$$

For the example shown in Figure 9.3, with five cycles completed in 8 weeks, $N_c = (5/8) \times 52 = 32.5$. In practice, this should be rounded down to 32, or even perhaps 30, to allow for additional holidays and other breaks in service. One bed will normally be provided to take the wet sludge delivered during a single working day.

7. Check the solids loading rate, using the equation:

$$\lambda_s = ZC_{TSS}N_C$$

where λ_s = solids loading rate in kg TS/m² year;
   Z = loading depth of wet sludge in m;
   N_c = number of beds required to accommodate regular loading; and
   C_{TSS} = solids concentration of the wet sludge, expressed in g/l or kg/m³.

If λ_s is less than around 100 kg/m² year, the options for increasing the solids content of the wet sludge, using the solids–liquid separation methods described in Chapter 7, should be explored. If λ_s is more than 300 kg/m² year, the assumed drying cycle time should be checked by either monitoring the drying cycle time required at existing drying beds treating similar sludge, or by building a small test drying bed to assess drying performance. If these activities show that the assumed drying cycle time is realistic, there is no need to limit the solids loading rate to an arbitrarily assumed figure.

Unplanted sludge drying beds: design example

A treatment plant is required to treat an estimated 450 m³ of septage per week. Sampling from suction tankers suggests that the septage will have an average solids content of around 1 per cent. Solids–liquid separation in hopper-bottomed gravity thickeners is proposed and is expected to produce a sludge with a 5 per cent solids content (50 g TS/l). The sludge will be dewatered on unplanted drying beds. Based on information collected from existing drying beds in the region, the time required to dewater sludge to achieve at least 20 per cent solids content is 9 days. The treatment plant is actively operated 6 days per week with no sludge treated on the 7th day. Key parameters for the design of the drying beds are as follows:

Parameter	Symbol	Value	Units
Hydraulic loading on drying beds	V_s	15	m³/d (six days/week)
Mean TSS concentration in separated sludge	C_{TSS}	50	g TS/l (or kg TS/m³)
Hydraulic loading depth, maximum	Z	200	mm
Dewatering time	t_d	9	days
Operating time per week	f_{op}	6	days/week

The steps in the calculation are as follows:

1. Determine the volume of wet sludge to be dewatered.
   The focus here is on sludge removed from hopper-bottomed gravity thickeners. Additional beds will be required to treat sludge produced at subsequent stages in the liquid treatment process but their design is not considered here. The 450 m³ of sludge delivered per week is at 1 per cent solids content. After solids–liquid separation, the solids content is 5 per cent, so the volume = 450(1/5) = 90 m³/week or 15 m³/working day.

2. Calculate the dewatering cycle time and hydraulic loading rate, assuming 1 day of loading and 2 days of desludging after sludge has dried:

$$t_{dc} = t_l + t_d + t_{ds} = 1 \text{ day} + 9 \text{ days} + 2 \text{ days} = 12 \text{ days}$$

3. Calculate the area required for the sludge produced during a single day:

$$SA = \left(\frac{V_s}{Z}\right) = \frac{15 \text{ m}^3}{0.2 \text{ m}} = 65 \text{ m}^2$$

Assume bed dimensions 11.5 m × 5.75 m, which will give a bed area of 66 m²

4. Determine the number of drying beds required.
The dewatering cycle time is 12 days and will encompass at least one non-working day. The minimum number of beds required will therefore be 11. One additional bed should be provided to allow for bed downtime to allow for repair and maintenance.

5. Calculate the total bed area required:
Area required = 12 × 66 m² = 792 m² plus the area required for sludge removed from liquid treatment units, which is not included in this example and would have to be calculated separately.

6. Determine the number of dewatering cycles per year:
First draw the loading diagram, as shown below.

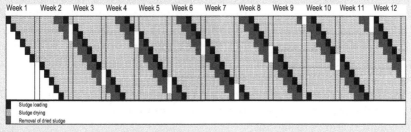

Week 1 Week 2 Week 3 Week 4 Week 5 Week 6 Week 7 Week 8 Week 9 Week 10 Week 11 Week 12

Sludge loading
Sludge drying
Removal of dried sludge

This shows that the loading cycle repeats after 11 weeks and that six complete dewatering cycles are completed in this time.

$$N_c \text{(cycles per year)} = \left(\frac{6 \text{ cycles}}{11 \text{ weeks}}\right) \times 52\text{(weeks in year)} = 28.36$$

Take the number of loading cycles as 28 per year.

7. Check the solids loading rate.
For a hydraulic loading depth of 200 mm, the solids loading rate is:

$$\lambda_s = 0.2 \text{ m} \times 50 \text{ kg TS/m}^3 \times 28 \text{ cycles/year} = 280 \text{ kg TS/m}^2\text{/year}$$

This loading rate is at the higher end of the loading rates quoted in the literature and it will be advisable to check that the assumptions regarding the dewatering cycle time are realistic.

Without solids–liquid separation, the solids loading rate would reduce by a factor of five, reducing λ_s to 56 kg TS/m² year and increasing the required drying bed area to almost 4,000 m². This TS loading is much lower than the 200 kg TS/m² year figure commonly assumed as a suitable solids loading design figure. This confirms the desirability of providing solids–liquid separation prior to sludge dewatering.

Planted drying beds

System description

Planted drying beds have been used to stabilize and dewater sludge from small activated sludge treatment plants in Europe since the late 1980s, most notably in Denmark, which has more than 140 full-scale systems. Other European countries with planted beds treating wastewater treatment plant sludge include Poland, Belgium, the UK, Italy, France, and Spain (Uggetti et al., 2010). To date, experience with the use of planted beds to dewater faecal sludge and septage in lower-income countries has mainly been at bench-scale and with pilot-scale initiatives. Full-scale planted drying beds were in operation from 2008 to at least 2011 at the Cambérène treatment facility in Dakar, Senegal (Dodane et al., 2011). In Belo Horizonte, Brazil, a constructed wetland intended for wastewater treatment was modified to act as a planted drying bed and was operated as such for 405 days from September 2013 to October 2014 (Andrade et al., 2017).

Planted beds are similar in construction to unplanted beds but are planted with emergent macrophytes, plants that are rooted in the bed but emerge above the sludge surface. They are sometimes referred to as constructed wetlands, but they operate rather differently from vertical-flow constructed wetlands and are sized using different design parameters. Water loss from planted drying beds takes place through a combination of evaporation, evapotranspiration from plants, and percolation through the bed. Like unplanted beds, they are loaded sequentially but they differ from unplanted beds in that dried sludge is removed at intervals of years rather than weeks. This is possible because the plant roots open up drainage paths in the sludge, facilitating both evaporation and percolation.

Evapotranspiration (ET) is a major contributor to the dewatering process, particularly in hot, dry climates. Chazarenc et al. (2003) estimated ET rates of 4–12 mm/d for a 1 m^2 pilot bed in France planted with *Phragmites australis*. Their findings compare with rates of 25–38 mm/d and 32–50 mm/d in north and south Italy recorded by Borin et al. (2011). ET rates are likely to be even higher in tropical and subtropical climates. These rates are significantly higher than evaporation rates of up to around 8 mm/d that can be expected from unplanted drying beds (see, for example, Simba et al., 2013). High ET rates reduce the length of the dewatering cycle and so allow higher hydraulic loading rates than are achievable on unplanted beds. In hot, dry climates there may be operational problems as the beds can dry out quickly, so creating conditions that are stressful for the plants.

Commonly used plants include reeds (*Phragmites* spp.) and cattails (*Typha* spp.). Cattails are an attractive option because of their high initial growth rate. Other options for use in tropical climates include antelope grass (*Echinochloa* spp.) and papyrus (*Cyperus papyrus*). Plant selection for a particular location is influenced by the types of plant that grow locally. For instance, a study of planted drying bed performance in Ouagadougou, Burkina Faso, used

Andropogon gayanus and citronella grass (*Cymbopogon nardus*), both locally available plants (Joceline et al., 2016). All the plants identified above grow from rhizomes – these are underground stems that send out shoots above and roots below. Shoots produce new stems, so the plant density increases over time.

The bed depth is typically in the range 60–80 cm, sufficient to accommodate the root systems of the plants. A typical bed formation consists of 10–15 cm of sand, overlying 15–25 cm of medium sized gravel and 25–40 cm of large gravel. To prevent leaching, the bottom of each bed is sealed, preferably with a waterproof membrane. Filtrate flows through the bed into perforated pipes, placed at intervals in the large gravel immediately above the bottom of the bed. To ensure good drainage, the bed should slope to the drainage outlet point, with a slope of 1 per cent or more. Sludge is fed by means of pipes which may be located in a corner of the bed, along one of the bed sides, or in the middle of the basin (upflow vertical pipes). Figure 9.4 shows a section through a typical planted drying bed.

As with unplanted beds, the number of beds required depends on the time required for dewatering. If each bed is loaded for 2 days and then left to dry for 10 days, the total loading period is 12 days and six beds will be required. Once the cycle is complete, sludge is again directed to the first bed. Increasing the number of beds allows a longer drying time and results in a drier sludge. However, it is important that the beds retain sufficient moisture at all times to meet the needs of the plants. If this requirement is neglected, plants will wilt and eventually die. One or more additional bed(s) should be provided to allow each bed to be rested for a period before desludging.

Potential advantages of planted drying beds over unplanted drying beds include the following:

- *Reduced labour requirement.* Labour will be required to harvest the plants, typically once or twice each year, but the effort required for this task will be much less than that required for regular desludging of an unplanted drying bed.
- *Income from plant sales.* This will be dependent on the existence of a market for the harvested plants and effective marketing systems. Income from the sale of harvested plants will offset the cost of harvesting, potentially making a small profit. A report on pilot-scale investigations in Cameroon states that a full harvest of *Echinochloa pyramidalis* shoots, harvested three times a year, could yield a biomass of at least 100–150 dry tonnes per hectare (Kengne and Tilley, 2014). Further investigation is required to determine the yield that can be achieved from full-scale beds under normal operating conditions.
- *Reduced health risk.* By reducing worker exposure to fresh sludge, planted beds will reduce their exposure to pathogens.
- *Good sludge mineralization.* This is a result of stabilization and dewatering during the long retention period on the bed. Together with dewatering,

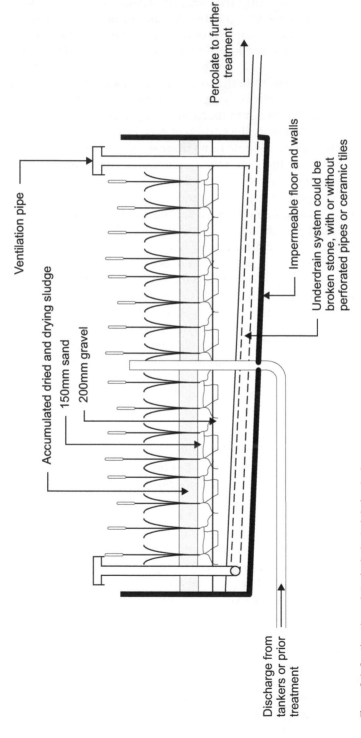

Figure 9.4 Section through typical planted drying bed

this may produce a final product that is suitable for land application as a Class B biosolid, either directly or after additional composting. It is unlikely that retention on a planted drying bed will produce a Class A biosolid. Research in Cameroon found that helminth egg concentration in dried sludge after a six-month loading period followed by six additional months' resting was 4 eggs/g TS, still above the World Health Organization (WHO) standard of ≤1 egg/g TS (Kengne et al., 2009). The heavy metal concentrations will not normally be a problem with domestic septage but the heavy metals concentration of biosolids should be checked if land application is planned.

* *Improved filtrate quality.* Heinss and Koottatep (1998) reported that BOD and COD concentrations in the water percolating from constructed wetlands were typically 35–55 per cent and 50–60 per cent, respectively: lower than those in water percolating from unplanted beds. They provided no information on how these figures were determined. The information on performance summarized below suggests that further research is required to assess the filtrate quality achieved under field conditions.

These advantages should be weighed against the possible drawbacks of planted drying beds, the most important of which is the potential for system failure if conditions are allowed to deviate too far from optimum operating conditions. In particular, careful management is required to ensure that plants do not dry out and wilt, and to maintain plant density at an acceptable level. These requirements are examined in more detail below.

Performance

The performance of planted drying beds can be assessed in relation to the solids and pathogen content of the dried sludge and the quality of the percolate. Research in Yaoundé, Cameroon found that dry solids contents of over 30 per cent could be achieved on yard-scale planted drying beds loaded with raw faecal sludge for six months at constant loading rates of 100–200 kg TS/m² year. Helminth egg concentrations in the dried biosolids remained high at 79 eggs/g TS (Kengne et al., 2009). Loading a 29.1 m² bed at the Arrudas plant in Belo Horizonte, Brazil at an average rate of 81 kg TS/m² year resulted in biosolids with 55 per cent dry solids content (Andrade et al., 2017).

Table 9.2 summarizes the findings of selected studies with regard to percolate quality. They show that removal of solids, COD, and nitrogen concentration will normally be insufficient to allow discharge to a watercourse or reuse without further treatment.

A further point to note regarding performance is that the performance of the full-sized bed at Belo Horizonte was inferior to those of various pilot-scale installations. One possible reason for this is that the loading on the Belo Horizonte beds was much more varied than those on the pilot-scale beds, which were mostly operated at carefully controlled solids loading rates. Andrade et al. (2017) suggest that another possible reason for

Table 9.2 Planted drying bed treatment performance for selected studies

Location	Influent characteristics (mg/l)	Solids loading rate (kg TS/m² year)	Removal in liquid effluent (%)	Notes and references
Bangkok, Thailand	TS: 15,350 COD: 15,700 TKN: 1,100 NH$_3$-N: 415	80–500 Most 250	TS: 74–86 COD: 78–99 TKN: 70–99 NH$_3$-N: 50–99	Koottatep et al. (2005) Nitrification indicated in sludge (Koottatep et al., 2005)
Yaoundé, Cameroon	TSS: 27,600 COD: 31,000 NH$_3$-N: 600	196–321	TSS: 92 COD: 98 NH$_3$-N: 78	Kengne et al. (2011) Mean figures – median TSS lower
Ouagadougou, Burkina Faso	COD: 952 BOD: 441	Not given	COD 71–77 BOD 75–90	Joceline et al. (2016)
Sarawak, Malaysia	TS: 24,573 COD: 31,957 TKN: 1,209 NH$_3$-N: 428	250	TS: 89 COD: 94.5 TKN: 76 NH$_3$-N: 76.8	Jong and Tank (2014) Slightly higher removal at 100 kg TS/m² year loading
Belo Horizonte, Brazil	TS: 2,349 COD: 2,937 BOD: 1,074 TKN: 88 NH$_4$-N[1]: 82	81	TS: 51 COD: 82 BOD: 77 TKN: 63 NH$_4$-N: 65	Andrade et al. (2017) Beds subject to wide variations in hydraulic and solids loading

Notes: TKN, total Kjeldahl nitrogen.
[1] Some researchers quote ammonia nitrogen as NH$_3$ and some as NH$_4$ but the key point is the nitrogen content, regardless of whether the ammonia is in un-ionized (NH$_3$) or ionized (NH$_4^+$) form.

the relatively poor performance of the Belo Horizonte plant was the use of coarse gravel for the bed media. The investigations on the Belo Horizonte plant revealed no improvement in either total coliforms or *Escherichia coli* in the percolate.

Operational and design considerations

Operational sequence. Operation of planted drying beds takes place over three phases (Brix, 2017):

- *Start-up phase* during which the plants are gradually acclimatized to withstand the full sludge loading. One option for acclimatizing beds is to load them with municipal wastewater combined with increasing amounts of sludge, until the loading rate reaches approximately 50 per cent of the design loading rate. Recommended lengths for the start-up phase range from 6 months (Kengne et al., 2011) to 2 years (Brix, 2017).
- *Operational phase* during which the beds are loaded cyclically, with a loading period followed by a longer resting period. The resting period must be long enough to allow the sludge to dry out and crack, so that

oxygen is available within the bed to support the aerobic microorganisms that contribute to the stabilization process. During the loading period the beds are loaded for periods of up to 2 hours and then left to dewater for a few hours before a new load is discharged. In temperate conditions, the loading and resting periods are typically 3–7 days and 3–7 weeks in duration, respectively, both increasing over time (Brix, 2017). The loading cycle in hot climates is shorter. Kengne and Tilley (2014) suggest loading 1–3 times per week with a resting period of between 2 days and several weeks, depending on weather conditions, the dry matter content of the sludge, and the plant species. Brix recommends a minimum of eight beds to ensure that the resting time is sufficient to allow sludge to dry and crack. The sludge accumulates slowly until the sludge level is just below the top of the side walls. In temperate climates this typically takes 5–10 years, depending on the sludge accumulation rate and the depth available for sludge storage. At this point, feeding is stopped and the resting and sludge removal phase begins.

- *Resting and sludge removal phase.* The resting period allows time for the sludge to dry and so increases the dry matter content of the sludge. It typically lasts a few weeks, although the actual time will depend on local climatic conditions. If sludge is removed carefully so that the underlying sand and gravel bed is not disturbed, it is possible that the plants will regrow. Regardless of whether plants can be regrown or have to be replaced by new plants, the loading rate on the bed must be reduced for the first few months following sludge removal (Brix, 2017).

Solids loading rate. Recommended loading rates in temperate and cold climate conditions range from about 60 kg TS/m^2 year (Brix, 2017) to 100 kg TS/m^2 year (Kinsley and Crolla, 2012). The results of the studies summarized in Box 9.2 suggest that loading rates of up to about 250 kg TS/m^2 year can be achieved in tropical climates. Keeping within this loading rate requires information on the volume and strength of the sludge delivered for treatment. Load assessment will be difficult where the sludge to be treated has highly variable characteristics (Sonko, el Hadji M et al., 2014). Assessment of sludge strength should be based on as many samples as possible.

Sludge accumulation rate. The sludge accumulation rate is strongly influenced by the solids loading rate. For the 50–60 kg TS/m^2 year loading rates used in Europe, the accumulation rate is typically about 10 cm/year (Brix, 2017; Troesch et al., 2009). Andrade et al. (2017) reported accumulation rate of 7.3 cm/year for a mean loading rate of 81 kg TS/m^2 year. Kengne et al. (2011) suggest accumulation rates of 50–70 cm/year for beds loaded at 100 kg TS/m^2 year and 80–113 cm/year for three beds loaded at 200 kg TS/m^2 year. Accumulation rates are likely to depend on local conditions and the Andrade et al. (2017) findings from Belo Horizonte in Brazil suggest that the accumulation rate for a given solids loading may be lower in hot climates than in temperate climates. The figures do show that the increased solids loading that is achievable in hot climates is likely to result

---

Box 9.2 Summary information on loading rate studies

Experimental work at the Asian Institute of Technology (AIT) on pilot-scale beds planted with cattails (*Typha angustifolia*) in the late 1990s with fairly strong septage (mean concentrations 15,700 mg/l COD, 15,350 mg/l TS, 1,100 mg/l total Kjeldahl nitrogen [TKN], and 415 mg/l ammonia nitrogen [NH_4-N]) found that the beds performed satisfactorily with loading rates up to 250 kg TS/m² year. COD, TS, TKN, and NH_4-N reductions in the bed were in the ranges 78–99 per cent, 74–86 per cent, 70–99 per cent, and 50–99 per cent, respectively. There was some tendency for performance to deteriorate at a loading rate of 500 kg TS/m² year. Cattail wilting was observed at this loading rate (Koottatep et al., 2005).

During research in Yaoundé, Cameroon, carried out between 2005 and 2006, beds planted with *Cyperus papyrus* and *E. pyramidalis* were loaded at rates of 100, 200, and 300 kg TS/m² year. The mean COD, TSS, and NH_4-N concentrations of the septage applied to the bed were 31,100 mg/l, 27,600 mg/l, and 600 mg/l, respectively. Performance of the beds was good, with COD, TSS, and ammonia reductions averaging 98 per cent, 92 per cent, and 78 per cent, respectively. Slight clogging of the beds started to become noticeable at the 200 kg TS/m² year loading rate and severe clogging was experienced in some beds at the 300 kg TS/m² year loading rate. The report on the research concluded that loadings of up to 200 kg TS/m² year were possible on beds planted with *E. pyramidalis* (Kengne et al., 2011).

Experimental work on pilot-scale beds in Malaysia showed that the proportion of drained water decreased at higher solids loading rates, from 59–81 per cent at 100 kg/m² year to 11–38 per cent at 350 kg/m² year (Tan et al., 2017).

---

in a reduction in the operating phase from the 10 years or more commonly achieved in European conditions to as little as 2 years.

Side wall height. As already indicated, sludge is allowed to accumulate for several years on planted drying beds. The sludge is typically allowed to reach a depth of 1–1.5 m before sludge is removed. Allowing for a bed depth of 800 mm, and 200 mm between the highest sludge level and the top of the walls, the total wall height required will thus lie in the range 2–2.5 m.

Planting and plant thinning. Plants are normally planted in pots at a density of between 4 and 12 plants/m² (Brix, 2017; Edwards et al., 2001). The plants used in drying beds grow from rhizomes – underground stems that produce roots and stems from nodes distributed along their length. Plant densities increase as new shoots are produced. Plant densities increase rapidly when the bed loading is within the prescribed range, to over 200 plants/m² in some instances. For instance, Sonko, el Hadji M et al. (2014) recorded *E. pyramidalis* densities of 211, 265, and 268 plants/m² for beds loaded once, twice, and three times per week, respectively. These densities are significantly higher than those recorded in natural conditions.

Loading arrangements. It is possible for tankers to discharge their loads directly onto drying beds. This is likely to result in overloading in areas close to the discharge points while areas that tanker hoses cannot reach are underloaded. It also means that it is difficult to adequately screen incoming sludge. Unequal distribution will also be a problem if sludge is discharged through a pipe in one corner of the bed or via a channel set in one end of the drying bed. The resulting sludge accumulation around the discharge point is likely to inhibit plant growth (Uggetti, 2011: 169). A better option is to discharge sludge through a series of vertical pipes, located at intervals in the bed, as shown in Figure 9.4. One potential difficulty with this arrangement is that of accessing distribution pipes laid under the bed to clear any blockages that might occur. The hydraulic design must allow for head losses through the distribution pipework. If these are ignored, differences in head may result in unequal distribution of flow between the different vertical pipes.

Loading regime. Sufficient water must be available to keep plants alive: plant die-off will occur if the solids loading rate is too high. This suggests that planted drying beds will be most suitable for lower strength septage with a high water content. Loading beds twice per week or more will help to reduce plant-wilting problems but may not allow the bed to dry and crack. A better approach will be to provide valves or penstocks on the outlets from the underdrain system to allow percolate to be impounded, so keeping the bottom of the drying beds wet. Koottatep et al. (2005) recommend that the percolate should be impounded for 2–6 days, but do not say how the impounding period should be determined. They speculate that impounding can cause anaerobic conditions in the percolate and hence result in denitrification. Percolate impounding did not have a significant effect on TS and COD removal performance.

Labour requirements. Labour will be required to maintain drying beds, thinning plants as necessary, and to harvest the plants, typically 2–3 times a year. One option for harvesting the plants is to outsource the task to local farmers or a small contractor. If there is a market for the harvested plants and effective marketing systems are in place, income from the sale of harvested plants will offset the cost of harvesting, potentially producing a small profit. The challenge will be to ensure the correct degree of thinning – too much thinning may result in the beds becoming denuded of plants.

Ventilation. Vent pipes should be provided to allow air to reach the lower bed layers. Heinss and Koottatep (1998) report research findings that reeds on non-ventilated planted beds loaded with activated sludge died at similar loadings to those at which reeds on ventilated beds survived. The average drying rate on ventilated beds was significantly higher.

Roofing. As with unplanted drying beds, provision of a transparent cover over the beds will improve drying efficiency.

Design criteria and design procedure

Most information on the performance of planted drying beds in hot climates is based on pilot-scale initiatives. Dodane et al. (2011) report experience with the use of full-scale planted drying beds, but there is a pressing need for further investigation of the practical issues associated with the implementation of

Table 9.3 Summary of planted sludge drying bed design criteria

Parameter	Symbol	Units	Recommended range	Notes
Bed depth	z_b	cm	70–90	Must provide sufficient depth to accommodate root growth
Solids loading rate	λ_s	kg TS/m² year	≤250	Build up to this load during start-up to allow plants to acclimatize
Number and configuration of beds (duty plus standby)	n_b	–	≥(2 + 1)	One standby cell allows resting of a bed before desludging
Hydraulic loading depth	z_h	mm	150–200	Wet sludge depth
Hydraulic loading frequency	f_H	loads per week	1–2	Interval between loads must be sufficient to allow sludge to dry and crack
Desludging interval		years	3–10	Depends on sludge accumulation rate, which in turn depends on solids loading rate

planted drying beds at scale. Table 9.3 sets out design criteria that take account of the currently available information.

For septage with a low solids content, the bed area required will usually be governed by hydraulic loading. Solids loading is likely to be critical for strong septage and faecal sludge. The required bed area based on hydraulic loading should be calculated using the approach already described for unplanted drying beds. An approach to the calculation of required bed area based on solids loading is set out below.

1. Calculate the annual solids loading, using the equation:

$$M_S = Q_d C_{TSS} N$$

where M_s = dry mass of solids in wet sludge delivered in one year (kg/year)

Q_d = volume of wet sludge delivered (m³/d)

C_{TSS} = mean solids concentration in wet sludge (g/l or kg/m³)

N = number of days per year on which wet sludge is delivered for treatment.

Where the material to be dewatered is septage or faecal sludge, rather than sludge removed from a treatment unit, it may be appropriate to calculate the volume to be dewatered directly, using the methods set out in Chapter 3.

2. Calculate the total bed area required, based on solids loading rate:

$$SA_s = \frac{M_s}{\lambda_s}$$

where: SA_s = total bed area required (m²)
λ_s = solids loading rate (kg TS/m² year)

3. Determine number of beds and surface area per bed.

The minimum number of beds required depends on the loading pattern and the length of the loading–resting cycle. For beds that are loaded daily, the length of the loading–resting cycle is given by the equation:

$$t_{L-R} = t_L + t_R$$

where: t_{L-R} = loading–resting cycle time,
t_L = loading time, and
t_R = resting time.

If one bed is loaded each day, the number of operational beds required will normally be equal to the number of working days within one complete loading–resting cycle. The area of one bed is given by the equation:

$$SA_{bed} = \frac{SA_s}{n}$$

where SA_{bed} = area of one bed
n = number of operational beds required

4. Check depth of each sludge application.

The depth of sludge at each application equals the volume of wet sludge divided by the area of the drying bed or beds to which the sludge is discharged. Thus:

$$Z_h = \frac{1,000\,Q_d}{SA_{bed}}$$

To ensure effective drying, Z_h should preferably be 200 mm or less and certainly not more than 300 mm. A high value of Z_h is an indication that hydraulic rather than solids loading will be critical.

5. Determine number of beds required to allow for bed acclimatization and resting.

Additional beds will be required to allow for bed acclimatization and resting at the beginning and end of the loading cycle, respectively. The number of additional beds required will depend on the length of the complete operational cycle for a single bed, the time required for acclimatization and final resting, and the number of beds in operation at any one time. Typically, one additional bed will be required when the number of years in the complete operational cycle equals or exceeds the number of beds. Two additional beds may be required for shorter operational cycles.

Planted drying beds design example

Design for planted drying beds, to accommodate sludge loading with the following characteristics and operated 6 days per week.

Parameter	Symbol	Value	Units
Mean daily flow rate (averaged over year)	Q_d	40	m³/d
Mean TSS influent concentration	C_{TSS}	15	g TS/l (or kg TS/m³)
Operating time per week	f_{op}	6	days/week

1. Determine the solids loading:

$$M_s = 40 \text{ m}^3/\text{d} \times 15 \text{ kg/m}^3 \times \left(\frac{365 \text{ d}}{1 \text{ year}}\right) = 219,000 \text{ kg/year}$$

2. Calculate surface area based on solids loading, assuming a 250 kg/m² year maximum solids loading rate:

$$SA_s = \frac{219,000 \text{ kg/year}}{250 \text{ kg/m}^2 \text{ year}} = 876 \text{ m}^2$$

3. Determine number of beds and surface area per bed.
   Assume a hydraulic loading frequency of once per week. Six beds will be required.

$$SA_{bed} = \frac{876 \text{ m}^2}{6 \text{ beds}} = 146 \text{ m}^2$$

Provide six 20 m × 7.5 m beds, giving an area of 150 m²/bed and total bed area of 900 m².

   Assume that each bed requires 6 months acclimatization before it can be fully loaded and 6 months resting between end of active loading and desludging.

4. Calculate depth of wet sludge loading.
   Calculate depth of sludge application and check against design criteria:

$$Q_{s\_load} = 40 \text{m}^3/\text{d} \left(\frac{365 \text{d/year}}{52 \text{weeks} \times 6 \text{ days loading/week}}\right) = 46.8 \text{ m}^3$$

$$Z_{h\_load} = \frac{46.8 \text{ m}^3}{150 \text{ m}^2} \times 1000 \text{ mm/m} = 312 \text{ mm}$$

This is slightly higher than the 300 mm figure that would normally be taken as the maximum figure for Z_h and suggests that hydraulic rather than solids loading might be critical.

5. Determine additional beds required to allow for bed acclimatization and resting.
   If the sludge accumulation rate is 300 mm/year and bed is desludged after 4 years' operation, the bed 'downtime' will be 25 per cent of active loading time. To cater for this, two additional beds, giving 33 per cent additional area, will be required.
   If the sludge accumulation rate is 200 mm/year and each bed is desludged after 6 years' operation, bed downtime will be 17 per cent of active loading time. One additional bed will be required to provide capacity to cover bed downtime.

Mechanical presses

Mechanical presses are routinely used to dewater sludge produced in sewage treatment plants and have also been used in septage treatment. To date, all examples of their use in septage treatment combine solids–liquid separation and dewatering and, in view of this, they are covered in Chapter 7. In principle, there is no reason why they should not also be used as a dewatering technology after solids–liquid separation. When receiving sludge from an upstream solids–liquid separation process, such as a gravity thickener, the relatively high solids concentration in the feed means that sizing of the equipment is likely to be based on solids loading rather than hydraulic loading.

Geobags as an aid to sludge dewatering

Geobags, or geotubes, have been used in industrialized countries to dewater sludge from wastewater treatment plants, and there have been pilot projects to test their suitability for dewatering faecal sludge in Malaysia, Bangladesh, Uganda, Tanzania, Kenya, and the Philippines. Geobags are long, relatively narrow, flexible bags fabricated from high-strength, permeable textiles. The only opening in a bag is a connection to allow sludge to be discharged into it at one end. Once sludge has been pumped into a geobag, solids are retained in the bag while free water drains out through the permeable walls of the bag. Geobags are available in a variety of sizes but all lie flat when empty and expand into a sausage shape when filled with sludge.

In the Malaysia pilot project, they were located on the sand drying beds at an existing sewage treatment works, an arrangement that allowed collection of filtrate in the drying bed under-drainage system and subsequent treatment. Sludge tanker crews discharged their loads into a geobag through a connecting hose. A single 14.8 m × 3.3 m geobag received over 90 truckloads of sludge. Exposure to the sun's heat increased the temperature inside the black bag and accelerated the dewatering process. Once the bag was full, it was left to dry, chopped up to aid transportation, and was then loaded onto a truck for removal to a suitable disposal site and replaced by an empty bag.

The Bangladesh initiative, implemented by WSUP Bangladesh, was smaller and included initial mixing of a polymer to improve the settlement properties of the sludge. An internal (unpublished) WSUP review states that when polymers were added, rapid dewatering took place for about 90 minutes, after which the dewatering rate declined, apparently because sludge particles were blocking the geobag pores. Performance without polymers was less satisfactory, with around 10 per cent reduction in volume after 30 minutes and little further dewatering after that. While polymer dosing was necessary to achieve good results, the workers found that mixing the polymer with the sludge was difficult and time consuming.

Geobags must be removed and replaced when they are full. This suggests that the permeable geobag option has a high operational cost, which reduces its viability as a dewatering option.

Key points from this chapter

Solids dewatering is required to increase the solids content of sludge to at least 20 per cent, at which point it can be handled as a solid. Dewatering options include sludge retention on planted and unplanted drying beds, and various types of mechanical press. To date, all examples of the use of mechanical presses in faecal sludge and septage treatment have combined dewatering with solids–liquid separation. Other key points to take from this chapter are listed below.

- Sludge drying beds, both planted and unplanted, provide a simple dewatering option, but have relatively high land requirements.
- Unplanted drying beds are typically loaded with wet sludge to a depth of around 200 mm. The sludge is left to dry until the solids content reaches 20 per cent or more. The sludge drying area required will be dependent on the hydraulic loading and the length of the drying cycle. The latter depends on climatic conditions, the nature of the sludge, and the required final solids content, and should be determined using information gathered from drying beds operating under similar conditions and field trials designed to emulate drying bed behaviour.
- The available evidence shows that the achievable solids loading rate on unplanted drying beds tends to increase with increased solids content of the raw sludge. Designs that start from an assumed solids loading rate without taking account of this effect are likely to result in incorrectly sized beds.
- Unplanted drying beds require labour to remove dried sludge at regular intervals. Labour requirements for planted drying beds are greatly reduced because sludge removal takes place at intervals of years rather than days.
- To date, most experience with the use of planted drying beds to treat faecal sludge in lower-income countries has been at a pilot scale and little information is available on the challenges of operating them at scale. One of these challenges will be to ensure that plants continue to grow. Both underloading and periodic overloading may lead to plant die-off and reduced performance. The management requirements of planted drying beds are therefore higher than those of unplanted drying beds.
- It is possible to use mechanical presses for dewatering after initial gravity solids–liquid separation. However, any potential benefits should be weighed against the increased complexity of a process involving both solids–liquid separation and mechanical press dewatering.

References

Adrian, D.D. (1978) *Sludge Dewatering and Drying on Sand Beds*, EPA-600/2-78-141, Cincinnati, OH: US EPA Municipal Environmental Research Laboratory <https://nepis.epa.gov/Exe/ZyPDF.cgi/9101CGM4.PDF?Dockey=9101CGM4.PDF> [accessed 27 January 2018].

Al-Nozaily, F.A., Taher, T.M. and Al-Rawi, M.H.M. (2013) 'Evaluation of the sludge drying beds at Sana'a wastewater treatment plant', paper presented at the *17th International Water Technology Conference, Istanbul* <http://iwtc.info/wp-content/uploads/2013/11/99.pdf> [accessed 21 December 2017].

Andrade, C.F., von Sperling, M. and Manjate, E.S. (2017) 'Treatment of septic tank sludge in a vertical flow constructed wetland system', *Engenharia Agrícola* 37(4): 811–9 <http://dx.doi.org/10.1590/1809-4430-eng.agric.v37n4p811-819/2017> [accessed 22 May 2018].

Badji et al., Dodane, P.H., Mbéguéré, M. and Koné, D. (2011) Traitement des boues de vidange: éléments affectant la performance des lits de séchage non plantés en taille réelle et les mécanismes de séchage, *Actes du symposium international sur la Gestion des Boues de Vidange, Dakar, 30 June– 1 July 2009*, Dübendorf, Switzerland: Eawag/SANDEC <www.pseau.org/outils/ouvrages/eawag_gestion_des_boues_de_vidange_optimisation_de_la_filiere_2011.pdf> [accessed 24 March 2018].

Borin, M., Milani, M., Salvato, M. and Toscano, A. (2011) 'Evaluation of *Phragmites australis* (Cav.) Trin. evapotranspiration in Northern and Southern Italy', *Ecological Engineering* 37(5): 721–8 <http://dx.doi.org/10.1016/j.ecoleng.2010.05.003> [accessed 22 May 2018].

Brix, H. (2017) 'Sludge dewatering and mineralization in sludge treatment reed beds', *Water* 9(3): 160 <http://dx.doi.org/10.3390/w9030160> [accessed 22 May 2018].

Chazarenc, F., Merlin, G. and Gonthier, Y. (2003) 'Hydrodynamics of horizontal subsurface flow constructed wetlands', *Ecological Engineering* 21: 165–73 <http://dx.doi.org/10.1016/j.ecoleng.2003.12.001> [accessed 22 May 2018].

Cofie, O.O., Agbottah, S., Strauss, M., Esseku, H., Montangero, A., Awuah, E. and 'Koné, D. (2006) 'Solid–liquid separation of faecal sludge using drying beds in Ghana: Implications for nutrient recycling in urban agriculture', *Water Research* 40: 75–82 <http://dx.doi.org/10.1016/j.watres.2005.10.023> [accessed 22 May 2018].

Crites, R. and Tchobanoglous, G. (1998) *Small and Decentralized Wastewater Management Systems*, Boston, MA: WCB McGraw Hill.

Dodane, P-H. and Ronteltap, M. (2014) 'Unplanted drying beds', in L. Strande, M. Ronteltap, and D. Brdjanovic (eds.), *Faecal Sludge Management: Systems Approach for Implementation and Operation*, London: IWA Publishing <https://www.un-ihe.org/sites/default/files/fsm_ch07.pdf> [accessed 26 January 2018].

Dodane, P-H., Mbéguéré, M., Kengne, I.M. and Strande Gaulke, L. (2011) 'Planted drying beds for faecal sludge treatment: lessons learned through scaling up in Dakar, Senegal', *Sandec News* 12 <www.eawag.ch/fileadmin/Domain1/Abteilungen/sandec/publikationen/EWM/Treatment_Technologies/Planted_drying_beds_Dakar.pdf> [accessed 22 February 2018].

Edwards, J.K., Gray, K.R., Cooper, D.J., Biddlestone, A.J. and Willoughby, N. (2001) 'Reed bed dewatering of agricultural sludges and slurries', *Water, Science and Technology* 44(10–11): 551–8.

Haseltine, T.R. (1951) 'Measurement of sludge drying bed performance', *Sewage Works Journal* 23(9).

Heinss, U. and Koottatep, T. (1998) *Use of Reed Beds for Faecal Sludge Dewatering*, Eawag/Sandec <https://www.sswm.info/sites/default/files/

reference_attachments/HEINSS%20and%20KOOTTATEP%201998%20
Use%20of%20Reed%20Beds%20for%20FS%20Dewatering.pdf>
[accessed 22 February 2018].

Heinss, U., Larmie, S.A. and Strauss, M. (1998) *Solids Separation and Pond
Systems for the Treatment of Faecal Sludges in the Tropics: Lessons Learnt and
Recommendations for Preliminary Design*, Sandec Report No. 5/98, 2nd edn,
Dübendorf, Switzerland: Eawag/Sandec <https://www.ircwash.org/sites/
default/files/342-98SO-14523.pdf> [accessed 21 March 2018].

Joceline, S.B., Koné, M., Yacouba, O. and Arsène, Y.H. (2016) 'Planted sludge
drying beds in treatment of faecal sludge from Ouagadougou: case of two
local plant species', *Journal of Water Resource and Protection* 8: 697–705
<http://dx.doi.org/10.4236/jwarp.2016.87057> [accessed 22 May 2018].

Jong, V.S.W and Tang, F.E. (2014) 'Septage treatment using pilot vertical flow
engineered wetland system', *Pertanika Journal of Science and Technology*
22(2): 613–25 <https://espace.curtin.edu.au/bitstream/handle/20.500.1193
7/46255/234719_234719.pdf?sequence=2> [accessed 23 March 2018].

Kengne, I.M. and Tilley, E. (2014) 'Planted drying beds', in L. Strande, M.
Ronteltap, and D. Brdjanovic (eds.), *Faecal Sludge Management: Systems
Approach for Implementation and Operation* <https://www.un-ihe.org/sites/
default/files/fsm_ch08.pdf> [accessed 22 February 2018].

Kengne, I.M., Dodane, P-H., Akoa, A. and Koné, D. (2009) 'Vertical-flow
constructed wetlands as sustainable sanitation approach for faecal sludge
dewatering in developing countries', *Desalination* 248(1–3): 291–7 <http://
dx.doi.org/10.1016/j.desal.2008.05.068> [accessed 22 May 2018]

Kengne, I.M., Kengne, E.S., Akoa, A., Benmo, N., Dodane, P-H. and Koné,
D. (2011) 'Vertical-flow constructed wetlands as an emerging solution for
faecal sludge dewatering in developing countries', *Journal of Water, Sanitation
and Hygiene for Development* 1(1): 13–19 <http://dx.doi.org/10.2166/
washdev.2011.001> [accessed 22 May 2018]

Kinsley, C. and Crolla, A. (2012) *Septage Treatment Using Reed and Sand Bed Filters,
Goulet Pilot Project*, Final Report to the Ontario Ministry of Environment,
Ontario Rural Wastewater Centre, Université de Guelph-Campus d'Alfred
<www.uoguelph.ca/orwc/Research/documents/Septage%20Treatment%20
Using%20Reed%20and%20Sand%20Bed%20Filters%20Final%20
Report%20to%20MOE.pdf> [accessed 26 February 2018].

Koné, D., Cofie, O., Zurbrugg, C., Gallizzi, K., Moser, D., Drescher, S. and
Strauss, M. (2007) 'Helminth eggs inactivation efficiency by faecal sludge
dewatering and cocomposting in tropical climates', *Water Research* 41(19):
4397–402 <http://dx.doi.org/10.1016/j.watres.2007.06.024> [accessed 22 May
2018].

Koottatep, T., Surinkul, N., Polprasert, C., Kamal, A., Koné, D., Montangero, A.,
Heinss, U. and Strauss, M. (2005) 'Treatment of septage in constructed
wetlands in tropical climate: lessons learnt after seven years of operation',
Water Science and Technology 51(9): 119–26.

Kuffour, R.A. (2010) *Improving Faecal Sludge Dewatering Efficiency of Unplanted
Drying Bed* (PhD Thesis), Department of Civil Engineering, Kwame Nkrumah
University of Science and Technology, Kumasi, Ghana <https://ocw.un-ihe.
org/pluginfile.php/4126/mod_resource/content/1/Kuffour_Improvement%20
Unplanted%20Drying%20Beds.pdf> [accessed 16 April 2018].

Lusaka Water and Sewerage Company (2014) *Scientific Monitoring of Quality of Sludge at Kanyama Water Trust: Comparing Efficacy of Different Beds Designs, Drying Beds Designs Performance*, Unpublished report for WSUP.

Metcalf & Eddy (2003) *Wastewater Engineering: Treatment and Reuse*, 4th edn, New York: McGraw Hill.

Nikiema, J., Cofie, O. and Impraim, R. (2014) *Technological Options for Safe Resource Recovery from Fecal Sludge*, Resource Recover and Reuse Series 2, International Water Management Institute (IWMI), CGIAR Research Program on Water, Land and Ecosystems (WLE) <www.iwmi.cgiar.org/Publications/wle/rrr/resource_recovery_and_reuse-series_2.pdf> [accessed 26 March 2018].

Pescod, M.B. (1971) 'Sludge handling and disposal in tropical developing countries', *Journal of the Water Pollution Control Federation* 44(4): 555–70.

Seck, A., Gold, M., Niang, S., Mbéguéré, M., Diop, C. and Strande, L. (2015) 'Faecal sludge drying beds: increasing drying rates for fuel resource recovery in Sub-Saharan Africa', *Journal of Water, Sanitation and Hygiene for Development* 5(1): 72–80 <http://dx.doi.org/10.2166/washdev.2014.213> [accessed 22 May 2018].

Simba, F.M., Matorevhu, A., Chikodzi, D. and Murwendo, T. (2013) 'Exploring estimation of evaporation in dry climates using a Class 'A' evaporation pan', *Irrigation & Drainage Systems Engineering* 2(2): #1000109 <http://dx.doi.org/10.4172/2168-9768.1000109> [accessed 22 May 2018]

Sonko, el Hadji, M., Mbéguéré, M., Diop, C., Niang, S. and Strande, L. (2014) 'Effect of hydraulic loading frequency on performance of planted drying beds for the treatment of faecal sludge', *Journal of Water Sanitation and Hygiene for Development* 4(4): 633–41 <http://dx.doi.org/10.2166/washdev.2014.024> [accessed 22 May 2018].

Strande, L., Ronteltap, M. and Brdjanovic, D. (2014) *Faecal Sludge Management: Systems Approach for Implementation and Operation*, London: IWA Publishing <www.eawag.ch/fileadmin/Domain1/Abteilungen/sandec/publikationen/EWM/Book/FSM_Ch0_Table_of_Contents.pdf> [accessed 2 March 2017].

Tan, Y.Y., Tang, F.E., Ho, C.L.I. and Jong, V.S.W. (2017) 'Dewatering and treatment of septage using vertical flow constructed wetlands', *Technologies* 5: 70 <https://doi.org/10.3390/technologies5040070> [accessed 22 May 2018].

Troesch, S., Lienard, A., Molle, P., Merlin, G. and Esser, D. (2009) 'Treatment of septage in sludge drying reed beds: a case study on pilot-scale beds', *Water Science and Technology* 60(3): 643–53 <https://hal.archives-ouvertes.fr/hal-00453160/document> [accessed 12 March 2018].

Uggetti, E. (2011) *Sewage Sludge Treatment in Constructed Wetlands: Technical, Economic, and Environmental Aspects Applied to Small Communities of the Mediterranean Region* (PhD thesis), Universitat Politècnica de Catalunya, Barcelona, Spain <http://gemma.upc.edu/images/downloads/thesis/tesis_enrica%20uggetti.pdf> [accessed 12 March 2018].

Uggetti, E., Ferrer, I., Castellnou, R. and Garcia, J. (2010) *Constructed Wetlands for Sludge Treatment: A Sustainable Technology for Sludge Management*, Barcelona: GEMMA Environmental Engineering and Microbiology Group <http://gemma.upc.edu/images/downloads/libros/constructed%20wetlands%20for%20sludge%20treatment-libro1.pdf> [accessed 13 February 2018].

Vater W. (1956) *Die Entwntwässerung Trocknung und Beseitigung von Städischen Klärschlamm*, Doctoral dissertation, Hannover Institute of Technology, Germany, p. 10.

Wang, L., Li, Y., Shammas, N.K. and Sakellaropoulos, G.P. (2007) 'Drying beds', in *Handbook of Environmental Engineering, Volume 6: Biosolids Treatment Processes*, Chapter 13, Totowa, NJ: The Humana Press Inc., <https://doi.org/10.1007/978-1-59259-996-7_13> [accessed 22 May 2018].

CHAPTER 10

Additional solids treatment for safe disposal or end use

The last link in the sanitation service chain is reuse or safe disposal of the products of treatment. Products with potential for reuse include dried sludge, treated supernatant water and leachate, and biogas. Previous chapters have included information on options for reuse of liquid and biogas. This chapter deals with the further treatment that is required to allow the safe end use of separated and dewatered solids. It first sets out basic principles and then describes technologies that use these principles to produce usable products. Some of these technologies have not yet been implemented beyond the pilot scale and so require further work to establish their technical and financial viability when implemented at scale.

Keywords: biosolids, end use, agricultural conditioner, biofuel, animal feed

Introduction

Separated faecal sludge solids, referred to here as biosolids, may be used in place of conventional resources including energy, nutrients, and water. In doing so, they will contribute to the Sustainable Development Goals (SDGs) on combating climate change, providing affordable energy, and reducing use of natural resources. It has been suggested that treated sludge might be used as a soil conditioner, building material, and biofuel and in the production of animal feed (Diener et al., 2014). To date, there are no known cases of the commercial use of treated faecal sludge as a building material and so this book does not consider this option. Researchers have explored the possibility of converting faecal sludge into biodiesel but have concluded that, while this is technically possible, it is not financially viable because of the high cost of drying and the low content of extractable lipids in the sludge (Tamakloe, 2014). This chapter therefore focuses on the treatment required prior to use of biosolids as a soil conditioner, a solid fuel, and an input to the production of animal feed. Its main concern is with the treatment of biosolids derived from faecal sludge and septage. However, most of the technologies and approaches described are equally applicable to the treatment of solids derived from wastewater treatment processes. They could therefore be used following septage and faecal sludge co-treatment at wastewater treatment plants. Additional treatment to remove heavy metals and other contaminants may be necessary where these are present in the sludge to be treated and the intention is to use biosolids as an agricultural additive. This is more likely to be the case for sludge from co-treatment plants than for those that only treat faecal sludge and septage.

http://dx.doi.org/10.3362/9781780449869.010

When added to the soil, biosolids increase its solids content and improve its structure. If added to a clayey soil, they can make the soil more friable and increase the amount of pore space available for root growth and entry of water. Conversely, if added to a sandy soil, they can increase its water-holding capacity and provide sites for nutrient exchange and adsorption (US EPA, 1995). Biosolids add some nutrients to the soil but are much less effective in this respect than artificial fertilizers. Dried sludge can be converted into fuel briquettes for industrial or household use. Alternatively, it is possible to use pyrolysis to produce charcoal and gas, both of which have potential for use as fuel, from dried sludge. To date, the main focus of attempts to develop the animal-feed option has been on growing black soldier fly larvae on faecal sludge. The larvae are a good source of protein and can be dried, packaged, and sold as animal feed.

Sludge that has been dewatered using the methods described in Chapter 9 typically has a solids content in the range 15–40 per cent and contains large numbers of pathogens. Further treatment will be required to ensure that separated solids are suitable and safe for the end uses identified above. Figure 10.1 shows possible treatment options for each of these end uses, together with the option of disposal to landfill without further treatment.

Some of the processes identified in Figure 10.1 require a high solids content. For sludge that is to be composted, this is achieved by mixing the sludge with a suitable 'bulking agent': a material with a relatively high solids content. Other options for increasing the solids content of sludge include extended retention on sludge drying beds and solar drying. Extended retention on drying beds involves the methods that have already been considered in Chapter 9. Achieving a high solids content, will require a longer time and, therefore, a large drying bed area. Solar drying is also considered in this chapter. It may be used either as a stand-alone drying option or to reduce the water content of sludge to the point at which other treatment options become feasible and financially viable.

Preconditions and requirements for solids end use

Preconditions for solids end use include those relating to finance and health. In addition to these preconditions, this section considers the dry solids content requirements of various processes, and examines the calorific value of dried biosolids, which is important when considering the possibility of using dried sludge as a fuel.

Financial preconditions

Initiatives to use biosolids, as either an agricultural input or a fuel will only be successful if they are financially viable. As already stated in Chapter 4, this requires that:

$$R_{TP} + S \geq C_{TP} - C_D$$

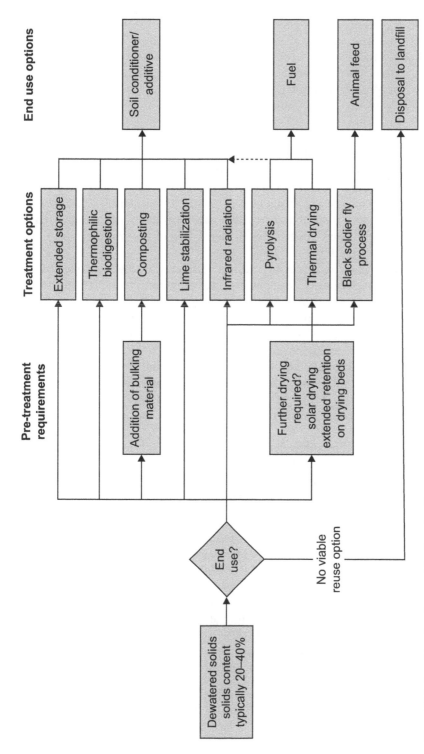

Figure 10.1 Overview of end-use and treatment options

where: R_{TP} is the revenue generated from the sale of treated products;

S is any subsidy that is available to promote the reuse of treated products;

C_{TP} is the cost of the additional treatment required to render the products of treatment suitable for reuse; and

C_D is the cost of disposal if no additional treatment for reuse is provided.

The term C_{TP} should normally include all recurrent costs, including equipment purchase and replacement costs. Subsidies might take the form of carbon credits provided to support efforts to replace fossil fuels with carbon neutral fuels. In theory, complete cost recovery is dependent on including an allowance for the amortized cost of capital investment in C_{TP}. In practice, the construction costs that constitute most or all of the required capital investment are often covered by higher levels of government and do not appear in the equation.

Subsidies may be direct or indirect. Direct subsidies will usually take the form of payments to operators to contribute to their day-to-day operating costs. One form of indirect subsidy will be funding for construction by a third party, typically government or an international agency. Another might be payment of a higher than market price for treated products. When assessing the financial viability of an end use option, it will be important to be clear about how initial capital costs and any future replacement costs will be funded. Regardless of the availability of government grants for capital construction, long-term financial viability requires that income covers future replacement costs as well as day-to-day operating costs.

Sales of treated products depend on the market for these products. If there is no demand for a product, it cannot be sold and so will generate no revenue. Market research will be required to assess current and potential demand for various end uses. This should include the following:

- Identification of any modifications required to existing technologies to allow them to use treated biosolids. (For example, would kilns need modification to allow the use of biosolids as a fuel?)
- Assessment of treated biosolids availability in relation to demand, taking account of seasonal variations in production and demand and likely supply shortfalls. Options for supplementing biosolids with other materials, for instance agricultural or municipal wastes, in order to reliably meet user demand should be explored.
- Assessment of marketing, distribution, and sales systems: what changes in existing systems will be required to ensure that treated biosolids can be sold to their intended users?

Schoebitz et al. (2016) provide further information on implementation of a market-driven approach to faecal sludge treatment products.

Health-related preconditions

A second precondition for biosolids end use initiatives is that they should pose no significant threat to the health of either workers or consumers. Reduction of health risk to an acceptable level will require treatment to reduce the pathogen content to safe levels as defined by international and national guidelines and standards. Table 10.1 sets out key points from the World Health Organization and US EPA guidelines on pathogen limits for biosolids that are to be used in agriculture. Where national guidelines exist, they are normally based on the WHO guidelines.

The WHO guideline figures quoted in Table 10.1 are conservative. As noted in Chapter 4, WHO now advocates the use of quantitative microbial risk assessment (QMRA) to assess health risks. Using this approach, Navarro et al. (2009) showed that higher helminth egg concentrations in biosolids did not significantly increase consumers' and farmers' health-risk exposure, concluding that the indicative guideline value of ≤1 helminth egg per gram total solids (TS) in biosolids was unnecessarily stringent. WHO now recognizes that health risks may be addressed using a lower level of solids treatment alongside a more holistic focus on biosolids management. This holistic approach might include a withholding period (a period when no new biosolids are added) to allow pathogen die-off prior to harvest, good food hygiene (such as washing with clean water), and cooking of food (WHO, 2006).

Local organizations will often lack the resources to gather the information required to carry out a QMRA. Where this is the case, it will usually be easier to define acceptable pathogen levels in relation to the intended end use of the treated biosolids, as recommended in the USA's Part 503 Biosolids rule (EPA, 1994). This distinguishes between Class A biosolids, suitable for unrestricted use, and Class B biosolids, suitable for use on arable land used to grow crops that are not to be consumed raw and to which there will be no public access for more than a year after application. Biosolids that meet Class B requirements are also suitable for use on forest land and spreading on woodlots which may be good options for the relatively small volumes of biosolids produced by many faecal sludge and septage treatment plants. Table 10.2 summarizes the requirements for biosolids to be accepted as Class A and Class B. The challenge with this approach, as with an approach based on meeting biosolids quality standards, will be to ensure that the various stakeholders comply with standards and guidelines and follow recommended procedures. Education may be as important as enforcement in this respect.

The Class A biosolids requirement for faecal coliforms is much more stringent than that for Class B biosolids. The discrepancy between the two standards appears to be greater than would logically be expected and it is arguable that it will normally be desirable to achieve lower faecal coliform concentrations for Class B biosolids than suggested by Table 10.2.

To achieve Class A biosolids status, US EPA requires that treatment options that rely on temperature alone must raise the temperature of biosolids with

Table 10.1 Recommended pathogen requirements for biosolids reuse: WHO and US EPA

Organization	Guideline requirements	Source
World Health Organization	Helminth egg count: ≤1 egg per gram of total solids *E. coli*: ≤1 000 count per gram of total solids	WHO (2006)
US Environmental Protection Agency (Part 503 biosolids rule)	Class A biosolids: faecal coliform density ≤1,000 per gram of total dry solids, or *Salmonella* subspecies (spp) density ≤3 per 4 grams of total dry solids Class B biosolids: faecal coliform density ≤2,000,000 per gram of total dry solids	US EPA (1994)

Table 10.2 US EPA Part 503 Biosolids Rule requirements for Class A and Class B biosolids

	Class A requirements	Class B requirements
Pathogens	Density of faecal coliforms ≤1,000 per g of total solids (dry weight basis) Density of *Salmonella* ≤3 most probable number (MPN) per 4 g of total solids (dry weight basis) Density of enteric viruses ≤1 PFU (plaque forming unit) per 4 g of total solids (dry weight basis) Density of viable helminth ova ≤1 per 4 g of total solids (dry weight basis)	Density of faecal coliforms ≤2,000,000 per gram of total dry solids
Vectors	The Part 503 Rule lists 12 options for reducing vector attraction to biosolids. Nine of these are intended to reduce the attractiveness of biosolids to vectors. They include anaerobic and aerobic composting, drying to high solids content, and alkaline treatment using lime. The remaining three work by preventing vectors from coming into contact with the biosolids by either injecting biosolids into the soil or covering them.	
Pollutants	All biosolids applied to agricultural land must not exceed ceiling concentrations for pollutants which include heavy metals. The guide to the Part 503 Rule lists maximum allowable concentrations for 10 heavy metals. Staying within these limits should not normally be a problem for biosolids derived from domestic sanitation facilities.	

a solids content greater than 7 per cent to a temperature of at least 50°C for a time t (days), which should not be less than either 20 minutes or the time given by the equation:

$$t = 131,700,000/(10^{0.14T})$$

where T is the temperature in degrees Celsius (US EPA, 1994: Table 5-3). The equation is very sensitive to temperature, giving values of t of 13.17 days, 12.58 hours, 30 minutes, and 71 seconds for temperatures of 50°C, 60°C, 70°C, and 80°C, respectively. The 20 minute requirement reduces to 15 seconds if the biosolids are in particle form and heated by contact with either warmed gases or immiscible liquid (liquid that will not combine with the biosolids). The requirements for biosolids with a solids content of less than 7 per cent are slightly less stringent.

Table 10.5 sets out the US EPA Part 503 Biosolids Rule requirements for processes that use a combination of raised temperature and high pH to remove pathogens.

Where it will be difficult to achieve Class A biosolids status, because a process is either difficult to control and monitor or has high operational costs, a more realistic objective will be to achieve the much lower standards required for Class B biosolids.

The need to reduce pathogen concentrations in products used for animal feed and solid fuel receives less attention than that for biosolids intended for use in agriculture. However, when contemplating such uses, there is still a need to consider the health risk to workers who come into contact with the biosolids. The best way to deal with this health risk will be to ensure that workers follow practices designed to protect their health. These include wearing protective clothing, particularly gloves, when handling potentially hazardous materials and hand washing with soap after every contact with such materials. Where direct worker contact with biosolids cannot be avoided, it will be advisable to ensure that the biosolids meet the Class B requirements set out in Table 10.2.

Dry solids content requirements

Depending on the proposed end use, further increase in the dry solids content of biosolids may be required after the dewatering processes described in Chapter 9. The requirements of specific treatment processes and end uses are as follows:

- *Combustion*. Dry solids content should be at least 80 per cent and preferably higher. The precise requirements will depend on the process used to burn the sludge.
- *Composting*. For optimum results, the dry solids content should be in the range 40–45 per cent. This corresponds to a water content which, in the case of compost, is normally referred to as its moisture content, of 55–60 per cent. It is possible to achieve solids contents in the required range by increasing the retention time on sludge drying beds; however, the more usual approach is to co-compost dewatered sludge with materials that have both a higher carbon to nitrogen ratio and lower moisture content.
- *Thermal drying*. It is possible to use heat to evaporate water from sludge with any water content but the energy requirement increases with increased water content. For this reason, it will usually be advisable to reduce the water content of sludge prior to thermal drying.
- *Pyrolysis*. As with thermal drying, the energy requirements of pyrolysis increase with increased water content and so further reduction of the water content of sludge from drying beds will normally be advisable.
- *Biological processing using black soldier flies*. The dry solids content of the sludge should be in the range 10–40 per cent (Dortmans et al., 2017).

It is possible to create a circular process in which the heat generated by burning dried sludge is used to dry wet sludge to the point at which it becomes combustible. This approach is used by technologies such as the Janicki Omniprocessor (Janicki Bioenergy, undated). The process typically becomes self-sufficient in energy when the sludge has a solids content in the range 15–20 per cent, with the exact figure depending on the calorific value of the sludge and the efficiency of the process. When the solids content of the sludge is below the level at which the process becomes self-sufficient in energy, an external source of energy will be required. When the solids content exceeds this level, the process can generate energy, clean water, or both. The volume of clean water produced will be less than the volume of sludge treated.

Calorific value

A precondition for proposals to create solid fuel from faecal matter is that the calorific value of the dried sludge is high enough to make the solid fuel option technically and financially viable. The calorific value of faecal matter is affected by the way in which it has been retained on site. It will thus vary between cities and between tanks and pits within cities. For example, investigations in three African cities, Kumasi, Dakar, and Kampala, revealed average calorific values for untreated faecal sludge of 19.1 MJ/kg TS, 16.6 MJ/kg TS, and 16.2 MJ/kg TS, respectively (Muspratt et al., 2014). The calorific value of digested sludge is less than that of untreated sludge. The average calorific value of samples collected from anaerobic waste stabilization ponds in Kumasi ranged from 14.6 MJ/kg for ponds that were currently in use to 11.3 MJ/kg for those that had been off-line for six months. These results represented a 25–40 per cent drop from the calorific value of raw faecal sludge. The loss in calorific value over time in the ponds is explained by the release of carbon in the form of methane and carbon dioxide during anaerobic digestion. These figures compare with typical calorific values of around 15 MJ/kg for lignite (poor quality coal) to around 43 MJ/kg for diesel and other oil-based fuels. The calorific values of methane and natural gas are about 40 MJ/m^3 and 43 MJ/m^3, respectively. These figures suggest that dried faecal sludge has potential as a solid fuel but that upstream anaerobic treatment should be avoided if biosolids are to be used as a fuel. The challenge is to develop processes and technologies that will realize this potential in a way that is financially viable. The Pivot Works initiative in Kigali, Rwanda, which is described in Box 10.7, is an example of the use of dried faecal sludge and septage biosolids as a solid fuel.

Options for reducing pathogen concentrations

The primary function of five of the technologies shown in Figure 10.1 is to reduce pathogen concentrations: storage for an extended period, composting, lime stabilization, infrared radiation, and thermophilic biodigestion. Thermal drying and pyrolysis are very effective at killing pathogens, but their main use to date has been to prepare biosolids for use as a fuel. Storage for an extended period is simple but is difficult to control and monitor, with the result that its effect on pathogen concentrations is similarly difficult to predict. Composting and lime stabilization are both considered in detail below. Information is also provided on a South African initiative that uses infrared radiation to produce safe biosolids.

The use of small-scale biogas digesters to reduce the odour and vector attraction problems associated with fresh, poorly digested sludge has already been described in Chapter 6. These small-scale systems usually operate in the mesophilic range and do not involve either externally powered mixing or heating. They are unlikely to have a large impact on pathogen concentrations and are not therefore an appropriate option for treatment prior to end use. Large-scale anaerobic digesters are widely used to reduce and stabilize solids at centralized wastewater treatment plants in industrialized countries. They rely on mechanical mixing and therefore require a reliable power source. Most operate in the mesophilic range and require a long retention time to inactivate pathogens. The US EPA (Part 503) specifies a minimum solids retention time of 15 days at 30–55°C and 60 days at 20°C to sufficiently reduce pathogens for Class B biosolids. The retention period required for pathogen inactivation will be reduced by providing external heating to maintain thermophilic temperatures in the digester. This reduces the digester volume required but results in higher operational costs. Due to their complexity and expense, large-scale anaerobic digesters will not be feasible for most faecal sludge and septage treatment applications in lower-income countries. For this reason, they are not considered further in this book.

Storage for an extended period

The simplest option for reducing pathogen concentrations is to store dried sludge for a long period. It may be considered in areas with a dry climate where space to accommodate stored sludge is available. The difficulty with this option is to determine the storage period required. In Cameroon, Kengne et al. (2009) concluded that the health risks associated with handling sludge from planted drying beds would be minimal if at least six months elapsed between the application of wet sludge to the drying bed and removal of the dried solids. Gallizzi (2003) quotes the findings of Veerannan (1977) that the *Ascaris* egg count in stored sludge was reduced by 50 per cent after 1 year and 100 per cent after 3 years. Other researchers quoted by Gallizzi recorded smaller egg-count reductions. Schwartzbrod (1997) found that storage of dried sludge for 16 months at a temperature of 25°C effectively eliminated *Ascaris* ova but that storage at 4°C was ineffective, indicating that die-off rates are temperature dependent. The die-off rate will also be influenced by moisture content and the size and shape of the storage heap. Pathogen regrowth may occur during storage depending on temperature and moisture conditions.

Given the difficulty of managing the conditions under which sludge is stored, it will normally be appropriate to allow a large margin of safety when assessing storage requirements. If the sludge is covered so that it remains dry, the storage period should not be less than 18 months. Where sludge may be subject to periods of wet weather, during which its moisture content rises, the storage period should be at least 3 years. These figures are provisional and may be amended if testing shows good pathogen reduction in a shorter period. In view of the uncertainties associated with extended storage, sludge that has been stored for an extended period should be assumed to meet only the requirements for a Class B biosolid and used accordingly.

To reduce the risk of surface water pollution, sludge should not be stored on sites where the slope of the ground exceeds 2 per cent or at locations that are subject to occasional flooding. The possibility of groundwater pollution should also be considered. To reduce the possibility, sites for extended storage should be located in areas where the water table is well below the surface, preferably at least 3–4 m below, throughout the year. Even so, for all but the most impermeable soils the provision of an impermeable 'pad' is desirable. Concrete and asphalt are commonly used for composting pads but they are relatively expensive. Other options include clay and filter fabric overlaid with gravel (Cornell Waste Management Institute, 2005). Drainage should be provided to direct leachate towards simple treatment facilities such as ponds and constructed wetlands. Where a risk of groundwater pollution cannot be avoided, groundwater monitoring wells or lysimeters should be installed (Olds College Composting Technology Centre, 1999). The challenge will then be to ensure that samples are regularly taken and analysed. The Canadian Code of Practice quoted by the Olds College Composting Technology Centre sets standards for chloride, nitrate, and pH. However, faecal coliforms, viewed as an indicator of pathogens, will be the main concern in most lower-income countries.

Berms should be provided to divert stormwater run-off around the drying area and provision should be made for collecting and safely disposing of any contaminated water that escapes from the drying sludge. Pathogens will die off more rapidly if the storage area is covered to keep off rain. However, the cost of roofing over the large area required must be taken into account when assessing this option.

Composting

System description

Composting uses aerobic decomposition to break down organic material under controlled conditions and produce stabilized products that do not smell. The activities of the aerobic microorganisms that use oxygen to convert carbon to carbon dioxide generate heat and raise the temperature of the compost. Pathogens in the composting material will be inactivated if the compost temperature can be maintained in the thermophilic range (40–70°C) over a sufficient time period, as explained in more detail below.

Achieving the required temperature conditions requires that the water content and carbon to nitrogen (C:N) ratio of the composting material are maintained within fairly restricted ranges and that sufficient free air space is available to provide the oxygen required for aerobic microbial activity. To achieve these conditions faecal sludge is usually co-composted with a suitable bulking agent: a material that has both a high carbon content and a low water content. It may also be necessary to add water to maintain the moisture content within the optimum range. Materials commonly used as bulking agents include municipal solid waste, agricultural waste, and sawdust. The volume of bulking agent required is typically 2–5 times the volume of faecal sludge, the ratio depending on the C:N ratio and the water content of the sludge and bulking agent. The stabilized product is a dark, humus-like material, which can be added to soil to increase its organic content and improve water retention.

Composting options include the following:

- *Windrow composting.* The material to be composted is formed into long piles, which are typically triangular or trapezoidal in section and 1.25–2.5 m in height, with a width to height ratio of roughly 2 to 1. The piles must be large enough to retain heat and ensure that thermophilic conditions are reached but porous enough to allow oxygen flow to its core. Windrows must be turned at regular intervals to maintain porosity and allow oxygen into the core of the windrow.
- *Aerated static-pile composting.* The material to be composted is placed in piles, typically around 2 m deep, and covered with 150–300 mm of a finished compost or another suitable material to reduce heat loss. Blowers are used to pump air into the piles through pipes laid under the piles. The use of aeration removes the need for labour to turn the compost. Additionally, the forced aeration better controls the process and the time needed is generally lower than for turned windrow composting. However, these systems are more expensive than turned windrow systems and require good maintenance systems, an effective supply chain, and a reliable power source.
- *In-vessel composting.* The material to be composted is placed in enclosed reactors with systems to control temperature, moisture, and odours. Commercial in-vessel composters are expensive and relatively complex and are unlikely to be suitable for treatment plants in lower-income countries.

To date, most initiatives to compost faecal sludge have used windrow composting. Box 10.1 provides information on initiatives to co-compost faecal sludge at scale.

The viability of composting depends on the availability of:

- land to accommodate the composting process;
- either labour or mechanical equipment to carry out the tasks associated with composting, particularly the turning of windrow piles;

Box 10.1 Examples of co-composting of faecal sludge

Balangoda, Sri Lanka. Treated septage is co-composted with municipal solid waste in a publicly owned compost plant, which produces 420 tonnes of compost annually. Sales are to small farmers, plantations, and government institutions (Rao et al., 2016).

Hanoi City, Vietnam. Dried faecal sludge is co-composted with market organic waste in Cau Dzien composting plant, a privately managed enterprise. The plant produces approximately 4,500 tonnes per year, significantly less than the design capacity of 13,600 tonnes per year. The compost is reported to exceed Vietnam standards of arsenic and coliforms for reuse (Nguyen et al., 2011).

Kushtia, Bangladesh. A pilot treatment plant has capacity to produce 4 tonnes of co-composted faecal sludge and organic waste per day (Enayetullah and Sinha, 2013).

Nairobi, Kenya. Sanergy, a company based in Nairobi, uses windrow composting to co-compost faecal sludge removed from its container-based sanitation systems with agricultural waste. It has also piloted aerated static pile composting (Kilbride and Kramer, 2012). Photo 10.1 shows the Sanergy windrow composting facility. In 2017, Sanergy removed about 5,000 tonnes of faecal waste from 'Fresh Life' toilets in Nairobi's slums and produced about 425 tonnes of composted soil conditioner/fertilizer from this waste (Jan Willem Rosenboom, personal communication, May 2018).

Photo 10.1 Sanergy windrow composting facility Nairobi
Source: photo by Jan Willem Rosenboom

Haiti. The NGO SOIL co-composts faecal sludge and agricultural wastes in a bin-composting system that uses neither turning of the compost nor induced aeration (Berendes et al., 2015; Remington et al., 2016). The temperature of the compost is checked regularly. After a minimum of two months in a bin, the compost is transferred to windrows where it is composted under less controlled conditions for a further 4–6 months (Kramer et al., 2011).

Accra, Ghana. A new composting plant, operated under a public–private partnership arrangement and with a design based on a decade-long research initiative by the International Water Management Institute (IWMI) in Kumasi and Accra (see Box 10.2), has the capacity to produce 500 tonnes of pelletized compost per year from 12,500 m³ of faecal sludge and 700 tonnes of sorted organic (food) waste (IWMI, 2017). The proportion of sorted food waste in the sludge/food waste mix appears to be lower than that in the other systems identified in this box.

- a market for soil-conditioning material produced from composted material;
- a reliable and inexpensive source of carbon-rich waste for use as a bulking agent; and
- operational capability and management support systems to monitor the composting process.

Composting objectives and performance

The overall objective of composting is to reduce pathogens to safe levels. However, testing for pathogens requires specialist equipment and skills and can be expensive. In view of this, the normal practice is to monitor temperature during the composting process and adjust process parameters to ensure that minimum temperature and time criteria are met. Table 10.3 sets out the US EPA (Part 503) temperature and time requirements for Class A and Class B biosolids. Meeting these requirements will be difficult but not impossible in cold climates.

Based on the review of field data compiled by Feachem et al. (1983), Vinnerås et al. (2003) derived equations to predict the relationship between composting temperature and time required for total removal of viable *Ascaris* and *Schistosoma* organisms. The equation for *Ascaris* is:

$$t = 177 \times 10^{-0.1922(T - 45)}$$

where t is time in days and T is temperature in degrees Celsius. It predicts that the time required to inactivate *Ascaris* eggs will be 19 days, 2 days, and 6 hours at pile temperatures of 50°C, 55°C, and 60°C, respectively. These requirements are less demanding than those of the US EPA Part 503 for Class A biosolids. This is, perhaps, because the US EPA requirements take account of, the need to allow time for compost to heat up. Studies of co-composted municipal sewage plant sludge in southern California found that windrows 1.2–1.5 m in height took around 20 days to reach a temperature of 55°C and that faecal coliform concentrations fell to <1/100 g dry solids after 25 days (Iacoboni et al., 1984). The WHO guideline of ≤1,000 FC/g dry solids was reached after about 15 days, at which point the temperature in the compost pile had reached about 50°C. The study in Kumasi, Ghana, described in Box 10.2, suggests that the time taken to inactivate *Ascaris* eggs is likely to be longer than the time predicted by the Vinnerås equation.

Table 10.3 US EPA Part 503 temperature and time criteria for composting

Class	Requirement
Class A (unrestricted use)	*Windrow composting*: Temperature must be >55°C for at least 15 days and windrows must be turned at least five times
	Aerated static pile or vessel: Temperature must be >55°C for at least 3 days
Class B (restricted use)	Temperature must be >40°C for at least 5 days and >55°C for at least 4 hours within the 5-day period

---

Box 10.2 Investigation of helminth egg inactivation, Kumasi, Ghana

In a study at Kumasi in Ghana (Gallizzi, 2003; Koné et al., 2007), two 3 m³ compost heaps were formed of 1 m³ of dewatered sludge and 2 m³ of organic waste from local markets. The sludge consisted of public toilet sludge and septage mixed at a 1:2 ratio and dewatered on a drying bed to achieve a solids content of about 20 per cent. The compost was monitored over two composting cycles, each comprising the following phases:

- an active phase during which the compost was regularly turned to aerate its contents and watered if the moisture content fell below 50–60 per cent; and
- a passive phase, during which it was left to mature without watering or turning.

During both cycles, the active phase lasted about 60 days, while the passive phase lasted for three weeks during the first cycle and six weeks during the second cycle. The first heap was turned when its temperature exceeded 55°C, initially around three times per week and later once per week. The second heap was turned at intervals of 10 days, irrespective of temperature. Samples taken from the inside and outside of the heap while turning the compost showed temperature differences of up to 10°C. Recorded temperatures exceeded 45°C for around 40 days on the inside and 20 days on the outside of both heaps. At the end of the second cycle, after about 110 days, the helminth egg numbers recorded in the final biosolids ranged from 0.2 to 1.7/g TS; i.e., below or very close to the WHO requirement.

Operational and design considerations

Active and passive composting. Many composting initiatives include an active phase, during which compost is regularly turned, followed by a passive phase during which compost is left in piles without turning. The inclusion of a passive composting phase increases the likelihood that pathogen concentrations in the finished compost will have been reduced to acceptable levels, but increases the area required for composting, typically by a factor of about two.

Turning and mixing options. When planning for a composting initiative, the options for procuring supplies of a suitable bulking agent, transporting it to the treatment facility, and mixing it with the sludge should be assessed. Manual turning of windrows is labour intensive and mechanical equipment in the form of front-end loaders will be required at larger facilities, the operation and maintenance needs of which must be assessed at the planning stage.

Larger windrows hold more compost mixture than smaller windrows and will achieve the temperature required for pathogen inactivation more quickly, but require a greater level of effort for turning. In view of this, windrows that will be turned by hand should be smaller than windrows that will be turned by machinery.

Moisture content. As already indicated, best results will be obtained when the compost moisture content lies in or close to the range 55–60 per cent. In order to maintain the moisture content within this range, operators must be able to assess it. Simple manual methods can provide a qualitative assessment of compost moisture content. If the compost water content is within the optimum range, the compost should have the feel of a 'wrung out' sponge. Squeezing a handful of compost should produce a trickle of water. Options for quantitative assessment include gravimetric methods, which require that compost is weighed before and after it has been dried. Gravimetric methods are accurate but require oven drying facilities and accurate weighing scales. Commercially produced moisture sensors provide another moisture content assessment option. For further information on these options, see Rynk (2008).

Aeration. Effective composting is only possible if the compost remains aerobic, providing sufficient oxygen for microorganisms to thrive. Free air space must be available in the compost pile to allow the circulation of air. The addition of a bulking agent helps to increase the free air space and so facilitates aeration. Forced aeration and turning the compost increase the air supply and improve air circulation. There are few examples of the use of forced aeration in lower-income countries. SOIL's experience in Haiti, which is briefly described in Box 10.3, suggests that the addition of a low-density bulking agent, such as bagasse, can provide sufficient air space to enable composting to proceed without either forced aeration or turning, but this point needs further research.

Testing and monitoring requirements. The C:N ratio and water content of composite samples of both the sludge to be composted and one or more potential bulking materials should be tested at the planning stage and the information obtained

---

Box 10.3 SOIL – Haiti: A simple approach to bin composting

The NGO SOIL operates a bin-composting system to treat faecal sludge collected from a container-based sanitation system. The system receives about 21 tonnes of faecal waste per month, which converts to about 4 tonnes of useful compost per month (Remington et al., 2016). Each compost bin is 3 m × 6 m in plan and about 1 m high at the sides and 1.5 m high at the centre. Each bin is filled with a mixture of faecal sludge and bagasse (the residue left after sugar has been extracted from sugarcane) over a period of two weeks. Once the bin is full, a 5–10 cm layer of sugarcane husk, mixed with palm fronds, is placed on top of the pile to help to retain heat and protect the pile contents from wind. The pile is not mixed over the 6-month composting period but the pile is frequently watered during the first 2–3 months, using urine collected from the urine-diversion toilets to maintain a C:N ratio of around 30:1. An investigation of bin performance in 2012 reported the following findings (Berendes et al., 2015):

- Temperatures in the centre of the bins were in the range 60–70°C for the first two weeks and remained above 58°C until the compost was moved to an open area pile after 6 months. Temperatures in the corners of the bins were lower, with none recorded at higher than 51°C.
- The moisture content of the untreated latrine waste averaged 79 per cent, while that in the bins averaged around 70 per cent during the first two weeks and then fell to an average of about 45 per cent in the final samples.

The baseline concentration of *E. coli* in untreated latrine waste samples ranged between 10^6 and 10^7 per g dry weight. Recorded levels after 10 days were mostly in the range 10^3–10^5 per g dry weight. After 75 days, *E. coli* levels were below the detectable limit of about 10^2 per g dry weight, regardless of depth or location within the compost pile.

After a minimum of two months in a bin, the compost is transferred to windrows where it is composted under less controlled conditions for a further 4–6 months (Kramer et al., 2011).

from testing should then be used to determine an appropriate ratio of sludge to bulking material, as described below. Once the composting process is operational, the temperature of the sludge should be regularly monitored to ensure that the requirements for inactivation of pathogens are met. Temperatures should be recorded at several points in the compost pile, including points close to the surface. This can be done using a long-stem compost thermometer. If the compost heap is correctly sized, failure to achieve the temperature required for pathogen reduction is an indication that the water content, the C:N ratio, or both are outside the range required for effective composting. Martin et al. (1995) describe a sampling protocol for compost.

Access. Space must be provided around windrows and compost bins to allow access. Where mechanical turning using front-end loaders is required, the access routes must be wide enough to allow them to work.

Rainwater exclusion. Placing windrows under cover will exclude rainwater, which might otherwise take the water content of the compost outside the optimal range. The sides of the covering structure should be open to allow cross-ventilation. Given the high cost of roofing, it may be appropriate to provide cover over the active composting area but leave the area required for subsequent passive composting open to the elements.

Environmental considerations. As already described in the sub-section on storage for an extended period, locations that are subject to occasional flooding and where the water table is close to the surface during the wet season should be avoided. Where there is a risk of groundwater contamination, monitoring wells or lysimeters should be provided to allow monitoring of groundwater quality.

Design criteria and procedure

As already noted, the composting process is affected by the compost moisture content, its C:N ratio, and the availability of air to ensure that the process remains aerobic. The moisture content and the C:N ratio are adjusted by mixing sludge with a suitable dry, carbon-rich bulking agent. Since the moisture content is the most critical factor and is also the easiest to test during operation, the normal practice is to select a sludge-to-bulking-agent ratio to achieve an optimum moisture content and then check that the C:N ratio is reasonably close to its optimum range. Determination of air requirements is not explicitly included in the calculation procedure outlined below. In lower-income countries, the availability of air will normally be ensured by a combination of selection of an appropriate low-density bulking agent and regular turning of the compost rather than forced aeration. With these introductory points in mind, the compost-mix design process is outlined below.

1. Calculate the mass of bulking agent required to give a mix with optimum moisture content for composting:
    The moisture content of the dewatered sludge is typically in the range 70–80 per cent. For effective composting, the moisture content

should lie in the range 55–62 per cent (WEF, 2010). The amount of bulking agent required to achieve a moisture content within the optimum range is calculated using the equation:

$$MC_{mix} = \frac{(m_s \times MC_s) + (m_{BA} \times MC_{BA})}{m_s + m_{BA}}$$

where: MC = moisture content (%);
$\quad\quad m$ = mass (kg/day);
$\quad\quad_s$ = dewatered sludge;
$\quad\quad_{BA}$ = bulking agent; and
$\quad\quad_{mix}$ = mixture of dewatered solids and bulking agent.

This formula can be rearranged to find the mass of bulking agent required to reach the chosen optimum moisture content:

$$m_{BA} = \frac{m_s (MC_s - MC_{mix})}{MC_{mix} - MC_{BA}}$$

The mass of sludge is calculated using the equation:

$$m_s = V_s \rho_s$$

where: m_s = mass of sludge to be composted (kg/d);
$\quad\quad V_s$ = volume of sludge to be composted (m³/d); and
$\quad\quad \rho_s$ = density of sludge (kg/m³).

2. Calculate the volume of the bulking agent (V_{BA}) required, based on its estimated bulk density (ρ_{BA}):

$$V_{BA} = \frac{m_{BA}}{\rho_{BA}}$$

Table 10.4 gives indicative information on the moisture contents of common bulking agents. The moisture content at a particular site will be affected by climate and storage conditions. When possible, tests to determine the moisture content of the proposed bulking agent should be carried out.

3. Determine the C:N ratio of the mix:

Composting is most effective when the C:N ratio is in the range 25–35 to 1 (WEF, 2010). At C:N ratios lower than 25, the temperature will not increase to sufficient levels for pathogen inactivation and ammonia gas is likely to form, producing an odour. Conversely, C:N ratios greater than 35 lead to reduced microbiological activity and lower temperatures in the compost (WEF, 2010). The C:N ratio of dewatered sludge is much lower than the optimum range required for effective composting: Nartey et al. (2017) reported a ratio of 11:1 for dewatered faecal sludge in Ghana, and Chazirakis et al. (2011) reported a ratio of 5.5:1 for dewatered sewage sludge in Crete.

To raise the C:N ratio to the figure required for effective composting, material with a high carbon content must be mixed with faecal sludge. Fortunately the materials used to adjust the moisture content of the compost mix are also rich in carbon. The C:N ratio of the mixture of dewatered sludge and bulking agent is calculated using the equation:

$$CN_{mix} = \frac{\left[m_s\left(100 - MC_s\right) \times c_s\right] + \left[m_{BA}\left(100 - MC_{BA}\right) \times c_{BA}\right]}{\left[m_s\left(100 - MC_s\right) \times n_s\right] + \left[m_{BA}\left(100 - MC_{BA}\right) \times n_{BA}\right]}$$

where: CN = carbon to nitrogen ratio;
MC = moisture content (%);
m = mass (kg/day);
c = proportion of carbon (as given in C:N ratio for component);
n = proportion of nitrogen (as given in C:N ratio for component);
$_s$, $_{BA}$ and $_{mix}$ denote dewatered sludge, bulking agent and mixture of dewatered sludge and bulking agent respectively

Table 10.4 gives typical values for a range of materials commonly used as bulking agents.

Studies have revealed large variations from some of the figures given in Table 10.4. For instance, Zhang et al. (2012) found the bulk density of rice husk, measured at locations on three continents, to lie in the range 332–381 kg/m³, three times the density given in Table 10.4. This variation in density perhaps reflects the effect of storage arrangements. Whatever the reason, it points to the need to determine the density of materials proposed as bulking material under the field conditions in which they are to be used.

4. Determine the area required for active composting:
After determining the volume of bulking agent required, the area required for an active composting facility can be determined.

Table 10.4 Typical moisture contents, C:N ratios and bulk density values of selected bulking agents

Bulking agent	Moisture content (%)	C:N ratio	Bulk density (kg/m³)
Paper/newspaper[1,2]	4–6	150–500:1	100–500
Vegetable waste[1,2,3]	80 (variable)	10–15:1	470–600
Grass clippings[1,2,3]	60–80	12–25:1	240–480
Corn straw[4,7]	9	30–60:1	50
Rice husk[4,5]	8–10	110:1	90–110
Bagasse[4,6]	9	170:1	100–200
Leaves[1,2,3]	10–50	30–80:1	90–400
Brush and tree trimmings[1,3]	40–50	200–500:1	150–300
Wood chips and sawdust[1,2,3]	5–20	100–500:1	180–360

Notes [1] CalRecovery Inc. (1993); [2] Hirrel et al. (undated); [3] Michigan Recycling Coalition (2015); [4] Danish et al. (2015); [5] NIIR (undated); [6] Hobson et al. (2016); [7] Thoreson et al. (2014)

Crites and Tchobanoglous (1998) give the following equation for estimating the area required for active composting:

$$A = \frac{1.1S(R + 1)}{H}$$

where: A = pad area for active compost piles (m²);
$\quad\quad S$ = total volume of sludge produced in 4 weeks (m³);
$\quad\quad R$ = ratio of bulking agent to sludge (m³/m³); and
$\quad\quad H$ = height of the compost pile, not including cover or base material (m).

This equation assumes a 28-day composting time, which is significantly shorter than the composting times used for the examples described in Boxes 10.2 and 10.3. A more accurate calculation of the area required for active windrow composting can be obtained by assuming a windrow profile, allowing an appropriate working space around each pile and working out the area required to contain the volume of combined sludge and bulking agent undergoing active composting. The area required for bin composting is likely to be smaller, since the bin sides will retain the compost.

5. Determine other space requirements:
The facility must provide space for:

- storage of dewatered faecal sludge and bulking agent;
- mixing the faecal sludge with the bulking agent;
- active composting;
- passive composting (maturation phase);
- final screening of the compost; and
- storage and bagging of the compost.

The layout must also provide space for access to move materials around the site and allow turning of compost piles. More space will be required when turning is done using a tractor fitted with a front-end loader. For typical passive composting times of 30–60 days, the area required for it will be at least as great as that required for active composting. The area required for sludge and bulking-agent storage and mixing will depend on the procedures for receiving and mixing the materials. In order to minimize space requirements, the aim should be to mix compost and move it to active composting areas within one or two days of it being received. Final screening and bagging will not require a large area. Bagged compost should preferably be stored under cover. The area required for this will depend on the speed with which bagged compost can be removed from the treatment facility for sale to customers. One way to maximize throughput of treated compost, and so minimize the storage area required, will be to establish relationships with retailers who will buy bagged compost in bulk and sell it on to customers.

Design example: co-composting

Prepare an outline design for a co-composting plant to treat 10 m³ of dried sludge per day. It has been determined that there is a viable market for biosolids use as a soil conditioner for landscaping applications and that rice husk is readily available as a co-composting material. Labour is relatively inexpensive and there is a poor supply chain for mechanical parts. Therefore, windrow composting is considered to be the most appropriate method. The target moisture content for the mix to be co-composted is 60 per cent. The basic design parameters and assumptions are listed below.

Parameter	Symbol	Value	Units
Volume of sludge after dewatering	V_s	10	m³/d
Density of dewatered sludge	ρ_s	1,050	kg/m³
Bulk density of bulking agent (rice husk)	ρ_{BA}	100	kg/m³
Moisture content of sludge	MC_s	75	%
Moisture content of bulking agent (rice husk)	MC_{BA}	9	%
C:N ratio of sludge	$C:N_s$	6	
C:N ratio of bulking agent	$C:N_{BA}$	110	

1. Calculate the mass of bulking agent (m_{BA}) required to reach the design moisture content.

$$m_{BA} = \frac{\left(10 \text{ m}^3/\text{d} \times 1050 \text{ kg/m}^3\right) \times (75 - 60)}{60 - 9}$$
$$= 3088 \text{ kg bulking agent required/day}$$

2. Calculate the volume of the bulking agent (V_{BA}) required according to its estimated bulk density (ρ_{BA}):

$$V_{BA} = \frac{3,088 \text{ kg/d}}{100 \text{ kg/m}^3} = 31 \text{ m}^3/\text{d bulking agent required}$$

3. Check if the C:N ratio of the dewatered sludge and bulking-agent mixture is within the optimum range:

$$CN_{mix} = \frac{\left[(10 \text{ m}^3/\text{d} \times 1050 \text{ kg/m}^3)(1 - 0.75) \times 6\right] + \left[(31 \text{ m}^3/\text{d} \times 100 \text{ kg/m}^3)(1 - 0.09) \times 110\right]}{\left[(10 \text{ m}^3/\text{d} \times 1050 \text{ kg/m}^3)(1 - 0.75) \times 1\right] + \left[(31 \text{ m}^3/\text{d} \times 100 \text{ kg/m}^3)(1 - 0.09) \times 1\right]} = 30$$

This C:N ratio of 30 is within the range for effective composting.

4. Estimate the area required for active composting:
   Assume the treatment plant operates 6 days per week and the height of the windrows is 1.5 m:

$$A = 1.1 \times 10 \text{ m}^3/\text{day} \times 4 \text{ weeks} \times 6 \text{ days/week} \times \frac{\left[(31 \text{ m}^3/10 \text{ m}^3) + 1\right]}{1.5 \text{ m}} = 720 \text{ m}^2$$

5. Determine the area required for storage of untreated sludge and bulking agent material.

Co-composting design example

Diaz et al. (2007) and Sunar et al. (2009) provide more detailed information on composting processes.

Assume that bulking agent is delivered at weekly intervals. The volume to be accommodated will be 186 m³ and that of sludge will be 60 m³. Assuming that the bulking agent is held in some form of bin, with an average depth of 1 m, a 15 m × 15 m bin will provide the required storage. Assuming that sludge is stored in a bin to a depth of 1 m, the required storage area will be about 60 m², requiring plan dimensions of about 8 m × 8 m. More space will be required if the sludge and bulking agent are to be stored in piles rather than bins. The best option for determining the space required for access will be to prepare a scale drawing showing the proposed layout of the composting facility.

Lime stabilization

System description

Lime stabilization involves the addition of either quicklime (CaO) or hydrated lime (Ca(OH)$_2$), also known as calcium hydroxide or slaked lime, to the sludge. Both increase the pH of the sludge and quicklime also reacts with the water in the sludge to raise its temperature. To ensure pathogen inactivation, the lime must be evenly mixed through the sludge. Lime-stabilized biosolids can be added to soil, increasing the pH, and so are particularly beneficial for acidic soils. They should not be added to alkaline soils. Lime-stabilized biosolids are generally lower in nitrogen than other biosolids products as nitrogen is converted to ammonia during processing (US EPA, 2000). Quicklime reacts violently with water and its use is potentially hazardous. To date, all lime-stabilization initiatives in lower-income countries have used hydrated lime and the focus of this brief introduction is on this option.

Lime can be applied to faecal sludge or septage prior to solids–liquid separation and dewatering, when the relatively high water content facilitates mixing. Adding lime to septage or faecal sludge at the start of the treatment process reduces odours but increases the volume of sludge to be dealt with at later in the treatment process. If lime is added at the end of the treatment process, the higher solids content of the dewatered sludge will make mixing more difficult. Specialized mechanical equipment, including pugmills, paddle mixers, and screw conveyors, is available to ensure effective mixing of lime with thicker, dewatered solids. As with other types of mechanical equipment, this equipment requires effective maintenance and repair procedures and good supply chains for spare and replacement parts. Regardless of the mixing method adopted, the use of lime as a long-term response to sludge stabilization and pathogen reduction needs will only be viable if hydrated lime is available at an affordable price.

Required and actual performance

Inactivation of pathogens by lime stabilization is dependent on the addition of sufficient lime to achieve a minimum pH and temperature for a minimum contact time. Table 10.5 sets out the US EPA guidelines for the results to be achieved for lime stabilization to produce Class A and Class B biosolids (US EPA, 2000).

When using hydrated lime, an external heat source will be required to meet the temperature conditions required to produce Class A biosolids. For this reason, lime stabilization with hydrated lime should normally be considered only as an option for achieving the less onerous Class B biosolids requirements. The findings on helminth egg ova reduction summarized in Box 10.4 show that lime stabilization does not reliably remove helminth ova.

Operational and design considerations
Lime availability and cost. Hydrated lime is produced by adding water to crushed quicklime, which in its turn is produced by heating crushed limestone in a kiln. In the past, kilns were small and fairly simple, but lime production is now an industrial process. Lime availability therefore depends on the existence of an in-county lime-production process. The cost of lime should be taken into account when comparing the operational costs of different treatment options.

Preparing the hydrated lime solution. Hydrated lime is available in the form of a powder. Good mixing of dry lime and sludge is difficult and the normal procedure is to mix the dry lime with water to form a slurry, which is then mixed with the sludge. The mixing ratio is typically one 20 kg bag of lime to 60–80 litres of water (USAID, 2015).

Mixing options. Complete pathogen inactivation is only possible if the lime is thoroughly mixed into the sludge. When mixing by hand, it is difficult

Table 10.5 US EPA Part 503 lime stabilization requirements

Class of biosolids	pH and contact time	Temperature	Additional requirements
Class A	>12 for 72 hours	52°C for >12 hours or 70°C for >30 minutes	Air dry to >50% dry solids
Class B	>12 for 2 hours	No requirement	None

Box 10.4 Examples of pathogen reduction using hydrated lime

Laboratory-scale trials in Blantyre, Malawi on pit latrine sludge with solids content in the range 9–12 per cent achieved reduction in *E. coli* levels to below the detectable limit of $10^4/100$ ml within 1 hour of treatment at pH 11 and above. Follow-up trials with 600 litres of sludge in a 1,000-litre container achieved 1,000 *E. coli*/100 ml within one hour at pH 12. In both cases an agitator was used to mix the lime with the sludge. Regrowth of bacteria occurred at lower pH values (Greya et al., 2016).

Removal of helminth ova is more difficult. Bean et al. (2007) found that faecal coliforms and salmonella were undetectable after 2 hours of lime stabilization at a pH of 12, but *Ascaris lumbricoides* ova and *Cryptosporidium parvum* oocysts remained viable after 2 hours at pH 12 followed by 70 hours at pH 11.5. Similarly, Bina et al. (2004) found that the reduction in the number of helminth ova after 5 days was only 56 per cent and 83.8 per cent at pH 11 and pH 12, respectively.

to ensure complete mixing of the lime with the sludge with the result that the sludge may not reach the pH of 11 or greater required for elimination of pathogens (USAID, 2015). Mechanical mixing will therefore be required for all but the smallest of facilities. Overdosing with lime does not compensate for poor lime mixing (North et al., 2008). The long-term viability of mechanical mixing is dependent on a reliable source of power, adequately skilled operators, and a good supply chain for spare and replacement parts.

Monitoring requirements. The pH of the mixture must be monitored at regular intervals to verify that it is held at the required level for the required time.

Health and safety issues. Hydrated lime can irritate the skin, eyes, lungs, and digestive system and it is therefore important that workers who handle lime, or work in close proximity to it, wear appropriate personal protective equipment. Workers should have access to an appropriately stocked first-aid box and guidance on the procedures to be followed in the event of eye and skin irritation (see National Lime Association (2004) for an overview of lime safety requirements).

Lime storage. Hydrated lime must be kept dry prior to use and so a dry lime-storage area must be provided on-site.

Design criteria and procedure
The key question for lime stabilization design is the lime dosage required to raise the pH of the sludge to the required level. This depends on the dry solids content of the sludge to be stabilized. Figures quoted in the literature for anaerobically digested sludge and septage fall within the range 0.1–0.5 kg of calcium hydroxide ($Ca(OH)_2$) per kg dry weight of sludge treated. Analysis of available figures for lime stabilization in lower-income countries suggests a narrower range, with 0.25–0.35 kg of hydrated lime typically required per kg of dry sludge.

A simple design example is shown below. Additional information on design criteria for lime stabilization of dewatered sludge is available from US EPA (2000).

For the calculation in the design example to be valid, the lime must be completely mixed with the sludge. Hand-mixing sludge with a 20 per cent solids content will be very difficult and a mechanical mixer will therefore be required. One option for facilitating hand-mixing with paddles will be to add water to the sludge but this will increase subsequent dewatering requirements. Where mechanical mixing is to be considered, it will normally be best to determine the basic design parameters and then request outline proposals from several manufacturers. The request for proposals should specify that manufacturers must demonstrate that they have some form of local presence and can thus provide operational support, including provision for supply of spare and replacement parts.

Design example: preliminary lime dosing assessment

Lime stabilization is to be considered as a treatment option for faecal sludge from pit latrines. The design load is 10 m³/d of faecal sludge with a solids content of 20 per cent (200 kg/m³). Hydrated lime with a 90 per cent $Ca(OH_2)$ content is available in 25 kg bags. Jar tests suggest that 0.3 kg of $Ca(OH_2)$ will be required per kg of dry solids to raise the pH of the sludge to the level required to produce Class B biosolids. To ensure continued operation in the event of a disruption in hydrated lime supply, storage for 14 days' supply of lime is to be provided. The table below summarizes the design parameters.

Parameter	Symbol	Value	Units
Faecal sludge loading rate	Q_s	10	m³/d
Sludge solids content		20	%
Contact time for Class A biosolids		pH >12 for 12 hours AND maintain temperature above 52°C for 72 hours AND final solids >50%	
Lime dose (determined through bench-scale testing)	D_{lime}	0.3	kg $CA(OH)_2$/kg sludge solids

1. Calculate amount of lime required per day.

$$\text{Dry weight of sludge to be treated} = 10 \text{ m}^3/\text{day} \times \frac{200 \text{ kg dry solids}}{\text{m}^3 \text{ wet sludge}} = 2{,}000 \text{ kg/day}$$

$$D_{lime} = \frac{2{,}000 \text{ kg dry sludge}}{\text{day}} \times \frac{0.3 \text{ kg}(OH)_2}{\text{kg dry sludge}} \times \frac{1 \text{ kg lime as supplied}}{0.9 \text{ kg } Ca(OH)_2}$$

$$= 667 \text{ kg lime as supplied/day}$$

2. Calculate lime storage required:
   Lime storage required = 667 kg/day × 14 days =9,338 kg
   Storage is thus required for 9,338/25 = 374 25-kg bags

Infrared radiation

Medium-wave infrared is an invisible form of electromagnetic radiation that is emitted by objects at high temperatures. It heats objects more rapidly than conventional heating and is used, for example, in the food industry to increase the surface temperature of food sufficiently to kill microorganisms without causing any substantial increase in interior temperature. Because of its low penetration, it will only be appropriate for pathogen inactivation in sludge if the sludge has first been processed to break it up into small particles. Box 10.5 provides information on a treatment process that incorporates infrared radiation.

Box 10.5 Infrared pasteurization: Latrine sludge dehydration and pasteurization (LaDePa)

In South Africa, eThekwini Water and Sanitation, a unit of eThekwini Municipality, working with Particle Separation Solutions (Pty) Ltd (PSS) to develop the LaDePa process, which uses medium-wave infrared irradiation to convert pit latrine sludge into a soil conditioner. The process is powered by a diesel generator (Septien et al., 2018) and is designed to deal with sludge containing a high percentage of garbage and other detritus. The feed sludge must have a solids content of 25–30 per cent, which is typical for faecal sludge removed from pit latrines in South Africa. The LaDePa system owned by eThekwini Water and Sanitation has a treatment capacity of 1.5 m³/h (or 12 m³/day) and was designed to treat the waste from 35,000 ventilated improved pit latrines (VIP) latrines, which eThekwini Water and Sanitation is responsible for emptying on a 5-year cycle. The stages in the process are as follows:

- Sludge and detritus taken from pits is compressed in a screw compactor that has lateral ports through which compressed sludge is ejected. Detritus is ejected through the end of the screw compactor.
- The separated sludge falls onto a porous steel conveyor belt, on which it forms a layer, typically 25–40 mm thick.
- The belt carries the sludge through a pre-dryer, heated by the exhaust gases from the diesel generator.
- The sludge then passes through a machine, patented by PSS, which subjects it to medium-wave infrared radiation. Power is provided by electricity produced by the diesel generator while a vacuum draws air through the sludge as it passes along the belt, extracting more water. The temperature of the sludge is raised by the combined effects of the infrared radiation and the exhaust gases from the diesel generator.
- The dried and pasteurized sludge falls off the far end of the moving belt and is then collected and bagged.

During the process, the sludge is heated to temperatures above 100°C for about 8 minutes. This, together with the exposure to infrared radiation, kills pathogens, including helminth eggs, and makes the bagged sludge safe for reuse as an agricultural conditioner.

The LaDePa system requires minimal labour, has a low footprint, and is housed in two standard shipping containers allowing the plant to be moved to other locations as necessary. Its main disadvantages are its power dependency and its reliance on mechanical equipment. At the time of writing (May 2018) eThekwini Water and Sanitation was finalizing a leasing agreement with the technology developer covering four LaDePa machines and including tests of the technology with wastewater treatment plant sludge (Teddy Gounden, personal communication, May 2018).

Drying options

Two drying options are considered in this section, solar drying and thermal drying. In addition to removing water, both reduce pathogen levels. Thermal drying is particularly effective in this regard and will produce Class A biosolids.

Solar drying

System description
Solar drying is an option for increasing the solids content of sludge to the levels required for some of the treatment options identified in Figure 10.1.

It can also be used as a stand-alone sludge drying technology. It differs from simple unplanted drying beds in the following respects:

- *The beds are housed within greenhouse-type structures*, which are typically formed from translucent polyethylene mounted on a metal frame.
- *It relies entirely on evaporation to remove moisture*. The transparent covering prevents the ingress of rain and increases the temperature of the air above the sludge, so increasing the evaporation rate. Ventilation is required to remove moist air from above the beds and replace it with dryer air, so maximizing the evaporation that can be achieved. Natural wind-based ventilation, based on wind, will have some effect, but most solar drying systems incorporate fans to circulate air and prevent warm air from rising.
- *The sludge must be regularly turned*. Turning brings wet sludge to the surface, thereby increasing the potential for evaporation.

Commercially available solar dryers may operate in either batch or continuous mode. Sludge is turned by a series of combs and paddles, which cut the surface of the sludge and allow aeration of the lower layers. In systems that operate in continuous mode, this 'tilling' mechanism also moves the sludge slowly along the length of the bed. The bed may be flat or may be provided with a gentle slope away from the end at which the sludge is delivered. Figure 10.2 shows a solar drying facility for septage and faecal sludge treatment.

Most of the understanding of performance of solar drying is based on studies and operational data from wastewater treatment plants. Since the basic mechanisms are the same, information obtained from assessing solar drying

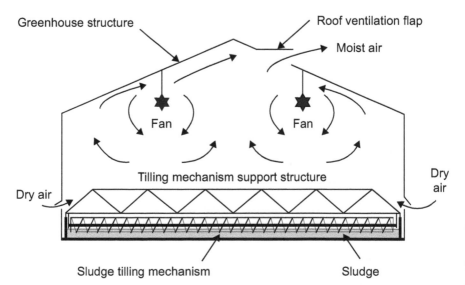

Figure 10.2 Solar drying in a greenhouse

performance at wastewater treatment plants should be generally applicable to septage and faecal sludge treatment plants.

Performance range
The main factors influencing the rate at which sludge will dewater on a solar drying bed are the amount of solar radiation, the air temperature, the relative humidity, and the depth of sludge. Relative humidity is strongly influenced by the ventilation flux, the rate at which saturated air is removed from the greenhouse and replaced by relatively dry air. There is some evidence that the initial total solids content also influences performance (Seginer and Bux, 2005). Studies in temperate climates show that, in favourable environmental conditions and with effective operation, sludge of approximately 15–20 per cent initial solids content can be dried to 70–95 per cent solids content in 15–30 days (Bux et al., 2001; Paluszak et al., 2012; Mathioudakis et al., 2013), report drying from 20 per cent initial solids to 70–80 per cent solids in 7 days in Kigali, Rwanda, using manual turning. Analysis of investigations of a pilot plant in Greece show that the depth of sludge has an important bearing on the drying time and that loadings in excess of 500 kg dry solids/m^2 year can be achieved at temperatures of 20°C and above when the solids content of the incoming sludge is greater than 15 per cent (Mathioudakis et al., 2013). Where possible, site-specific pilot trials should be conducted to determine the actual drying time.

Solar drying reduces pathogen numbers but studies reach varying conclusions as to the extent of this reduction (see Box 10.6). In view of the uncertainty about the degree of pathogen reduction achieved, the solids produced by solar drying should at best be considered as Class B biosolids, to be applied to fields that are not used to grow vegetables that are eaten raw.

Operational and design considerations

Solar drying requires mechanical equipment and a reliable electricity supply. Manual operation of solar drying facilities is labour intensive, requiring manual conveyance of dewatered sludge to the solar drying area, and regular manual mixing and turning of the sludge. For all but the smallest facilities, mechanical tilling devices will be required to turn the sludge. Maintenance systems, supported by reliable supply chains for spare parts, must be in place to ensure the continued functioning of all mechanical equipment. A reliable electricity supply must be available to provide power for ventilation fans and tilling devices.

Mechanical tilling devices can be automated to ensure optimum drying performance. Automated systems can provide effective and efficient performance, but have additional operational requirements and require trained operators with a good understanding of the monitoring instruments and the automation system.

Number and configuration of drying beds. Multiple beds in parallel should be provided so that beds can be loaded sequentially. At least one additional

---

Box 10.6 Examples of pathogen removal by solar drying

Solar drying of sludge from the Maroochydore sewage treatment plant in Queensland, Australia achieved reductions in virus, helminth, salmonella, and *E. coli* counts sufficient to meet the New South Wales EPA Guidelines on use of sludge as a Grade A soil conditioner. The results for bacterial indicators, particularly faecal coliforms, were inconclusive. The tests were carried out on two rectangular drying beds, with the sludge depth varying from 150 mm to 300 mm. Roll-down plastic sheets were used to exclude rain without blocking solar radiation and it is possible that these blocked short wavelength ultra violet radiation, which is most effective in killing off pathogenic microorganisms (Shanahan et al., 2010).

A study of the impact of solar drying of sludge at a sewage treatment plant in Poland found limited impact upon faecal streptococci and *E. coli*, with only a 2-log reduction in concentration recorded after 4 weeks. Deactivation of *Ascaris suum* eggs was even more limited, with more than 90 per cent of live eggs remaining after 28 days (Sypuła et al., 2013).

A study of pilot-scale solar drying beds in Lusaka, using sludge from Manchinchi wastewater treatment plant and ecological toilets (Phiri et al., 2014), found that oocysts for the protozoon *Cryptosporidium parvum* were reduced by 62 per cent after 1 week, and were totally eliminated from the biosolids after 2 weeks of treatment. No viable *Ascaris lumbricoides* eggs were found after 4 weeks. The research team noted that the time taken to eliminate pathogens was longer than that recorded by other studies, suggesting as a possible reason that the study had been carried out in the rainy season when long overcast periods reduced exposure to sunlight.

---

bed should be provided in addition to the number required for continuous operation to allow beds to be taken out of commission for maintenance and repair.

Other maintenance needs. The greenhouse covering should be cleaned regularly to ensure that a build-up of dust and grime does not block solar radiation and hence reduce drying performance.

Design criteria and procedure

The design procedures for solar drying beds are similar to those for unplanted drying beds, which have already been set out in Chapter 9. Critical design parameters are the solids content of the incoming sludge, the required solids content of the dewatered sludge, the depth to which the incoming sludge is loaded on the bed, and the dewatering cycle time. Drying performance will also be influenced by the ventilation rate. As with unplanted drying beds, design of solar beds should be based on hydraulic/volumetric loading rather than an assumed maximum solids loading rate.

Dewatering cycle time. The drying time is a key design variable and this, in turn, influences the dewatering cycle time and determines the number of times a bed can be loaded in a year. The drying time depends on a number of factors, including the required solids content of the treated sludge, the solids content of the untreated sludge, the evaporation rate, and the sludge depth. The evaporation rate similarly depends on a number of factors, the most important of which are solar radiation, air temperature, ventilation rate, and dry solids content of the sludge (Seginer and Bux, 2005).

Sludge depth. This should lie in the range 150–400 mm, with higher depths possible for systems with mechanical mixing. Mathioudakis et al. (2013) report using a sludge depth of 150–200 mm for sewage sludge solar drying in Greece, achieving up to 95 per cent dry solids content after 8–31 days, depending on weather conditions. Mehrdadi et al. (2007) suggest a depth of sludge of 150–350 mm. The effort required to turn the sludge increases with sludge depth and this means that deeper beds will be dependent on mechanical systems to mix and turn the sludge. In some systems, sludge is moved along the bed by the mixing and turning equipment, getting progressively drier as it moves along the bed. This will result in a reduction in sludge depth with distance along the bed. The difference in depth between the two ends may be 100 mm (Hoffman et al., 2014).

Ventilation rate. A study by Bux et al. (2001) on modelling of evaporation rate found that, for the study location in Füssen, Germany, the optimal ventilation rate was at least 150 m³/m² floor space. The ventilation rate may range below and above these examples, depending upon the specification.

Seginer and Bux (2005) developed the following equation to predict evaporation from a solar drying bed:

$$E = 0.000461R_o + 0.00101Q_v + 0.00744T_o - 0.22\sigma + 0.000114Q_m$$

where: E = evaporation rate (mm/h);
R_o = outdoor solar radiation (W/m²);
Q_v = ventilation rate (m³/m² h);
T_o = air temperature (°C);
σ = dry solids content (kg solids/kg sludge);
Q_m = air mixing rate (m³/m² h).

In theory, this equation could be solved to determine the evaporation rate, which could then be used to calculate the dewatering rate. Integrating the dewatering rate over time would allow the change in water content of the sludge to be calculated. The calculation is complicated by the fact that the evaporation rate is influenced by the dry solids content, which changes over time. In practice, it will be easier to determine solar drying bed requirements using information on drying rates obtained from field studies. If specialized electromechanical and automated equipment is to be used, the supplier should be asked to propose the size of facility required and provide a performance guarantee based on that sizing.

Thermal drying

System description
Thermal drying involves heating of dewatered biosolids to evaporate water and hence reduce their water content. It serves to:

- reduce the sludge volume, so reducing any onward transportation costs for the treated product;

- raise temperature levels sufficiently to kill pathogens; and
- increase the specific (per unit volume) calorific value of the biosolids, an important consideration if the intention is to use dried solids as a fuel.

Thermal dryers fall into two basic categories: direct thermal dryers, in which hot air is directly blown over the sludge, and indirect thermal dryers, in which heat is transferred to the sludge from a heat transfer medium such as oil by conduction through the metal wall of the vessel holding the sludge. The heat transfer medium has no direct contact with the solids. The most commonly used types of direct dryer are rotary and belt dryers. The simplest form of dryer is the direct rotary dryer. This consists of a cylindrical steel shell that rotates on bearings and which is mounted horizontally, with a slight slope down from the feed end to the discharge end. The feed sludge is mixed with hot gases produced in a furnace and is fed through the dryer. As it passes through the dryer, flights (fin-like attachments to the wall of the cylinder) pick up and drop the sludge, causing it to cascade through the gas stream. Moisture in the sludge evaporates, leaving a much dryer material at the discharge end of the dryer. The dried sludge is separated from the warm exhaust gas, part of which is recycled to the dryer while the remainder is treated to remove pollutants and is then vented to the atmosphere. A rotary dryer was used in the Pivot Works plant in Kigali, Rwanda (see Box 10.7). Belt dryers operate at lower temperatures than rotary drum dryers. The heat from the furnace is transferred to a thermal fluid, which heats the air in the dryer. The dewatered cake that is to be dried is distributed onto a slow-moving belt, which exposes a high surface area to the hot air.

Indirect drying options include paddle dryers, vertical tray dryers, and an indirect type of fluidized-bed dryer (WEF, 2014). From the 1940s onwards, flash dryers were installed in the USA to dry municipal wastewater sludge, but few remained in operation by the end of the 20th century (WEF, 1998, quoted in Metcalf & Eddy, 2003). Fluidized-bed dryers have also been used in Europe and the USA to produce a pelletized product from sewage works sludge. They are more complex and require more energy than rotary dryers.

Both direct and indirect dryers require an outside energy source to provide the heat that is needed for drying. An electricity supply is typically also required to turn the dryer and to power a blower or pump to move the heating medium around the material to be dried.

Performance range

Metcalf & Eddy (2003) state that rotary dryers require a sludge feed with a water content of around 65 per cent to allow the sludge to move through the dryer without sticking. However, the experience of Pivot Works in Kigali is that solids content should be around 60 per cent (Ashley Murray Muspratt, personal communication, November 2017). To reduce energy requirements,

---

Box 10.7 Using a thermal dryer for beneficial solids reuse in Rwanda

In 2015, Pivot Works, a private company based in Kigali, Rwanda, reached agreement with Kigali Municipality to build and operate a facility to convert faecal waste from septic tanks and pit latrines into fuel. The facility produced about 1 tonne of biomass fuel per day, which was sold to private customers, mainly to a cement producer that used the dried sludge to fuel its kilns and a textile manufacturer that used the dried sludge to fire steam boilers. The price was competitive with the customers' alternative fuels, including seasonal biomass and imported coal.

The Pivot Works pilot plant was located at the site where vacuum tankers previously discharged septage removed from the city's septic tanks. On average, about 100 m^3/d of this septage was delivered to the Pivot Works factory. The factory also received 1–2 m^3/d of faecal sludge removed from pit latrines by its own team of workers. Typical solids contents of the septage and faecal sludge were 1 per cent and 7–12 per cent, respectively.

Septage and faecal sludge were dewatered using a microscreen and then passed through a solar drying process before a direct heat drum dryer was used to further increase the solids content to about 95 per cent. In addition to reducing the water content of the sludge, the dryer eliminated pathogens, making the product safe for handling by customers.

The Pivot Works approach was founded on the belief that it is possible to harness the economic potential of human waste and that facilities should be viewed as factories rather than treatment plants (Muspratt et al., 2017). This requires that fuel sales cover the operational costs of the plant. Pivot Works estimated that this objective could be achieved with a throughput of about 10 tonnes of dry solids per day. In practice, it proved difficult to achieve this level of throughput and the operation remained dependent on funds provided by international donors and investors. These proved to be either insufficient or unreliable and the company was dissolved and the plant ceased operations in December 2017. Several important lessons emerge from the Pivot Works experience. The first is that a private company with a focus on running a successful business can innovate and successfully operate technologies such as mechanical dewatering devices, solar drying beds, and sludge dryers. The second is that it is unrealistic to expect sales from treated products to cover the whole cost of treatment. Prior to the Pivot Works initiative, there had been no septage and faecal sludge treatment in Kigali. The company was therefore faced with the challenge of meeting the whole cost of treatment from solid-fuel sales. This is a much more onerous challenge than that suggested at the beginning of this chapter of meeting the additional cost of treatment to allow reuse. It suggests that there will be few situations in which facilities can be viewed purely as factories rather than treatment plants. Rather, there is a need for partnerships that recognize the role of public finance in rendering septage and faecal sludge safe for disposal (Muspratt, 2017). Public sector finance should arguably cover most or all of the public good aspect of treatment, in other words the treatment required to ensure that treated liquid and solids can be safely returned to the environment. The challenge will be to develop procedures and contract arrangements that ensure equitable sharing of costs, benefits, and risks between the partners.

---

solar drying can be used to reduce the water content of the sludge prior to thermal drying. The solids content of the dried sludge is typically in the range 90–95 per cent. Its pathogen content should be undetectable so that solids dried using a rotary dryer should achieve Class A biosolids status. The Pivot experience in Kigali shows that dried sludge with this solids content can be marketed as a solid fuel.

Operational and design considerations

Thermal dryers have a high energy requirement. 4.186 kJ (1 kcal) per degree Celsius is required to raise the temperature of one kilogram of water to boiling point. A further 2,260 kJ (540 kcal)/kg is required to evaporate the 90–95 per cent of the water content of the sludge that is removed during drying. Because bound water is both physically and chemically bound to the sludge, energy is required to release it from its bonds. Chun et al. (2012) report drying efficiencies of up to 84.8 per cent for a rotary drum dryer operating under optimum conditions and Crawford (2012) reports boiler thermal efficiencies up to 87 per cent for fluidized bed combustors. However, a combination of the additional energy required to release the bonds of bound water, heat losses in the exhaust and through the dryer body, steam generation and distribution losses, condensate losses, losses during start-up, shut-down, and low load periods, and other ancillary factors, means that the energy required for evaporation may only amount to 50 per cent of the total process energy requirement (Kemp, 2011).

Health and safety considerations. Thermal drying systems produce dust, particularly when the solids content exceeds 95 per cent. Dust removal, often using baghouse filters, is required for direct dryers. The system must be designed in a way that ensures that the equipment does not pulverize the product and produce more dust.

Operator training and skill requirements. Thermal drying equipment requires skilled operators who have been trained to operate the equipment correctly and safely, are able to troubleshoot problems, and who can repair simple equipment faults.

Manufacturer support. Technical support from the equipment manufacturer is highly desirable, and a reliable supply chain for spare and replacement parts is essential. If these conditions are not in place, thermal drying is unlikely to be viable. Manufacturer support should be sought at the design stage. The normal procedure is to specify the volume of sludge to be dried and the initial and final required water contents and ask manufacturers to produce a priced proposal for a dryer system to meet the specified performance requirements.

Design criteria and procedure
The energy required to evaporate the water from 1 kg of wet sludge is given by the equation:

$$E_{r,e} = \frac{\left[4.186(100 - T_a) + 2260(c_i - c_f) \right]}{\varepsilon}$$

where: $E_{r,e}$ = total energy requirement for evaporation (kJ/kg of wet sludge);
c_i = water content of the dewatered sludge;
c_f = water content of the dried sludge;
T_a = ambient temperature (°C);
ε = efficiency of the drying process;

4.186 = energy required to heat water (kJ/kg °C);

2,260 = energy required for vaporization (kJ/kg).

For an ambient temperature of 25°C and initial and final solids contents of 60 per cent and 95 per cent, respectively, the energy requirement to dry one kilogram of wet sludge is:

$E_{r,e}$ = 4.186 × (100 − 25) + [2260 × (0.95 − 0.6)] = 1,105 kJ/kg wet sludge
This equates to 1,105/0.6 = 2,762 kJ/kg of dry solids

This is the amount of heat energy transferred to the water. If the overall process efficiency is 60 per cent, the power requirement will be 2,762/0.6 = 4,603 kJ/kg of dry solids, equivalent to a little over 1.25 kWh.

It is possible to burn the dried solids to provide the energy required for the drying process. This principle is used in the Janicki Omniprocessor, of which one has been installed in Dakar, Senegal. This will reduce the considerable fuel bill that would otherwise be incurred to power the dryer. The energy produced through incineration ($E_{p,i}$) can be calculated as:

$$E_{p,i} = (1 - c_i) \times CV \times \varepsilon$$

where: $E_{p,i}$ = energy produced by incineration (per kg wet solids);

c_i = water content of the sludge (kg water/kg wet sludge);

CV = calorific value of sludge (MJ/kg TS); and

ε = efficiency of the process.

An example of a calculation to determine the sludge water content required for a system to be energy neutral is shown below. The calculation is simplified and is sensitive to the assumptions made regarding dryer and furnace efficiencies. At the assumed efficiencies, it suggests that an initial solids content of around 16.5 per cent is required for the system to be self-sufficient in energy. This is in line with the results quoted for the Janicki Omniprocessor. Bearing in mind the other factors that are likely to influence system efficiency identified by Kemp (2011), this calculation may represent a best-case scenario.

Box 10.7 describes an initiative that used a direct heat rotary drum dryer to produce biosolids that were successfully marketed as a solid fuel. The process incorporated solar drying prior to thermal drying.

Calculation for self-powered drying system

Set energy produced by incineration and energy required for evaporation equal to each other:

For the system to be energy neutral, the energy required for evaporation must be equal to the energy produced by incineration. To find the initial water content of the dewatered sludge at which the system will be energy neutral, set the energy required to evaporate water ($E_{r,e}$) equal to the energy produced by incineration:

$$E_{r,e} = E_{p,i}$$

Expanding the relationship using the equations given in the text:

$$E_{r,e} = \frac{\left[4.186(100 - T_a) + 2260(c_i - c_f)\right]}{\varepsilon(\text{dryer})}$$

$$= (1 - c_i) \times CV \times \varepsilon(\text{furnace})$$

For the assumptions in this example:

$$\frac{\left[4.186(100 - 30) + 2260(c_i - 0.05)\right]}{0.85} = (1 - c_i) \times 17,300 \times 0.85$$

Solving for c_i, the initial water content gives a c_i value of 83.5 per cent, indicating that a solids content of 16.5 per cent will be required to ensure that the system is energy neutral.

Basic design criteria and assumptions:

The average ambient temperature is 30°C, the final solids content of the dried sludge is 95 per cent, and efficiency of the process is 85 per cent for a rotary dryer and 85 per cent for the furnace used to incinerate the dried sludge. The sludge is a fresh faecal sludge with an assumed calorific value of 17.3 MJ/kg TS (note that this value would be ~12 MJ/kg TS for well-digested sludge derived from septage).

Two further examples are given below to illustrate the influence of the sludge water content on the energy balance. Both assume the same efficiencies as for the main example.

If the sludge solids content is 5 per cent, the energy required for evaporation is 2,738 kJ/kg wet sludge, while the energy produced by incineration is 735 kJ/kg wet sludge, giving an energy shortfall of 2,003 kJ/kg wet sludge. An external power source will be required to provide this energy. Alternatively, the sludge could be dewatered prior to thermal drying to achieve an energy-neutral system.

If the solids content of the sludge to be treated is 50 per cent, the energy required for evaporation is 1,541 kJ/kg wet sludge, while the energy produced by incineration would be 7,352 kJ/kg wet sludge, which gives an energy surplus of 5,811 kJ/kg wet sludge.

Pyrolysis

Pyrolysis is the thermal decomposition of material at high temperatures in the absence of oxygen. It may be classified as fast, intermediate, or slow. Fast and intermediate pyrolysis require that the material undergoing decomposition remains in the reactor for seconds or minutes. Slow pyrolysis, the main focus here, requires a retention time measured in hours and a temperature of at least 200°C and typically more, up to around 700°C. Pyrolysis differs from combustion in that little or no carbon dioxide is released during the process. Organic material instead undergoes carbonization, or conversion into carbon in the form of hard, porous charcoal. This material, which is called biochar, can be used as a soil amendment or as a fuel source.

Pyrolysis produces a mixture of gases that are used as the fuel to power the process. Research at the Cambèréne treatment plant in Dakar, Senegal found that solids contents of 58 per cent, 62 per cent, and 70 per cent would be required at highest heating temperatures (HHTs) of 700°C, 500°C, and 300°C, respectively, to meet process heat demands without recourse to an external heating source (Cunningham et al., 2016). These figures suggest that pyrolysis requires a dry solids content of at least 60–70 per cent if it is to be self-sufficient in energy. The solids content required in practice may be higher. Most pyrolysis plants operating in low-income countries operate in batch mode. This simplifies their operational requirements, but increases the need for an external fuel source to heat the reactor contents to the required reaction temperature.

Biochar increases the soil's ability to retain water and nutrients and release them slowly. A meta-analysis of the results of 109 studies revealed that biochar application in tropical conditions resulted in an average increase in crop yield of about 25 per cent at a median biochar application rate of 15 tonnes/ha. This was in marked contrast to the situation at temperate latitudes, where the average effect of biochar application was a small decrease in crop yield. The benefits in tropical areas were greatest in low-nutrient acidic soils, suggesting that the increased yield associated with biochar application derives from a soil-liming effect, similar to that found for natural chars in wildfire-affected ecosystems (Jeffrey et al., 2017).

The high temperatures reached during pyrolysis completely remove pathogens, ensuring that the biochar produced is safe to use. Other potential benefits include volume reduction, carbon sequestration, and the production of liquid that may be processed to produce a solid fuel. Potential challenges include the difficulty of controlling emissions and the maintenance challenges arising from the nature of the liquid produced during pyrolysis. This is normally referred to as tar and consists of a mixture of complex hydrocarbons and water (Basu, 2013).

Several pilot-scale initiatives have focused on the possible use of biochar to produce solid fuel briquettes. Box 10.8 provides brief information on some of these initiatives. Many poor people in urban areas of low-income countries, particularly African countries, use either wood or charcoal produced from wood as a household fuel. It is possible that biochar briquettes produced from a faecal sludge or a mixture of faecal sludge and solid waste will offer a cheaper alternative. One advantage of a switch to biochar produced from faecal sludge would be a reduction in deforestation around towns and cities.

In the short term, it is likely that the focus of initiatives involving pyrolysis will be on pilot-scale initiatives, designed to explore the technical and financial viability of the option. Clearly, the latter will depend on demand for biochar and the existence of effective marketing systems. The carbon content of biochar breaks down much more slowly than typical organic material and therefore carbon is considered to be 'sequestered' in biochar. It is possible that some of the costs of biochar production can be recovered through carbon sequestration credits.

Box 10.8 Biochar production from faecal sludge using pyrolysis

To date, most initiatives using pyrolysis to produce biochar or fuel briquettes from faecal sludge have been at the pilot scale. One such initiative is operated by Water for People with support from the Water Research Commission (WRC) in Uganda and involves production of sludge briquettes. Prior to pyrolysis, the incoming faecal sludge is dewatered on unplanted drying beds to a solids content of approximately 60 per cent and then further dried on racks to achieve a solids content of 80 per cent, which is suitable for the pyrolysis process. Currently the organization is experimenting with two types of small kilns that have previously been used for carbonization of wood: a masonry insulated retort kiln and a metallic kiln. The process involves the following steps: (1) a start-up fuel (wood or charcoal) is burned at the base of the kiln, (2) dried sludge is added until the kiln is full, (3) additional sludge is added as sludge burns down (4–5 hours), and (4) when the fire penetrates the topmost sludge, the unit is air-locked to allow the pyrolysis process to continue overnight. In the final step of the process the carbonized biochar is crushed into fine particles and then blended with a binder such as cassava or molasses. Clay may also be added as a filler to reduce the burning rate of the briquettes, although this may not be necessary as the lack of pit lining means that sludge may already contain a high proportion of filler. Crushed charcoal can be added to increase the energy content of the mixture. After blending and addition of water to increase the moisture content, the briquettes are produced using either a mechanized extruder, screw extruder, hand/manual press, or honeycomb press. The calorific value of the briquettes is reported to be 7.5–15.5 MJ/kg compared with a calorific value of 12.5 MJ/kg for charcoal dust. The organization reports the selling price for charcoal to be 5.8 times the selling price for the briquettes, although it is not clear what the revenue and operating costs are for the system. Other initiatives using pyrolysis to produce briquettes from faecal sludge include those of Slamson Ghana Ltd (https://www.slamsonghana.com) and Sanivation in Kenya (http://sanivation.com).

Black soldier fly treatment

Description

The black soldier fly (*Hermetia illucens*) (BSF) is a fly of the family Stratiomyidae. In nature, its larvae play an important role in breaking down organic material and returning nutrients to the soil. BSF systems harness this activity to convert organic material such as food wastes, agricultural wastes, manures, and human faeces into usable by-products. In BSF processing facilities, the larvae of the BSF feed on decomposing organic material, growing from a few millimetres to around 2.5 cm in 14–16 days while reducing the wet weight of waste by up to 80 per cent (Dortmans et al., 2017). The larvae are harvested prior to the prepupal stage using a mechanical agitator to separate them from organic wastes. They are high in protein (around 35 per cent) and fats (around 30 per cent) and can be used as an animal feed similar to fishmeal (Dortmans et al., 2017). The residue can also be used as a soil conditioner but requires further treatment prior to reuse. Processing of faecal sludge by BSFs is reported to effectively reduce *Salmonella* spp. but has minimal effect on *Ascaris* ova (Lalander et al., 2013). BSFs occur naturally in tropical and sub-tropical environments worldwide and do not transmit diseases to humans.

A facility to raise and process BSFs typically consists of the following:

- A nursery in which BSFs reproduce and are reared.
- A grow-out unit in which larvae mature in shallow containers known as larveros while feeding on waste, in the process converting organic material to biomass.
- Processing units for larvae harvesting, refining, and residue processing.

The area required for these processes is approximately 500–750 m^2 per tonne of dry solids processed per day with an additional 60 m^2 per tonne required for a waste receiving area and to accommodate a laboratory, office and storage space, and employee facilities (Dortmans et al., 2017; Khanyisa Project, personal communication, November 2017).

Operational and design considerations

Management requirements. BSF processing does not require sophisticated technologies. However, breeding colonies can be difficult to establish and BSF reproduction and growth cycles are sensitive to a range of environmental and other conditions. Regular monitoring of BSF reproduction and growth is required to ensure a reliable and steady supply of larvae to process waste.

Environmental conditions. BSF reproduction and growth are sensitive to the following aspects of the environmental conditions within which they are grown:

- *Temperature and humidity.* The temperature should ideally be within the range 25–30°C with an optimum temperature for larvae pupation of 27.8°C. To encourage BSF mating, the humidity should lie in the range 30–90 per cent. The optimum humidity for BSF larvae development is 70 per cent (Bullock et al., 2013).
- *Light.* In nature, adult BSFs need an abundant amount of direct sunlight for effective reproduction. When reared indoors, they require supplementary artificial lighting. A 500 watt, 135 µmol/m^2 s quartz-iodine lamp stimulates mating and oviposition at rates and times comparable to those under natural sunlight (Park, 2016). Larvae prefer a shaded environment. If their food source is exposed to light, they will try to move deeper into the food source to escape the light (Dortmans et al., 2017).
- *Depth of organic waste.* BSF larvae do not thrive at depths of more than 225 mm beneath the surface of their food source (Bullock et al., 2013).
- *Ventilation.* This is required to allow oxygen supply to the larveros and replacement of moisture-saturated air. Additional ventilation using fans is desirable for the last few days before harvesting to increase evaporation and produce a crumbly waste residue that can easily be sieved from larvae (Dortmans et al., 2017).

The system requires a feedstock with a dry solids content of 20–30 per cent and free of detritus and hazardous materials. Faecal sludge from dry pits or urine-diversion toilets in locations with a low ground water table may be within this dry solids range. Sludge from other types of facility, including pit latrines in areas with a high ground water table, will require dewatering prior to BSF treatment.

Screening should be provided prior to BSF treatment to remove solid waste. It will also be important to remove contaminants such as chemicals, used engine oil, and detergents, which are sometimes used for odour and mosquito control in pits. Box 10.9 describes the operational constraints due to solid waste and grit content in faecal sludge for a pilot BSF processing facility in Durban, South Africa.

Because of the difficulties associated with BSF breeding, and the sensitivity of the process, it is arguable that BSF treatment is best viewed as a commercial activity to be run by a private sector organization or a public company with the specialist skills required to successfully implement the treatment process.

Box 10.9 Treatment of faecal sludge by BSF: Khanyisa Projects, Durban, South Africa

In Durban, South Africa, BioCycle, in partnership with the eThekwini Municipality, and with support from Khanyisa Projects, has been operating a BSF facility for the treatment of faecal sludge since 2017. The facility treated 3 tonnes of faecal sludge (wet weight) per day in the later part of 2017, and is designed to eventually treat 20 tonnes per day. It was initially operated with a mixture of food waste and faecal sludge. The use of food waste was discontinued and in May 2018 the plant was treating a combination of 80 per cent faecal sludge and 20 per cent wastewater treatment plant primary sludge (Teddy Gouden, personal communication, May 2018).

The faecal sludge processed does not require dewatering prior to BSF processing as it is sourced primarily from urine-diversion pits and has a low water content. Indeed, BioCycle report having to use primary sludge as an additive in order to increase both nutrient levels and the moisture content of the material. During the start-up period, Khanyisa and BioCycle encountered operational challenges including large amounts of sand and detritus from urine-diversion pits. These have to be separated from the organic material prior to loading the mixer if the organic content of the sludge is to be sufficient to allow an efficient feeding process to take place. Other challenges included the settling of residue in the mechanical agitation bin provided to separate larvae from organic waste at the time of harvesting. The organization estimates a revenue of R350–525 (US$28–39) per tonne of faecal waste, based on a payment by the municipality per tonne of faecal sludge processed and revenue from protein, oil, and residue products, all of which are in development.

Source: based on personal communications with Nick Alcock of Khanyisa Projects and Marc Lewis of Agriprotein (March 2018)
For further information on BSF processing see Dortmans et al. (2017).

Key points from this chapter

Treated faecal sludge solids have potential uses as a soil conditioner, animal feed, solid fuel, biofuel, and building material. There are no commercial examples of the last two and this chapter has focused on the options for treating sludge solids to render them suitable for use as a soil conditioner, solid fuel, and animal feed. Key points emerging from the chapter include the following:

- It will be difficult to sustain any initiative based on end use of treated faecal sludge solids unless it is financially viable. At the very least, the aim should be to ensure that the recurrent cost of converting treated sludge into a safe and saleable product is less than the sum of the income generated by the sale of the product and the cost of disposal to landfill if no treatment is provided. Subsidy may be justified, either as a short-term expedient to support development of systems or to facilitate achievement of wider environmental and climate-change goals.
- Costs will only be recoverable from product sales if there is demand for the product that can be realized through effective marketing and sales systems.
- Use as an agricultural additive/soil conditioner is often assumed to be the default end use option for dewatered faecal sludge. The challenge with this option will be to generate enough income to meet the financial viability criterion. There are few examples of this option being used at scale.
- Dried sludge for use in agriculture must be substantially free of pathogens. The options for achieving this condition include composting, lime stabilization, and infrared radiation. Reliable production of a Class A biosolids by composting is difficult and the aim should therefore normally be to produce a Class B biosolid and to restrict its use.
- In order to be used as a solid fuel, sludge must be dried to a solids content of at least 80 per cent and preferably higher. Drying options include solar drying and thermal drying. Both require mechanical equipment, which will require skilled operators, effective maintenance, and reliable spare- and replacement-part supply chains. The solid fuel will only be viable if there is sufficient incoming sludge to produce biosolids in marketable quantities and there is a market for those biosolids.
- If the solids content of the sludge is high enough, typically in the range 15–20 per cent, depending on process efficiency, it is possible to fuel thermal drying processes using dried sludge, thus creating a circular process with no requirement for an external energy source. When the sludge solids content is lower than the break-even level, the process will require an external energy source. When the sludge solids content is higher than this level, the process may become a net producer of energy.
- Pyrolysis has been implemented at a pilot scale but has not yet gone to scale in any city. It requires a feedstock with a high solids content. Like other technologies described in this chapter, it will not be effective without pre-treatment using the technologies described in earlier chapters.
- Investigations into the use of black soldier flies to treat dried sludge are ongoing at both the household and the municipal scale. The product of the process is high in protein and has a potential use as an animal feed. The challenge with this option will be to ensure that effective systems are in place to manage the process.

References

Basu, P. (2013) *Biomass Gasification, Pyrolysis, and Torrefaction: Practical Design and Theory*, 2nd edn, Amsterdam: Elsevier.

Bean, C.L., Hansen, J.J., Magolin, A.B., Balkin, H., Batzer, G. and Widmer, G. (2007) 'Class B alkaline stabilization to achieve pathogen inactivation', *International Journal of Environmental Reseach and Public Health* 4(1): 53–60 <http://dx.doi.org/10.3390/ijerph2007010009> [accessed 19 July 2018].

Berendes, D., Levy, K., Knee, J., Handzel, T. and Hill, V.R. (2015) '*Ascaris* and *Escherichia coli* inactivation in an ecological sanitation system in Port-au-Prince, Haiti', *PLoS ONE* 10(5): e0125336 <https://doi.org/10.1371/journal.pone.0125336> [accessed 19 July 2018].

Bina, B., Movahedian, H. and Kord, I. (2004) 'The effect of lime stabilization on the microbiological qaulity of sewage sludge', *Iranian Journal of Environmental Health* 1(1): 34–8 <www.bioline.org.br/pdf?se04007> [accessed 27 March 2018].

Bullock, N., Chapin, E., Evans, A., Elder, B., Givens, G., Jeffay, N., Pierce, B. and Robinson, W. (2013) *The Black Soldier Fly How-to-Guide*, Chapel Hill, NC: Institute for the Environment, University of North Carolina <https://ie.unc.edu/files/2016/03/bsfl_how-to_guide.pdf> [accessed 19 March 2018].

Bux, M., Baumann, R., Philipp, W., Conrad, T. and Mühlbauer, W. (2001) 'Class A by solar drying: recent experiences in Europe', in *Proceedings of the WEFTEC (Water Environment Federation) Congress, 14–18 October 2001, Atlanta, GA*.

CalRecovery, Inc. (1993) *Handbook of Solid Waste Properties*, New York, NY: Governmental Advisory Associates.

Chazirakis, P., Giannis, A., Gidarakos, E., Wang, J-Y. and Stegmann, R. (2011) 'Application of sludge, organic solid wastes and yard trimmings in aerobic compost piles', *Global NEST Journal* 13(4): 405–11 <https://journal.gnest.org/sites/default/files/Journal%20Papers/405-411_793_Giannis_13-4.pdf> [accessed 17 May 2018].

Chun, Y.N., Lim, M.S. and Yoshika, K. (2012) 'Development of high-efficiency rotary dryer for sewage sludge', *Journal of Material Cycles and Waste Management* 14(1): 65–73 <https://link.springer.com/article/10.1007/s10163-012-0040-6> [accessed 24 May 2018].

Cornell Waste Management Institute (2005) *Compost Fact Sheet #6: Compost Pads*, Ithaca, NY: Department of Crop and Soil Sciences, Cornell University <www.manuremanagement.cornell.edu/Pages/General_Docs/Fact_Sheets/compostfs6.pdf> [accessed 23 May 2018].

Crawford, M. (2012) 'Fluidized-Bed Combustors for Biomass Boilers', <https://www.asme.org/engineering-topics/articles/boilers/fluidized-bed-combustors-for-biomass-boilers> [accessed 25 May 2018].

Crites, R. and Tchobanoglous, G. (1998) *Small and Decentralized Wastewater Management Systems*, Boston: McGraw-Hill.

Cunningham, M., Gold, M. and Strande, L. (2016) *Literature Review: Slow Pyrolysis of Faecal Sludge*, Dübendorf: Eawag/Sandec <https://www.dora.lib4ri.ch/eawag/islandora/object/eawag%3A14834/datastream/PDF/view> [accessed 8 February 2018].

Danish, M., Naqvi, M., Farooq, U. and Naqvi, S. (2015) 'Characterization of South Asian agricultural residues for potential utilization in future "energy mix"', *Energy Procedia* 75: 2974–80 <https://doi.org/10.1016/j.egypro.2015.07.604> [accessed 19 July 2018].

Diaz, L.F., Bertoldi, M., Bidlingmaier, W. and Stentiford, E. (2007) *Compost Science and Technology*, Amsterdam: Elsevier.

Diener, S., Semiyaga, S., Niwagaba, C.B., Murray Muspratt, A., Gning, J.B., Mbéguéré, M., Ennin, J.E., Zurbrügg, C. and Strande, L. (2014) 'A value proposition: resource recovery from faecal sludge – Can it be the driver for improved sanitation', *Resources Conservation and Recycling* 88: 32–8 <https://doi.org/10.1016/j.resconrec.2014.04.005> [accessed 19 July 2018].

Dortmans, B.M.A., Diener, S., Verstappen, B.M. and Zurbrügg, C. (2017) *Black Soldier Fly Biowaste Processing: A Step-by-Step Guide*, Dübendorf: Swiss Federal Institute of Aquatic Science and Technology, Dübendorf, Switzerland <www.eawag.ch/fileadmin/Domain1/Abteilungen/sandec/publikationen/SWM/BSF/BSF_Biowaste_Processing_HR.pdf> [accessed 19 March 2018].

Enayetullah, I. and Sinha, A.H.M.M. (2013) 'Co-composting of municipal solid waste and faecal sludge for agriculture in Kushtia Municipality, Bangladesh', presentation at *ISWA 2013 World Congress Conference, Vienna, Austria* <www.unescap.org/sites/default/files/Co-Composting%20Kushtia_Waste%20Concern.pdf> [accessed 17 May 2018].

Feachem, R.G., Bradley, D.J., Garelick, H. and Mara, D.D. (1983) *Sanitation and Disease: Health Aspects of Excreta and Wastewater Management*, Chichester: John Wiley & Sons.

Gallizzi, K. (2003) *Co-Composting Reduces Helminth Eggs in Fecal Sludge: A Field Study in Kumasi, Ghana, June–November 2003*, Dübendorf: Sandec/Eawag <https://www.eawag.ch/fileadmin/Domain1/Abteilungen/sandec/publikationen/SWM/Co-composting/Gallizzi_2003.pdf> [accessed 176 May 2018].

Greya, W., Thole, B., Anderson, C., Kamwani, F., Spit, J. and Mamani, G. (2016) 'Off-site lime stabilisation as an option to treat pit latrine faecal sludge for emergency and existing on-site sanitation systems', *Journal of Waste Management* article ID: 2717304 <http://dx.doi.org/10.1155/2016/2717304> [accessed 19 July 2018].

Hirrel, S., Riley, T. and Andersen, C.R. (undated) *Composting*, Division of Agriculture, University of Arkansas <https://www.uaex.edu/publications/PDF/FSA-2087.pdf> [accessed 28 June 2018].

Hobson, P.A., McKenzie, N., Plaza, F., Baker, A. East, A. and Moghaddam, L. (2016) 'Permeability and diffusivity properties of bagasse stockpiles', in *Proceedings of the 38th Conference of the Australian Society of Sugar Cane Technologists*.

Hoffman, R., Hildreth, S., and Salkeld, C. (2014) 'New Zealand's first full-scale biosolids solar drying facility', *Proceedings from the Water New Zealand 2014 Annual Conference & Exposition*.

Iacoboni, M., Livingston, J. and LeBrun, T. (1984) *Project Summary: Windrow and Static Pile Composting of Municipal Sewage Sludges*, US EPA Report No. EPA-600/S2-84-122, Cincinnati, OH: US EPA Municipal Environmental Research Laboratory <https://nepis.epa.gov/Exe/ZyPDF.cgi/2000THYG.PDF?Dockey=2000THYG.PDF> [accessed 15 February 2018].

International Water Management Institute (IWMI) (2017) *Where There's Muck There's Gold: Turning an Environmental Challenge into a Business Opportunity*, Battaramulla: IWMI <www.iwmi.cgiar.org/Publications/wle/fortifier/wle-rrr-where-there-is-muck-there-is-gold.pdf> [accessed 17 May 2018].

Janicki Bioenergy (undated) *How the Janicki Bioprocessor Works*, Sedro-Woolley, WA: Janiki Bioenergy <https://www.janickibioenergy.com/janicki-omni-processor/how-it-works> [accessed 17 May 2018].

Jeffery, S., Abalos, D., Prodana, M., Bastos, A.C., van Groenigen, J.W., Hungate, B.A. and Verheijen, F. (2017) 'Biochar boosts tropical but not temperate crop yields', *Environmental Research Letters* 12(5): #053001 <http://iopscience.iop.org/article/10.1088/1748-9326/aa67bd/meta> [accessed 17 March 2018].

Kemp, I.C. (2011) 'Fundamentals of energy analysis of dryers', in E. Tsotsas and A.S.I. Mujumdar (eds.), *Modern Drying Technology, Volume 4: Energy Saving*, pp. 1–45, Weinheim: Wiley-VCH Verlag <https://pdfs.semanticscholar.org/ff7a/53005d365e319a66bf587f7175537dedd5e0.pdf> [accessed 9 April 2018].

Kengne, I.M., Dodane, P-H., Akoa, A. and Koné, D. (2009) 'Vertical-flow constructed wetlands as sustainable sanitation approach for faecal sludge dewatering in developing countries', *Desalination* 248(1–3): 291–7 <https://doi.org/10.1016/j.desal.2008.05.068> [accessed 22 May 2018].

Kilbride, A. and Kramer, S. (2012) 'Wrapping up the toilet tour in Nairobi, Kenya', Sebastopol, CA: Sustainable Organic Integrated Livelihoods <https://www.oursoil.org/wrapping-up-the-toilet-tour-in-narobi-kenya-2/> [accessed 7 October 2017].

Koné, D., Cofie, O., Zurbrügg, C., Gallizzi, K., Moser, D., Drescher, S. and Strauss, M. (2007) 'Helminth eggs inactivation efficiency by faecal sludge dewatering and co-composting in tropical climates', *Water Resources* 41(19): 4397–402 <https://doi.org/10.1016/j.watres.2007.06.024> [accessed 19 July 2018].

Kramer, S., Preneta, N., Kilbride, A., Page, L.N., Coe, C.M. and Dahlberg, A. (2011) *The SOIL Guide to Ecological Sanitation*, Sebastopol, CA: Sustainable Organic Integrated Livelihoods <www.oursoil.org/wp-content/uploads/2015/07/Complete-Guide-PDF.pdf> [accessed 17 May 2018].

Lalander, C., Diener, S., Magri, M.E., Zurbrügg, C., Lindstrom, A. and Vinnerås, B. (2013) 'Faecal sludge management with the larvae of the black soldier fly (*Hermetia illucens*): from a hygiene aspect', *Science of the Total Environment* 458–60: 312–8 <https://doi.org/10.1016/j.scitotenv.2013.04.033> [accessed 19 July 2018].

Martin, J.H., Collins, A.R. and Diener, R.E. (1995) 'A sampling protocol for composting, recycling, and re-use', *Journal of the Air & Waste Management Association* 45: 864–70 <https://doi.org/10.1080/10473289.1995.10467416> [accessed 19 July 2018].

Mathioudakis, V.L., Kapagiannidis, A.G., Athanasoulia, E., Paltzoglou, A.D., Melidis, P. and Aivasidis, A. (2013) 'Sewage sludge solar drying: experiences from the first pilot-scale application in Greece', *Drying Technology* 31(5): 519–26 <https://doi.org/10.1080/07373937.2012.744998> [accessed 19 July 2018].

Mehrdadi, N., Joshi, S.G., Nasrabadi, T. and Hoveidi, H. (2007) 'Application of solar energy for drying of sludge from pharmaceutical industrial waste water and probable reuse', *International Journal of Environmental Research* 1(1): 42–8 <http://dx.doi.org/10.22059/IJER.2010.108>.

Metcalf & Eddy (2003) *Wastewater Engineering Treatment and Reuse*, 4th edn, New York, NY: McGraw Hill.

Michigan Recycling Coalition (2015) *Compost Operator Guidebook: Best Management Practices for Commercial Scale Composting Operations*, Lansing, MI:

Michigan Department of Environmental Quality <https://www.michigan.gov/documents/deq/deq-oea-compostoperatorguidebook_488399_7.pdf> [accessed 14 May 2018].

Muspratt, A. (2017) 'Make room for the disruptors: while desperate for innovation, the sanitation sector poses unique structural challenges to startup companies', LinkedIn publication <https://www.linkedin.com/pulse/make-room-disruptors-while-desperate-innovation-sector-muspratt/> [accessed 24 May 2018].

Muspratt, A.M., Nakato, T., Niwagaba, C., Dione, H., Kang, J., Stupin, L., Regulinski, J., Mbégueré, M. and Strande, L. (2014) 'Fuel potential of faecal sludge: calorific value results from Uganda, Ghana and Senegal', *Journal of Water, Sanitation and Hygiene for Development* 4(2): 223–30 <http://dx.doi.org/10.2166/washdev.2013.055> [accessed 19 July 2018].

Muspratt, A., Miller, A. and Wade, T. (2017) 'Leveraging resource recovery to pay for sanitation: Pivot Works demonstration in Kigali, Rwanda', presented at the *4th International Faecal Sludge Management Conference (FSM 4), Chennai, India, February 2017*.

Nartey, E.G., Amoah, P. and Ofosu-Budu, G.K. (2017) 'Effects of co-composting of faecal sludge and agricultural wastes on tomato transplant and growth', *International Journal of Recycling Organic Waste in Agriculture* 6: 23–6 <https://doi.org/10.1007/s40093-016-0149-z> [accessed 19 July 2018].

National Lime Association (2004) *Fact Sheet: Lime Safety Precautions*, Arlington, VA: National Lime Association <https://www.lime.org/documents/lime_basics/fact-safety_precautions.pdf> [accessed 14 May 2018].

Navarro, I., Jiménez, B., Lucario, S. and Cifuentes, E. (2009) 'Application of helminth ova infection dose curve to estimate the risks associated with biosolids application on soil', *Journal of Water and Health* 7(1): 31–44 <http://dx.doi.org/10.2166/wh.2009.113> [accessed 19 July 2018].

Nguyen, V.A., Nguyen, H.S., Dinh, D.H., Nguyen, P.D. and Nguyen, X.T. (2011) *Landscape Analysis and Business Model Assessment in Fecal Sludge Management: Extraction and Transportation Models in Vietnam – Final Report*, Hanoi: Institute of Environmental Science and Engineering, Hanoi University of Civil Engineering <www.susana.org/_resources/documents/default/2-1673-vietnam-fsm-study.pdf> [accessed 7 April 2018].

NIIR (undated) *Rice Husk, Rice Hull, Rice Husk Ash (Agriculture waste) based Projects*, New Delhi: NIIR Project Consultancy Services <www.niir.org/project-reports/projects/rice-husk-rice-hull-rice-husk-ash-agricultural-waste-based-projects/z,,70,0,64/index.html> [accessed 7 April 2018].

North, J.M., Becker, J.G., Seagren, E.A., Ramirez, M., Peot, C. and Murthy, S.N. (2008) 'Methods for quantifying lime incorporation into dewatered sludge II: field scale application', *Journal of Environmental Engineering* 134(9): 750–1 <http://dx.doi.org/10.1061/(ASCE)0733-9372(2008)134:9(750)>.

Olds College Composting Technology Centre (1999) *Midscale Composting Manual*, 1st edn, Calgary: Alberta Environment and Parks <http://aep.alberta.ca/waste/legislation-and-policy/documents/MidscaleCompostingManual-Dec1999.pdf> [accessed 23 May 2018].

Paluszak, Z., Skowron, K., Sypuła, M. and Skowron, K.J. (2012) 'Microbial evaluation of the effectiveness of sewage sludge sanitization with solar drying technology', *International Journal of Photoenergy* 2012: #341592 <http://dx.doi.org/10.1155/2012/341592> [accessed 19 July 2018].

Park, H.H. (2016) *Black Soldier Fly Larvae Manual*, Amherst, MA: University of Massachusetts, <https://scholarworks.umass.edu/cgi/viewcontent.cgi?article =1015&context=sustainableumass_studentshowcase> [accessed 19 March 2018].

Phiri, J.S., Katebe, R.C., Mzyece, C.C., Shaba, P. and Halwind, H. (2014) 'Characterization of biosolids and evaluating the effectiveness of plastic-covered sun drying beds as a biosolids stabilization method in Lusaka, Zambia', *International Journal of Recycling of Organic Waste in Agriculture* 3: #61 <https://doi.org/10.1007/s40093-014-0061-3> [accessed 19 July 2018].

Rao, K.C., Kvarnström, E., Di Mario, L. and Drechsel, P. (2016) *Business Models for Fecal Sludge Management* (Resource Recovery and Reuse Series 6), Colombo: International Water Management Institute <https://dx.doi.org/ 10.5337/2016.213> [accessed 19 July 2018].

Remington, C., Cherrak, M., Preneta, N., Kramer, S. and Mesa, B. (2016) A social business model for the provision of household ecological sanitation services in urban Haiti, in *Proceedings of the 39th WEDC International Conference, Kumasi, Ghana*, Loughborough: Water, Engineering and Development Centre, University of Loughborough <https://wedc-knowledge.lboro.ac.uk/resources/conference/39/Remington-2529.pdf> [accessed 7 October 2017].

Rynk, R. (2008) 'Monitoring moisture in composting systems', *BioCycle Magazine* <http://compostingcouncil.org/wp/wp-content/uploads/2014/02/7-MonitoringMoisture.pdf> [accessed 24 May 2018].

Schoebitz, L., Andriessen, N., Bollier, S., Bassan, M., Strande, L. *Market Driven Approach for Selection of Faecal Sludge Treatment Products*, Eawag: Swiss Federal Institute of Aquatic Science and Technology. Dübendorf, Switzerland. June 2016. <www.eawag.ch/fileadmin/Domain1/Abteilungen/sandec/ publikationen/EWM/Market_Driven_Approach/market_driven_approach. pdf> [accessed 21 December 2017].

Schwartzbrod, J. (1997) 'Agents pathogènes dans les boues et impact des différents traitements', in *Actes des Journées Techniques – Epandage des Boues Résiduaires*, pp. 81–9, Paris: Agence de l'Environnement et de la Maîtrise de l'Énergie.

Seginer, I. and Bux, M. (2005) 'Prediction of evaporation rate in a solar dryer for sewage sludge', *Agricultural Engineering International* VII: #EE05009 <www.cigrjournal.org/index.php/Ejounral/article/view/590/584> [accessed 20 December 2017].

Septien, S., Singh, A., Mirara, S.W., Teba, L., Velkushanova, K. and Buckley, C. (2018) "LaDePa" process for the drying and pasteurization of faecal sludge from VIP latrines using infrared radiation', *South African Journal of Chemical Engineering* 25: 147–58 <https://doi.org/10.1016/j.sajce.2018.04.005> [accessed 19 July 2018].

Shanahan, E.F., Roiko, A., Tindale, N.W., Thomas, M.P., Walpole, R. and Kurtböike, D.I. (2010) 'Evaluation of pathogen removal in a solar sludge drying facility using microbial indicators', *International Journal of Environment Research and Public Health* 7(2): 562–82 <https://doi.org/10.3390/ ijerph7020565> [accessed 19 July 2018].

Sunar, N.M., Stentiford, E.I., Stewart, D.I. and Fletcher, L.A. (2009) 'The process and pathogen behaviour in composting: a review', in *Proceedings of the*

UMT-MSD 2009 Post Graduate Seminar, pp, 78–87, Terengganu: Universiti Malaysia Terengganu <https://arxiv.org/ftp/arxiv/papers/1404/1404.5210. pdf> [accessed 11 March 2018].

Sypuła, M., Paluszak, Z. and Szala, B. (2013) 'Effect of sewage sludge solar drying technology on inactivation of select indicator microorganisms', *Polish Journal of Environmental Studies* 22(2): 533–40 <www.pjoes.com/ Effect-of-Sewage-Sludge-Solar-Drying-Technology-r-non-Inactivation-of-Select-Indicator,89007,0,2.html> [accessed 28 June 2018].

Tamakloe, W. (2014) *Characterization of Faecal Sludge and Analysis of its Lipid Content for Biodiesel Production* (MSc thesis), Kumasi, Ghana: Department of Chemical Engineering, Kwame Nkrumah University of Science and Technology <http://dspace.knust.edu.gh/bitstream/123456789/6686/1/WILSON%20TAMAKLOE.pdf> [accessed 17 May 2018].

Thoreson, C.P., Webster, K.E., Darr, M.J. and Kapler, E.J. (2014) 'Investigation of process variables in the densification of corn stover briquettes', *Energies* 7: 4019–32 <https://doi.org/10.3390/en7064019> [accessed 19 July 2018].

USAID (2015) *Implementer's Guide to Lime Stabilization for Septage Management in the Philippines* [online], Manila: USAID <http://forum.susana.org/media/ kunena/attachments/818/ImplementersGuidetoLimeStabilizationforSeptag eManagementinthePhilippines.pdf> [accessed 3 March 2018].

US EPA (1994) *A Plain English Guide to the EPA Part 503 Biosolids Rule*, Washington, DC: Office of Wastewater Management, United States Environmental Protection Agency <https://nepis.epa.gov/Exe/ZyPDF. cgi/200046QX.PDF?Dockey=200046QX.PDF> [accessed 17 May 2018].

US EPA (1995) *Process Design Manual: Land Application of Sewage Sludge and Domestic Septage*, Washington, DC: Office of Research and Development, United States Environmental Protection Agency <http://nepis.epa.gov/ Adobe/PDF/30004O9U.pdf> [accessed 17 May 2018].

US EPA (2000) *Biosolids Technology Fact Sheet: Alkaline Stabilization of Biosolids* Washington, DC: Office of Water, United States Environmental Protection Agency <https://nepis.epa.gov/Exe/ZyPDF.cgi/901U0R00.PDF? Dockey=901U0R00.PDF> [accessed 11 March 2018].

Veerannan, K.M. (1977) 'Some experimental evidence on the viability of *Ascaris lumbricoides* ova', *Current Science* 46(11): 386–7 <http://www.jstor. org/stable/24215840> [accessed 19 July 2018].

Vinnerås, B., Björklung, A. and Jönsson, H. (2003) 'Thermal composting of faecal matter as treatment and possible disinfection method: laboratory-scale and pilot-scale studies', *Bioresource Technology* 88: 47–54 <https://doi. org/10.1016/S0960-8524(02)00268-7>.

Water Environment Federation (WEF) (2010) *Design of Municipal Wastewater Treatment Plants* (Manual of Practice No. 8), 5th edn, Alexandria, VA: Water Environment Federation Press. <https://www.accessengineeringlibrary.com/ browse/design-of-municipal-wastewater-treatment-plants-wef-manual-of-practice-no-8-asce-manuals-and-reports-on-engineering-practice-no-76-fifth-edition> [accessed 17 May 2018].

WEF (2014) *Drying of Wastewater Solids Fact Sheet*, Arlington, VA: Water Environment Federation Press <www.wrrfdata.org/NBP/DryerFS/Drying_of_ Wastewater_Solids_Fact_Sheet_January2014.pdf> [accessed 7 April 2018].

WHO (2006) *Guidelines for the Safe Use of Wastewater, Excreta and Greywater*, Geneva: World Health Organization <www.who.int/water_sanitation_ health/sanitation-waste/wastewater/wastewater-guidelines/en> [accessed 17 May 2018].

Zhang, Y., Ghaly, A.E. and Li. B. (2012) 'Physical properties of rice residues as affected by variety and climatic and cultivation oonditions in three continents', *American Journal of Applied Sciences* 9(11): 1757–68 <http:// dx.doi.org/10.3844/ajassp.2012.1757.1768> [accessed 19 July 2018].

Index

Page numbers in *italics* refer to boxes, figures and tables.

Milton Keynes UK
Ingram Content Group UK Ltd.
UKHW020626210924
1771UKWH00008B/51